St Petersburg and the Russian Court, 1703–1761

St Petersburg and the Russian Court, 1703–1761

Paul Keenan
Lecturer in International History, London School of Economics, UK

First published 2013 by
PALGRAVE MACMILLAN

Palgrave Macmillan in the UK is an imprint of Macmillan Publishers Limited, registered in England, company number 785998, of Houndmills, Basingstoke, Hampshire RG21 6XS.

Palgrave Macmillan in the US is a division of St Martin's Press LLC, 175 Fifth Avenue, New York, NY 10010.

Palgrave Macmillan is the global academic imprint of the above companies and has companies and representatives throughout the world.

Palgrave® and Macmillan® are registered trademarks in the United States, the United Kingdom, Europe and other countries.

ISBN 978–1–137–31159–7

This book is printed on paper suitable for recycling and made from fully managed and sustained forest sources. Logging, pulping and manufacturing processes are expected to conform to the environmental regulations of the country of origin.

A catalogue record for this book is available from the British Library.

A catalog record for this book is available from the Library of Congress.

Typeset by MPS Limited, Chennai, India.

To the memory of Lindsey Hughes (1949–2007)

Contents

List of Maps

Acknowledgements

This book would simply not have been possible without the involvement of a large number of individuals and academic institutions. The Arts and Humanities Research Council provided the funding for my initial work on this project and the Department of International History at LSE was generous in providing funds for subsequent research trips. This project would not have been possible without the assistance of the staff in a variety of Russian archives and libraries. These institutions were: the Russian State Archive of Ancient Acts (RGADA), the Russian State Historical Archive (RGIA), the Russian State Military Historical Archive (RGVIA), the Institute of History of the Academy of Sciences in St Petersburg, the National Library of Russia, the State Public Library, the State Public Historical Library, the Academy of Sciences Library, and the State Theatrical Library. Similarly, in the United Kingdom, I am indebted to the staff of the School of Slavonic and East European Studies library, the British Library and the National Archives at Kew for their help.

Most Ph.D. students would consider themselves lucky to have one good supervisor, whereas I have had the privilege to work with two. Roger Bartlett was the main driving force behind the first two years of my research and has continued to offer his support ever since. Lindsey Hughes then took responsibility for me and ensured – in her characteristically encouraging and practical manner – that my thesis reached a successful conclusion in 2005. Her untimely death in 2007 means that I can only attempt to repay her investment in me in some small manner by dedicating this book to her memory. She is sadly missed.

I owe many other individual debts to those who have taken time out of very busy schedules to read and comment on part or all of this work. In particular, I would like to thank Tim Hochstrasser, Simon Dixon, Janet Hartley, Isabel de Madariaga, Dominic Lieven, Gary Marker, Wendy Rosslyn and Richard Butterwick. Whilst in Russia, my research work was made considerably more productive by the efforts of Ol'ga Kosheleva, Aleksandr Kamenskii, Evgenii Anisimov and Boris Morozov, whose advice on my topic and guidance on the location of relevant material was very welcome. In the UK, the Study Group on Eighteenth-Century Russia has provided a friendly and constructive atmosphere for discussing my research over the last 10 years. At Palgrave Macmillan, I am grateful for the help provided by Jenny McCall, Holly Tyler and Clare Mence, who have been very patient with me over the last two years. Similarly, at LSE, I owe considerable thanks to Mina Moshkeri, who provided invaluable technical expertise in redrawing and clarifying the maps for this volume.

Finally, and most importantly from a personal perpective, I must thank my parents and brothers, my wife Róisín and our daughter Naoimh, who have all lived with this book, in one form or another, for as long as I have. Their love and understanding has kept me going throughout this process – I will always be grateful.

Abbreviations

Printed Sources

AKV *Arkhiv kniazei Vorontsovykh*, ed. Petr. I. Bartenev (Moscow, 1870–95), 40 vols.

ChIOIDR *Chteniia v Imperatorskom Obshchestve Istorii i Drevnostei Rossiiskikh pri Moskovskom universitete* (Moscow, 1846–1918), 258 vols.

KfZh *Kamer-fur'erskie Zhurnaly, 1726–1771 goda*, ed. B. M. Fedorov (St Petersburg, 1853–5), 40 vols.

MIIAN *Materialy dlia istorii Imperatorskogo Akademii nauk*, ed. Mikhail V. Sukhomlinov (St Petersburg, 1890–1900), 10 vols.

MP *Muzykal'nyi Peterburg. Entsiklopedicheskii slovar': XVIII vek*, ed. Anna L. Porfir'eva (St Petersburg, 1999–2000), 3 vols.

PiBIPV *Pis'ma i bumagi imperatora Petra Velikogo* (Moscow, 1887–), 13 vols to date.

PoZh *Pokhodnye i putevye zhurnaly imperatora Petra I-go, 1695–1726*, ed. A. Th. Bychkov (St Petersburg, 1853–5), 32 vols.

PridZh *Pridvornye zhurnaly... 1741–42, 1743–48*, ed. Ivan A. Cherkasov (St Petersburg, 1883 and 1913).

PSZ *Polnoe sobranie zakonov rossiiskoi imperii... 1649–1825* (St Petersburg, 1830), 46 vols.

SEER *Slavonic and East European Review*

SGECRN *Study Group on Eighteenth-Century Russia Newsletter*

SIRIO *Sbornik Imperatorskogo Rossiiskogo Istoricheskogo Obshchestva* (St Petersburg, 1867–1926), 148 vols.

SK *Svodnyi katalog katalog russkoi knigi grazhdanskoi pechati XVIII veka, 1725–1800*, ed. I. P. Kondakov et al. (Moscow, 1962–7), 5 vols.

Slovar' *Slovar' russkogo iazyka XVIII veka*, ed. Stepan G. Barkhudarov et al. (St Petersburg, 1984–), 19 vols. to date.

Sochineniia *Sochineniia imperatritsy Ekateriny II, na osnovanii podlinnykh rukopisei*, ed. A. N. Pypin (St Petersburg 1901–7), 12 vols.

SPV *Sanktpeterburgskie Vedomosti*

SR *Slavic Review*

TZhRAI	*Teatral'naia zhizn' Rossii v epokhu Anny Ioannovny.* *Dokumental'naia khronika, 1730–40,* ed. Liudmila M. Starikova (Moscow, 1995).
TZhREP	*Teatral'naia zhizn' Rossii v epokhu Elizavety Petrovny.* *Dokumental'naia khronika,* ed. Liudmila M. Starikova (Moscow, 2003–), 3 parts, in progress.
ZhDGA	*Zhurnaly dezhurnykh general-ad"iuntantov: tsarstvovanie imper-* *atritsy Elizavety Petrovny,* comp. Leonid V. Evdokimov (St Petersburg, 1897).

Archives

RGADA	Rossiiskii gosudarstvennyi arkhiv drevnikh aktov
RGIA	Rossiiskii gosudarstvennyi istoricheskii arkhiv
RGVIA	Rossiiskii gosudarstvennyi voenno-istoricheskii arkhiv
StPb IRI RAN	Sanktpeterburgskii filial Instituta Rossiiskoi Istorii Rossiiskoi Akademii Nauk

Archival references

f.	fond
op.	opis'
d.	delo
kn.	kniga
l. or ll.	list(y)

Introduction

There has been an enduring fascination with St Petersburg in the course of the three centuries since its foundation in 1703 and, at first glance, it is not difficult to understand why this should be the case. It is a relatively recent city, founded only at the beginning of the eighteenth century, and yet it rapidly grew to become the famed capital city of one of Europe's Great Powers. Several aspects of this process help to explain the continuing allure of St Petersburg. It has often been described as Russia's 'window' into Europe, a phrase first coined by Francesco Algarotti who visited St Petersburg in the 1730s and one that neatly encapsulates the situation of the city, geographically and culturally.[1] The mythology associated with the creation and development of St Petersburg has also attracted considerable interest over the intervening centuries.[2] One popular example is the myth of the city's foundation, which presents Peter creating his new city in a wilderness and has featured in numerous literary treatments of St Petersburg. This image conveniently overlooks two considerations: that Peter may not have been present on this momentous occasion in May 1703 and that the proposed site contained a Swedish fortress, known as 'Nienschants', as well as a number of small settlements, principally the town of Nien.[3] Instead, this topos has its origins in the work of successive eighteenth-century writers, beginning during the reign of Peter himself, that celebrated the achievement of the city's founder and it subsequently gained widespread currency through its inclusion in Aleksandr S. Pushkin's famous *Bronze Horseman*.[4]

Yet, despite the poetic licence or mythology at work in these presentations of the city, such images of St Petersburg have played an important part in influencing its interpretation. For example, the city's distinctive architecture reflects the influence of a variety of European styles, while its location on the Baltic coast meant that it played an important commercial and diplomatic role in Russia's relationship with northern and western Europe. These interactions were a deliberate and essential influence on St Petersburg during the decades immediately following its foundation. Likewise, in the seventeenth century, only Moscow was comparable in size and population to other European cities and Russia remained a predominantly rural society until the late nineteenth century. Although hardly created from 'nothing', the building of a new city like St Petersburg was a major project and therefore a symbol of considerable significance. According to my interpretation, the first half of the eighteenth century set the tone for St Petersburg's development as a leading European capital city thereafter. Before introducing the broad themes of this study, I want to address two questions that occurred to me at an early stage in my research and that have subsequently helped to situate the book in a wider scholarly context. The questions surround the choice of the period – the first half of the eighteenth century – and the subject matter – the cultural life of St Petersburg.

The significance of Peter I (or 'the Great') and his reign as Tsar of Russia has long been debated. Both in the popular imagination and in academic studies, he continues to be the focus of considerable attention. His dynamic character and his eccentricities are writ large in the popular treatments of his reign.[5] The scholarly analysis instead dwelt on the impact of Peter's reforms, with positive and negative assessments about the legacy that they created for Russia's subsequent development.[6] During the Soviet period, scholarship in Russia chiefly discussed Peter I's role in transforming Russia, a process in which culture was considered less significant than the military or the economy.[7] While several important works, particularly in the late Soviet period, explored the costs of these 'revolutionary' reforms – examining the violence and surveillance of the Petrine system, for instance – the fundamental paradigm had not altered significantly since the late imperial period.[8] However, in the last two decades, there have been a number of major works on the Petrine era that have demonstrated the merits of adopting a different approach to this period, while acknowledging their debt to previous writings. In particular, their analysis has integrated previously understudied aspects of the period, such as the influential political networks and the complex cultural expressions of power at the Petrine court.[9] Other recent work has further contextualised the period in terms of the important developments of the preceding seventeenth century and the influence of foreign examples.[10]

A related aspect of the debate on Peter I's significance spotlights the period between his death in 1725 and the accession of Catherine II in 1762. This period between Russia's two 'Great' reigns of the eighteenth century has often been overlooked because of the perception, both scholarly and popular, of the weakness and instability of the rulers, memorably described by one historian as 'ignorant, licentious women, half-witted German princes, and mere children'.[11] This attitude proved both widespread and resilient, with the middle decades of the eighteenth century remaining relatively understudied as a result. There were some important exceptions to this historiographical trend that attempted to rehabilitate or at least better contextualise these rulers.[12] More recently, there has been a concerted effort to re-examine the 'era of palace revolutions' using an impressive array of archival and printed materials in order to analyse and unpick some of its mythology, such as the question of stagnation and the influence of favourites.[13] Just as the revisionist scholarship on Petrine Russia stresses the need to examine the extent and nature of change during his reign in a wider context, so too the significance of the post-Petrine period lies in exploring the aftermath of those reforms, when their impact and longevity can be properly assessed. Given the considerable changes that Russia underwent in this period, not least in the demands placed on its populace, it is hardly surprising that one leading historian talks of the need for a 'breathing space' during this period when the various reforms could be consolidated and adapted for purpose.[14]

The city of St Petersburg was one of these changes, introduced by Peter, that would require this period of consolidation, even if it subsequently became the most visible and enduring of all of his endeavours. While Peter's desire to found a new city had its roots in the 1690s, St Petersburg is nevertheless a clear example of an innovation that had no roots in the pre-Petrine era. In addition, its location and intended function explicitly reflects a desire to engage directly with the rest of Europe, whether militarily, commercially or culturally.[15] It is therefore tempting to view the city as a physical manifestation of the wide-ranging goals of the reforming Tsar. While the reality is necessarily more complicated than this broad characterisation suggests, the idea that the city was founded and developed as part of an attempt to create a new image of Russia, domestically and internationally, is a striking and, to my mind, persuasive one.[16] St Petersburg has been the subject of an extensive and varied literature since the early decades of its existence, with both inhabitants and outsiders keen to learn more about the history and characteristics of the city, particularly around one of its anniversaries, as in 1903 and 2003.[17] The modern histories of the city have generally presented a narrative of St Petersburg's development, from the early imperial era to the Soviet period and beyond, while exploring its role as a crucible for political, social or cultural change in Russia.[18]

The city became an important theme for successive generations of Russian authors and the question of what St Petersburg represents has been explored in a number of works dealing with its literary portrayal over the same period. These works analyse the rhetorical and symbolic presentation of St Petersburg, which is so often reflected in accounts of the city.[19] For my chosen period, in the early eighteenth century, the standard starting place remains Petrov's magnum opus on St Petersburg's history up to 1782, which not only provides a wealth of information but also a critical view on some of the city's mythology.[20] Likewise, the construction and early life of the city during the Petrine era has been covered by the pioneering work of Luppov.[21] This subject has been further developed in two major recent works by Ageeva and Anisimov that include much greater consideration of the social and cultural life of the early city.[22] Each of these works, both general and specific, has been important in shaping my view on the city and in suggesting areas for further discussion.

This book examines St Petersburg as a conscious attempt to create a forum for certain social and cultural changes in Russia, while further developing the latter's relationship with the rest of Europe. This is not to suggest either that these attempts were a coherent or cohesive set of policies, or that St Petersburg should be seen as a microcosm for the Russian Empire as a whole. In a country where the official urban population was only 3 per cent of the total population in this period, St Petersburg was hardly typical in its composition and growth.[23] As a result, my argument examines St Petersburg's development from a number of related perspectives, with particular focus on the role of the court in promoting and regulating the city's cultural life. My work focuses on the period between St Petersburg's foundation and the death of Peter I's daughter Elizabeth, because the significance of this period has often been overlooked in studies of this topic. In my view, the developments of the preceding period are crucial to understanding the priorities and actions of Catherine II, both for the city and the court.[24] In order to provide some context for the discussion that follows in subsequent chapters, the following sections briefly introduce the three concepts that provide a backdrop to this book: the question of Russia's relationship with 'Europe'; recent developments in studying the early modern court, particularly in Russia; and the comparison between St Petersburg and other *Residenzstädte* ('court cities').

Russia and Europe

When comparing Russia to a broadly defined region, be it Europe or 'the West', one must question what that region meant to contemporaries, rather than applying that definition anachronistically. At risk of gross understatement, 'Europe' was a complex term in the early modern period, as now. The religious divisions of the Reformation challenged the unitary concept of (Latin) Christendom of the medieval period, and attempts to create a 'universal monarchy' were undermined by the dynastic rivalries of the sixteenth and seventeenth centuries.[25] Yet, religious and Classical ideas continued to inform the discourse about 'Europe' amongst early modern scholars. In their view, Europe was the heart of the 'civilised' world and was thought to be defined by certain values, such as 'liberty', that emphasised its civilisation, as compared with its 'barbaric' rivals in Asia and north Africa.[26] Russia presented an interesting test case for these ideas. It had been part of the European order during the medieval period, when Kievan Rus' had an established, if fractious relationship with a number of leading powers, such as the Byzantine Empire.[27] Grand Prince of Moscow Ivan III's aggressive assertion of sovereignty after two centuries of Mongol domination led to renewed relations with other European rulers during the fifteenth century. As a result,

Muscovy forged commercial and diplomatic contacts with a number of German states and, from the mid-sixteenth century, with England and the Dutch Republic.

Ivan's dynastic marriage to the Byzantine Empire's ruling family, the Palaiologoi, was an important step toward greater recognition on the European stage. With the fall of Constantinople in 1453, Muscovy claimed the role of leading Orthodox Christian polity and the eastern successor to the imperial legacy of Rome.[28] However, at the same time, Muscovy remained very much on the periphery of continental Europe for much of the early modern period and its staunch Orthodoxy created tension with the Latin Christian Church that it had anathematised in 1054. A small but growing number of foreigners travelled to Russia, including craftsmen, merchants, soldiers and diplomats. The accounts written by these travellers played a key role in shaping the debate on Russia, its form of government and the question of its status as 'civilised' (or otherwise) during the early modern period.[29] While such foreigners were the subject of mistrust, not to say xenophobia, their expertise was employed by the Muscovite elite throughout this period, as reflected in the Italian influence on the Kremlin and its cathedrals.[30] The foreign presence was consolidated with the establishment of a 'foreign quarter' in Moscow by the mid-seventeenth century, which proved an important, if restricted conduit for these personnel, their expertise and practices.[31]

The relationship developed in several important ways from the mid-seventeenth century onward. There was a growing awareness of Muscovy across Europe. Its involvement in the Holy Alliance, albeit as an ally of Poland, against the Ottoman Empire in the 1680s was hardly successful in military terms, but reflected a recognition of its utility in international affairs and guaranteed its possession of Left-Bank Ukraine.[32] This acquisition also brought Russia geographically closer to 'Europe', although the generally-acknowledged eastern boundary of Europe had been gradually shifting in that direction anyway, from the River Don in the fifteenth century to the Ural mountains in the eighteenth century.[33] This boundary was proposed on the basis of the differences between the physical geography on either side of the mountains by both Philip Johann von Strahlenberg, a Swedish officer and prisoner of war in Russia, and by Vasilii N. Tatishchev, a Russian geographer and proponent of the Petrine legacy, thereby giving Russia a voice in this debate for the first time.[34] Although Russia stretched across both continents, its heart lay on the European side of this divide. While Muscovy had extensive contact with and a degree of admiration for Asian powers throughout this period, there was a clear sense of distinction between them, not least on the grounds of religion. Similarly, in its dealings with Siberia and its maritime exploration from the late eighteenth century, there are many similarities between imperial attitudes in Russia and in other European cases.[35]

Another facet of this relationship revolves around the 'Europeanisation' of Russia during this period. The use of 'Europeanisation' has now become slightly more common in its application than its bedfellows 'Westernisation' or 'modernisation', but it naturally raises the spectre of the debatable nature of such concepts (or processes) for Russia.[36] The imprecision of such overarching terms has been highlighted in the long-running debate on the subject, which has raised very important questions about the chronology of the process, the areas that it affected and the extent of its impact.[37] Bushkovitch is right to highlight the danger of defining Russian developments in terms of an abstract 'Europe', often based on the exceptional, rather than the typical.[38] With that in mind, I have drawn on the work of Cracraft, whose recent monograph on Russia's cultural development during the Petrine era and its relationship with a variety of influences from across Europe, provides a brief, but useful working definition of 'Europeanisation': 'assimilation or, more appropriately, appropriation in some degree of European cultural practices and norms'.[39] My study places St Petersburg and its cultural life during this period in the broader context of other case studies from across contemporary Europe in order to understand the nature and extent of its development.

Russia and the early modern court

For contemporaries, there was no question about the centrality of the royal court in the early modern world. For popular audiences, then as now, the lives and activities of 'the royals' was a source of a certain fascination, whether motivated by devoted loyalty, righteous indignation or idle curiosity. This interest was fed by the publication of royal histories, biographies and collections of historical anecdotes, a trend that continues to the modern day despite the fading of monarchy as a political institution. However, it was rarely the focus of scholarly attention, often being associated with the study of the court's ceremonial setting and trappings at a surface level. The serious academic study of royal courts has only emerged in recent decades. The influence of Elias's work on the 'court society' was undoubtedly a major contribution to this endeavour, even if it has subsequently been extensively critiqued by historians of the period.[40] Elias's importance lies in prompting a re-examination of certain basic assumptions about the composition and functions of the royal court, in order to better understand its significance as an institution in the early modern period.[41] What has emerged from this 'new court history' is a detailed, more nuanced picture of the early modern court as a key forum for the developments of the period and the revision of previous assertions about the ruler's relationship with the elite, the role of religion and the influence of new cultural practices.[42]

The historiography of the Russian court presents a similarly mixed picture. Historians of the late imperial period produced a number of important scholarly works on the rulers and their court in preceding centuries, some of which remain the standard starting point for modern treatments of the subject.[43] Although there was a tendency toward biographical studies, blending anecdotal and archival evidence, they reveal something of the official and popular discourse on certain rulers, notably Catherine II.[44] During the Soviet period, there was a relative paucity of works on the royal court, an institution usually identified with arbitrary cruelty, corruption and profligacy in Marxist historiography. The important contributions to our understanding of the court during the eighteenth century from this period focused instead on its institutional and financial structures.[45] Such work was undoubtedly valuable, not least for highlighting the complexity and partial nature of relevant materials on this area. In the last two decades, this approach has begun to change, as the royal court has become a topic for serious study again, gradually engaging with the growing court historiography outside Russia.[46] The rise of this 'new court history' in Russia has been complemented by an upsurge of interest in other aspects of the early modern period that had previously been neglected or sidelined, such as religion, gender and identity.[47]

The importance of such studies has been to challenge previous assumptions or oversights about these subjects, on the basis of extensive work in Russian archives – now more accessible than ever before – and comparative analysis, as informed by other historical case studies or academic disciplines. The court provides a useful focal point from which to approach a number of these areas. Several historians have challenged the widely held view that Peter I had little time or patience for elaborate ritual and therefore introduced a new 'secular' court, in contrast to its religious Muscovite predecessor.[48] Instead, as noted above, Peter adapted existing Muscovite practices, where they suited his purposes, while simultaneously innovating in other respects, as reflected in the reform of the Muscovite ritual calendar and the introduction of new anniversaries.[49] Similarly, far from Peter's reign being a period of secularisation in Russian culture, recent work has clearly demonstrated the religious foundations of his close circle's activities and the continuing importance of Orthodoxy in the court's major rituals.[50] In a similar vein, Marker's study of the cult of St Catherine in eighteenth-century Russia presents a sophisticated analysis of the relationship between Orthodoxy, female rulership and its expression in Russian court culture.[51]

Detailed archival work has provided a great deal of previously unseen material on the question of the Russian court's evolution as an institution during the eighteenth century. Ageeva has examined this process in two complementary monographs in the last 10 years. The first analyses the court's 'Europeanisation' by examining the titles of court posts and the introduction of new regulations, often informed by courtly practices elsewhere.[52] The second is an exhaustive examination of the court's administration, chief offices and financial affairs, in a manner similar to Duindam's work on the courts of Versailles and Vienna.[53] While the comparative context of other European courts is largely unexplored, there is no doubt that these two monographs have established a new gold standard for archival studies of the Russian court. They have been joined by other, similarly detailed archival studies, of which Pisarenko's recent book on Elizabeth's court is a welcome addition to a neglected period that provides a wealth of new details about the wide-ranging scope of court life.[54] While my work draws on the fruits of this new approach, particularly in shaping my view of its complexities, I will instead explore the court's role in creating and fostering the ceremonial and social life of St Petersburg. The organic relationship between the court, its elite and the city bears comparison with other European examples, which are discussed in the next section.

Russia and the *Residenzstadt*

The promotion of St Petersburg by Peter I and his successors has been viewed by some historians as an attempt to create a version of the German *Residenzstadt* or 'court city' in Russia.[55] At its most basic, the term *Residenz* was used to indicate the permanent, or at least long-term, presence of the ruler and their court in a given location, in contrast to the itinerant medieval and Renaissance courts that often moved to different centres across their realms on a regular basis.[56] There were a number of reasons for this trend. The growing size and cost of the court made a permanent base more attractive, while such *Residenzstädte* could be used to reflect the wealth, status and, ultimately, power of their ruler in material and symbolic terms.[57] Commonly, these towns or cities were transformed by the presence of the ruler and their court or, as in the case of St Petersburg, built specifically for this purpose. There are prominent examples across early modern Europe.[58] An early example of a royal court choosing a permanent location and then transforming the site to fit this purpose was the development of Madrid under the Spanish Habsburgs, where royal investment from Philip II onwards turned a small town into a major capital city.[59] Louis XIV's palace and garden complex at Versailles presents a high-profile, influential example of a *Residenz* created anew, on the site of an old hunting lodge, and one that was deliberately located beyond the *Stadt* of Paris.[60]

While it was undoubtedly one of the most impressive examples of its type, Versailles was not as dominant an influence as traditionally suggested. The Bourbons' main dynastic rivals, the Austrian Habsburgs, provided an alternative with their more austere but equally significant *Residenz*, based around the Hofburg palace in Vienna.[61] Similarly, the style of Italian architects, as reflected in Gian Lorenzo Bernini's commissions in seventeenth-century Rome, may not have satisfied Louis XIV's tastes but it proved influential in central and northern Europe throughout this period.[62] This multiplicity of influences can be seen at a range of courts of varying size and significance, as demonstrated by a host of princes, dukes, bishops and other rulers across the German lands during the second half of the seventeenth century.[63] An appropriately magnificent residence represented an assertion of the ruler's status – whether a reality, an aspiration or, occasionally, a compensation – in order to be acknowledged by contemporaries, domestically and internationally. The ambitions of the Bavarian Wittelsbachs and the electors of Saxony found expression in the extensive redevelopment of Munich and Dresden from the 1680s onward.[64] Prussia's claim of a royal title in 1701 led to considerable investment in Berlin as Frederick I sought to reinforce his new status through extensive building projects and major court celebrations. On the other hand, Prussian rulers continued to be crowned in Königsberg, a tradition that bears comparison with the Russian case.[65]

With regard to St Petersburg, there are certainly similarities between Peter's new city and the seats of other contemporary rulers across Europe. In common with the smaller court cities across the German lands, it was a city that owed its entire existence to the ruler's will. The rapid development of St Petersburg was less an organic process than it was the result of investment by successive rulers and the city's wealthy elite. St Petersburg was firmly established as the principal seat of the royal court and the main administrative bodies within two decades of its foundation. However, contrary to popular belief, there was no formal declaration of St Petersburg's assumption of the title of capital city during Peter's reign.[66] St Petersburg's position came under scrutiny following the death of its founder in 1725, with speculation at the end of the decade that these institutions might return to Moscow permanently when the young Tsar Peter II preferred to reside there before his death in 1730. Instead, the triumphant return of Anna Ivanovna and her court to St Petersburg in 1732 confirmed the new city's ruling status, with the court spending only three of the next 30 years in Moscow.

Yet, despite claims to the contrary by some later commentators, Moscow was hardly neglected during this period.[67] It was the site of numerous construction projects – including state buildings, palaces and churches – that had much in common with those commissioned in St Petersburg.[68] It also continued to play an important ceremonial role for the Russian court by hosting a number of major celebrations, most importantly the ruler's coronation.[69] This overlapping status is reflected in the terms used to refer to both St Petersburg and Moscow during this period. To take one example, the titles of the maps produced of the two cities by both Russian and foreign cartographers use similar words to indicate their role as seats of the court and capital cities. St Petersburg is referred to as *la Capitale* (Nicholas de Fer, 1717), *Haupt-residenz* (Johann Homann, 1720), *Residentz Stadt* and *stolichnyi gorod* (Joseph de L'Isle, 1737 and John Truscott, 1753) – the latter phrase was also applied to Moscow (Ivan Michurin, 1739), along with its variant *tsarstvuiushii grad* (1763). These maps were subsequently reproduced across Europe in a number of forms.[70] Their titles are therefore significant in that they established St Petersburg as akin to Europe's other capitals – by using the same terms to define the city – while maintaining the existing status of Moscow, the 'old' capital.

Chapter outline

Chapter 1 provides an overview of the creation of St Petersburg and its component spaces. The planning and appearance of St Petersburg reflect one aspect of the relationship between Russia and the rest of Europe during this period. However, such plans, whether for St Petersburg's layout or the designs commissioned for its main buildings, had to contend with the natural and practical restrictions imposed by the chosen location. St Petersburg was the site of several new, constructed spaces that provided important forums for related reforms. The chapter examines the creation and development of the city's social, intellectual and ceremonial spaces in order to provide a context for the more detailed discussion of these areas in later chapters. Chapter 2 examines another aspect of the relationship between Russia and the rest of Europe through a discussion of 'police' legislation that was introduced by a number of European states to promote 'good order' amongst their population. The chapter discusses the introduction of Russia's first 'police' institution in St Petersburg in 1718. The Police Chancellery was created by Peter I to oversee a number of key areas in the new city's development, which included the physical, economic and moral well-being of its inhabitants. By examining several specific concerns – excessive drinking, gambling and immoral behaviour – the chapter argues that Russia attempted to tackle these problems in a similar manner to other European states, although its results were very mixed.

Chapter 3 focuses on the Russian court and its annual celebrations. The eighteenth-century Russian court was related to, but distinct from its Muscovite predecessor as an institution, with the establishment of new ranks and offices with European titles and functions. The court calendar displayed a similar development, as new celebrations were added to the existing religious Muscovite court ceremonies. The latter were reshaped to include a greater emphasis on the state and the ruling dynasty under Peter and, particularly, under his successors. The chapter examines several case studies of large-scale public celebrations in St Petersburg relating to specific major events – royal entries, weddings and funerals – that established a strong connection between the dynasty and the city. The argument is that the planning, organisation and symbolic imagery associated with these events were a reflection of the Russian court's desire to establish itself on the courtly map of Europe. Chapter 4 turns to the question of the court's relationship with the regular social life of St Petersburg. The analysis centres on a number of related sociable activities, in which the ruler actively encouraged participation during this period, a practice continued under

Catherine II and beyond. Finally, St Petersburg hosted many traditional, popular forms of entertainment, such as ice slides and other seasonal festivities. The chapter discusses their ongoing presence to emphasise the theme of continuity, alongside the innovations elsewhere in St Petersburg's social and cultural life.

Finally, Chapter 5 shifts the focus of discussion from the spaces of the city to the people expected to participate within them. The novelty of certain 'Europeanised' aspects of St Petersburg's social life, such as the 'assemblies', meant that their intended attendees were initially ill-prepared for the experience. The chapter deals with several aspects of their process of adaptation. Education was a crucial means to acquire the skills considered appropriate to aid sociable interaction. New educational institutions for the elite, such as the Cadet Corps, and the increased use of foreign tutors by leading noble families facilitated this process. Advice on suitable behaviour was also available through foreign conduct literature, sometimes published in Russian translation. Dancing became an important part of education during this period, since it informed movement, comportment and behaviour in social situations. The chapter finishes by examining the changes to dress and grooming, the most visible symbol of change in Russian society during this period. European fashions became a mainstay amongst elite and urban groups during this period and access to certain events or areas within St Petersburg often listed dress requirements, thereby excluding the lower social groups. These reforms helped to minimise the physical and, to a certain extent, cultural distinctiveness between Russians and their contemporaries elsewhere in Europe.

Returning to Algarotti's description of the city, he notes several aspects of the city's construction: 'There reigns in this capital a kind of bastard architecture, which partakes of the Italian, the French, and the Dutch...' and 'It has been wittily enough said, that ruins make themselves in other places, but that they were built in Petersburgh.'[71] While typical of Algarotti's literary style, these observations nevertheless touch on two important themes that have influenced opinion on St Petersburg throughout its history. The first questions the nature of Russia's relationship with Europe, characterising it as imitating a hodge-podge of styles, while the second is a comment on the foundations of the city, which are presented as ill-conceived and unstable. The following chapters explore the questions raised by both of these characterisations, while challenging their conclusion.

1
Location: Situating the City

As founder of St Petersburg, Peter I consciously, and arguably also subconsciously, attempted to control both the city's space and its inhabitants, in pursuit of certain goals. These goals were in part related to his wider reform agenda – that of transforming Russia into a stronger entity, domestically and internationally – but were also emblematic of a desire to use the city as a testing ground for certain specific ventures. Whilst St Petersburg began life as a fortified port on the Baltic coast, considerable efforts were made by Peter I and his successors to provide it with the appearance, institutions and activities of something much more in keeping with a royal residence or a capital city. The cities that Peter himself visited during the Grand Embassy of 1697–8 provided a natural starting point for some of the inspirations for his new project. This list of cities includes both large capitals and some of the smaller, but significant cities in central Europe: Riga, Mitau, Königsberg, Amsterdam (specifically Zaandam), London, Leipzig, Dresden, Prague, Vienna and Rawa. These cities provided a range of experiences and examples that would prove important, to varying degrees, in Peter's planning. Whether as international ports, commercial centres, seats of learning or sites of courtly culture, they provided a tangible flavour of the possibilities available to the young Tsar.

This chapter examines the creation of the various spaces, buildings and institutions within St Petersburg and how they subsequently influenced the development of the city. As a newly founded city, St Petersburg offered a prime opportunity to plan and regulate its existence. The location of the major organs of the Russian state in the new city naturally led to an increase in official scrutiny in this respect also. Arguably the most important institution for such attention – the royal court – will be examined separately in Chapter 3. From the layout of its street plan to the appearance of its major buildings, from the question of how to populate the city to the emphasis on 'well-ordered' behaviour in everyday life, St Petersburg was a deliberate, if not always well-coordinated or consistent project. One of the principal stumbling blocks for the planning process was the natural situation of the city. The Neva River occupied a central place in the city's geography and divided the city into distinct sections, which were not always well connected or easy to navigate. As a result and almost by necessity, the river became a major element in both the everyday and the festive life of the city. An alternative 'natural' space within St Petersburg was provided by the royal gardens, which were used as a symbolic representation of the harnessing of nature for beneficial purposes, and as part of Peter I's attempt to portray the new city as an earthly 'paradise'. They were also an important social space within the city, which will be examined in more detail in Chapter 4.

The relocation to St Petersburg also had an impact on the social life of the elite, in particular with the emergence of several new types of social gathering, both at court and in the houses of leading noble families. The developments of this period highlight the relationship between compulsion, regulation and acceptance of the new social context by the Russian elite. The city also housed the newly established Academy of Sciences, which was to help establish the city as an important centre for scientific study during the eighteenth century. However, on an exemplary level, the Academy also served as a model of educated, not to mention civilised behaviour, and its public activities served to highlight this to a domestic and international audience. Finally, as a result of the presence of both the royal family and the military, civil and court elite, the new city naturally hosted many of the celebrations associated with them. Whilst the specifics of the court calendar will be addressed in Chapter 3, it is important to give some context for the spaces in which these state occasions took place. While the setting of St Petersburg was 'new', in chronological terms, the form and content of these aspects reflects a more complex relationship between tradition and innovation.

A 'regular' city?

The example of Europe is frequently highlighted as an influence on Peter I's thinking about his new city. Its architectural appearance and various institutions also drew on existing models, in one form or another. St Petersburg has often been compared to other European cities, despite a lack of any clearly discernible influence on Peter I or any of his close advisers. For example, Italian visitors to the city during the eighteenth century did not share the views of some contemporary commentators who drew comparisons between St Petersburg and Venice on account of the city's waterways and canals.[1] According to some contemporary observers, Peter's preferred model was Amsterdam – a seaport built on international trade.[2] But these cities had evolved over centuries, whereas St Petersburg was a new project – it allowed the possibility of planning its overall design, rather than redeveloping an established urban site.[3] Another source of inspiration came from the various architectural and fortificatory treatises in the Kremlin library.[4] Peter added to his personal library by purchasing a considerable number of works on architecture during the Grand Embassy. Several of these texts were then translated into Russian, thereby establishing a new lexicon of architectural terms in the Russian language. To take one example, Giacomo da Vignola's famous *Regola delli cinque ordini d'architettura* ('Canon of the Five Orders of Architecture', first published in 1562) was printed in Russian translation in 1709 and reprinted twice more during Peter's reign, in 1712 and 1722.[5]

The next step was to put these plans into action, which began very early in the city's existence. Almost as soon as the earthworks for the fortifications had been dug, Peter was ordering plans from his military engineers for what would soon become the Sts Peter and Paul Fortress (1; see Key to Maps on page 217). More extensive planning was hindered by the exigencies of war, with Russia's position on the Baltic the subject of a series of successful campaigns and sieges under Field-Marshal Boris P. Sheremetev. In order to coordinate the various elements in the construction of St Petersburg, Peter I had established the Chancellery of Urban Affairs in 1706, renamed the Chancellery of Construction in 1723, under the direction of Ul'ian A. Seniavin, with the Italian Domenico Trezzini as its chief architect.[6] The Chancellery was responsible not only for city planning and building designs, through its architects, but also with managing the wider workforce and building materials. As a result, it had a very large budget, by civilian standards, of around 5 per cent of state revenue by the early 1720s.[7]

Victory at the battle of Poltava, in late June 1709, was the turning point in the Great Northern War that convinced Peter himself that the city was securely established and that he could turn his attention to its overall design.[8] From this point onward, there was a move to commission unified plans for certain sections of the city, such as the Admiralty (2), or for the city as a whole, in line with Peter's desired features and, crucially, financial constraints. The desired features of the 'regular' Baroque city, discussed above, were reflected in the well-known plan submitted by the French architect Jean LeBlond in 1716. It was based largely on the development of Vasil'evskii Island, thus reflecting another of Peter's initial ideas for the centre of his new city, with a geometric pattern of streets and canals, surrounded by extensive fortifications in the contemporary French 'Vauban' style. The geographical situation of the city, particularly the complications associated with the marshy terrain and the width of the Neva River, and the enormous expense that such a plan would have incurred made it impossible to adopt fully, especially since construction work in the city was already well underway by the time that LeBlond arrived in Russia. Nevertheless some elements were retained, as shown by the canal and street grid that developed on Vasil'evskii Island from the middle of the eighteenth century onward.[9]

Contemporary legislation also reflected the intention to create a regular appearance for the new city. The types of houses that should be built by different groups in society and what sort of materials they should use was legislated on from 1714 onwards. House plans were commissioned from the architect Domenico Trezzini for groups such as 'common' (*podlye*) and 'notable' (*imenitye*) people.[10] From April 1714 onwards, these plans were used as the basis for orders on the types of houses to be built by different groups in society and what sort of materials were to be used. Such laws also indicate the ongoing presence of the European influence on this process – one of the laws on the construction of 'wattle and daub' (*mazanka*) houses specifically notes that this is 'the Prussian style'.[11] There was also an attempt to legislate on where in the city houses should be located, which was linked to the role of their inhabitants within society. A decree of June 1712 stipulated that the nobility should build their houses along the Neva upriver from Peter's original Winter Palace (4), whilst the merchants and artisans were to build their houses on the opposite bank of the river, on Vasil'evskii Island.[12] However, as with the commissioned plans for St Petersburg in the same period, such laws proved difficult to enforce. At the end of the following year, an official reminder was issued to these groups about their required relocation and such reminders were a common feature of this period.[13]

Similarly, Trezzini's house plans served only for those who could afford to build such houses and only really applied to the façades of buildings in highly visible parts of the city, such as the banks of the main waterways. The decree on the desired location of houses was reissued in March 1720, but it continued to prove very difficult to make people move to certain parts of the city, notably Vasil'evskii Island.[14] Foreign visitors to St Petersburg noted the relative neglect of this part of the city. After a visit to Vasil'evskii Island in March 1725, Friedrich-Wilhelm von Bergholz, a member of the Holstein delegation in Russia, described the considerable number of stone houses standing empty, since their noble owners had residences elsewhere in the city.[15] Sir Francis Dashwood, who came to St Petersburg as part of an English trade delegation in the early 1730s, also noted these fine but uninhabited houses in 1733, as well as the fact that, although the island was supposedly the commercial centre of the city, many merchants did not live there. He believed that this was linked to the construction of a pontoon bridge (25), which allowed them to travel easily from the Admiralty side to the island to conduct their business at the Exchange (28).[16]

As a result of the speed with which the city sprang up, the implementation of Peter's requirements was haphazard at best, not helped by the inhospitable climate and the vagaries of the city's population. It was only after major fires around the Admiralty in the summers of 1736 and 1737 had destroyed much of the existing wooden housing, which lay behind the regulated stone buildings along the city's main waterways and housed the lowest rungs of the city's population, that a major overhaul could begin. The 'Commission for Construction' was established in St Petersburg in mid-1737 to regulate construction of streets and squares so as to ensure a more unified appearance to the central parts of the city.[17] One of the leading architects on the Commission was Petr M. Eropkin, who had been sent abroad to study the arts in Amsterdam and in several Italian cities by Peter I between 1716 and 1724. Upon his return, Eropkin was a prolific architect, working on buildings throughout the city and on the royal estates around it, including Peterhof and Oranienbaum.[18] He drafted a manuscript treatise on architecture, 'Duty of the Architectural Expedition' (*Dolzhnost' arkhitekturnoi ekspiditsii*), several sections of which have been linked to the influence of Andrea Palladio's famous 'Four Books of Architecture' (*I quattro libri dell'architettura*, 1570).[19] The Commission's work was affected by Eropkin's arrest and execution for political conspiracy in 1740, but it succeeded in establishing five separate administrative areas for the city – Admiral'teiskaia, Vasil'evskaia, Peterburgskaia, Vyborgskaia and Moskovskaia – and consolidated the three-pronged street pattern emanating from the Admiralty fortress as the central axis of St Petersburg.[20]

Another outbreak of fires in the late 1740s cleared yet more of the ramshackle housing from St Petersburg's centre, allowing further development to take place. In particular, this period saw the consolidation of Nevskii Prospekt **(16)**, as it became known from 1738 onwards, as the main arterial route in the city, excepting the Neva. The prospekt stretched from the Admiralty to the city limits just beyond the Fontanka river, continuing on to the St Aleksandr Nevskii monastery **(5)**. While the banks of the Neva and the city's lesser waterways, like the Moika and the Fontanka, remained a desirable location for major building projects, by the middle of the century Nevskii Prospekt was the site of a growing number of important buildings. Several major palaces that survive to the present day were constructed in this period. For example, the Anichkov Palace **(33)** was commissioned for Elizabeth's favourite, Count Aleksei G. Razumovskii, shortly after her seizure of the throne in late 1741. The architect of the project was Mikhail G. Zemtsov, a former student of Domenico Trezzini and a colleague of Eropkin's on the 'Commission', who also designed a number of the smaller stone houses on Nevskii Prospekt. The construction of the palace took 12 years and was overseen by Bartolomeo Rastrelli, a French-born architect who had been invited to Russia by Peter I. He was also responsible for designing and building the Stroganov Palace **(31)** at the behest of Baron Sergei G. Stroganov, who commissioned him in 1753.[21] The influence of Rastrelli's elaborate style can be seen in a range of projects throughout the city during Elizabeth's reign, particularly in his work on the royal residences, discussed below.

A unified overall appearance for St Petersburg was naturally hampered by the mixture of architectural styles throughout the city, unsurprising in view of the range of backgrounds of the various architects – French, German, Italian and Russian. However, by the early 1760s, the most prominent aspects of the city's overall appearance improved considerably, aided by earlier mapping efforts, the draft plans for different parts of the city as part of the work of the 'Commission' and the projects of its various contributors, all of which contributed to the famous 1753 map of the city.[22] These changes also affected the lives of the city's inhabitants and the experiences of the early population of St Petersburg will be examined in the next section.

A populated city

The process of populating the new city was also subject to official regulation and it was conducted in a manner similar to conscription. Building work was initially begun by troops and local inhabitants, but the numbers were insufficient for both Peter's plans and his patience. Beginning with 40,000 workers mentioned in a law issued in March 1704, tens of thousands of workers were sent to work on the new city, and a pattern of two annual 'shifts' of three months (between April and October) was established in 1705. Although the number of workers was increased in 1707, the demands of the war against Sweden and the high rate of desertion, despite the use of armed guards to escort workers to the site, meant that the required number was always lower than that stipulated.[23] Seniavin wrote repeatedly to the Tsar, and later to the Senate, about the need for more workers to replace losses.[24] The miserable working and living conditions, the considerable distance from their homes, and the nature of the conscription itself meant that it proved difficult to keep up with this demand. A large number of workers were also believed to have died during the construction process due to the poor working conditions, a view which featured strongly in foreign accounts of the city.[25] Luppov's conclusion that the numbers given by foreigners were undoubtedly exaggerated is a persuasive one.[26] The exact number of deaths caused by disease and squalid working conditions has been somewhat difficult to establish, not least because of the lack of accurate information.[27] However, an excessively high mortality rate seems unlikely given that St Petersburg had only a small resident population during the early years – around 8000 in 1710 – that was bolstered by the biannual influx of workers, and the fact that the number of inhabitants in the city rose rapidly to approximately 40,000 by 1725.[28]

In addition to these conscripted workers, both the nobility and the merchantry were expected to populate Peter's new city and carry out their new 'useful' functions there. For example, Charles Whitworth, the English ambassador to Russia, noted a decree in late May 1712 that ordered 1000 of the 'best' noble families, a similar number of merchants and 2000 artisans to build houses in St Petersburg.[29] Another decree, in 1714, again ordered 1000 of the wealthiest noble families to move from Moscow to St Petersburg and build houses in the city.[30] Peter's long-term planning for the move to St Petersburg was reflected in the submission to the Senate in August 1712 of a list of 1212 members of the military and civil officials, merchants and artisans, who were ordered to move to St Petersburg after the conclusion of the war against Sweden. These plans were then put into action in the later stages of the war, with the Senate responsible for overseeing the transfer process.[31] Peter allowed for very few exceptions to these orders, although heavily pregnant women and the very ill were allowed to delay (but not avoid) their departure. A further decree stated that nobles who had failed to move to St Petersburg by 1725 would have their property demolished and then be forced to live in huts (*chernye izby*) on Vasil'evskii Island.[32] However, the fact that laws ordering moves to the new city were reissued until Peter's death and the Senate received a steady stream of noble petitions requesting leave to return to their estates indicates that the move to St Petersburg continued to meet with resistance.[33]

There were good reasons for this reluctance on the part of the prospective inhabitants of the new city. Leaving aside the hardships involved in the move itself and the challenges posed by the different climate of the Petersburg region, there were serious financial implications attached to this relocation. In addition to the transport of a household to St Petersburg, the expense of constructing a new house and the higher cost of living in the new city could challenge even the more wealthy members of the elite. Friedrich Christian Weber, a Hanoverian member of the English embassy in the city between 1714 and 1719, wrote that some noble families believed that they had lost almost two-thirds of their capital in making the move.[34] One explanation for this expense may be that the geographical location of St Petersburg made it much further from the majority of noble estates than Moscow, which had an impact on the income and produce generated for use by the nobility. Dashwood, writing in the early 1730s, noted the example of Prince Fedor A. Lopukhin, who had an annual income of 30,000 rubles from his Siberian estates but could use less than half of that in St Petersburg.[35] The other part of Lopukhin's income doubtless included some form of payment 'in kind', such as foodstuffs, fuel and other goods. Whilst a noble was resident in Moscow, it was relatively straightforward to send such goods from an estate, and thereby keep costs down, but the relocation to St Petersburg made the nobility more reliant on cash income.[36]

There was some official recognition of this issue by 1719, when nobles owning fewer than 100-serf households, and middling-income merchants were excused from the compulsory move.[37] Nevertheless, the population transfer continued to be subject to official scrutiny throughout this period. A census was taken of each house and its inhabitants in 1717, although in a growing city with a large migrant population, the information for some parts of the city was difficult to keep up to date.[38] Ageeva highlights a Senate report which listed nobles who had failed to make the move to St Petersburg by 1723 and prompted an investigation into the circumstances behind their absence, including claims of illness made through the Medical Chancellery.[39] The move of the court back to Moscow briefly for the coronation of Catherine I in 1724 and for a longer sojourn during the short reign of the young

Peter II interrupted this transfer. However, the clear statement made by the triumphal entry of Anna Ivanovna into St Petersburg in 1732 (discussed in Chapter 3) marked a decisive shift in this process. The presence of both the court and the main bodies of the state administration underlined the importance of St Petersburg as a location for the nobility, despite the considerable resentment at the expense and discomfort it incurred. The increase in building activity from the 1730s onwards, discussed below, bears this out.

In terms of the population of the city, the city grew at a rapid rate, given its humble origins. From 40,000 inhabitants in 1725, the city grew to have around 70,000 inhabitants by 1737, according to information collected by the Holy Synod.[40] The Police Chancellery was also responsible for collecting such information in this period. Chancellor Aleksei P. Bestuzhev-Riumin ordered the office to compile information about the city's population, including not only Russian inhabitants (either residents or visitors), but also military personnel and foreigners, be they diplomats, merchants or naval personnel. General-Policemaster Aleksei D. Tatishchev responded by outlining the various difficulties of such a task.[41] He then wrote to Elizabeth's Cabinet Secretary, Ivan A. Cherkasov, requesting that the College of Foreign Affairs ask the foreign representatives directly for the required information.[42] The resulting report gave the official figure (with the attendant caution about the precision or veracity of such data for this period) as 74,283.[43] For the sake of comparison, Johann Georgi, in his celebrated study of St Petersburg in the 1790s, gave a population figure of 74,273 (excluding children) for the city in 1750.[44] Thereafter, the city's population appears to have stayed around the same level, despite the official number of inhabitants often reported as around 120,000 by the beginning of Catherine II's reign, because of the lower number of military personnel in the city during the Seven Years War.[45]

To put the extent of St Petersburg's growth into context, it is worth comparing with some of its contemporaries by 1750. Although it was still dwarfed by the major European capital cities, like London (population 675,000), Paris (576,000) and Vienna (175,000), it was on a par with the capitals of its neighbouring states, including Stockholm (60,000), Copenhagen (93,000), Berlin (90,000), Dresden (52,000). It was also considerably larger than the small residential cities of the German states in this period, like Braunschweig (21,000), Kassel (19,000), Mannheim (20,000) and Würzburg (15,000).[46] The latter examples are important, in that their creation and development occurred in a similarly short period of time to that of St Petersburg. Although it would flourish as a major European city during the reign of Catherine II, thanks in no small part to her policies, it is important to note at this point that this period was fundamental, not only in creating the city, but also ensuring that it continued to develop after Peter I's death with the consolidation of the presence of key institutions and their personnel.

Nature and its uses

The Neva River was a major geographical feature of St Petersburg. Its impact on St Petersburg's development and on the lives of its inhabitants owed much to its sheer physical presence at the heart of the city. Unlike the narrower Moskva River, which ran through Moscow, the width of the Neva and the fact that it flowed directly into the Baltic Sea made it very difficult to bridge. The inclement climate also made crossing the river a dangerous prospect during the spring and autumn months. The situation was further complicated by Peter's desire for the inhabitants of his new city to become capable, not to say enthusiastic sailors. A system of fines was devised to ensure that military officers sailed, rather than rowed their vessels in good weather.[47] On a wider level, a law in April 1718 provided boats for people of 'various ranks' so that they could sail every Sunday. There were punishments for those who missed these outings more than twice in one month.[48] Even the city's distinguished residents were not exempt. In order to participate in Peter's marine celebrations, most notably the 'naval assemblies' (*vodiannye assamblei*), members of the elite were expected to have their own vessels, including a yacht and two launches. Failure to attend these events was punished in typically Petrine terms. After a poor showing at one such event to celebrate the Tsar's return to the city in late July 1723, Peter instructed the city's General-Policemaster Anton M. Devier to collect fines of 50 roubles from future absentees who did not have an adequate excuse.[49]

Peter's active stance against the construction of bridges in the city was another means of 'encouraging' the use of boats amongst the populace. As a result, the only bridges built during his reign were over St Petersburg's minor waterways, such as the wooden footbridge linking the Sts Peter and Paul Fortress to the Petersburg side of the city.[50] The first to span the Neva was a pontoon bridge (25), built in 1727 and renovated in 1734, which ran between the Church of the Resurrection of Christ, on Vasil'evskii Island, and the Church of St Isaac of Dalmatia (11).[51] Despite the appearance of bridges, the river remained a major transport route throughout this period. In the 1730s, Dashwood noted that the state monopolised the hire of 'boat ferries' and that the city's merchants tended to own their own boats, in part due to their need to negotiate the various waterways to reach the Exchange on Vasil'evskii Island. Interestingly, he added that 'publick houses' – by which he presumably meant *traktiry* or *avsterii* (in other words, hostelries) – also had their own vessels.[52] This provision was not unusual in other contemporary cities beside major rivers – for example, in London, they were used for a variety of roles, such as providing transport for those individuals wishing to explore the 'delights' of Southwark. They also indicate the integral role of water transport in the everyday life of St Petersburg.

Peter used the Neva as a central part of many celebrations, again reflecting his enthusiasm for sailing, as with the celebrations for the major naval victory at Hangöudd organised in the city in September 1714. Attendance at the event was clearly expected, as the plans were formally announced on 8 September in a printed declaration, read out in churches and distributed with the newspaper, *Vedomosti*. Events began the following day with a procession of ships into St Petersburg, greeted by cannon salutes from both fortresses, followed by a parade (in carriages) with Swedish prisoners of war through a specially constructed triumphal arch to the Senate building, then located near the Sts Peter and Paul Fortress (**1**).[53] Peter was promoted to vice-admiral and the celebrations culminated with a banquet in Aleksandr D. Menshikov's palace (**13**), during which there was a display of fireworks.[54] St Petersburg also hosted the celebrations for the other major naval victory of the Great Northern War, the battle of Grengram in 1720, which had a similar procession of captured ships and victorious troops on 8 September, followed by fireworks for three days.[55] The naval theme was even present in several of Peter's land-based celebrations. For example, as part of the ongoing celebrations for the Peace of Nystadt, there was a carnival parade in St Petersburg in February 1722 that featured floats in the form of ships. On several other occasions, Peter or members of his close circle attended court masquerades in naval costume.[56] Even after Peter I's death, the river played a part in his funeral ceremony (discussed in more detail in Chapter 3), when an 'avenue' (*prospekt*) was marked out on the frozen river to allow the procession to travel from the Winter Palace to the Sts Peter and Paul Cathedral.

The rulers that followed Peter I were much less personally involved in navigational matters than Peter. They did not themselves build ships or initiate impromptu 'maritime assemblies', but the launching of new ships continued to be celebrated on occasion, as during the Petrine period. For example, Anna Ivanovna attended the launch of a ship bearing her name in June 1736. The same vessel was then used to host a court banquet and a ball the following week, which was attended by the Persian ambassador and other foreign ministers.[57] On a grander scale, the opening of the Peter the Great Canal at Kronstadt in late July 1752 emphasised the importance of the continuation of his naval legacy by his daughter, Elizabeth, and was the focus of several days of celebrations, attended by both Russian and foreign dignitaries.[58] As with the other inhabitants of the city, the ruler and members of the royal family also regularly used the river for transport purposes, either to move between different parts of the city or from the city to the royal estates at Petergof and Oranienbaum.[59]

The Summer Gardens were another symbol of the city's relationship with the natural world. As early as March 1704, Peter wrote to Tikhon N. Streshnev, head of the *Razriadnyi prikaz* and one of his trusted confidantes, asking him to send various bushes, trees and plants in order to establish gardens in his new city, which were to be located on the southern bank of the Neva, opposite the fortress.[60] Over the next decade, Peter continued to collect plants for the gardens from the warmer areas of the Empire and also imported more exotic specimens from abroad, along with gardeners to ensure their survival in the harsh climate. In particular, Dutch gardeners, such as Jan Roosen in 1712, had an important influence on the early development of the gardens. However, in 1716, Peter decided to create a regular garden in the French style and chose a design proposed by the architect LeBlond. His plan for the gardens consisted of a central alley lined with Classical busts and statues, parallel to the 'Swan' canal that separated the garden from Tsaritsyn Meadow (6), from the Neva River to the Moika River. The rest of the gardens were arranged symmetrically on either side of the alley, featuring fountains, pavilions and a wide variety of plants and trees.[61]

The Poperechnyi canal divided the gardens into two, although they were linked by a small bridge. From this canal to the Neva was the 'first' Summer Garden (8), as begun by Ivan Matveev in 1707, which contained Peter's stone Summer Palace (7) and the 'grotto', a common feature in contemporary European gardens.[62] This part of the gardens was often used to host the court's outdoor celebrations, discussed in Chapter 4. The other half, from the canal to the Moika River, was developed after 1716 as the 'second' Summer Garden (9). The 'third' Summer Garden (10), also known as Tsaritsyn Garden due to its origins as a gift from Peter to Catherine, lay on the other side of the Moika and was subsequently connected to the main Summer Gardens by a covered footbridge. This garden housed an orangery used for the court kitchens and later became the site of Elizabeth's 'new' wooden Summer Palace (22), designed and built by Rastrelli in 1742. The final major royal garden lay on the other side of the Fontanka and was known as the 'Italian' Gardens (12), after the style of the small palace built there in 1712 for the infant Tsarevna Anna Petrovna.[63]

These gardens played two important roles in the wider context of the city. Firstly, the gardens were used by the court to host a number of social events and other celebrations, even if the fickle nature of the weather occasionally dampened the tone of proceedings.[64] During the summer months, when the court resided in the city, rather than at Tsarskoe Selo or Petergof, the Empress and the royal family would be based in the two Summer Palaces, hence the use of the surrounding gardens for banquets, illuminations and even theatrical performances was appropriate. Secondly, the gardens can be linked to the wider theme of regulation and control within the city's spaces, since the regular design implicitly represented a control of nature. The Dutch influence on the early Summer Gardens, through both personnel and design, can be linked to this theme.[65] This endeavour was continued in the area surrounding St Petersburg, with Peter involved in both planning and constructing the estates at Petergof, Ekateringof and Strel'na.[66]

This theme was also reflected in early depictions of the city, which could also be used to show the new city as a means of controlling and using nature to create something significant. This approach is perhaps most clearly reflected in the work of another contemporary engraver, Aleksei F. Zubov, whose 'Panorama of St Petersburg' (1716) featured Peter and Catherine in one of the boats on the Neva. Kaganov argues convincingly that this depiction of the city should be considered alongside the imagery used by Archbishop Feofan Prokopovich, likening the city to the ship of St Peter, as part of the wider efforts to present the city as both a sacred space and a source of calmness in an otherwise wild (in the sense of uncontrolled) environment.[67] As part of the same collection, Zubov also produced a contemporary image of the Summer Gardens, stretching out from the river's bank toward the horizon. The view of the gardens arranged in neatly defined sections with regular, geometric avenues may have been idealised, to some extent, but it is a clear image of order and one which was very much in keeping with later images of the city.

The city's developing relationship with nature was also present in such depictions. The Dutch artist Pieter Picart contrasted the large empty space of the river with the city, represented by a small number of isolated buildings as a thin line against the horizon, in an early engraving of St Petersburg from 1704. This image of the city dominated by its natural surroundings continued, despite St Petersburg's considerable development during this period. A 1725 engraving by Christopher Marselis showed St Petersburg from the perspective of an observer on the island of Kronstadt, with the city reduced to a shoreline sandwiched between the river and the sky.[68] By the middle of the century, the famous engravings by Mikhail Makhaev focus instead on the city's principal perspectives, emphasising the ordered, constructed nature of the city. The river is still present, naturally, but it is no longer dominant, being hemmed in by stone embankments and quaysides.[69] By mid-century, St Petersburg was being presented as firmly established and in control of its environment.

A new social setting

Relocation to St Petersburg had a disruptive effect on the social life of its inhabitants. The familiar setting of Moscow, with its established neighbourhoods and the presence of many palaces of the leading noble families, was now replaced with the unfamiliar and imposed setting of St Petersburg. However, the legislation governing the transfer and settlement of the nobility and other social groups in the new city was only part of the picture. St Petersburg was also intended to host a number of new social settings, mainly for the elite, in order to encourage interaction in an explicitly European fashion. These forms of sociable interaction were familiar to contemporary foreign visitors to the city and drew comments to that effect in their accounts. The residences of the court and the leading nobility were expected to provide the setting for such occasions, which had an impact on their subsequent development.

The Winter and Summer Palaces provided important focal points for the court in St Petersburg, although their Petrine incarnations were modest in comparison with their successors. Between 1711 and 1762, there were five incarnations of the Winter Palace. Four of them were stone buildings on the site of the modern Winter Palace on the banks of the Neva, beginning with the small Petrine Palace (4) in 1711. This building was rebuilt and extended between 1732 and 1735, incorporating the nearby palaces formerly belonging to the Apraksin, Iaguzhinskii and Kikin families, before Rastrelli undertook a further renovation at the end of Elizabeth's reign (20). The other Winter Palace (21) was a temporary wooden structure, built on the Moika River for the Empress Elizabeth between February and November 1755 by Bartolomeo Rastrelli during the construction of the 'new' stone Winter Palace.[70] The Petrine Summer Palace (7) was built in 1712 within the Summer Gardens on the banks of the Fontanka, and continued to be used throughout this period. However, a second Summer Palace (22), a much larger building, was built by Rastrelli between 1741 and 1743 at the other end of the gardens, where the Moika met the Fontanka.[71] Although it was initially commissioned by Anna Leopoldovna, it was completed and subsequently used extensively during Elizabeth's reign.

In addition to the individual tastes of the rulers in question, another reason for the number of renovations of the royal palaces was the related desire to reflect the grandeur of the Russian court and the increase in its social activities. Whilst Peter had made use of Menshikov's palace to host major celebrations – like the wedding of his niece Anna Ivanovna to the Duke of Courland in 1710 – the development of the court as an institution and its associated social events, such as balls, masquerades and the theatre, required the royal palaces to provide a grander setting. At the same time, the close proximity of these royal palaces to the houses of the nobility, an aspect of St Petersburg's development that had no precedent in Moscow, had an important influence on the development of these 'new' social spaces.[72] Nobles were not accustomed to opening their homes to large numbers of guests and even the process of 'visiting' was conducted in a formal manner in Muscovite Russia. For example, the influential sixteenth-century text on household management, the *Domostroi*, contains advice for both receiving and being a guest.[73] However, this situation changed with the introduction of new forms of social gathering, from 1699 onward, following Peter's return from his Grand Embassy.

These developments were embodied in the law on 'assemblies' (*assamblei*), issued on 26 November 1718, although this was probably a confirmation of existing Petrine practice.[74] The law was most likely the result of Peter's second foreign trip in 1717, where he observed social practices at other European courts. The foreign influence was highlighted in the text of the *ukaz* itself, when it was noted that a French term had to be used to describe these events because there was no Russian equivalent.[75] It is probably no coincidence that the first assembly was held in the St Petersburg residence of the 'Prince-Pope' of the 'All-Drunken Synod' Petr I. Buturlin, an appropriately laid-back host for such a social evening, on 27 November.[76] In general, the 'assemblies' were to be held two or three times a week, as an informal gathering in a noble's house at which both men and women of various social backgrounds (Peter was careful to include master shipwrights and prominent merchants) could talk amongst themselves, play games, dance and generally interact together, regardless of the usual social barriers.[77] The informality of the occasion was encapsulated in certain practices, such as permitting any gentleman to ask any woman (including the Empress) to dance. The law had been signed by Devier, in his new role as the General-Policemaster of St Petersburg, which will be discussed in the next chapter, and the element of control was still present at even these supposedly informal events. All prospective houses were carefully checked beforehand, to ensure that they met the appropriate criteria, and, as with several Petrine social occasions, participants were 'encouraged' not to leave by armed guards.[78]

Nevertheless, the 'assemblies' were a significant development since they effectively represented an attempt to extend sociable and inclusive forms of interaction into the previously exclusive space of the home. They were more accessible than previous social gatherings had been, by virtue of their location in the houses of prominent nobles, as opposed to the main royal palaces, and the explicit inclusion of a number of non-noble social groups. They also provided a forum for the consolidation of European social practices, encapsulated in activities like polite conversation and the various forms of entertainment, like dancing and parlour games. Bergholz provides some of the most detailed descriptions of these events in his diary, with the evening of 18 February 1722 being a useful example. The assembly took place at Count Andrei A. Matveev's house and was well attended by both men and women, although not by the Tsar. Bergholz compliments the host's daughter, Mariia A. Rumiantseva, on her education and social graces – he is less kind about the Court Physician Laurentius Blumentrost's young bride, who is described as a 'coquette'. Importantly, he is also clear about the shortcomings of such events, complaining that men and women continue to sit separately in the hall and that, when not dancing, they are neither willing nor able to conduct conversation.[79] Nevertheless, such social activities and particularly the presence of women also meant that the 'assemblies' were an important contribution to the development of new behavioural values amongst their participants, which will be discussed in more detail in Chapter 4.

Although the process of change within Russian social life continued after Peter's death, attendance at such events was narrowed to exclude all but members of the nobility, in particular the court elite. On 11 January 1727, Catherine I issued a law that replaced the 'assemblies' with regular evening receptions at court, referred to as *kurdakhi* (later *kurtagi*) or *s"ezdy* – the two terms are used interchangeably in official accounts of this period.[80] The inspiration for these occasions may have come from her visits to Western courts in Germany and France with Peter, since the term has its origins in the Franco-German hybrid term 'courtag' used to describe receptions held at court.[81] There were a number of important differences between the 'assemblies' and their replacements: firstly, they took place only in the royal residences; secondly, they were held on a fixed day (Thursday) of every week; and thirdly, access was restricted to distinguished guests and other individuals holding a high rank.[82] In other respects, however, social life at court had not changed tone from the Petrine era, with the emphasis still very much on drinking on certain occasions, much to the chagrin of foreign observers like the Saxon minister, Count Johann Lefort.[83]

This pattern of regular access to the court for high-ranking members of the nobility continued for the rest of this period. For example, as dowager duchess of Courland, Anna Ivanovna held two weekly court evenings at her palace in Mitau, on Sundays and Wednesdays, according to Bergholz in September 1724.[84] Lady Rondeau, the wife of the British resident in Russia during the 1730s, noted that she continued this practice as Empress. In her *Letters*, she provides a brief description of their informal atmosphere, with the assembled court playing cards and socialising 'freely', although she stressed that Anna kept her dignity at all times.[85] Karl Berch, a contemporary Swedish visitor to St Petersburg, noted how the relatively open 'assemblies' had fallen into disuse following Peter I's death and how this type of socialising continued only amongst the city's resident foreign ministers. He also noted the contrast between these occasions and the more regular 'courtags', which took place behind closed doors.[86] Elizabeth's court continued this trend and these events were regularly held on Sundays as part of the Empress's extensive social calendar. During her reign, the distinction between the *kurtag* and the *s"ezd* was clarified: the latter took place in the morning, while the former was an evening event. These occasions were intended for the Empress's enjoyment, as highlighted in laws issued in 1732 and 1752, which stated that she should not be petitioned on such occasions.[87]

Access to such events appears to have relied on several factors and rank undoubtedly played an important role. The official documentation is not entirely clear on this issue, often simply referring to the attendees of such events as 'distinguished' (*znatnye*) people. This term had previously been used to indicate a specific group within the nobility on ceremonial occasions, such as at Catherine I's coronation in 1724.[88] The term continued to be used throughout the post-Petrine period.[89] The likely composition of this group is suggested by an order sent by Baron Cherkasov to the Police Chancellery in January 1748 on the need to compile a list of all members of the first five Ranks of the Table of Ranks, plus their wives and children.[90] Since the Police Chancellery was the body responsible for notifying 'the usual' attendees for the *kurtagi*, it seems reasonable to conclude that this list identifies at least part of this 'distinguished' group.[91] By contrast, the lower orders were kept well away from such events, with guards posted near the palace to ensure that passers-by and traffic could not interfere with arrivals.[92]

Although there was undoubtedly an element of compulsion in the creation of and participation in the new social spaces in St Petersburg, they played an important part in changing elite social life and the various forms of interaction within it. The fact that they were initially open to other social groups during the Petrine era is also important, since it represents an attempt to create a wider sociable group within urban society, albeit one that did not always quite work as intended. That this 'openness' was subsequently restricted was due in no small part to the increasing dominance of the court in the city's social life and arguably served as a symbol of the nobility's desire to ensure that the key forums of power and influence, close to the ruler, remained very much in their hands alone. However, by the latter stages of this period, such events would again be made accessible to groups beyond the traditional court elite of the wealthy high-born nobility, albeit with important restrictions still in place. Further issues concerned with access to and participation in these spaces will be examined in detail in Chapter 4.

A learning environment

The importance of education in the Petrine worldview, with its emphasis on the acquisition of skills useful for the development of the state, meant that St Petersburg's space was influenced by the various educational institutions spread across the city. The dispersed locations of these establishments – the Naval Academy housed in the former Kikin Palace on the Admiralty side (**14**), the school attached to the Artillery Laboratory on the Liteinyi side (**34**), and the St Aleksandr Nevskii seminary (**5**) attached to the monastery outside the city limits – meant that the early city did not have a consolidated 'academic' space. However, from 1729, the housing of the Academy of Sciences (**18**) in the former palace of Tsaritsa Praskov'ia Fedorovna, alongside the Kunstkamera and its library, on the Strelka on Vasil'evskii Island was a major step toward providing an academic centre for the city. This process was further aided by the founding of the Cadet Corps (**13**), which was housed in the Menshikov Palace from 1731 onward after its previous owner's exile to Siberia in 1727.[93]

The Academy of Sciences had been the subject of discussions in correspondence between Peter I and the German philosopher Gottfried Leibniz since the last years of the seventeenth century.[94] The intended model drew on established European examples, such as the Royal Society (London), the Académie Royale des Sciences (Paris) and, in particular, the Academy of Sciences in Berlin.[95] The role envisaged for the Russian Academy of Sciences has been extensively discussed by historians, taking into consideration the nature of the situation in Russia and Peter's personal motivation to 'modernise' Russia.[96] However, more recent work has convincingly argued that the purpose of the Academy was not merely to establish Russia on the academic map of Europe, although it was undoubtedly an important scientific research institution, but to contribute to the 'civilisation' of the Russian elite.[97] As part of its role as an educational establishment in a wider sense, the Academy and its members were also intended to serve as an example or model (*obrazets*) for Russia, according to the 'Project' of its foundation, signed on 22 January 1724.[98] Peter's experience of such scientific institutions during his Grand Embassy had shown him that such bodies encouraged a type of civilised discourse and internal order which he wished to see develop in Russian society.[99]

This wider role for the Academy was reflected in the activities set out in the 'Project'. In addition to weekly meetings, which were to be attended by academics and the ruler to discuss progress and view results, academics had to participate in open meetings (referred to as 'assemblies') three times a year and also give a number of public lectures.[100] Although the identity of the prospective audience of such meetings and lectures was not elaborated in the 'Project', the staffing of the Academy itself made clear that this was to be a small and well-educated elite group. The fact that foreign scholars dominated the personnel of the early Academy meant that the languages of academic discourse were Latin or German, thereby restricting access to proceedings.[101] The shortage of Russians with the necessary knowledge or interest to participate in these events reduced the prospective audience further still. However, the 'Project' included plans to create both a school (*gimnaziia*) and a university attached to the Academy, with the aim of eventually producing educated Russian students.[102] The law establishing the Academy was issued by Peter on 28 January 1724, although the institution was officially opened on 2 November 1725, just over 10 months after his death.[103]

The Academy's first 'public' assembly took place shortly afterwards, on 27 December 1725, in the house of Petr P. Shafirov and was attended by Tsarevna Anna Petrovna (Peter's eldest daughter), her husband, the Duke of Holstein, and around 400 other dignitaries.[104] The varied composition of this audience makes clear that not all of them were present purely for intellectual reasons. While Archbishop Feofan Prokopovich's educated credentials are beyond reproach, Aleksandr D. Menshikov, although an honorary Fellow of the Royal Society, could be said to represent the members of the court elite attending for either political or social reasons.[105] The proceedings of this meeting were published in Königsberg later in the same year. The opening speeches emphasised the beneficial nature of such assemblies. Georg Bernhard Bilfinger, Professor of Physics, unsurprisingly noted Peter's benign legacy in establishing order and discipline in Russia, using the Academy as an example, whilst Jacob Hermann, Professor of Mathematics, highlighted the need for such civilised discussions in the public arena, before moving on to more concrete academic matters.[106] The account of the Academy's second public assembly, also held in Shafirov's house, on 1 August 1726 followed a similar pattern – a distinguished audience (this time including the Empress), praise for the ruler and then papers on scientific subjects.[107]

Although these public assemblies established a link between the Academy and its role as an exemplary institution, Werrett convincingly argues that the response from beyond the academic community in St Petersburg was hardly positive, since the intended audience for the public assemblies proved largely uninterested in their findings.[108] As a result, the assemblies were allowed to lapse between February 1732 and November 1749, when they began to be held again regularly, usually on an annual basis (with a short gap between 1753 and 1754).[109] The revived assembly, which was timed to coincide with the celebration of the Empress's accession to the throne, had a familiar content. Georg Wilhelm Richmann gave a speech on the laws of evaporation, with a response from Stepan P. Krasheninnikov, and Mikhail V. Lomonosov spoke in praise of the Empress. These speeches were subsequently published, along with a description of the fireworks from the celebrations.[110] The other assemblies from the 1750s generally took place in early September, which coincided with the Empress's name-day celebrations. The published accounts of these assemblies and the other celebrations ended in 1751, but the activities of the Academy continued to be described in the *Sanktpeterburgskie vedomosti*, the official newspaper, for the rest of the period.[111] On a wider European level, the Academy promoted itself by establishing links with its fellow institutions in Paris, Berlin and Uppsala, and publishing its academic work in an annual journal, the *Commentarii academiae scientarum imperialis Petropolitanae*, from 1728 (renamed the *Novi commentarii academiae scientarum imperialis Petropolitanae* in 1747).[112]

The Academy's subsidiary activities were another area where the question of access was directly addressed, principally the library and the museum. Both of these institutions originated in Peter's private collections, which had been transferred from Moscow to the Summer Palace during the first decade of St Petersburg's existence. The collections steadily grew as more items were purchased and, in 1718, they were moved to the newly constructed palace of Aleksandr V. Kikin, who had been arrested and executed for treason earlier that year, before finally finding a permanent home in the new Academy of Sciences building in 1729.[113] The museum began as Peter's collection of curiosities, or Kunstkamera. Such collections were a means to reflect a ruler's wealth, status and civilisation and rulers at courts across Europe, large and small, spent considerable sums in putting them together throughout the early modern period.[114] The collection of Rudolph II, initially housed in Prague before being moved to Vienna after the Thirty Years War by his successors, was one of the most extensive and famous in this period.[115]

Linking these famous collections to Peter I was King Augustus II of Saxony-Poland, who had visited the extensive Habsburg collection in Vienna, as well as the collections of Louis XIV at Versailles and of the Medici in Florence during his travels in the 1680s. The court at Dresden already had an impressive collection, begun by Elector August in 1560, and Augustus took a keen interest in developing it further.[116] Such collections of curiosities had had predecessors in Russia, notably that of Peter's father, Aleksei Mikhailovich.[117] Peter's own interest had been further fuelled by his visits to a number of such collections, including Dresden, during his Grand Embassy in 1697. The anatomical collection of Frederik Ruysch which he saw in Amsterdam proved particularly fascinating and Peter subsequently purchased it in 1717 for 30,000 ducats.[118] The Kunstkamera gradually grew in size through the acquisition of existing collections, such as that of Ruysch, gifts from foreign dignitaries, like the famous Globe of Gottorp (installed in the Kunstkamera in 1717), and Peter's own enthusiasm and scientific curiosity.[119] For example, he issued a decree on 'monsters' (*monstry, to est' urody*) in 1718, which ordered that any creatures, including humans, displaying deformities or other unusual characteristics should be reported to local officials, with a financial reward based on their condition. They would then be collected and sent to St Petersburg for analysis.[120]

However, the Kunstkamera was distinctive in two respects, both of which are significant for this discussion of the Academy's role within St Petersburg. Firstly, the collection illustrates the wider European interest in the relationship between science and nature in the early modern period, highlighted by Peter's own experiences in the Netherlands with Ruysch's controversial collection. Russian Orthodox tradition forbade the dissection of corpses and storage of body organs, because of the fear of the corpse rising to reclaim its component parts, and it has thus been suggested that the Kunstkamera symbolises Peter's desire to demonstrate the scientific control of nature (and its discontents).[121] Secondly, and closely related to the latter point, the Kunstkamera has traditionally been viewed as Russia's first public museum, in contrast to the largely private collections of the Muscovite Tsars, mentioned above. The collection was to be open to visitors, importantly with no entrance fee, despite suggestions to the contrary by Pavel I. Iaguzhinskii, a member of Peter's close circle and later General-Procurator of the Senate. As an incentive, visitors were to be offered complimentary coffee, wine or vodka, although given the nature of the collection, the latter may have been necessary to steady the nerves.[122] The visual and visceral nature of the displays in the Kunstkamera also made it potentially accessible to a wider group of people than either the academic or printed output of the Academy, although again it is difficult to draw firm conclusions in terms of numbers from the limited information available.

The library was initially based on Peter's own collection and the collection of the Duke of Courland, which had been sent from Mitau to St Petersburg in 1716.[123] Again, this base was supplemented by foreign purchases and further expanded with legacies of books in the wills of scholars and other state officials, such as the extensive personal library of the court doctor, Robert Erskine.[124] As with the Kunstkamera, the library was purposefully made open to visitors and the records of the Academy contain the names of early readers, such as Feofan Prokopovich and James Bruce.[125] Both the library and the Kunstkamera were promoted on a wider scale with the publication of a descriptive booklet (or brochure) in 1741. This short work described the history of both the Academy of Sciences and the two collections, followed by a brief catalogue of their holdings and engravings of the building.[126] Such catalogues were as important as a statement about the extent and highlights of these collections as they were about their scientific import or organisation.[127]

In each of the above cases, these institutions presented St Petersburg to an audience that stretched beyond the domestic sphere. The lack of interest in their scientific pursuits from the average inhabitant of the city can be tempered, to an extent, by a recognition that they played an important role in attracting attention to what was happening in this previously under-active part of Europe. Foreign visitors during this period visited these institutions and commented, generally favourably, on their facilities and activities.[128] The Academy, seeking the financial security of ongoing patronage, played an active role in promoting the ruler and their court through a variety of means, which will be discussed further in Chapter 3.

A ceremonial city

With the presence of the court and the social elite in St Petersburg, the city naturally became an important space in which the regular rituals and celebrations associated with the ruler took place. The ceremonial space of the city, however, presents a series of complex relationships which defy a straightforward characterisation. The creation process and the influence of foreigners in its design led some historians to conclude that St Petersburg should be seen as a modernising project, as discussed in the Introduction. Similarly, one might expect tensions to emerge between the officially mandated regularity of St Petersburg and the traditionally spontaneous nature of the festivities that it hosted. Instead, recent work has stressed the importance of religion as a component part of the new state celebrations, rather than as the target of supposedly secularising reforms.[129] Similarly, the raucous behaviour associated with popular festivities was also present in a number of the court's activities during this period, particularly during the Petrine era, even if its seemingly chaotic nature masked a complex set of rituals and symbolic relationships.[130] As with many of its contemporaries across Europe, St Petersburg proved to be both a continuation and an innovation on what had preceded it in the Russian context.

Certain elements have been used to try to differentiate official and popular celebrations, but instead, these only demonstrate the degree of overlap within the St Petersburg setting. One interpretation, proposed by Mazaev, contrasts the organisation of popular celebrations – typically circular (unregulated movement around a defined centre) – with the more linear nature of state celebrations (consciously controlled movement towards a fixed destination).[131] However, in both cases, the nature of the spaces described by this model is not as clear-cut as it suggests. Whilst the distinction was certainly present in St Petersburg, and it is clear in the number of triumphal marches and processions that occurred within the city, making use of the arterial routes, there is a sense in which these two types of movement become confused with regard to the nature of the city itself. In other words, the centre of St Petersburg effectively served as the centre of its festive space, albeit the movement around it was more tightly regulated than in Mazaev's characterisation of popular celebrations. This did not apply to the (linear) military celebrations, where there was a defined destination, as with the Cathedral of the Holy Trinity and the large square around it (3), which were used for many of the early victory celebrations in St Petersburg. One could also point to the military exercises that took place on Trinity Square and Tsaritsyn Meadow as evidence of organised movement around a fixed centre, again challenging Mazaev's formulation.

The architecture of the city has already been discussed in relation to its intended role as an ideal, regulated, early modern city, but such architecture also had an impact on its ceremonial and festive life. Keller refers to St Petersburg's streets, buildings and embankments as 'an original ballroom costume' in her examination of the city's festive life, since they provided a splendid background for the city's numerous celebrations.[132] The 'regularity' of the buildings, and therefore the spaces between them, cannot fail to have had an influence on events occurring within them, whether they were state celebrations or traditional festivities.[133] However, particular events also played an important part in shaping the spaces in which they occurred. Triumphal arches provide one example of this – drawing on the Classical model, they were built to commemorate a victory and were then used as part of the victory celebrations. Although often temporary structures, increasingly there was a move in the second half of the seventeenth century to use these arches as permanent monuments to military prowess.[134] This was certainly the case in Russia, where temporary arches were built for the celebration of major victories during the seventeenth century. This practice was consolidated during the Great Northern War when they were constructed in both Moscow and St Petersburg for such celebrations, as for Hangöudd and Grengram (noted above). By the mid-eighteenth century, however, two permanent triumphal arches were constructed on Nevskii Prospekt as the latter assumed the function of St Petersburg's main ceremonial route for major events in this period. These arches thereafter served as a lasting reminder of the state's achievements for the city's inhabitants.[135]

A question might be raised about the traditionally open nature of popular festivities, related to the issue of free movement, when considered alongside the controlled and regulated nature of St Petersburg, where such regulation existed to a greater degree than in other Russian cities of the same period. Although popular festivities in St Petersburg occurred in largely the same types of places as in other Russian towns – the main square(s) – it has been argued that the overall space of the new 'regular' city imposed restrictions of its own, whether through its physical geography or the close attentions of the city's authorities.[136] However, there is no indication that any of these factors affected the conduct of such festivities in St Petersburg. While the spaces used for festivities, such as the main squares (including Tsaritsyn Meadow within this category) and the arterial routes (principally the Neva and Nevskii Prospekt), dominated the centre of the city, it was hardly unusual in a wider European sense that such areas could be transformed for the purposes of a given holiday.[137] For example, the perception of the Neva in the everyday lives of the city's inhabitants was not the same as when it was illuminated during a firework display for a state celebration, or when it was the site of popular festivities whilst frozen during the winter months. In this sense, then, in common with most other cities, the everyday and festive spaces of St Petersburg became interlinked. The question of regulation, with particular reference to the city's police and their relationship with certain aspects of public behaviour, will be discussed in the next chapter.

A particular aspect of St Petersburg's development that has generally been overlooked is the fact that, as in other Russian cities, churches were a key element in the formation of the city's spaces, as well as its ritual and everyday life.[138] In her discussion of what she has termed the 'aural landscape' of St Petersburg, Chudinova highlights the importance of cannon fire from the city's two fortresses as a secular means of telling the time, but she also points out that church bells remained a key part of everyday life, as in other Russian cities. The bells were rung not only to summon the congregation for daily and weekly services, but also at certain points during the church service itself, and they remained an established part of celebrations on feast days and public celebrations in general. Similarly, the centre of the city had originally been focused on the Cathedral of the Holy Trinity and the open area immediately surrounding it on the Petersburg side. The church was founded in October 1703 and played a central role in many of the city's important early ceremonies.[139] For example, Peter was granted the title of *Imperator* after a service in the church during the celebrations for the Peace of Nystadt in 1721.[140]

However, under Peter's successors, the focus gradually shifted toward the Admiralty side, as the location of the Winter Palace, many of the city's leading palaces and its main avenue. The Church of the Nativity of the Virgin (30), on Nevskii Prospekt, was consecrated in 1737 and soon became the centre of court worship. It took possession of the icon of the Virgin of Kazan, which was associated with the Romanov family, in the early 1740s and was subsequently known by that name.[141] It was the site of royal weddings, coronation anniversaries, name-day and birthday celebrations. The church also played a significant role in other major religious occasions celebrated by the court in St Petersburg, such as serving as the starting point for the annual procession to the St Aleksandr Nevskii monastery on the saint's feast day.[142] The church's position on Nevskii Prospekt also led to its incorporation into other important celebrations, such as the ceremonial entries of both Anna Ivanovna and Elizabeth following their coronations in Moscow, which will be discussed further in Chapter 3. The major points throughout the city – the royal palaces, the Summer Gardens and the main churches – highlight the considerable degree to which the various spaces within St Petersburg – official, festive and religious – overlapped within the city.

The Petrine and post-Petrine period saw considerable developments with regard to St Petersburg and its constituent spaces, albeit not unproblematic in their outcomes. The city had been properly established, both as a physical entity and in terms of its population, but the pace of both processes had taken its toll on the city's supposed regularity. Some parts of the city, particularly on the outskirts of its central region, remained quite underdeveloped or haphazard in their execution. The natural world, while tamed to an extent during the construction phase, was nevertheless an unescapable and occasionally dangerous presence in the city. In other respects, however, St Petersburg had proven a success in establishing new spaces in the Russian context, particularly in playing host to the first formal 'assemblies' and as the site of the Academy of Sciences. Crucially, it had also become the main focus of the Russian court's festive calendar by hosting many of its leading ceremonies. As with the seats of other European courts, these aspects of St Petersburg were crucial to gaining recognition and, ultimately, some measure of prestige on an international stage. As a result, in both cases, although the initial results were mixed, they represented clear examples of the direction that Russia would take over the remainder of the century and beyond.

2
Regulation: Policing the City

The numerous reforms introduced by Peter I have been linked to the concept of the early modern *Polizeistaat*, or 'well-ordered police state', wherein 'police' refers to the 'institutional means and procedures necessary to secure peaceful and orderly existence for the population'.[1] However, as one of the leading historians of eighteenth-century Russia has noted, 'police' (*politsiia*) was not merely an institution, it was also a way of thinking about the authority and role of the state.[2] This interpretation can be linked to the concept of social discipline insofar as the strong central authority of the state – a key part of the *Polizeistaat* – was able to control social behaviour effectively. St Petersburg provided an important staging ground for the implementation of such a system, since it was the first city in Russia to have a dedicated 'police' institution to enforce the component laws. However, the requirements of such a system often meant that the reality of everyday life in St Petersburg often fell short of the ideal, particularly in the consistent application of that system.

Following a discussion of the broader themes of such 'police' administrations and related concepts, such as social discipline and surveillance, this chapter examines the role of the Police Chancellery in St Petersburg in influencing and thereby helping to control a number of aspects of everyday life in the city. In particular, the concepts of 'regularity' and 'good order' – discussed in the last chapter in relation to the planning of St Petersburg – were central to the activities of the Police Chancellery. The attempt to regulate public life in this way can be seen through the 'police' legislation introduced in this period. The 'good order' of St Petersburg society relied upon its health and safety, which meant that the police were responsible for dealing with any potential threats, including fire, disease and crime. The chapter focuses on three aspects of public life that were subject to repeated attempts at regulation during this period – drinking, gambling and lewd behaviour. The policies adopted by the Russian authorities bear comparison with contemporary efforts elsewhere in Europe, both in their aims and outcomes. The specific reactions of the populace to such laws is not examined in this chapter, since there has been some excellent recent research on the inhabitants of the city and their use of the law courts to assert their views on a range of concerns during Peter's reign.[3]

Police administration and social discipline

There has been some debate over the motives behind Peter I's reforms, most notably in relation to the state's need for more efficient means to generate revenue to fund its military activities during the Great Northern War.[4] Whatever the motivation, it seems clear that, in order to achieve his aims, Peter drew on the example of earlier 'police' regulations (*Polizeiordnungen*) in other European states. Such regulations had been introduced initially in the Holy Roman Empire as a response to the disruptions brought about by the events of the Reformation. The example provided by these ordnances, introduced at Reich level, then prompted the introduction of more detailed legislation in the imperial territories in the second half of the sixteenth century.[5] Later, in states like Sweden and Prussia, during the seventeenth century, such regulations reflected the attempt to assert the central authority of the ruler over their domains, as well as to benefit society with a more rational and orderly system that targeted certain abuses, whether economic, practical or moral.[6] For some states, particularly Prussia, this process was crucial in order to recover from the devastation of the Thirty Years War and stake its claim for greater prominence, both within the Holy Roman Empire and also within Europe.[7] For others, the introduction of similar types of regulation was prompted by the need to increase domestic productivity to meet the growing costs and other demands of military developments in the same period, with the rise of the 'fiscal-military state'.[8]

Although early modern Russian society did not undergo quite the same process of change, two important factors altered the situation in Russia from the mid-seventeenth century. The first factor was the 'Schism' (*Raskol*), which undermined the Church's position as the principal source of moral and cultural authority within Russian society. The second factor was the gradual recognition of the need to engage with the rest of Europe amongst the upper reaches of Russian society. This recognition was reflected in increased trade with Western Europe, the larger number of Europeans coming to Muscovy, and the appearance of some European elements in elite Russian culture. Both of these factors contributed to a loss of 'cultural identity', which can be linked to a wider sense of crisis in the 1670s and 1680s, as reflected in popular protests against taxation, unrest amongst the military elite, the contested succession to Tsar Fedor Alekseevich in 1682 and the failure of campaigns against the Crimean Tartars in 1685 and 1686. Raeff argues that, in the face of this crisis, there appeared to be no means within the Muscovite system to deal with the situation adequately.[9]

At the same time, this process of change within late Muscovite cultural identity – in particular the challenge to the centrality of the Orthodox Church – raises the related subject of social discipline. A distinction should be drawn between 'social discipline' and 'social control', although they are certainly linked and often reinforce one another. 'Social discipline' has been defined as a 'conscious effort' by a central authority to change social attitudes and behaviour. 'Social control' refers instead to the traditional rules and practices within any society.[10] The upheaval within European society as a result of the Reformation and the attendant changes which both contributed to and followed from it, such as the rapid development of printing, the rise of humanist education and the challenge to the Church's authority over moral matters, led to a change both in social relationships and in the state's relationship with society. The desire to define and regulate these relationships can therefore be seen in state measures like the *Polizeiordnungen* and, later, Cameralism. This narrative has been critiqued in several respects – its emphasis on the regulations, rather than the responses to them, for example – and there were certainly limitations on such measures in practice. Equally, however, it is important to recognise such legislation as an embodiment of the desire to tackle perceived problems in the economic and moral spheres.[11]

With regard to Russia, the Orthodox Church was arguably the strongest influence on social discipline throughout the early modern period, but its position of moral authority was undermined by the Schism and the inclusion of secular punishments for crimes formerly under the jurisdiction of the Church in the Law Code (*Ulozhenie*) of 1649.[12] During the reign of Peter I, and particularly after the death of Patriarch Adrian in 1700, the state steadily reduced the Church's autonomy – while it remained a major influence on Russian society, the Church's policies were arguably increasingly driven by state concerns. This process was encapsulated in the establishment of the Holy Synod in 1721 and the issuing of the Spiritual Regulation, as a result of which the Orthodox Church was brought under the administrative authority of the state.[13] Indeed, for Peter and his leading advisers, the Church was to become a means to extend the Tsar and the state's authority as part of a 'conscious effort' to influence and, in some cases, change the attitude and behaviour of Russian society.[14] During Peter's reign, the emphasis placed on 'good order', as embodied in a 'police' administration, was part and parcel of the general reform agenda. Contemporary practice in other states, such as Sweden, provided important examples of how public life could be regulated by 'good government' to make the state and society more efficient.[15] The early Cameralist writers provided another model – to maximise the state's economic potential through efficient government – although such work featured more prominently in Catherine II's reforms in the 1770s and 1780s.[16]

Peter's attempts to introduce this 'modernising' European *Polizeistaat* were necessarily limited by the nature of the Russian context and the cooperation of its social groups, upon whom he had to rely for its effective implementation.

A number of measures introduced by Peter highlight the desire for greater regularity. For example, the revision of the existing census information between 1719–24 was intended to serve two important functions: to aid the efficient collection of the new 'soul' tax, from 1724, and to prevent unauthorised peasant migration, following the introduction of 'passports' in April 1722.[17] The collection of the new tax was the responsibility of the army; appropriately, as they were the main recipient of this income. However the system soon developed difficulties, with protests at the amount having to be paid and the lack of flexibility in the system for regional variations and differing levels of income. The resulting arrears soon mounted up, reaching almost 2 million rubles in late 1738 and 2.5 million rubles by 1746. Despite the threat of severe punishments and exile to Siberia for those who failed to pay, the state was unable to find an effective means to tackle these difficulties, and the arrears continued to be a problem throughout this period.[18]

The desire for 'good order' was also reflected in the administrative reforms introduced by Peter in the second half of his reign. For example, the central administration was re-organised into nine 'colleges', which covered the essential functions of government – war, foreign affairs, finance and so on. This model had been devised by Peter and his advisers from contemporary German and Scandinavian examples in order to provide clear jurisdictions and responsibilities.[19] Such institutions also required detailed instructions. Given the military emphasis of this period, it is natural that he chose to begin with the 'Military Regulation' (*Ustav Voinskii*, 1716) and the 'Naval Statute' (*Morskoi Ustav*, 1720).[20] However the same principles were applied to the civil sphere in the 'General Regulation' (*General'nyi Reglament*, 1720), a set of procedures to be adhered to by members of the state administration. These regulations dealt not only with official procedures, but also the organisation of office space and one's behaviour within it.[21] Although appearing over-meticulous to a modern observer, the 'General Regulation' sought to remove the possibility that personal concerns could influence the efficient function of the state. This principle was also featured in the 'Table of Ranks', introduced in January 1722, which established a unified, rational system assessing social hierarchy, with education and competent service intended to be the main determinants of a man's rank on the table.[22] It drew on the examples provided by contemporary Swedish, Prussian and Danish models, which were analysed by Heinrich (Andrei) Ostermann. Further examples from England and France were also examined but were not considered appropriate for Russia.[23]

The 'Table of Ranks' was a departure from previous practice in several respects. Most notably, it established a link between state service and the attainment of noble status, specifically for all military officers and civil officials reaching Rank 8. Officials below the latter rank were designated as 'personal' nobles, so their title was not hereditary. It also introduced a formal division between military and civil service, and created a separate hierarchy of court ranks, discussed in Chapter 3. It was not, however, an attempt to introduce a meritocratic system to the Russian administration, since the state was the only intended beneficiary.[24] Although competition at the lower levels of the civil administration meant that ability and education could play some role in promotions, the explanatory points included in the law that set out the 'Table' carried an implicit recognition of the importance of family lineage.[25] For example, members of princely or other titled families and other 'distinguished' (*znatnye*) servitors always took precedence over their equivalent ranks at major celebrations.[26] Similarly, despite Peter's promotion of non-nobles, like Menshikov, scholarship on the *Generalitet* (Ranks 1–4 of the military and civil administration) in 1730 indicates that there were relatively few 'new men' at the highest levels of the Petrine administration and that their numbers gradually decreased in the period following 1725.[27] The impact of this measure was further limited by the persistence of extensive patronage networks from the Muscovite period, with the numerous members of the military and civil hierarchy, connected by marriage, history or financial concerns, largely able to continue to serve their own interests within the new system.[28]

The regulating principles embodied in such legislation encountered considerable problems in Russia during this period. The existing system of traditional patrimonial authority, with the Tsar atop the hierarchy, proved very difficult to overcome. The new institutions and protocols were not always more efficient than their predecessors and their role (not to mention their terminology) was not well understood by the Tsar's personnel, or by his subjects. But Russia was hardly unusual in this respect – such issues of personal authority, inefficiency and nepotism also affected other states across Europe in the same period.[29] Instead, they should be viewed as expressions of the state's assumption of the lead role in promoting social discipline. From the Petrine era onwards, there were repeated attempts to push Russian administration and society in a different direction, influenced by the new demands of the state and the example of its neighbours. These reforms enjoyed only mixed success, since the influence of the established system remained very strong. Their impact on certain regions or groups (i.e. the rural peasantry) was mitigated by distance, relevance, funding and the perennial shortage of trained personnel in the provinces throughout this period. However, their impact on St Petersburg was rather more realisable, as the Police Chancellery had a defined and supported role within St Petersburg society, owing to the city's status as the capital and the residence of the court.[30] The Chancellery was also given a clearer definition of its duties, which are discussed in the next section.

Police in St Petersburg

The police legislation that was subsequently introduced in St Petersburg dealt with issues that had long been a concern for the Muscovite state and many of its contemporaries around Europe. Peter I's father, Aleksei Mikhailovich, had issued legislation that addressed a number of concerns for the early modern city, with specific reference to Moscow – fire, theft and disease. Those who failed to respond quickly to such circumstances faced punishments, ranging from the stocks to the death penalty.[31] Similarly, the problems of disorderly conduct and violence on the streets were dealt with by legislation during the regency of Sophia Alekseevna.[32] However, these measures were piecemeal and the responsibilities for their execution were divided between a number of institutions, depending on which issue or group they dealt with. Instead, the first concerted effort to create a formal 'police administration' came in 1718, coinciding with the implementation of the new College system (discussed above).

The new institution was announced in late May, when a list of duties was issued to the new General-Policemaster 'for the best order(s) in this city'. These duties were also to be publicised to all inhabitants so that they could not feign ignorance of them.[33] This new office was made responsible for most aspects of public life in the city, including hygiene (proper disposal of waste), safety (preventing fires and dealing with criminals) and conduct of business (ensuring order in the city's markets, regulating prices and standardising weights). In addition, it was charged with overseeing the appearance of the city itself – to approve and monitor all new building work, to ensure that the city's embankments and streets were properly maintained, and to keep its waterways clear.[34] Subsequently, the new institution was to be responsible for monitoring all movement within, into and out of the city. This was especially so in the case of foreigners, who were expected to register with the Police Chancellery.[35] The list clearly encapsulated many of the aspects of regulation that had been dealt with in the earlier *Polizeiordnungen*. However, another inspiration for this new institution came from a French, rather than a German model. Peter had recently visited Paris, in 1717, and seen the work of the office of the *lieutenant-général de police* at first hand. Nicolas de la Mare, first appointed by Louis XIV in 1667, subsequently published one of the most influential treatises on the subject, the four-volume *La Traité de la Police*, between 1705 and 1738.[36]

The new body was headed by Antonio M. Devier (de Vieira), a Portuguese sailor who had come to Russia with Peter I from Amsterdam following the Great Embassy and had risen through the ranks of the army. He took the position very seriously, not least in fear of being held directly responsible for its failings by the Tsar, but was hampered from the outset by the sheer range of duties and limited resources. He continued in this post after Peter's death, but was exiled to Siberia in 1727 for opposing the growing political influence of his brother-in-law, Menshikov. He was pardoned by Elizabeth and again became General-Policemaster in 1744, but was beset by illness and died the following year.[37] His two main successors as General-Policemaster were both related to the imperial family and wielded considerable influence as a result of their position. Vasilii F. Saltykov served under Anna Ivanovna, from 1732 onwards, and was involved in a number of major projects, including the 'Commission on Construction', discussed in the last chapter. From 1745 until 1760, the post was held by Aleksei D. Tatishchev, a courtier under Anna Ivanovna who was subsequently promoted by Elizabeth. During his tenure, the post became more privileged, with its promotion from Rank 5 to Rank 3 on the Table of Ranks (equivalent to a lieutenant-general or vice-admiral) and its holder was able to report directly to the Empress.[38] With greater power came greater responsibility and the post remained a demanding one – Tatishchev died *in officio* in 1760.

One of the problems that the Police Chancellery faced was the small number of personnel available. The actual staff of the Chancellery numbered 88 people in 1723, which also included its administrators.[39] By 1727, this number had risen to 122, of which 94 were troops.[40] Since their responsibilities included the maintenance of public order, which involved not only preventing fights and other disturbances, but also pursuing thieves and brigands, the police were able to call on two additional groups to bolster this number. Firstly, the army regiments garrisoned in the city provided additional numbers for police duties, including dragoons for mounted patrols.[41] Secondly, the inhabitants of St Petersburg were used to keep watch at night when sentries and night watches were posted at various points around the city. These checkpoints (*shlagbaum*, of German origin) were manned by chosen men from the city's inhabitants, who were responsible for ensuring that only authorised people, carrying lanterns, were allowed to pass, and for reporting suspicious behaviour.[42] Although the system was not ideal because of the inexperience of the chosen men, the outcome was reasonably effective.[43] Their efforts were aided by another innovation when Russia's first street lights were introduced in St Petersburg's main squares, around several important buildings and along some of its main streets.[44]

Anti-social groups, principally vagrants and beggars, were another concern for the police. Within urban society, these groups did not fulfil a 'useful' function and could actually prove counterproductive to 'good order'. The question of how to deal with such groups in an urban setting had been current since the early 1690s, when Peter I issued a number of laws ordering them to be thrown out of Moscow and other towns – if they tried to return, they were to be flogged and sent to Siberia.[45] There were several reasons for this attitude. These people lacked a permanent address and the appropriate papers to stay in towns, so they were impossible to tax and contributed little to the state. As a result, they were frequently linked to criminal activities and, in the case of beggars, the feigning of injury to gain alms. In both cases, this behaviour flew in the face of Peter's well-established 'work ethic' and such people were targeted by a series of laws throughout his reign.[46] In the early 1720s, beggars and young people who were not engaged in work were banned from seeking alms in the streets, which was equated with theft, and anyone caught giving them money was to be fined five roubles. The official advice to charitable individuals was to give such money to worthy institutions instead, like the city's hospitals.[47] The subject of 'fake cripples' was addressed in the Spiritual Regulation, which stated that anyone giving alms to a 'fake cripple' was complicit in their fraudulent crime and would be punished as a result.[48] However, with a considerable section of the population consisting of migrant workers and with the hardships common in any early modern city, the problem of itinerants on the streets persisted throughout the period and successive rulers sought to deal with it. During Elizabeth's reign, such offenders were to be punished by being sent back to their former owners (if they were serfs), into the army or to work in a factory, depending on their physical condition.[49]

As with the more general attempt to regulate the administration and population of Russia, the implementation of the Police Chancellery was a mixed success in St Petersburg. The institution itself drew some positive comments from foreign visitors during this period, such as Weber who, having earlier commented on the dangerous nature of the streets at night, praises the introduction of a night watch in St Petersburg 'after the method of Hambourg'.[50] Other areas remained more problematic. Repeated exhortations to notify the Chancellery of new buildings or of arrivals in the city suggests that the new regulations were not being followed. The dangers of fire and public disturbances remained current throughout this period and the Chancellery was under constant pressure to respond. Nevertheless, the existence of the Chancellery, and the continued emphasis on regulation through legislation, again placed St Petersburg squarely in the European context of the early eighteenth century.[51] The focus of official scrutiny also included the everyday conduct of the inhabitants and the following sections deal with the developing official attitude toward several important aspects that came to prominence during this period.

Drinking

Drinking has a long and infamous association with the Russian people, even to the point where it was recorded as one of the reasons for Prince Vladimir's decision to convert to Orthodox Christianity, rather than Islam, by the Russian Primary Chronicle.[52] Certainly, early foreign observers, such as Adam Olearius, were quick to note the drunken behaviour of the Russians in the days immediately before the start of one of the major fasts, such as Shrovetide (*Maslenitsa*).[53] Whether or not this was part of a wider negative stereotype of the Russians as a 'barbaric' people, there can be little doubt that alcohol was a common feature of everyday life in Russia, as it was across early modern Europe. Alcohol served as an important component in the average diet. It was safer to consume than water, since the brewing (or distilling) process removed many impurities, and it was also an important source of calories for both young and old.[54] The production of alcohol depended upon several factors, not least a surplus of grain and the timber necessary to build the distilling equipment, and consequently most production took place in rural areas where these resources were located. However, certain types of alcohol, particularly beer and mead, were also produced in urban communities for several reasons, including convenience and the limited 'shelf-life' of these drinks in comparison with their bottled brethren.[55]

In either setting, therefore, alcohol was generally readily available, except when the harvests were poor, and consequently the Russian state was not slow to realise its economic potential. Its production was strictly controlled by a state monopoly on sales, with producers paying an excise (*aktsiz*) on all alcohol produced for sale in the various establishments, discussed below.[56] The system was refined in 1753, when the supply of alcohol became the sole provision of the nobility, cutting out the merchantry almost entirely.[57] Such regulation of alcohol production was not unusual, since it had financial implications in the form of excise and resource implications in the form of grain, but production elsewhere was divided between guilds and private individuals, rather than the domain of any one social group.[58] In light of this background, this section examines the change that took place in the first half of the eighteenth century with regard to official attitudes to drinking and drunkenness. On the one hand, alcohol was an important, traditional element in both everyday and particularly festive life for the majority of the populace, even within the court elite, especially during Peter I's reign. However, at the same time, the development of the court, influenced by ideas on appropriate behaviour and more sophisticated forms of entertainment, and the desire of the state to curb excessive drunkenness resulted in a desire to regulate this facet of life in the new city.

Peter himself had developed his drinking prowess in the convivial surroundings of the Foreign Quarter (*Nemetskaia sloboda*) in Moscow, which was not far from the palace at Preobrazhenskoe where he spent much of his youth. It is perhaps not surprising that his social acquaintances in this setting included a vintner, Mr Mons (father of Anna and Willem, both of whom were later to become intimately connected with the imperial family), and such hard-drinking military men as the Swiss Franz Lefort and the Scotsman Patrick Gordon. In particular, Lefort's close relationship with Peter meant that the former's palace was used to host receptions, banquets and other celebrations that featured 'drunkenness so great that it is impossible to describe', according to one contemporary.[59] At the same time, such pursuits were hardly unknown in contemporary European courts. One need only think of the crude activities of Frederick William I's *Tabakskollegium* at the Prussian court, in which alcohol played a considerable role.[60] Although Peter's enthusiasm may have been disconcerting, not to say dangerous on occasion, the complaints contained in the accounts of Olearius, Bergholz and other foreign observers should be balanced with the common foreign perception of Russians as inveterate drunkards.[61] Peter was certainly able to moderate his behaviour when necessary. For example, during the Grand Embassy, Princess Sophia of Hanover noted after meeting Peter in Koppenbrücke, 'he did not get drunk in our presence, but we had hardly left when the people of his suite made ample amends.'[62]

The infamous 'All-Drunken Synod' has long been associated with Peter's hedonistic tendencies and had its origins in the early 1690s, when Peter was still relatively free to indulge his passions away from a number of ritual duties that could be performed by his brother and co-Tsar, Ivan V. Recent work on the 'Synod' has moved away from its traditional interpretation as either bacchanalia or religious parody to focus on its role as an important part of court life, since many of its members occupied key positions within Peter's civil and military administration.[63] It has also been persuasively argued that, far from being merely hedonistic or irreligious, both the 'Synod' and Peter's other 'parodic' entertainments, such as the war games and mock weddings, were intended to bind his company of 'disciples' together and demonstrate their role in 'bringing order out of chaos'.[64]

An excerpt from the account of the Danish envoy at Peter's court, Just Juel, suggests another possible motivation for these heavy drinking sessions. 'But (as in this case) the Tsar himself rarely drinks more than one or, in a rare case, two bottles of wine, so that in many drinking sessions I rarely saw him, as they say, drunk as a cobbler. Meanwhile the remaining guests are compelled to drink until they see or hear nothing, and then the Tsar starts to probe them, trying to find out what each one has on his mind. Fights and arguments between the drunks are also to the Tsar's liking, as their accusations between one another reveals their stealing, swindling and cunning, and he uses the opportunity to punish the guilty.'[65] Anisimov links this comment to his wider point on the importance of surveillance and denunciation in Petrine Russia. In a similar vein, he later notes the example of Count Petr A. Tolstoi, whom Peter accused of feigning drunkenness in order to observe his companions in a compromised state to his advantage.[66]

Peter was keen to ensure that other participants matched (or, as in the case noted by Juel, exceeded) his considerable intake. Bergholz noted the comments made by the Tsar, during the celebrations after a naval review in St Petersburg on 11 August 1723, that those who did not get drunk with him were 'good-for-nothings' and that he forced all present to keep drinking until the break of dawn the following day.[67] Several reasons can be put forward, some of which have wider resonance in the context of Peter's reign. The trials that guests were put through can be linked to a form of cruel (not to say tortuous) entertainment, intended for the Tsar's amusement. In particular, the enforced drinking of toasts on a given occasion left very little leeway for the guests to refuse the Tsar's request.[68] These trials were applied equally to men and women. Bergholz notes with some horror the example made of the Marshal of the Court (*gofmarshal*) Vasilii D. Olsuf'ev's

German wife, Eva, who was punished (along with 29 other women) for failing to attend a masquerade in November 1721 by having to drink a penalty, despite being heavily pregnant. The result was the birth of a stillborn baby the following morning.[69] The use of alcohol – whether to loosen the tongues of his subjects or foreign representatives, or to promote a sense of unity and common purpose amongst his social circle, or even as a source of crude entertainment for the Tsar – undoubtedly played a central part in court life under Peter. It is telling that several of Peter's close circle died as a result of their alcohol intake – for example, Franz Lefort and Fedor A. Golovin – a fact which Peter himself noted in warning Admiral Fedor M. Apraksin about his enthusiastic imbibing.[70]

Several other aspects of drinking culture changed during Peter's reign and these were gradually refined throughout the eighteenth century. French and German wine was imported into Russia from the late seventeenth century onward. Peter had a particular taste for such drinks, as shown in an early letter in which he orders bottles of Sack and Rhenish wine from the governor of Archangel'sk in 1694.[71] The strong Hungarian wine was used for toasts (or trials) at many celebrations. During this period, therefore, wine became an established part of the court's inventory, with its status enhanced by its association with elite drinking fashions in the rest of Europe.[72] Alongside other imported drinks, notably cognac, wine enjoyed a status as something of a luxury item, demonstrated by the fact that the quantity imported stayed relatively low throughout the eighteenth century.[73] Both the court and leading members of the nobility were keen to stress this luxury at receptions, particularly for foreign guests. On more than one occasion, Bergholz remarks on the range and quality of the wine served to him or to the duke of Holstein, which included champagne, Burgundy and claret (Haut-Brion, although the Russian uses the English version, Pontack).[74]

Information on drinking beyond the immediate confines of the court is more difficult to find. The demands of the Great Northern War and the failure of harvests (for example, in 1708) had a direct impact on alcohol production, but, as with other elements of traditional culture during Peter's reign, in general drinking habits simply did not change, particularly in rural areas. Similarly, despite the introduction of new regular celebrations on the calendar, such as the anniversaries of major victories and the ruler's coronation, during Peter's reign (discussed in the following chapter), many aspects of popular festivities remained essentially the same and drinking was no exception. The venues for drinking in St Petersburg therefore initially followed the traditional pattern. For example, the terms used to refer to public drinking places in Russia during the sixteenth and seventeenth centuries generally had their origins in older Slavic terms, such as 'hostelry' (*avsteriia*), 'drink shop' (*fartina* or *piteinyi dom*) and 'tavern' (*korchma* or *kabak*).[75]

Although these words were still used in the early eighteenth century, there is some evidence to suggest that new terms were gradually being introduced.

A law issued in April 1734 refers to the ownership of 'taverns' (*traktiry*) and the collection of the alcohol excise by using another term – 'free houses' (*vol'nye domy*).[76] The distinction between the different establishments is not entirely clear from contemporary documents, but it is clear that some measure of difference existed, as reflected in the terms used to identify them. For example, a former 'tavern' (*kabak*) known as the 'Petrovskii', located on the corner of the future Nevskii Prospekt on the Admiralty side, was bought by the Treasury Office (*Kamer-kontora*) in April 1737 with the aim of building a stone tavern (*traktir*) for use by visiting merchants and foreigners.[77] The term *kabak* was supposedly replaced in official language with *piteinyi dom*, by a decree in 1746, although there is little evidence to suggest that this new convention was followed in either official or everyday usage. Subsequent legislation on the subject in 1765 and 1779 indicates that the terms continued to be used interchangeably.[78]

Concerns about the social and financial side effects of alcohol and excessive drunkenness can be seen in the legislation of the post-Petrine period. A Senate decree of August 1735 outlawed the practice of accepting items of clothing, household items or other goods in place of payment in drinking establishments. Weber had noted this practice in his description of the city's 'public tap-houses' in 1716.[79] Not only did such pawning often lead to overindulgence, but it was also linked to theft, as items sat in the open until redeemed by their owner. As a result, lists of prices were to be issued by the Treasury Office for spirits, beer and mead, which proprietors and their staff had to use when charging patrons.[80] More seriously, in October 1740, following the murder of a sentry at the Sts Peter and Paul Fortress and the theft of several hundred roubles, there was another proclamation banning noisy behaviour and fighting during the night. As a result, drinking establishments were only permitted to sell alcohol between 9 a.m. and 7 p.m. Those who failed to observe this ban were to be reported to the Police Chancellery.[81] This particular law directly referenced the link between violent crime and alcohol, stressing that the enforcement of these measures to prevent such crimes was the duty of the Police Chancellery in St Petersburg.

On a wider social scale, drinking was a common feature of feast-day celebrations and official concerns were raised about raucous behaviour on such occasions. In July 1743, the Senate, acting on the advice of the Holy Synod, addressed the issue of taverns opening to sell drinks during the Liturgy, or the procession of the Cross, at monasteries and in large parishes as part of the religious celebrations on church holidays. The same law also mentioned other unsuitable activities that took place at the same time – fist fighting, horseracing, peasant dances (*pliaski*) and other 'unrefined' (*bezchinnyi*) activities. The law noted that this issue had previously been addressed in a debate in the Holy Synod in September 1722, followed by a ruling from the Senate, but the implication is that it had not been effective. Finally it stated that the Empress had also ordered a ban on fist fighting in both

St Petersburg and Moscow on 3 July.[82] A law prohibiting the construction of drinking establishments near churches or graveyards in early 1747 was most likely motivated by the desire to ensure respect for sanctified land, but it certainly also fits with the other legislation on anti-drunken behaviour issued in the same period.[83]

There are other contemporary examples that suggest that Elizabeth took the issue of public drunkenness in St Petersburg seriously. In December 1742, she issued a decree regarding the appearance of the streets in St Petersburg, in which she noted her disapproval at the presence of taverns (*kabaki*) and food stalls (*kharchevny*) on the city's 'distinguished' (*znatnye*) streets, presumably meaning the main avenues that contained the houses of the leading noble families. In the case of taverns, she ordered that they should be moved to particular areas away from the city's elite residence; in the case of food stalls, that they should be confined to the marketplace.[84] However, in 1746, Elizabeth again issued a decree stating that no taverns should be situated on these 'distinguished' streets, but instead should be restricted to side streets, and that those currently occupying such a location should be moved.[85] A further decree in October 1752 reiterated the need to move both types of establishment away from these 'distinguished' streets. The fact that it specifically noted the location of a tavern on Millionnaia Ulitsa, beside the old Winter Palace and several leading noble residences, suggests that the failure of the previous legislation was readily apparent to the Empress.[86]

The situation came to a head in December 1758, when General-Fieldmarshal and General-Procurator Prince Nikita Iu. Trubetskoi submitted a report to the Senate about the action that he had undertaken against taverns that he considered to be in contravention of the existing laws. Following reports of a tavern owned by the merchant Ivan R. Chirkin, housed in *Kamer-fuer'er* Vasilii K. Rubanovskii's house on Millionnaia Ulitsa, he had launched an investigation to find out which houses on the city's main streets contained taverns or similar establishments. Two other taverns were subsequently discovered on Lugovaia Ulitsa in the houses of the merchant Prokhor I. Gnevyshev, opposite the Admiralty, and Nikolai G. Zherebtsov (vice-governor of Moscow), on the Moika. The intent was not to close these establishments but to ensure that they were moved to more suitable premises in nearby, but less high-profile streets. Hence, the tavern in Gnevyshev's house was moved to a property belonging to Princess Mariia Cherkasskaia on Malaia Morskaia Ulitsa, whilst Chirkin's tavern was moved to a stone building on a vacant lot beside Konniushennyi Bridge.[87] The impact of this action can be seen in a follow-up report from the Treasury Office to the Senate, stating that there had been a 24,500 rouble loss in profits from the sale of alcohol.[88] The cosmetic element was also addressed in a further decree, which tried to reduce the number of stalls (*budki*) by the turnpikes on the city's main avenues with specific mention of those selling food and drink on Millionnaia Ulitsa that had to be kept off the street front.[89]

Drinking remained a central part of both everyday life and the celebrations of the social elite during this period. Although some of the excesses of the Petrine era were scaled back under his successors, drinking remained an essential part of the court's activities, whether in the regular drinking of toasts on particular anniversaries or as part of the desire to show the wealth of the court through the quality of wines and liquors used at its banquets. The frequent characterisation of the Russians as a people with a penchant for drunkenness needs to be put in context, since many other contemporary states enjoyed a similarly familiar relationship with the fruit of the vine. For example, there was no episode in Russia during this period that generated the hysteria of the 'Gin Craze' in England.[90] The repeated concerns over excessive consumption, inappropriate behaviour and the location of premises selling alcohol were motivated by a desire to ensure the maintenance of 'good order' in the city – such issues were dealt with in other states and, as in Russia, with varying degrees of success.[91]

Gambling[92]

Gaming and gambling have long been recognised as an important part of the social life of early modern Europe, although they generally developed despite official disapproval.[93] Objections sprang from a number of sources, usually displaying a combination of moral outrage at its excesses and a practical concern for the victims of a bad run of luck.[94] The establishment of gaming and gambling as popular recreations was in part due to their prominence at leading courts across Europe, principally that of Louis XIV of France which contributed to the popularity of its principal card games, such as quadrille.[95] However, such games were just as popular in the taverns, coffee houses and private houses in this period, thereby enabling the participation of players from a variety of social backgrounds.[96] Gambling was also not simply restricted to particular games – any number of activities could form the basis for a wager, from sporting events to the mortality of acquaintances.[97] Certain games such as chess and various dice games had a long tradition in Russia, owing to their cultural relationship with Asian powers like the Mongol Empire in the medieval period.[98] However, increased contact between Muscovy and the rest of Europe from the sixteenth century onwards meant that other games and gambling practices were introduced to Russia, including a variety of card games, draughts and other table games.[99]

Scholarship on gambling in the eighteenth century has often focused on its symbolic meaning and cultural importance. One such area of investigation is the relationship between gambling and literature, in particular on the desire of some gamblers to portray themselves as challenging Fate by throwing caution to the wind and playing at high stakes, an established literary theme of the period.[100] The history of gambling has also been examined in

Russia, albeit concentrating on the latter stages of the eighteenth century and the first half of the nineteenth century.[101] Such interest in the literary portrayal of gambling during this period is also present in the Russian context.[102] However, apart from some passing mentions of a later period in the introductions to these studies, the early to mid-eighteenth-century background to gambling has most often been the subject of 'antiquarian' collections of Russian and foreign anecdotes.[103] The history of card playing has been somewhat better covered, but even in such cases the focus has usually been on the extravagant nature of gambling at the imperial court.[104] Therefore, whilst all of the above works include some interesting details, this section instead focuses on the emergence of gambling as a social pastime during the early eighteenth century as part of a wider cultural development in Russia.

As elsewhere in contemporary Europe, the official attitude was largely hostile to this type of activity – the Orthodox Church distrusted objects and pastimes of foreign origin and the wager of money was considered sinful. Gambling was condemned by Tsar Ivan IV's 1551 Church Council in Moscow, the written proceedings of which became known as the 'One Hundred Chapters' (*Stoglav*).[105] From the state's perspective, the Law Code (*Ulozhenie*) of 1649 made clear that gambling with cards or dice was associated with thieves (*vory*) and was to be punished in the same way as theft – a beating with the knout, the removal of the left ear and two years in prison, followed by hard labour.[106] Nevertheless it is clear from contemporary accounts that such games persisted in Russia, even if gambling remained problematic. Patrick Gordon describes how several soldiers billeted in the Foreign Quarter in Moscow were caught playing cards by a Russian officer, Afanasii K. Spiridonov, who confiscated the gambled money and a further 60 rubles.[107] In the latter stages of the seventeenth century, a number of factors allowed for the gradual spread of both games and gambling practices. The education of young noblemen abroad during the Petrine era exposed them to the common practice of gambling in other European countries. Petr Tolstoi visited one of the numerous gambling houses in Venice during his visit of 1698, noting both the card games being played and the amount of money being wagered.[108]

By the early eighteenth century, Russia was clearly familiar with such games and domestic card games had also emerged. For example, Bergholz notes the details of one such game that his hosts taught him – it is referred to as 'the game in kings', which involves the swapping of cards to complete 'tricks'.[109] There was also a growing recognition that these games were an integral part of the social experience. This was particularly the case in a city like St Petersburg where foreign travellers, merchants and naval personnel were common. A decree that ordered the establishment of a certain number of hostelries (*gerbergy*) in St Petersburg and on Kronstadt for use by foreign visitors in 1750 made specific mention of the need to provide billiards for this purpose.[110] The introduction of the 'assemblies', discussed in Chapter 1, provided a social forum in which these games could be played. Weber's description of these social occasions indicates that there was supposed to be a separate room for playing chess and draughts, and another room for 'parlour games', such as forfeits and cross-purposes.[111] Although the emphasis in both the original proclamation and in Weber's account was on social interaction, it was noted by other contemporaries that this was not always possible, albeit for largely practical reasons; smoking, gaming and dancing in close proximity to one another hindered conversation. Peter himself was not keen on gambling, preferring chess or draughts to cards at court social gatherings, and it was not permitted at the 'assemblies' as a result.[112] However, members of both Peter's close circle, such as Menshikov, were enthusiastic card players, although much of the evidence for this activity comes from the period after Peter's death in 1725.[113]

With the development of the court's social life during the 1730s and 1740s, such games, in particular cards, became a prominent feature of an evening of entertainments as part of a *kurtag* or masked ball. The close circle of players around a card table allowed for privileged access to the Empress for those who were selected.[114] It has also been suggested that card playing, by its very nature a static pursuit, was generally favoured by the more mature and hence less energetic members of the court.[115] This is certainly borne out by the fact that both Anna Ivanovna and Elizabeth increasingly favoured cards as an alternative to dancing at court events as their reigns progressed. Although all of the Empresses during this period were keen players, this enthusiasm did not always translate into skill at the card table. Christoph von Manstein, who served in the Russian army during the 1730s and attended Anna Ivanovna's court, noted that the Empress tended to lose quite quickly and thus favoured being the banker during games at court.[116] As was the case at other European courts, the fact that the ruler played such games meant that their courtiers were usually obliged to participate, regardless of the financial implications. For example, Louis XV's court evenings were dominated by the royal couple's enthusiasm for card playing (particularly lansquenet and cavagnole), but such games then ceased shortly after they retired for the evening.[117] However, as several contemporary writers make clear, it was a common and largely unavoidable activity for all ages and abilities as part of the daily round of court life.

A 1761 law dealing with the regulation of gambling amongst the nobility, discussed in more detail below, provides a convenient overview of many of the popular card games in Russia during this period. The listed games included faro, quintiche, ombré, quadrille, piquet and pamphile.[118] Some of these games were designed to be played by a small number of people and emphasised skilled play over pure chance, notably quadrille, which involved only four players.[119] However, the element of risk was much stronger in other card games, particularly faro, in which the odds strongly favoured the banker.[120] The very nature of such games meant that it could prove an expensive pastime, even for members of the elite.[121] Such expenditure was potentially very harmful for a family's fortunes in the longer term as there was little to be gained and much to be lost. Yet such incidents were hardly unusual in contemporary Europe. At Versailles, the royal court's enthusiasm for gambling meant that serious losses could be incurred. High profile examples included Madame de Montespan, believed to have lost 400,000 *pistoles* in one night, and Orry de Fulvy, *directeur de finances*, who lost a sum of 20,000 *louis* in one evening that was mysteriously paid off the following day.[122] Similarly, the leading political and society figures of Georgian London would commonly incur heavy gambling debts amounting to thousands of pounds by playing cards at establishments such as White's and Brooks's.[123] The potential consequences of risking one's livelihood, or family fortune in the case of the nobility, on a game of cards prompted the series of laws on gambling during this period.

A law issued by Anna Ivanovna in January 1733 tackled some of the concerns surrounding gambling for high stakes and the importance of the issue was highlighted by the specific instruction for the law to be promulgated in public. It began by referring to a previous ban on playing games for money, issued by Peter I in 1717, in which participants were to be fined triple the amount of money wagered in the game. However, the law stated that gambling had continued in spite of this prohibition, both in a public and presumably social setting, and also in private houses. More seriously, from an official point of view, gamblers had begun to wager not only money and household goods, but also serfs and villages whilst playing cards, dice and other games of chance. The law makes clear that such gambling will not only bring financial ruin, but also represents 'a most grave sin', with reference to the example of 'God's law'. The description of the games as 'wicked and harmful' (*bogomerzkiia i vreditel'nyia*) leaves little doubt about the official attitude toward such practices. Consequently all gambling for money, goods or property was banned, both in private dwellings and in 'public' (*vol'nykh*) houses. The law also listed the prescribed punishments. For a first offence, the precedent of 1717 was followed, with two-thirds of the fine to be given to a hospital (not specified). A second offence was to be punished by a month in prison for officers and other 'distinguished' (*znatnye*) people, or a merciless beating with sticks for common (*podlye*) people. A third offence involved doubling the monetary value of the fine, and subsequent punishments were left to the discretion of the Police Chancellery, the local governor or the commanding officer.[124]

The prohibitions on gambling were not only intended to apply to the general populace. The activities of card playing and billiards were noted specifically in another law, issued in March 1735. It prohibited pages and chamber-pages of the royal household from frequenting taverns and other drinking establishments where they could play billiards, cards and similar

games. Offenders were to be placed under arrest (the law cited the punishment of the page Ivan Volkov as an example) and the owner of the premises
also faced the prospect of a severe punishment, including a fine.[125] However,
as with other aspects of the city's police legislation, there are signs that these
gambling practices continued to be a problem, despite the prohibitions
against them. The law of 1717/1733 was reissued in June 1743 and again in
March 1747, adding that people of all ranks (*vsiakogo china liudi*) had continued gambling for money in such places, despite the restatement of the
fines and punishments.[126]

However, there was also a recognition of the difference between gambling,
particularly card playing, as a vice and its role as a social activity. A law
issued in mid-1761 ordered that card games, namely faro, quintiche and
other similar games, were not to be played under any circumstances for
money or for goods, except in the Empress's apartments. Importantly, an
exception was made for a number of other card games, including ombré,
quadrille, piquet and pamphile, which could be played for very small
sums of money in aristocratic houses (*v znatnykh dvorianskikh domakh*).
However this exception was only for 'the purposes of passing the time',
rather than in order to win something. Anyone playing for larger sums was
to be fined twice their annual salary and the amount of money gambled
(or the value of any goods that were pawned to cover debts), while the
owner of the premises in which the game took placed was to be fined as
well. This fine was to be divided in four – one part was to be given to 'the
hospital', a second part was to be used for the upkeep of the police, and
the other two parts were to be used to reward informers who could provide
adequate written proof of the illegal activity.[127] Any attempt to use promis-
sory notes (*vekseli*) or bills of exchange in place of money, or any kind of
pawned goods, would result in their confiscation by the Treasury and a
fine for those involved. Although the Police Chancellery or local officials
were responsible for enforcing this ban, the final point added that the
Senate should be informed about any fines, as should the War College, the
Admiralty or the regimental chancelleries for the Guards, since these could
have a bearing on rank and promotion.[128]

There are several important points arising from this law, which illustrate
the official attitude toward gambling throughout this period. Firstly, card
playing was clearly perceived as a social pursuit and there were only certain
spaces where this was considered appropriate, namely at court, in the apartments of the Empress, and in the houses of distinguished nobles. Secondly,
there was a clear preference for games involving small groups or a high
degree of skill – such as quadrille – that promoted a sociable atmosphere,
over those with a high degree of chance – like faro – which carried the risk
of high losses and debt. Thirdly, the law made clear that improper gambling
could have a negative effect on one's career, besides the financial implications of any fine imposed. This type of regulation is typical of the period.

For example, the French law on gambling was typified by an *ordonnance* issued in late 1717, which prohibited dice games and various specified card games, and then vaguely referred to other similar activities. This was followed by similar *ordonnances* issued in 1757, 1759 and 1765, with only the specified card games altered.[129] A similar set of measures were undertaken in Georgian England, where the official response can be seen simultaneously as an attempt to protect victims and to penalise rapacious behaviour at the gaming table.[130]

There were, however, some differences between Russia and the rest of Europe in the treatment of gambling. No attempt was made to license gambling houses during this period, as they had been in the Austrian Crown lands, so that the state (not to mention the court official responsible) could profit from what was recognised as a widespread and therefore largely unavoidable practice.[131] A related venture, the lottery, which had proven very useful for raising funds in a number of states in the early modern period, was not as successful in Russia.[132] The first state lottery was introduced in 1760 to support invalided officers from the Seven Years War, but it was subsequently abandoned in 1764 on the grounds of poor administration, which had resulted in a poor financial return.[133] Instead, in the Russian context, the importance of the developments in this period were in establishing gaming and gambling as social pursuits, with a definite emphasis on their role as a forum for interaction, albeit one with defined roles and accepted behaviour. As such, although the introduction of this practice was relatively recent, it quickly became a central part of court life by the end of this period and would remain so thereafter.

Immoral behaviour

The final area of police regulation of everyday life in St Petersburg in this chapter deals with two aspects of the moral conduct of its inhabitants. As with the previous sections, this area was the focus of considerable official scrutiny during this period, but it was also an aspect which saw a shifting pattern of behaviour at court as well. The public façade of respectability and morality often masked a plethora of sexual intrigues and flexible arrangements at many early modern courts.[134] However, the disapproval of the Church and the influence of traditional institutions, from individual households to whole communities, meant that there was a strong sense of moral economy in the handling of these matters.[135] The practical outcomes of such behaviour, particularly the spread of certain debilitating diseases, also attracted the attention of the state. Brothels that had been tolerated within towns and cities during the medieval period were closed in the wake of a religiously inspired official backlash in the sixteenth century. Such actions did not lessen the incidence of prostitution in early modern cities, but instead simply made it illegal.[136] As with the case of gambling, the difficulty of policing such activity led some states to pursue a regulatory policy, wherein they could license and thereby profit from prostitution, as in Florence.[137] Regardless of official sanction or otherwise, prostitutes were a common element of everyday life in an urban setting, with their numbers in the thousands for some of the larger cities of this period.[138]

The history of prostitution in Russia has tended to focus on the nineteenth century, when there was a concerted effort to tackle the problems associated with it through a new regulatory system in the major towns and cities.[139] The earlier period has not been as comprehensively studied, although some welcome work on the legal archives has been done recently.[140] As with other European states, the religious component loomed large in the promulgation of sexual mores. The last Patriarch of Moscow, Adrian, devoted a number of paragraphs to this in his instructions of 1697, although prostitution was not specifically mentioned.[141] Didactic religious literature also raised the subject, as the presence and tacit toleration of such activities within a community was held to have serious implications for its inhabitants. This aspect featured in a number of moral tales from the seventeenth century, such as the story of a village that turned a blind eye to the presence of a prostitute and was consequently punished by God through the corruption of their water supply.[142] However, specific mentions of prostitutes in contemporary documents are somewhat difficult to find. Legislation, such as the 1649 Law Code, refers instead to 'licentious' behaviour, which is nevertheless to be strongly punished.[143]

Foreign accounts of the period certainly do focus on the loose morals on display on the streets of Moscow, particularly during the celebration of feast days, but the comments are general in scope, rather than specifically focusing on incidences of prostitution.[144] Instead, they tend to be oblique. For example, Johann-Georg Korb notes the execution of an army officer for 'libidinous congress' with an eight-year-old girl in September 1699.[145] Later in his work, when discussing the morals of the Russian people, he records a comment from the Governor-General of Moscow wondering why, with so many prostitutes around, the officer had forced himself on someone.[146] During the reign of Peter I, official concern for the 'good order' of both the state and society meant that such religiously inspired disapproval was combined with the need to tackle the practical problems created by prostitution. Of particular concern was the question of sexual disease, carried both by prostitutes and their regular clients, which could have a serious impact on the public health of the urban community. With the high demand on manpower throughout the Great Northern War, it is hardly surprising that steps were taken by Peter and his military staff to minimise the impact of such diseases on their troops by tackling the problem of prostitution.

The punishments for a number of sexual crimes, including rape and homosexual activity, were contained in the various regulations or statutes issued to the military forces in the second half of Peter's reign. The punishments for these crimes were typically unequivocal – hard labour in the galleys or beheading, in the worst cases. Article 175 of the Military Statute deals specifically with prostitutes (*bludnitsi*) who were to be expelled from the camp upon discovery.[147] The Naval Statute contains similar prescriptions.[148] The link between the existence of brothels in St Petersburg and the large number of unmarried military personnel was again made in a 1730 report to the city's main administrative body, the Magistracy, on the subject of prostitution. To prevent the spread of disease, it advised that the brothels should be closed, prostitutes should be beaten with rods and any woman infecting three men should be sent to a 'house of correction'.[149] Later in Anna's reign, there was a further measure against prostitutes who were using the city's taverns for business. The Senate ordered that these women should be removed from these premises, flogged and sent to the authorities, since they were often runaway serfs. Anyone found harbouring them would face a severe fine and further punishment.[150]

The most high-profile campaign against organised prostitution in this period was conducted during the reign of Elizabeth, supposedly instigated on the advice of her influential confessor Fedor Dubianskii.[151] This action was taken in June 1750, when the Empress ordered State Counsellor Vasilii I. Demidov to oversee an investigation of the activities of a German 'madame', Anna-Cunegonda Felker, also known as 'Dresdensha' (after her city of origin).[152] The Police Chancellery were also instructed to search the city for prostitutes and arrest them.[153] His operation, based in the *Kalinkin dom*, set to work – Felker was arrested at an apartment that she had hired in the house of Major General Ivan Golovin on Vasil'evskii Island less than a week later. The police rounded up more than 50 prostitutes, most of whom were from north German ports, and Demidov noted how quiet the streets were at night.[154] Felker's interrogation by the Police Chancellery revealed a great deal of information about the operation that she had run and who exactly had taken part in it. She had rented a number of properties around the city, which she then used to host 'social evenings' over the course of the 1740s. These events were organised for a paying clientele (men had to pay one ruble to attend) and included entertainments, such as music and dancing. These evenings were a means to allow her clients to view and select women on offer. The women were a mixture of Russian and foreigners (mainly Germans), who had been recruited by Felker for this purpose.[155]

An example from 1748 provides a useful overview of her methods. She rented rooms in the house of Prince Mikhail A. Belosel'skii for a month and held three 'social evenings' in them, applying for the usual permission from the Police Chancellery and bribing the official. Tickets were sent to those who knew about such events and she provided a list of the attendees, which included noblemen, Guards officers and even two court pages.[156]

Although she maintained that such events were not intended for soliciting purposes, other parts of her testimony provide a list of her regular clients, who approached her specifically to find women of a flexible moral nature. This list includes a number of Russian and foreign dignitaries, such as the Imperial ambassador Count von Brettlach, the Saxon minister Count von Vitzhulm, Count Fedor A. Apraksin and Prince Boris V. Golitsyn.[157] This information fed into the ongoing police operation throughout the city, which was extended to include Kronstadt in August.[158] By November, there had been around 250 arrests and the number was expected to grow as the investigation continued.[159] Action had to be taken, and those found guilty of immoral behaviour were sentenced to a series of punishments – pimps were beaten with the knout, while prostitutes were flogged publicly. The foreign prostitutes were then deported by ship through Riga, while those of Russian origin were exiled to Orenburg.[160] Measures against prostitution also featured in the proposed law codes during the latter stages of Elizabeth's reign: brothels were to be closed, their owners whipped and the prostitutes sent to a mill.[161]

Another area related to the issue of public decency, and accessible to a paying clientele, was the city's commercial bathhouses (*torgovye bani*, as distinct from privately-owned bathhouses). These were dotted across St Petersburg; according to Bogdanov's description from 1751, there were at least nine examples in the city and its immediate surroundings. They were generally located either in peripheral areas, such as by the Galernyi Dvor on the Moika River, by the Obukhov Bridge or on Vasil'evskii Island, or attached to larger institutions, like the St Aleksandr Nevskii monastery or the garrisons of the Preobrazhenskii and Semenovskii Guards regiments.[162] Although the origins of the Russian bathhouse (*bania*) are obscure, they begin to appear in traveller's accounts from the sixteenth century onwards. Such foreign descriptions tended to focus mainly on the coarse behaviour of the bathers and the other seedy aspects of Russian bathing. In particular, the tendency of the sexes to mingle in close proximity to one another (around the entrances to segregated bathhouses) was thought to lend itself all too easily to immoral activities, in the opinion of observers such as Olearius and Korb.[163] On the other hand, Russians generally had a relaxed attitude toward mixed bathing throughout the sixteenth and seventeenth centuries. However, this began to change at the turn of the eighteenth century, partly as a result of the influence of Western attitudes and the greater awareness of appropriate behaviour. It also reflects a recognition that bathhouses were commonly used as a meeting place by prostitutes and their clients.[164]

As a result, mixed bathing was addressed in two laws during Elizabeth's reign, initially in 1743 in relation to St Petersburg and subsequently in 1760 for the rest of the Empire. The first regulation arose from a debate in the Senate about the existence of mixed bathing in the city's commercial baths, which was described as 'absolutely disgusting' (*ves'ma protivno*). Procurator Batiushkin from the Police Chancellery was summoned to explain whether an inspection had taken place, and he confirmed that this practice had been discovered in one of the baths. The Police Chancellery had issued an order regarding the proprietors of the offending baths to the Court Office, which was responsible for their regulation. The Senate confirmed this order in law and recommended the strict imposition of fines on the guilty parties in future.[165] The second law was issued by the Senate in August 1760 and noted that, despite prohibitive legislation, the practice of mixed bathing had continued. Both the Police Chancellery and the Court Office were instructed to redouble their efforts and the ban was extended to all cities.[166]

However, both these aspects of public behaviour clearly remained a concern for the authorities after this period. A 1771 law ordered that any prostitutes caught by the authorities were to be sent to work in factories, mirroring the similar treatment of such women in other contemporary states.[167] Most notably, Catherine II dealt with both issues in her 'Police Statute' (*Ustav blagochiniia*) of 1782. Article 71 contained the stipulation that bathhouses were to be kept removed from other buildings and should have clearly marked separate entrances for men and women. Prostitution was covered by a number of articles, in particular prohibiting the establishment or use of houses as brothels. The 'Police Statute' set out clear punishments for those who broke these regulations, ranging from fines to a prolonged spell in a house of correction.[168] Overall, both prostitution and mixed bathing highlight prominent examples of inappropriate and immoral practices to which members of all of St Petersburg's social groups had access. The social, moral and medical consequences of these activities excited considerable attention from the authorities in this period, driven in part by the ruler's moral outrage. The extensive reach and prominence of these activities in St Petersburg by the mid-1750s led to concerted efforts towards their prohibition, but the scale of the problem meant that this necessarily had to remain an ongoing project for Russia's rulers.

Overall, the institution of the Police Chancellery had a major impact on public life in St Petersburg. It embodied the desire of the state to regulate many aspects of everyday life, principally in relation to health and safety, in order to maintain 'good order' in society. However, as the case studies of drinking and gambling have demonstrated, there were continued efforts to restrict the potential for excess in the case of the wider population, whilst tolerating them as part of the social life of the nobility. In part, these restrictions reflect the recognition that the more refined atmosphere at court and in the houses of the nobility imposed its own regulation, with the imposition of fines and losing favour in influential circles providing a suitable incentive. The aspects of this regulation which applied to sexual conduct proved more complicated, with the state struggling to find a coherent, practical approach to a widespread problem. The moral dimension also complicated this issue, with the social mores of the elite proving rather more flexible than the official stance on the activities of the rest of the population. The gradual refinement of the nobility through suitable education, with its emphasis on self-regulation and appropriate behaviour – discussed in Chapter 5 – had to be balanced against the reality of everyday life in St Petersburg.

3
Organisation: the Court and its Celebrations

The royal court was the centre of the early modern state, both politically and culturally. As an institution, the court evolved out of the traditional late-medieval ruler's household to become a more extensive and sophisticated entity during the late fifteenth and sixteenth centuries. The importance of the court, and therefore of studying it as an institution, lies in the scope of its activity. The ruler remained the principal political decision-maker in most states throughout this period. The administration of the state emerged from the management of the ruler's affairs and expanded as the state became more centralised. Loyal service and proximity to the ruler remained important factors in exercising influence over decision-making, so attendance at court became increasingly important for ambitious nobles. The creation of new posts and responsibilities created a formal hierarchy at court, with prospects akin to the traditional military careers. By the end of the seventeenth century, the elaborate court of Louis XIV at Versailles embodied these developments, with its nobility serving the king in a large number of court posts, and its court celebrations glorifying his image.[1]

Yet, this image serves to disguise a much more nuanced reality. The traditional interpretation of the early modern court as a reflection and assertion of the ruler's absolute authority over the elite has been systematically challenged by detailed work on the complexity of courtly practices across Europe throughout this period.[2] The early modern court instead embodied a series of intricate and often tense relationships: between the interests of the ruler and those of the leading noble families; between the religious authority of the Church and the secular authority of the ruler's government; between the ideology of absolute royal authority and the reality of politics. The successful courts in this period were the result of careful negotiation that took account of these complexities. Rulers who tried to override them ran the risk of serious opposition or even being overthrown. This revisionist approach to the court and its activities has prompted a closer examination of courtly display, in particular the spectacle created by the court's major ceremonial occasions and celebrations. This 'representational culture' was an important means of displaying the achievements and status of a court, particularly to its competitors across Europe.[3]

In common with a number of other second-rank or peripheral courts in Europe, the Russian court actively sought to increase its international standing throughout this period. This chapter examines the Russian court as an evolving institution, and as the centre of St Petersburg's ceremonial life in the first half of the eighteenth century. The court underwent considerable changes during this period, as its relocation to St Petersburg was mirrored by its changing structure, size and appearance. The chapter therefore begins with these developments in relation to its predecessor and other contemporaries across Europe to place the early eighteenth-century Russian court in context. It then examines one of the aspects of 'representational culture' in the public court celebrations held in St Petersburg. During this period, St Petersburg became the primary stage for many major court ceremonies and celebrations, which had an impact on public life in the city. These events were elaborately planned and the decisions taken about their form and content often reflected the use of the court as a stage to project a particular image or message. The city's inhabitants, whether members of the elite or not, were part of these ceremonies, either as active participants or as members of the audience.

The nature of such celebrations was affected by the fact that St Petersburg was still a city under construction. Elaborate or widespread festivities were restricted in the first decade of its existence because of the lack of sufficiently developed areas in which they could be held. Consequently, many of the major celebrations in early St Petersburg were focused on certain areas, notably Troitskii Square during Peter I's reign and Nevskii Prospekt from the late 1730s onward. The focus here is on court celebrations that either occurred in central, open areas of St Petersburg or that were publicised in some form. Celebrations conducted in enclosed areas with limited access, such as the Summer Gardens and the city's palaces, are discussed in the following chapter. The major celebrations of the court in St Petersburg were consciously planned as public spectacles, often involving large processions and illuminations. Details of these celebrations were then printed in lavish commemorative publications and, for those outside the court elite, through descriptions carried in the city's newspaper, the *Sanktpeterburgskie Vedomosti*. These printed accounts carried the Russian court's ceremonial activities to a wider audience and were part of a wider bid for prestige in the eyes of other royal courts across Europe.

The court as an institution

Trying to generalise about a typical early modern royal court is a risky prospect, since there were many variations on that theme across Europe that encompassed a considerable range of personnel and offices. Nevertheless, by the early eighteenth century, a large number of courts displayed areas in common, from the functions assigned to courtiers to the administrative bodies responsible for their finances and activities. As well as being a leading patron and consumer of goods, the royal court employed a large number of personnel. However, while physically close to the ruler, the role and influence of court staff was very different to that of the courtiers. This division could be considered in terms of an inner court and an outer court. The inner court consisted of the ruler, their family and the high-ranking court office holders (men and women) who served as their companions and performed official roles in their chambers, at banquets and on ceremonial occasions. The outer court was much broader in its composition, including the lower ranks of the court administration and the large number of servants, craftsmen, musicians, gardeners and other retainers required for the practical everyday running of the court.[4] The overall size of the major European courts, such as those of France and the Holy Roman Empire, numbered in the thousands.[5]

In Muscovite Russia, the Tsar's household was chiefly run by the 'Great Palace Chancellery' (*Prikaz Bol'shogo dvortsa*), which dealt with everyday matters such as provisioning, while separate chancelleries dealt with clothing, regalia and other court treasures, its history and commemorations, and the service records of courtiers. There were also long-established offices to organise the court hunts, a favourite pastime in the Muscovite period, and to administer the Tsar's personal estates, including income.[6] This overall court structure did not change significantly during the early years of Peter's reign. However, with the deaths of Peter's mother and his brother Ivan V by 1696, and the demands of the Great Northern War from 1700 onwards, the court administration changed to suit the Tsar's frequent travels and his preference for the practical over the ceremonial. In October 1704, Peter created his Cabinet to organise the routine elements of his frequent travels, but it soon became responsible for overseeing and, more importantly, funding his various interests, which included projects like the Kunstkamera. Its new responsibilities also included aspects relating to court life – paying for Catherine I's wardrobe and servants, issuing gifts to court servants and hiring personnel.[7] The posts of 'orderlies' (*denshchiki*) and 'court couriers' (*pridvornye kur'ery*) soon served the same function as the 'table attendants' (*stol'niki*) of the traditional Muscovite court.[8]

However, this blend of the traditional and the expedient was hardly a long-term solution, particularly for a ruler with a penchant for organisation and regulation. Peter had experienced the atmosphere at several other European courts during the Grand Embassy (1697–8) and his later visits to Western Europe (1711–12 and 1716–17), when he visited impressive examples at Dresden, Vienna and Versailles. Whilst Peter was never particularly comfortable in formal court settings, whether Muscovite or European, he was also aware of the importance of the court as a political forum, whether domestically or internationally. A revised structure and appearance for the court could provide a more familiar setting for dealing with foreign diplomats and could also serve as an important stage to reflect Russia's ambitions and achievements, dynastic, military or otherwise. An important step in developing a new court structure was taken in March 1711, when Peter publicly declared that Catherine was a 'true sovereign' – given her common origins and the fact that they were not yet married, this was a significant statement.[9] The following day, Semen G. Naryshkin was appointed to Catherine's personal entourage using a new title – 'chamberlain' (*kamerger*) – although the new position had no officially defined duties as yet.[10]

Later in the same year, Alexander notes that the marriage of Tsarevich Aleksei Petrovich to Princess Charlotte of Brunswick-Lüneberg, sister-in-law of the Holy Roman Emperor Charles VI, in October 1711 meant that her German entourage came to Russia with her.[11] Gerhard Johann von Löwenwolde was appointed as her Chief Steward (*ober-gofmeister*) later that year, becoming the first man to fulfil that role in Russia. Other new positions were gradually created for other members of Catherine's circle, such as that of 'Groom of the Chamber' (*kamer-iunker*), a position that was occupied from 1716 by her lover Willem Mons.[12] A new administrative body – the 'Main Palace Chancellery' (*Glavnaia dvortsovaia kantseliariia*) – dealt with this revised court structure and its personnel gradually subsumed the responsibilities of the existing Great Palace Chancellery and several other chancelleries.[13] By 1724, it had effectively become the centre of the court administration under the authority of Matvei D. Olsuf'ev, a childhood friend of Peter's who was appointed the Chief Steward in 1723. This measure was intended to prevent the problem of overlapping jurisdiction, as was the closure of the Cabinet in 1727.[14]

During the same period, Peter ordered the compilation of a list of new court ranks, whose titles displayed a decidedly German influence and reflected the efforts of Russian diplomats in collecting a large amount of information about the structures and ranks of many leading European courts, including the examples visited by Peter himself.[15] This process formed part of the new hierarchy enshrined in the Table of Ranks for the three main strands of state service – military, civil and court – although it involved some consultation with the military and the Senate on the standings of the posts at each rank.[16] However, at this point, the court hierarchy contained in the Table of Ranks was essentially a list of titles and their corresponding ranks. Many of the posts were not filled during either Peter or Catherine I's reigns, despite Menshikov's efforts to form a proper court staff in 1726, and the duties of many court posts were left undefined.[17] Although several more court posts in this new hierarchy were appointed during Peter II's reign, albeit by his Chief Steward Heinrich Ostermann (author of the draft court hierarchy that subsequently informed the Table of Ranks), it remained very small, with only 19 courtiers.[18] However, it established the general pattern that was followed by the other rulers of this period, particularly in the number of Chamberlains and Chamber Grooms.

The reign of Anna Ivanovna heralded several major developments for the court as an institution. At the beginning of her reign, formal regulations were introduced for the two major ranks in the organisation of the court – the Chief Steward and the Chief Marshal of the Court (*ober-gofmarshal*).[19] The Chief Steward was particularly important, since he was the head of the Palace Chancellery and therefore in charge of the court's finances. He also dealt with the reception of foreign ambassadors. However, on a practical level, the everyday running of the court relied more on the figures of the Chief Marshal of the Court and his deputy, the Marshal of the Court (*gofmarshal*). The Chief Marshal was in charge of the Court Office, which oversaw the various servitors and servants at court, with the exception of the female courtiers, who were supervised by the Chief Stewardess (*ober-gofmeisterina*). The sheer number of areas covered by the court – the residences and gardens, the stables, the various estates, each of these with their attendant staffs – meant that there were a considerable number of people involved beyond the ruler and their courtiers.[20] Anna's reign also saw the formal appointment of many court posts for the first time, steadily increasing the overall size of the court.[21]

There were several means by which one could enter court service. During the early stages of the court's existence, many of its personnel were reassigned from the military and serving as an officer in one of the Guards regiments provided an opportunity to distinguish oneself in the eyes of the ruler. For example, Dmitrii A. Shepelev, who was made Chief Marshal of the Court by Elizabeth in July 1744, began his service in the Guards before being ordered to join Catherine's court, where he was made firstly a Chamber Groom in 1721 and then Marshal of the Court in 1726.[22] Rank could be gained either by promotion from within one of the court's subsidiary bodies, by leaving to join the army or, from the 1730s onwards, by means of education in the Cadet Corps.[23] The ranks associated with these court posts were revised upwards during this period. Under Peter I, Chamber Grooms were deemed equivalent to captains and Chamberlains to colonels. Anna Ivanovna raised the rank of both positions in 1737, with the former now equivalent to colonels and the latter to majors-general. Elizabeth subsequently raised Chamber Grooms to the rank of brigadiers in 1743.[24] Nevertheless, the military continued to enjoy the favoured position in elite society that had been established during Peter I's reign. A law issued in November 1731 ordered that, if ranks were equal according to the Table, the military officer was to take precedence over both the civil official and the courtier in all circumstances.[25]

However, the importance of the ruler's patronage in such matters meant that it was possible to rise very quickly through the court ranks if one had the requisite ability or charm. At this time, such promotion was usually associated with the favourites of the rulers, with high-profile examples such as Aleksandr D. Menshikov, Ernst von Biron and Ivan I. Shuvalov featuring prominently in the scholarship on this period.[26] The practice also applied elsewhere in the court structure. Vasilii I. Chulkov began his career as a servant at court under Anna Ivanovna, but his efficiency (or good looks) apparently caught Elizabeth's eye and she put him in charge of her wardrobe in September 1731, with the rank of 'valet' (*kamerdiner*). Elizabeth then created a new post for him in February 1742, Master of the Wardrobe (*metr-de-garderob* or *garderobmeister*, deemed of equivalent rank with a Chamber Groom). This promotion highlighted his ability to please her in this undoubtedly demanding role, especially in view of the Empress's well-known passion for elaborate and expensive clothing. He was subsequently made a Chamberlain in September 1751 which, given his humble origins and the privileged access to the Empress that his specialised duties entailed, may have caused some resentment.[27] There is considerable evidence to suggest that, with an awareness of the influential patronage networks at court and the right marriage connections, lesser noble families could establish themselves alongside their wealthier, more prestigious counterparts.[28]

Another means of gaining experience and standing at court was by serving as a page in the imperial household. This new position was created at around the same time as the other posts in the revised court establishment for Catherine I in 1711. The practice was then adopted by other members of the imperial family and even some high-ranking dignitaries, such as Menshikov. As with other court posts, the initial duties of the pages were not clearly defined, but they appear to have been used in a similar manner to their other European counterparts.[29] Their role was both practical and ceremonial. They participated in major court celebrations, along with the other court post-holders, but they were also used as personal servers at banquets, to direct guests at entertainments in the imperial residences, or to run specific errands, as required.[30] This role gave them privileged access to court events and pages were also used in preference to other court servants during the court's evening entertainments, such as *kurtagi* and balls.[31] This experience was important, as many pages subsequently held other court posts later in their career. Although their ranks were never the sole domain of the elite, with foreigners and middling nobles dominating their numbers in the first decades, leading families such as the Naryshkins, Golitsyns, Meshcherskiis and Vorontsovs were increasingly represented from the 1740s onwards.[32] The value of this position as a prelude to further service, whether with the court or elsewhere, was formalised with the foundation of the 'Corps of Pages', under the directorship of the Frenchman Louis Théodore de Tschudi, in 1759.[33]

These developments at the heart of the court establishment were mirrored at the various subsidiary courts attached to the heir to the throne and other members of the ruler's family. These 'satellites' were a typical feature of other contemporary European courts, albeit of varying size, cost and significance.[34]

Members of the Tsar's family had traditionally maintained a small personal court on their private estates, such as that of Tsaritsa Praskov'ia Fedorovna at Izmailovo during Peter I's reign.[35] The tastes of the individual dominated the composition of these personal courts, as there was no impetus to regulate them, and they frequently contained more 'dependents' – wise women, entertainers and family retainers – than officials. Indeed, one could argue that Peter himself had such a court during the 1680s, as he gathered his close circle of confidants and pursued his own interests on the royal estate at Preobrazhenskoe.[36] However, with the gradual expansion of the revised court by the 1720s, this situation began to change. Peter II appointed a salaried staff of courtiers for his sister Natal'ia Alekseevna in late 1727, including a Chamberlain, four Chamber Grooms and two 'Court Grooms' (*gof-iunkery*).[37] The extent of these personal courts is highlighted by the example of Tsarevna Elizabeth during Anna Ivanovna's reign. She had a large staff of around 200 people, including courtiers, maids, liveried servants and huntsmen, which required its own administrative office.[38]

For the 'young' court of her heir, Grand Duke Peter, Elizabeth was quick to appoint the senior posts in 1743. This responsibility was entrusted to members of her close circle and relations, such as Semen K. Naryshkin (as Marshal of the Court). Following the arrival of his future wife Catherine in 1744, the same pattern was followed for the appointment of the latter's court ladies, like Maria S. Choglokova (Chief Stewardess from 1746). Chancellor Aleksei P. Bestuzhev-Riumin compiled a series of instructions for the other members of this suite.[39] This scrutiny was important, as such 'young' courts could become a haven for (tacit) criticism of the main court, as demonstrated by the strained relations at other contemporary courts.[40] The Russian court had experienced this with the case of Peter's heir, Aleksei Petrovich, whose close circle was identified by his father as a focal point for discontent amongst certain 'conservative' elements in the Russian elite.[41] While the extent of any concrete conspiracy within Russia was limited, there is little doubt that the situation was treated very seriously, as reflected in the creation and investigations of the Secret Chancellery from 1718 onward and the unfortunate death of the Tsarevich in the same year.[42] Several of the 'young' courts later in this period displayed some level of discontent, albeit with less tragic outcomes. Thus, Grand Duke Peter's admiration for Frederick II of Prussia may have placed him at odds with Elizabeth's personal opinion and her foreign policy in the 1750s, but he was not disinherited.[43]

This period saw the gradual development of a more organised and European-style court, in marked contrast to its Muscovite predecessor. The establishment of new court ranks and titles under Peter I was subsequently consolidated during the reigns of Anna Ivanovna and Elizabeth. The regularity of the court was also addressed, with the issuing of instructions to the senior courtiers in the early 1730s and to the members of the heir's 'young' court in the late 1740s. Although many of the court's aspects continued to reflect the personality and preferences of the ruler, not least in the appoint-ment of personnel and its activities, this was hardly unusual in eighteenth-century Europe. Yet, there were clear areas of concern by the early 1760s. In particular, the Russian court struggled with the increased cost of its enlargement. The annual cost of the salaries paid to the court's officers and servants had risen from around 23,000 rubles in 1725 to 168,000 rubles in 1742. When added to the court's other expenses – provisioning, furniture, clothing, gifts – the overall spending per year was ruinously high.[44] Other courts spent extensively to reflect their prestige, as with France and the larger German courts (excepting Prussia, after Frederick I's death). Russia adopted a similar approach to its large-scale celebrations in this period, despite the strain that these placed on its underdeveloped economic resources.

Court celebrations

The festival calendar

The Muscovite court calendar was consolidated during the sixteenth century and was primarily linked to the Orthodox liturgical year, with due promi-nence given to the saints' days linked to the individual rulers and their relatives, as well as other events of significance, such as the major annual monastic pilgrimages.[45] One high-profile example, the Palm Sunday proces-sion, was an important part of the Muscovite court calendar and was noted by several foreign travellers during the seventeenth century.[46] The proces-sion was conducted from the Kremlin to St Basil's Cathedral and reflected the hierarchy at such ceremonial events. It was led by low-ranking courtiers, followed by a float bearing a tree with fruit tied to it representing fertil-ity. The float was then followed by parish clergy, high-ranking courtiers, the Tsar and the patriarch, members of the Church hierarchy, and finally, distinguished Moscow merchants.[47] Although many of these Muscovite celebrations were restricted to members of the social and religious elite, there were some public ceremonies such as the blessing of the waters on Epiphany (6 January). This was both a major state celebration and an important religious occasion that was celebrated at a symbolic 'river Jordan', recreated using the Moskva River outside the Kremlin. Although the court was the main focus of proceedings and participated in the procession of the Cross, the celebrations also attracted large crowds of faithful Muscovites to watch and then to collect the blessed waters after the ceremony had fin-ished.[48] There was also an exemplary element to such celebrations, with the Tsar's participation reflecting his adherence to the Orthodox faith and his humility in the service of God.

Peter I sought to harness this public, representational side of such rituals in his reorientation of the calendar of official celebrations, but here the sym-bolic message was slightly different. Although religious ritual and imagery remained a significant part of these events, their focus became the earthly military power of the monarch and the state as the chief agents of divine providence.[49] Peter's reign saw the introduction of troops being paraded before the 'blessing of the waters' for the feast of the Epiphany on 6 January, and the incorporation of the raising of the Russian standard, and cannon salutes, into the celebrations on Easter Sunday.[50] Victory celebrations represented a clear blend of religious and secular military elements. Although triumphal parades had occurred in seventeenth-century Russia, such as those to celebrate Prince Vasilii V. Golitsyn's return from the Crimean campaigns in the late 1680s, the victory celebrations for the capture of Azov in 1696 began this process of change, with military success being attributed to the Tsar and the army's achievements as much as to God's favour. The prominent use of Classical imagery in such celebrations – drawing comparisons with Hercules and Mars, for example – highlighted the shifting symbolic context.[51]

The major victories of the Great Northern War celebrated in St Petersburg reflect this melding of the two influences, as with the commemoration of Charles XII's defeat at Poltava. Although this victory had already been celebrated in Moscow in December 1709, further celebrations were held in St Petersburg in June 1710. The day began with a church service, accompanied by cannon salutes from both fortresses and ships on the Neva. Later, there was a regatta of these ships and a fireworks display, followed by a banquet in the evening.[52] Thereafter, the victory was celebrated annually on 27 June. The major Russian naval victories of the Great Northern War at Hangöudd (1714) and Grengram (1720) have already been discussed in Chapter 1. The signing of the Peace of Nystadt with Sweden in August 1721 led to impromptu celebrations in St Petersburg. A church service in the Sts Peter and Paul Cathedral was followed by cannon salutes, with beer and wine subsequently distributed amongst the people of the city.[53] The formal celebrations, which began on 22 October, have been well documented both by contemporaries and historians because of their significance in Peter I's acceptance of the title *imperator*. A service in the Sts Peter and Paul Cathedral was followed by cannon salutes from the fortress and 125 ships on the Neva, along with musket volleys from assembled regiments. In the evening, there was a banquet for 1000 dignitaries in the Senate house, and a large-scale fireworks display, with the city illuminated at night.[54]

Alongside the introduction of regular celebrations of major successes, there was also a conscious move to celebrate the person of the ruler and the dynasty as a whole in a more high-profile manner. Name days, birthdays and significant anniversaries, such as the ruler's coronation day, became important elements in the court calendar from Peter's reign onwards. The religious heart of the Muscovite court's celebrations was still present on such occasions, particularly for the feast days of saints associated with the ruler or their families, but it was supplemented by a range of new elements. For example, Peter's birthday on 30 May 1723 began with his attending matins at the St Aleksandr Nevskii monastery, before travelling by boat to the Cathedral of the Holy Trinity for mass. He was saluted three times by cannon fire from both fortresses and musket volleys from the Guards regiments on Trinity Square. He then dined at the Senate, after which there was a fireworks display on the river.[55] The following year, there were similar celebrations for his coronation anniversary (25 June) and his name day (29 June) – mass at the Cathedral of the Holy Trinity was followed by cannon and musket salutes, then the reception was held in the Summer Palace and gardens, which featured fireworks.[56]

The celebration of these events continued to dominate the official calendar during the reigns of Peter's successors because of their link to his legacy, both dynastic and imperial. In a period that has often been characterised as a succession of rulers whose claims to the throne could be (and often were) disputed, the emphasis on continuity and legitimacy contained in these regular celebrations was very important. During the 1730s, Peter I's name day – 29 June – became a regular celebration at court for the Order of St Andrew, the first Russian chivalric order established by Peter in 1699.[57] Continuity was also emphasised in the celebration of the birthdays and name days of the nominated heir to the throne. During Elizabeth's reign, the Order's feast was also the name day of Grand Duke Peter, so these celebrations could be combined.[58] The legitimacy of the ruler's reign was repeatedly stressed in the major annual celebrations of their accession to the throne, as well as in those marking their coronation.[59] Although the precise dates and details changed according to the individual reign, such celebrations usually followed similar contours. The day would begin with mass, followed by congratulations from those invited to attend for the subject of the anniversary, be it the Empress or a member of the imperial family. Later in the day, there was a banquet in one of the imperial palaces, at which toasts were made to the health of the Empress and to the subject of the event, and this was usually followed by a ball and a fireworks display or illumination.

At the same time, the Orthodox festive cycle remained an essential component in the major celebrations of the court. Although Peter had certainly reduced the overall number of religious holidays, compared with the mid-seventeenth-century court of his father, the major Orthodox feasts continued to be celebrated publicly by the court.[60] Examples included Epiphany (6 January), Candlemas (2 February), the Annunciation (25 March), the moveable feasts associated with Easter (including the Ascension), the Dormition (15 August) and the Nativity of the Virgin (8 September).[61] Away from the court setting, these occasions also maintained other traditional elements. A decree issued by Anna Ivanovna in 1735 served as a reminder of the importance of the religious commemoration of the major feasts of the ruler and the court in churches and religious communities across Russia, including those in remembrance of the deceased members of the dynasty.[62] Similarly, the religiosity of the ruler had an important bearing on the nature of the official calendar. For example, Elizabeth ensured that her court observed the important feast days of the Orthodox calendar and adhered to the fasting periods throughout the year.[63]

By the early 1760s, the Russian court calendar was a hybrid of traditional and new elements. While there was undoubtedly a greater emphasis on state-centric occasions as a legacy of the Petrine era, regular celebrations of the dynasty were very much in keeping with the traditional personalised nature of authority in Russia. The extensive religious calendar of the Muscovite court had been scaled back somewhat, but religious feasts and imagery remained very important parts of the Russian court's celebrations. Although Peter I's reign saw the introduction of new elements, like Classical symbolism and large-scale illuminations, to the repertoire of the regular court celebrations, its foundation remained Orthodox. The focus of the following sections moves from the court's regular anniversaries to instead consider the planning and execution of specific celebrations that attracted considerable domestic and international attention. Although conducted on an occasional basis, these events were major projects in their own right, involving extensive planning and investment by the court administration. As major spectacles conducted in the middle of St Petersburg, they drew in participants from the city's social elite and an audience from the rest of the city's population. The specific events have been chosen to illustrate the court's relationship with the city, embodying its triumphant return after the coronation in Moscow, the celebration of the dynasty's future happiness, and the final resting place of the ruler.[64]

Triumphal entries

A ruler's coronation is arguably the most important ceremony of their reign, since the symbolism of its celebrations focuses attention on the qualities and aspirations of the new monarch.[65] In Russia, imperial coronations were held in their traditional surroundings in Moscow, a practice that continued until the fall of the Romanov dynasty in 1917.[66] However, the relocation of the court and the social elite to St Petersburg as their primary residence in the first decade of the eighteenth century created a new circumstance, as the ruler had to return to the northern city after the coronation, rather than staying in Moscow. Russia was not the only state where the coronation took place in a city that was not the court's residence. For example, the French king was traditionally crowned in Rheims Cathedral, but ruled from Paris (later Versailles), while the Prussian elector (then king) was crowned in Königsberg, but ruled from Berlin. In such cases, the ruler and the court marked their return to the ruling city with a ceremonial entry. This event was essentially a variation on the triumphal entry, originally a Classical celebration associated with military victories. This had risen to prominence again during the fifteenth and sixteenth centuries, when it was used both in its military context and also as a demonstration of a ruler's power.[67]

In the aftermath of a coronation, this type of procession symbolised the assertion of the new ruler's authority over the seat of his power, while his reception in the city reflected the acceptance and loyalty of their subjects.[68] However, while these large-scale royal entries were an established part of European ceremonial for much of the early modern period, they were becoming less common at leading courts by the second half of the seventeenth century. The practice had fallen out of favour in England during Charles I's reign, after he cancelled his entry into London in 1625.[69] Similarly, Louis XIV's entry into Paris in 1660 was the last of its kind for well over a century.[70] There were several reasons for this decline, not least the considerable cost, which outweighed the symbolic value of this rather old-fashioned display. This decline was not absolute and, in a given context, the royal entry could still make an important statement of intent. The elaborate celebrations for Frederick I's coronation as 'King in Prussia' in 1701 were carefully planned, with the court ceremony-master Johann von Besser drawing on a range of other European examples for each element. The total cost was an estimated 6 million talers.[71] The court's triumphant return to Berlin was an integral part of the celebrations and was planned with the same level of detail.[72]

Russia had staged triumphal entries for major military victories, notably from the reign of Ivan IV onward, and a ceremonial entry into Moscow had become part of the coronation process during the reign of Peter II.[73] However, in focusing on the coronation celebrations in Moscow, the question of the court's return to St Petersburg has often been overlooked. At first glance, it is not difficult to see why this should be the case. Ceremonial entries were not held for either Catherine I, crowned in May 1724, or Peter II, crowned in February 1728.[74] During the latter's reign, his extended residence in Moscow left some contemporaries to wonder about St Petersburg's future.[75] However, with Peter's death and the accession of Anna Ivanovna in Moscow in 1730, the court planned its return to St Petersburg, heralded by a ceremonial entry in January 1732. Field-Marshal Burkhard C. von Münnich, governor of St Petersburg since 1727 and head of the Office of Artillery and Fortifications since 1729, had already organised the illuminations for Anna's coronation, and her planned return to St Petersburg in early 1732 provided another opportunity to gain her favour.[76] He drew up plans for the disposition of the procession and the various stages of the ceremonial entry.[77] A description of this event was then published as a supplement to the city's bi-weekly newspaper, *Sanktpeterburgskie vedomosti*.[78] The details of this event illustrate some of its influences on the planning and execution of Elizabeth's entry a decade later.

On the morning of 16 January, the procession's participants drew up along Bol'shaia Artilleriiskaia Ulitsa, either mounted on horseback or in carriages, in the order established by the plans. The procession then began at the triumphal arch at the Anichkov Bridge (32) at 1 p.m., led by St Petersburg's

Post-Director and his officials, who announced the procession with their post-horns. The procession involved representatives of the groups symbolically returning to the city. Merchants 'of all nations' were near the front of the procession, followed by foreign ministers and members of the *Generalitet*, in carriages, with each group divided by mounted dragoons and military musicians. Proximity to the Empress's carriage indicated a privileged status and was reserved for members of her family and court officials. Her favourite, Ernst von Biron (officially her Chief Chamberlain) and the Chief Marshal of the Court, Karl von Löwenwolde, rode alongside her carriage on horseback, while she was followed by her relations and her court ladies.[79]

The route followed Nevskii Prospekt through another triumphal arch, near the Admiralty, before diverting to the Church of St Isaac of Dalmatia. The Empress was met there by members of the Holy Synod and attended mass, before resuming the journey to the Winter Palace. At three stages during the procession (at the start, by the Admiralty and when approaching the Winter Palace), three rockets were to be fired to signal cannon salutes from the two fortresses. A fourth rocket signal heralded a musket salute from the troops lining the Nevskii Prospekt route, followed by the troops removing their hats with the traditional shout of 'Vivat'. These troops were drawn along the route, two ranks deep. This salute began, from the Winter Palace, with members of the four Guards regiments (starting with the Preobrazhenskii), then midshipmen from the Naval Academy (*gardemariny*) and marine grenadiers, and finally soldiers from other line regiments (such as Ingermanlandskii). The maintenance of order was clearly of concern, with the city's four garrison regiments designated as a security reserve. Similarly, several days prior to the event, each regiment was ordered to line up in its appointed spot to perfect both its line and distancing from the parade route.[80] To commemorate the event, the inscriptions from the engravings on the triumphal arches were subsequently published in the supplemental series (*Primechaniia*) to the *Sanktpeterburgskie Vedomosti* later that year.[81]

Münnich's detailed plans for the ceremonial procession in 1732 provided an important precedent for those planning the equivalent entry a decade later. In particular, the disposition of the ceremonial procession, the route that it followed, and the use of both military and sacral elements to create an audio-visual spectacle demonstrate the relationship between the two events. However, the 1742 entry was a larger event and incorporated some new elements. Its planning began with the design and construction of the triumphal arches along the route of the procession, and of the illuminations on the evening of the procession.[82] Their production began in September 1742, when Elizabeth indicated her wish to have two new arches built for the occasion of her return. The project was to be overseen by a special committee, using personnel from the Chancellery for Construction, although the creative input was left to specialists, mainly from the Academy of Sciences. Prominent amongst them were the architect Pietro Trezzini and the engraver Johann Stenglin, who were in charge of the overall style of the arches and of the prominent allegorical panels, respectively. In this endeavour, as with the ceremony and procession, they were able to work from precedent; the new arches were intended to replace those that had been constructed for the 1732 entry. The large amount of money assigned to these projects (10,000 rubles) reflects their importance.[83]

The planning of the ceremonial entry itself began much closer to the date. The disposition of the procession was originally written in French and then translated into Russian in order to be sent to the relevant participating bodies.[84] The author of this plan was given as Admiral Count Nikolai F. Golovin, who had been the Head of the Court Stables (*ober-shtalmeister*) since November 1740. The Court Stables were in charge of providing the horses for the procession and so this was not an unusual choice. The other prominent figure in the planning of the procession was Prince Nikita Iu. Trubetskoi, the General-Procurator of the Senate. He was certainly familiar with court ceremonial, having served as a Chamber Groom from November 1726, but had also served as a senior military officer in the 1730s. Trubetskoi was a reasonable choice, since the triumphal entry combined ceremonial and military elements in its planning. Although not marked as such on the original, a short register of the documents relevant to the ceremonial entry, which follows immediately after these documents in the bound volume that contains them – dated 23 December 1742 – attributes the composition of the order of the procession to Trubetskoi.[85] However, more unusually, the court's 'Chief Master of Ceremonies' (*ober-tseremoniimeister*) Franz Santi was only consulted on the evening of 21 December, when he was summoned to Trubetskoi's residence.

The disposition of the procession was essentially the same as in 1732, albeit larger due to the increased number of court officials and their servants. The route was also similar, following Nevskii Prospekt from the Fontanka River to the Winter Palace. However, the principal difference between this and the first procession was the more distinctive nature of the stages along the route where military, administrative, spiritual and commercial representatives of St Petersburg greeted the Empress. The first stage was at the first triumphal arch on Nevskii Prospect, by the Anichkov Bridge, where the Empress was met by the senior and staff officers of the regiments garrisoned in St Petersburg, most prominently those of the Guards. The second was at the new Gostinyi Dvor (**23**), where the city's merchants were drawn up in two lines, with Russians on the right-hand side and foreigners on the left-hand side of the prospekt. The third was at the Church of the Virgin of Kazan, where members of the Holy Synod were assembled, with 20 seminarians on elevated platforms on either side of the prospekt singing a specially composed hymn of praise to the Empress.[86] The fourth was at the second triumphal arch, by the Zelennyi Bridge over the Moika River, where ranks six to eight of the state administration were assembled. Finally, the top six ranks of the administration and further court officials received the Empress in front of the Winter Palace.[87]

As in 1732, the audio-visual elements were an integral part of the 1742 celebrations. The musicians of each regiment began to play as the Empress's cortège approached and continued until she had passed. As Chudinova notes, this created a rolling wave of music following her progress through the city. All of the city's churches were instructed to ring their bells and sound their chimes continuously during the procession. This musical accompaniment was joined by cannon salutes at the three main stages, fired by the regimental guns at each stage and the heavier guns of the two fortresses, alerted by rocket signals. At the final signal, as the Empress's carriage arrived at the Winter Palace, troops lining the procession route loosed a musket volley.[88] The visual element was reflected in the clothing of the different groups represented at each of the main stages, who were required to dress in their full uniforms. For example, the seminarians that sang in front of the Church of the Virgin of Kazan had to dress in white, which provided a contrast to the robes of the members of the Holy Synod and other clergy present. The city's merchants, who did not have a formal uniform, were instructed to wear brown, but distinctions were drawn between Russian, English and other foreign merchants. The lining of their kaftans was different (light blue for Russians, red for the others) and each group was allowed a certain amount of gold brocade, embroidery and other decorative features. On a wider visual scale, in addition to the fireworks display, the city and the triumphal arches were illuminated for the following eight nights.[89]

The procession was clearly intended to be a public celebration of the ruler's return to the capital. The large volume of gunfire throughout the day, as well as the illumination of the city at night, ensured that the city's wider population was made well aware of the occasion. However, evidence of contemporary reaction to the event is limited. The court journals are largely silent on the matter, merely noting that the Empress arrived in the city on 20 December and stayed in her old palace at Smol'nyi that evening.[90] Contemporary foreign observers do not provide any more detail. Cyril Wyche, the English resident at the Russian court, only travelled back to St Petersburg on 28 December, having previously complained of illness and transport difficulties, and so missed the event entirely.[91] His French counterpart, D'Alion, was also still in Moscow at the time. D'Alions' dispatch to the foreign minister, Jean-Jacques Amelot de Chaillou, on 27 December explained that he would only arrive at St Petersburg in 'five or six days'.[92] His colleague L'Estocq had arrived back from Moscow on 20 December, but his dispatch of 28 December did not mention the entry celebrations.[93] Similarly, the event was not described in the *Sanktpeterburgskie vedomosti*, in contrast to the description of the 1732 entry in the supplemental *Pribavleniia*.[94]

Santi, the Chief Master of Ceremonies, wrote a report in which he noted the issues discussed at the meeting on 21 December and some of the problems that subsequently occurred on the day of the procession itself.[95] Santi initially noted that he advised Trubetskoi to liaise with the other leading court officials, in order to ensure that the liveries of the various equipages and horses for the procession were ready. Trubetskoi replied that orders had been issued which participants were obliged to carry out. Santi then expressed his reservations about Golovin's proposed disposition, which he had apparently already sent to Trubetskoi in a letter. He was concerned about the orderly conduct of the ceremony at each stage. For example, he highlighted that the court gentlemen had been given no instructions about their arrival and function at the Church of the Virgin of Kazan. Similarly, the description of the procession contained no mention of which staircase the Empress would use to alight from her carriage when she arrived at the church. To the former point, Trubetskoi replied that members of the court should know their duties and then ignored the latter point entirely.[96]

Santi's report then proceeded to describe the confusion and 'extreme disorder' that occurred as the result of ignoring his advice. Principally, this took place outside the church, where there was no court official to escort the Empress when she alighted her carriage. Santi had to fulfil this role himself until relieved by Count Mikhail I. Vorontsov. Further confusion ensued when the rocket signal to indicate the Empress's departure from the church was not fired on time. As a result, Santi was unable to get back to his carriage in time before the procession moved off, meaning that he had to run for 'half a verst' in order to catch his carriage. The report ends with the pointed comment by Jean Armand de L'Estocq, echoed by several unnamed Russian officials, that if a court has *une grande maître des ceremonies*, then it should let him carry out his duties.[97] This account, whilst hardly objective, nevertheless provides a useful alternative to the ideal version of events represented by the planning documents. In particular, it includes details on the practical problems, such as the mistimed signals or confusion over specific duties, that were created by events on this scale and that are not recorded anywhere else.

In fact, the evidence of wider awareness of this event centres on one of the lasting visual reminders of the entry: the triumphal arches. In his description of St Petersburg, written just under a decade later, Andrei Bogdanov notes the construction of the two arches, linking them not only to the entry but to the conclusion of peace with the Swedes the following year.[98] A description of the engravings on the two arches was published by the Academy of Sciences in January 1743, having been composed by Christian Crusius as part of the preparation process for the entry.[99] Although only around 300 copies were printed, according to the records of the Academy of Sciences, this decision nevertheless provides evidence of an attempt to highlight the importance of the meaning of the engravings by reproducing the inscriptions that accompanied them on the arches.[100] The presence of the arches served to confirm Nevskii Prospekt's position as the main arterial and ceremonial route through St Petersburg, with the incorporation of its architectural features as the main stages of the procession. Although the prospekt had been used for the 1732 entry, extensive rebuilding during the late 1730s and the consecration of the Church of the Virgin of Kazan in 1737 – subsequently used as one of the main sites of the court's religious ceremonies in the city – ensured that it consolidated this position in St Petersburg's landscape.

Elizabeth's return to St Petersburg carried a slightly different meaning to that of Anna Ivanovna. The latter's ceremonial entry in 1732 essentially represented the return of the court and the Russian elite to the city, following a period of uncertainty about its future role in the late 1720s. However, Elizabeth and her court were already resident in St Petersburg when she took power in late 1741, and they had returned to Moscow in order to celebrate her coronation in the traditional manner. Her status as Peter I's daughter, particularly in light of her claim to represent his legacy during her overthrow of Ivan VI, meant that the return to 'his' city had both personal and political significance. There was also a military side to the occasion with the recent victories in the war against Sweden, which linked this event to the traditional triumphal entry. The presentation of Elizabeth as the defender of her father's legacy and a victorious ruler in her own right was a powerful image with which to complement the existing 1732 model.

Both ceremonial entries into St Petersburg in the first half of the eighteenth century bear comparison with the example of the Prussian court entering Berlin in 1701. The two cities were newly established as the principal seats of their respective royal courts and the respective monarchs were keen to firmly establish a link between the court and its main residence. The extensive planning and considerable financial investment indicates the importance of this spectacle at the outset of both monarchs' reigns. In the Russian case, the comparison between the 1732 and 1742 entries demonstrates the development of both the court and the city in the intervening decade, particularly in the larger number of participants in the second procession and the physical commemoration of the entry, in the form of triumphal arches, on Nevskii Prospekt. However, one further similarity between the Berlin and St Petersburg entries was that they did not prove to be a lasting feature of court ceremonial. Frederick I's successors, starting with his son Frederick-William I, eliminated extravagant ceremonies as a waste of money and the entry into Berlin was one of the victims.[101] For the Russian court, Peter III did not last long enough to have a formal coronation in Moscow and so Catherine II was the last ruler to have a triumphal return to St Petersburg after her coronation in 1763.[102] By the end of the century, the court was firmly established in St Petersburg and the ceremonial entry's symbolic statement of intent was no longer necessary.

Weddings

The planning of a royal wedding was a major undertaking for any early modern court. It had wide-ranging domestic and international implications, with the choice of the ruler's new spouse usually hinging on political considerations rather than the suitability or attractiveness of the two individuals. Such weddings provided an important opportunity to reflect the wealth and status of the host court through the scale and splendour of the celebrations. The joining of two dynasties through a marriage alliance was also a well-established means of cementing alliances or pushing for greater recognition on the international stage. As a result, such wedding matches were explored and carefully planned, so that both parties could agree on the intended outcome, often before the couple ever met. The resulting marriage did not have to be happy, but it did at least have to produce a suitable heir. Yet one of the peculiarities of the Russian court in the eighteenth century is that relatively few royal weddings took place. The circumstances of Russia's rulers in this period provides an explanation. Amongst Peter I's successors after 1725, Catherine I and Anna Ivanovna were widowed, Peter II died before his wedding, Ivan VI was a child and Elizabeth remained officially single.

Russia was also quite distinctive in its royal wedding traditions. The Muscovite court adopted the 'bride show' from the Byzantine tradition, with the Tsar selecting his future wife from a range of candidates from throughout his realm. Although theoretically open, this selection process was strongly influenced by advisers and family members. It favoured candidates from domestic, noble backgrounds in order to prevent instability caused by marrying into a particular *boiar* family, or one with problematic foreign ties.[103] Muscovite wedding celebrations were religious in nature. Peter I's wedding to his first wife Evdokiia in 1689 provides a typical example of the traditional ceremony and associated imagery.[104] As a result, there were no major public wedding celebrations in Russia on a par with those of Louis XIV in 1660 or Leopold I in 1666, 1673 and 1676.[105] This situation began to change in the early eighteenth century in two important respects. Peter I's desire to push Russia onto the European stage through reform and military action against Sweden meant that marriage alliances were a viable means of gaining international support and influence. In the same period, the court's move to St Petersburg meant that the new city became the likeliest setting for royal weddings. Since the ruler was already married, for the time being the focus of any potential weddings at the Russian court fell on the other members of the royal family, in particular the heir to the throne.

The first major court wedding in St Petersburg was that of Peter's niece, the future Empress Anna Ivanovna, who married Friedrich Wilhelm, Duke of Courland, on 11 November 1710. The ceremony and the subsequent celebrations were both held at Menshikov's palace on Vasil'evskii Island. The Tsar was the marshal of the wedding, with all members of the military establishment (down to the rank of lieutenant) and other dignitaries invited to attend. The marriage ceremony was followed by a banquet, with toasts and cannon salutes to the newly-weds.[106] The Danish envoy Just Juel was a guest and his account reveals some interesting details. For example, the service was conducted in Russian, but the vows were translated into Latin for the Courlanders by Juel's secretary Rasmus Ærebo, and there were no fireworks after the banquet as Menshikov was not well.[107] In terms of its setting, personnel and content, this wedding has been identified as a significant departure from the traditions of the previous century.[108] The new elements were then echoed in the arrangements for Peter's second wedding, to his consort Catherine, in February 1712. Again, the celebrations were conducted publicly in European fashion, with the overall theme of the wedding reflecting Peter's personal interests, rather than tradition; he wore his rear-admiral's uniform and naval officers dominated the guest list.[109] There was a short, private church ceremony followed by a banquet in the Winter Palace – although Menshikov's palace is depicted in the famous engraving of the event by Aleksei Zubov – with Menshikov serving as the marshal. There were fireworks and other illuminations later that night.[110]

These two events established the pattern for royal weddings for the remainder of this period, virtually all of which took place in St Petersburg, rather than Moscow. The new city's European stylings provided a suitable setting for these weddings, as the Russian court sought to forge connections with other northern European dynasties through marriage. Anna Ivanovna's marriage to the Duke of Courland established a pattern: her sister Catherine married the Duke of Mecklenburg in 1716, Anna Petrovna married the Duke of Holstein shortly after her father's death in 1725, and Anna Leopoldovna married the Duke of Brunswick in 1737. The latter two weddings took place in St Petersburg.[111] However, one royal wedding in particular dominated this period – that of Grand Duke Peter Fedorovich to his German fiancée, Princess Sophie of Anhalt-Zerbst, the future Catherine II, in 1745. Peter had been chosen as Elizabeth's heir in late 1742 and the Empress was keen to ensure the dynasty's future through his marriage and offspring, so the wedding held great significance for the Russian court.[112] These concerns were also reflected in other high-profile royal weddings of the royal heirs at some of Europe's leading courts in this period: Prussia in 1733, Britain and the Holy Roman Empire in 1736, Sweden in 1744 and France in 1744 and 1747.[113] The Grand Duke's wedding in 1745 encapsulates some important aspects of the Russian court's relationship with European court ceremonial. In particular, Santi's notes on the occasion, as the court's Chief Master of Ceremonies, provide an important insight into the planning process that is not available for the earlier court weddings in St Petersburg.

Planning for the wedding of the Grand Duke probably began in earnest after his fiancée's conversion to Orthodoxy in Moscow on 28 June 1744, when she took the name Ekaterina Alekseevna and received the title of Grand Duchess. Catherine wrote in her *Mémoires* that, by the spring of

1745, wedding preparations had already begun.[114] Count Santi and his Deputy Master of Ceremonies, Fedor P. Veselovskii, held a meeting on the subject with Count Aleksei P. Bestuzhev-Riumin at his house at 6 p.m. on 26 February. The Empress had ordered that the wedding should be based on that of Grand Duchess Anna (the Empress's sister and Grand Duke Peter's mother) to the Duke of Holstein-Gottorp, which had taken place in May 1725. Santi wrote to the Marshal of the Court Dmitrii A. Shepelev to ask for the records of the occasion from the Court Office. Shepelev replied that the office did not have records from the time of the previous wedding and Santi was therefore obliged to consult recollections of events (*des traditions orales*) and devise a new plan with 'irrefutable foundations'.[115] This plan was then to be reviewed by the College of Foreign Affairs.[116]

The resulting plan, submitted and discussed in March 1745, raised 14 'points' or questions that needed further input from the Empress. These points dealt not only with practical concerns, but also important questions about the appropriate protocol. The practical points usually sought clarification on the physical aspects of the plan, such as the nature of the travelling arrangements, the order of the carriages in which the royal family would travel and where they would be placed in relation to the Empress's carriage. A later point queried the seating arrangements for the royal family at the wedding banquet, in particular the placement of Catherine's mother and Prince August. Santi suggested that they might be placed at a separate table, either opposite the throne or to the left of it, citing the example of the seating for the coronation of Catherine I and referring to the glorious memory of Elizabeth's father. For other participants, the tenth point addressed the carriages to be used by each rank in the procession. Questions were raised about the use of six horses (rather than four), the need for gold and silver ornamentation on both carriage and livery, and how many servants should be allowed per participant. This point also highlighted the need to inform these people in sufficient time to make the necessary preparations.[117]

The points dealing with protocol indicate a broader concern with perception, particularly how Russia should engage with the example of other European courts. The wedding was to be publicly proclaimed by two heralds for three days prior to the event, accompanied by trumpets and drums. A marginal note adds that this point had been extensively debated by the College of Foreign Affairs and, although Santi was unable to recall a previous example of such a proclamation in Russia, it was considered necessary because of the number of ambassadors and foreign ministers in attendance. The seventh point, on the choice of church for the ceremony, had a note in the margins that such weddings usually took place in one of the royal churches at other European courts. The ninth point, on the question of who should carry the trains of the Empress and the Grand Duchess, noted that, in the principal courts of Europe, this role was performed by court ladies.[118] More explicitly, the final 'point' noted that the custom observed at Anna's wedding, of the bride receiving congratulations from guests and presenting each of them with a glass of wine, was not considered appropriate for this occasion. As Santi put it: 'This practice, while ancient, is preserved mostly in the eastern or middling peoples of Europe [and] is very much opposed to good practice in the courts of Sovereigns.'[119] This aspect of the planning process reflects Russia's awareness of and desire to engage with the practices of other European courts. The College of Foreign Affairs had been responsible for gathering such information since Peter I's reign and its role in qualifying Santi's plans indicates that the court was keen to ensure that it presented an appropriate image.

Two decrees issued on 16 March 1745 relate to this planning process and concern the appearance of the distinguished guests and their mode of transport for the wedding celebrations. In the first decree, from the Empress to the Senate, members of the first four ranks and court gentlemen were given a monetary grant in order to ensure that their equipage was in a suitable condition for the occasion.[120] The second decree required the Senate and the distinguished ranks of the Empire to begin their preparations for the wedding ceremony and celebrations in the early days of July. The first four ranks and court gentlemen were allowed to use gold and silver ornamentation, in both their clothing and their equipage, according to their means. In addition, since the celebrations were to take place over a number of days, each participant was to have at least one new set of clothing made, although those who wanted to could make more. With regard to the points raised by Santi's plan, it was stipulated that each person should have a carriage, with those who could afford it also providing one for their wives, and the plan listed how many servants each rank could have to accompany them. Finally, the guidelines on dress and equipage were extended to members of the fifth and sixth ranks, who were not taking part in the ceremonial procession, but who would be participating in the other celebrations.[121]

This concern for the appearance of the participants, in the ceremonial procession and in the wedding celebrations in general, shown in the documents above, was very much a reflection of both the wealth and the status of the Russian elite. Although the guidelines clearly disregard the *ukaz* on the need for moderation in one's dress, issued by the Empress only two years previously, it is equally clear that the occasion was considered sufficiently important to merit such an exception. The importance of the preparations was restated several times during the build-up to the wedding. On 9 August 1745, the *Sanktpeterburgskie Vedomosti* contained a reminder to all participants that their preparations for the Grand Duke's wedding should be completed by 19 August.[122] Similarly, in the week preceding the wedding, specifically on 14 and 16 August, there were masquerade balls incorporating rehearsals of the dance quadrilles that subsequently featured in the wedding celebrations.[123] With such extensive planning, it is surprising that several of the plans and projects for the wedding celebrations suggest that the ceremony was originally set for 18 August.[124] Catherine noted in her *Mémoires* that 21 August was chosen after the preparations had been mostly completed, but gives no further explanation.[125] The English envoy, Lord Hyndford, provides the likeliest explanation when he noted that the weather had been poor in the days preceding the wedding and it was delayed as a result.[126]

In preparation for the wedding, and at the Empress's request, Peter and Catherine attended confession and took communion in the Church of the Virgin of Kazan (the venue for the wedding) on 15 August, and heard Vespers at the St Aleksandr Nevskii monastery on 17 August.[127] On 21 August, a five-gun salute from the Sts Peter and Paul Fortress at 6 a.m. signalled the members of the first four ranks (*Generalitet*) to gather in front of the 'new' wooden Winter Palace on Nevskii Prospekt. At 11 a.m., a 21-gun salute from the Admiralty signalled the start of a carriage procession to the Church of the Virgin of Kazan. This procession involved the royal family and their courtiers, members of the *Generalitet* and foreign ministers, with their wives. The order of the procession provides a useful list of the notable members of St Petersburg society, their rank and some indication of their relationship with the Empress. Unsurprisingly, the closest people to Elizabeth – aside from Peter and Catherine, who travelled in her carriage – were her court ladies and gentlemen, along with her personal guard from the Life Company.

Following the church ceremony, the assembled regiments fired three volleys in conjunction to cannon salutes from 24 galleys, two transports and two yachts on the Neva River. The procession then returned to the Winter Palace for the wedding banquet, spread across the gallery and four other rooms. There were a number of toasts to both the Empress and the newly-weds, accompanied by cannon salutes from both fortresses (51 guns for the 'happy' couple, 101 guns for Elizabeth).[128] Afterwards there was a ball until 11.45 p.m., whereupon the couple were led away to their newly prepared rooms, where they were expected to consummate the marriage, according to Catherine's *Mémoires*.[129] The celebrations continued the following evening, with a ball at 9 p.m. in the gallery of the 'new' Winter Palace, to which the first four ranks and foreign ministers were invited. It was followed by a banquet in the hall at 1 a.m., where the guests dined at a large, specially made table, incorporating fountains, cascades and pyramids of candles. Seating at this table was controlled by ticket and there were 130 guests from the court ranks, foreign ministers and the members of the first four ranks. The meal was accompanied by Italian music played from the balcony of the hall. The Empress did not dine at this table, but in a side room with Church dignitaries and other select (unnamed) guests – 35 people in all.[130]

The next major event in the celebrations was the performance of the *opera seria, Scipio,* in the opera house near the Summer Palace on 25 August. It was the work of composer Francesco Araja to a libretto by the poet Giuseppe Bonecchi. The rather more fitting ballet *The Wedding of Psyche and Cupid* was performed during the intermission. The Empress, the Grand Duke and Duchess, her mother and Prince August of Hessen-Homburg all attended, along with other distinguished guests. The libretto was printed in a handsome edition for distribution to the guests in Russian, French and Italian.[131] However, the centrepiece of the court celebrations occurred on 26 August in the form of the masked quadrilles, which had been rehearsed earlier in the month. This elaborate dance formed part of a ball held in the 'new' Winter Palace at 7 p.m. There were four quadrilles, each with 17 pairs, a total of 136 people. As with the seating at the banquet discussed above, partners were decided by tickets. The quadrilles were led by the Grand Duke, the Grand Duchess, her mother and Prince August; each group had its own colours – the Grand Duke's were rose and silver, his wife's white and gold, her mother's light blue and silver, and Prince August's were pale yellow and silver. There was a banquet after the ball, with seating by number, with each quadrille sitting in a row. The Empress instead went to dine with Count Aleksei G. Razumovskii at his residence near the 'old' Winter Palace, with 40 other guests.[132]

The impression given by this description is of a colourful and well-organised dance spectacle, another reflection of the court's grandeur; yet, oddly, ambassadors and foreign ministers were not invited to the ball. No reason for this omission was given in the official account of the celebrations.[133] Catherine's description of the occasion in her *Mémoires* calls into question the impact of the masked ball as a spectacle, but her memory had evidently been affected either by the unhappy nature of events or the passage of time. For example, although she correctly remembered her dance partner of the evening, Count Peter Lacy, she complained that none of the gentlemen present was capable of dancing and that they were all aged between 60 and 90. She added: 'I never saw a sadder and more tasteless spectacle in my life as the quadrilles; there were only 48 pairs of the most lame, gout-ridden and decrepit people in a huge room, and all the rest were spectators in ordinary [i.e. not in the quadrille's colours] dress, not daring to interfere with the quadrilles. However the Empress found it so beautiful that she had it repeated for a second time.'[134] This description hardly seems flattering to Prince Nikita Iu. Trubetskoi (aged 48), Vice-Chancellor Count Mikhail Vorontsov or Petr I. Shuvalov (both aged 35), to name a few examples that were members of her quadrille.[135] Doubtless Catherine's description applied to some of the participants, in view of their age and health, but equally her own memories of the celebrations may not have been entirely free of the ambivalence that she subsequently felt towards her marriage.

Overall, royal weddings were an ideal opportunity to showcase the court in a display that worked on a number of different levels. Such a marriage often represented a symbolic union of dynastic interests between two courts and while Russia was still not at the level of the French, English or Austrian courts as a prospective partner, it was clearly an established and credible presence in northern Europe by the end of this period.[136] The celebrations provided a glorious display of the court's wealth and sophistication, with St Petersburg now providing the stage for both domestic and international audiences. The event certainly drew comment from both the foreign ambassadors in attendance and the foreign press.[137] Santi's notes make clear that the planning in 1745 dealt with many aspects of the wedding's conduct and appearance, with the example of other European courts looming large as an influence. Royal weddings were therefore a microcosm of sorts for Russia's growing prominence and its suitability as a potential ally; they also demonstrated its adherence to a familiar set of courtly practices on such occasions.

Funerals

Royal funerals occupied the opposite end of the emotional spectrum from the joyful celebration of royal weddings, but they were no less important in highlighting the themes of dynastic continuity and splendour. Although the ceremonies frequently had medieval origins, their form and content continually evolved throughout the early modern period as their symbolic messages began to focus increasingly on the glory of the monarchy and its achievements. During the same period, the highly visible public celebration of royal funerals emphasised these themes and conveyed them to a wide audience, through a variety of media (text, image and sound).[138] Although the broad outline of these funerals was similar across Europe, there were some important differences in tone during this period. For example, from the mid-seventeenth century, the Habsburg court was very concerned with following the established protocol of previous imperial funerals, as seen in the funerals of Leopold I, Joseph I and Charles VI.[139] By contrast, the English monarchy increasingly sought to minimise the public nature of royal funerals, and moved toward a smaller, more private ceremony during the eighteenth century. The elaborate and very expensive funeral for Queen Mary in 1695 was not repeated for her husband, William III (who left specific instructions to that effect), or by any of their successors during the eighteenth century.[140]

Muscovite funerals were traditionally conducted entirely within the walls of the Kremlin, with the burial taking place in the Cathedral of the Archangel Michael, a short distance from the royal palace. Muscovite funeral processions were exclusively religious affairs, within the enclosed space of the Kremlin, and only involved members of the ruling family, the Church and court hierarchy. The funeral ceremony generally took place within two days of death, after which groups of courtiers and members of the clergy maintained a vigil by the tomb of the deceased around the clock for 40 days, in accordance with Orthodox tradition.[141] Peter I's funeral in March 1725 stood in stark contrast to the traditional funerals of his father and half-brothers, which had taken place in January 1676, April 1682 and January 1696 respectively. It was held in St Petersburg, with his body interred in the Sts Peters and Paul Cathedral, and the ceremony explicitly drew on European sources for its procedures and symbolism.[142] It provided a model for the future conduct of Russian royal funerals and established the Sts Peter and Paul Cathedral in St Petersburg as the main burial place for the Romanovs until the fall of the dynasty in 1917.

Peter had already organised European-style funerals for a number of his close associates, most notably General Patrick Gordon and Franz Lefort in the late 1690s and Admiral Fedor A. Golovin in 1707, all held in Moscow.[143] However, the establishment of St Petersburg thereafter meant that the funerals of members of his family or close circle were firmly centred on his new city. European influences can be detected in the funerals of members of the royal family in St Petersburg during the last decade of Peter's reign. Examples include the numerous funerals of those of Peter and Catherine's numerous children who died in infancy, and the major ceremonies for the interment of Peter's half-sister Natal'ia Alekseevna, in November 1717, and his son Aleksei Petrovich, in June 1718.[144] The scale of these occasions caught the attention of contemporaries. Weber witnessed the funeral processions of Peter's daughter-in-law, Princess Charlotte of Brunswick-Lüneberg, in October 1715 and of Marfa Matveevna, widow of Tsar Fedor Alekseevich, in January 1716, which was conducted from the 'house of mourning' to the Sts Peter and Paul Cathedral across the frozen Neva River, with the route lined by 'a double row of Flambeaus'.[145]

Peter devoted a considerable (not to say morbid) amount of time to planning for his own funeral. He issued an *ukaz* in April 1723 ordering information to be gathered about funeral practices at other European courts – reports were then submitted from Berlin, Vienna, Paris and Stockholm. Ageeva highlights Prince Sergei Dolgorukii's notes on the funeral ceremony of the Elector of Saxony, dated February 1724, although it presumably refers to John George IV, who died in 1694. His notes paid particular attention to the *castrum doloris* and the funeral procession to the church.[146] The eventual plan for Peter's funeral was written by General James (Iakov) Bruce and recent scholarship has noted the influence of Swedish and German models for elements such as the imagery surrounding the deceased and the public presentation of the royal body.[147] Peter's death from an infection in late January 1725 moved these plans into action. His corpse was first embalmed, a standard technique at other European courts but one that proved controversial with the Orthodox Church. The body then lay in state for almost six weeks, prior to the funeral procession, in a specially designed 'chamber of mourning' (using the transliterated Latin term *castrum doloris*) in the large hall of the Winter Palace. The coffin was surrounded by symbols of military and imperial power, and the room was decorated with allegorical sculptures, featuring grieving Classical figures and representations of Peter's virtues. This decor also proved unpopular with the Church hierarchy, who believed such symbols were 'pagan'.[148]

A vigil was kept by groups of senators and soldiers, with a priest reading from the psalms and the gospels. This *castrum doloris* was also open to the public and the coffin was raised up to allow access for mourning by the large crowds of people.[149] A contemporary source on Peter's death, attributed to Archbishop Feofan Prokopovich, describes this public mourning, albeit with some rhetorical licence, with people of all ranks and ages coming to kiss the late Tsar's hand and weep.[150] The actual funeral took place on 10 March, a week after the death of Peter's youngest daughter Natal'ia, who was buried in the same ceremony. The funeral procession was a major public event, as it was conducted from the Winter Palace to the Sts Peter and Paul Cathedral across the frozen Neva River on a specially-laid wooden 'prospekt'. It was publicly announced two days beforehand and a list of participants had been drawn up, consisting of 166 different groups of mourners. Alongside members of the ruling family, the court and the top ranks of the civil/military administration, the list included members of a number of social groups, like the merchantry (both Russian and foreign), representatives from other major towns and the Baltic German nobility. The military side of the late Tsar's reign was presented prominently in the funeral procession, as it was led by regimental musicians and the route was lined by over 10,000 troops from the regiments based in the city.[151] The planning clearly had an impact, as the city's foreign ministers were impressed with how well the court had handled the situation.[152]

By contrast with her late husband, there is very little detailed information about Catherine I's funeral in St Petersburg in May 1727. The river was no longer frozen by this stage in the late spring and so the procession had to be conducted by boat, accompanied by cannon fire from both fortresses and boats moored on the Neva, whilst the regiments garrisoned in St Petersburg played music and beat drums.[153] As the funeral of the young Peter II took place in Moscow, the next major royal funeral to occur in St Petersburg was that of Anna Ivanovna in December 1740. A special commission was convened shortly after the Empress's death on 17 October to coordinate the various elements of the funeral preparations, with an overall budget of 65,000 rubles.[154] The resulting funeral largely followed the Petrine model, to the extent that proceedings were delayed until the ice on the Neva had hardened sufficiently to enable the funeral to process to the Sts Peter and Paul Cathedral. However certain details were changed, particularly in the public presentation of the royal corpse for public mourning. The Empress's body was moved to the small hall of the 'old' (i.e. Petrine) Summer Palace in mid-November and there lay in state with only limited access for members of the court and the Church hierarchy. Then, on 16 December, the body was transferred to the burial coffin and displayed along with the imperial Russian crown (as redesigned in 1731 on Anna's orders) and other items of royal regalia. During the following week, people from all social groups were allowed to visit this room every day between 9 and 11.30 a.m. and

2 and 5 p.m. Indeed, so many people came to mourn that the black drapery at the entrance was damaged and had to be replaced.[155]

The final royal funeral of this period was that of Elizabeth and, despite her aversion to anything associated with death, it was an elaborate, expensive ceremony. Elizabeth died after a period of illness on Christmas Day, 1761, and the court followed the precedent set by Anna Ivanovna's death two decades earlier. Peter III established a funeral commission with an increased budget of 100,000 rubles and the academic Jakob von Stählin oversaw the design of the funeral's imagery. The body was moved by Chamberlains from the deathbed to a specially designed state room in the Winter Palace on 14 January, so that members of the court could visit it to mourn.[156] One contemporary, who was a sentry for the corpse in the Winter Palace, remarked that the cold weather had helped to keep it well preserved, except for the mouth.[157] On 25 January, the body was moved to a *castrum doloris* where it lay in state and crowds were allowed to view it twice per day.[158] The funeral then took place on 5 February with the now familiar procession by the court elite across the frozen river to the Sts Peters and Paul Cathedral, with the route lined by the military. The coffin was placed on a catafalque in the middle of the cathedral and was interred only on 27 February.[159]

Royal funerals provide another example of the Russian court engaging with contemporary European practice and incorporating a number of elements into their ceremonial tradition during the first half of the eighteenth century. The desire to alter the established funerary tradition was not unique to Russia. For example, the funeral of Frederick I of Prussia in 1713 was a deliberately spectacular occasion, with a scale and expense quite out of keeping with his predecessors and indeed his successors.[160] The Russian reorientation proved much more durable and the creation of a funeral spectacle gave royal funerals from Peter I onward a much more public profile than their Muscovite predecessors. The use of the *castrum doloris*, with its emphasis on the earthly achievements of the ruler, enabled a large number of people to actively participate in the mourning process alongside the traditional religious commemoration of their blessed memory. Symbolically, the use of St Petersburg as the new official resting place of the ruler and of leading members of the imperial family during this period meant that, even in death, they remained resident in the city.

Reporting court events

The importance of courtly spectacle for each of these occasions raises the question of its audience. Although the point of major court celebrations was to make an immediate impact on the audience present at the event itself, there was also a recognition that a wider audience could be reached through the medium of print.[161] European courts commissioned special publications for major events, such as coronations. These works embodied a number of themes: celebratory, with their glorification of the subject of events; explanatory, in providing a description of the symbolic imagery used in the celebrations; and commemorative, in presenting the event for posterity.[162] But these works were not intended only for domestic audiences. Instead, they presented their celebrations as a display to other courts across Europe in a bid for recognition and prestige.[163] For courts with ambition, as with Prussia in 1701, these albums were not intended to be merely a record of events, but instead make a statement about their status.[164] This trend holds true for Russia in the same period, when the Academy of Sciences prepared commemorative albums for Anna Ivanovna and Elizabeth's coronations. These albums resembled their counterparts elsewhere, with a description of the celebrations accompanied by engravings of the procession, illuminations and other festivities.[165] In the case of Elizabeth's album, the initial print run was 1200 copies, 600 in Russian, 300 in French and 300 in German. Copies were then sent to the administrative Colleges and to other European courts.[166] In exporting an idealised form of the Russian court's most important ceremony, these albums were entirely in keeping with contemporary courtly practice.

The expense of these commemorative works meant that only the wealthiest could afford them and so they were not a suitable means for widespread dissemination of the court's celebrations. Instead, other publications presented a similar type of information for a broader audience. Short pamphlets describing illuminations and firework displays were first published during Peter's reign and, when the Academy of Sciences took charge of their compilation and publication, they appeared regularly throughout the first half of the century.[167] Even then, such pamphlets were not bestsellers – they typically had a print run of only 300 copies and were sold through the Academy's bookshop on Vasil'evskii Island.[168] In addition to these occasional publications, there were other, more regular outlets for this type of information. Newspapers in this period often carried descriptions of court celebrations, with the reports on the court at Versailles in the *Mercure galant* from 1672 onward being a particularly notable example.[169] Although levels of detail varied and commentary was not always possible, the royal court's position at the centre of government and public life in most states meant that it remained an important subject for the European press in the eighteenth century.

St Petersburg's newspaper, the *Sanktpeterburgskie Vedomosti* (hereafter *SPV*), began life in late 1702 as simply *Vedomosti*, a handwritten (from 1710, printed) newsletter for military and diplomatic reports during the Great Northern War. Its coverage of foreign news had an earlier precedent in the form of the *Vesti-Kuranty*, the translated compilations of foreign news from European newspapers that were produced for officials during the seventeenth century.[170] Unlike its seventeenth-century predecessor, *Vedomosti* was intended for distribution. After the war ended in 1721, *Vedomosti* remained an important part of the state's means of disseminating official information. From 1728, it became the *Sanktpeterburgskie Vedomosti* and its coverage began to shift, with major announcements and foreign news joined by commercial information for the city's merchant population. The newspaper was produced by the Academy of Sciences and Gerhard Friedrich Müller, then a student at the Academy, served as its first editor.[171] The *SPV* was distributed twice a week on the regular post days, Tuesday and Friday. The paper was typically eight pages in length and print runs gradually increased from 300 copies in the late 1720s to 600 by the 1760s.[172] Distribution was through subscription, with the annual price of between two roubles fifty kopecks and three roubles fifty kopecks by the 1750s, depending on paper quality.[173]

The lists for 1749–51 and 1753 provide a broad outline of the pattern of subscriptions, although such figures do not reflect the actual readership since such publications were often shared between family members or the subscriber's close social circle.[174] The lists note the subscriber's position within state service, according to the Table of Ranks. If this information was not available or relevant, their place of work, their regiment or some other information was recorded in its place. In this period, there was a roughly equal divide between noble and non-noble subscribers. Within these two broad groups, the largest sections were in the military and 'political' ranks within the nobility, and the 'non-noble intelligentsia' (teachers, musicians, doctors, translators, low-level administrative and clerical staff, engravers and artists) and merchants in the non-noble groups. There was a steady increase in the number of merchant subscribers so that, by 1753, they outnumbered noble subscribers.[175] The increase in the number of notices about goods and services in the newspaper from the 1740s onwards explains this trend.

Seen as an official publication, albeit filtered through the prism of the Academy's editors, the *SPV* provided its readers with a source of information about the court's activities during this period. The descriptions of its ceremonies and celebrations in the *Vedomosti* generally focused on details of what had occurred and who was present, although the picture presented is the ideal, rather than the reality of the event. The descriptions noted details about the individuals and, more usually, the broader groups of people who attended these events (such as foreign ministers and various distinguished groups within Russian society like the *Generalitet* and other senior ranks in the military) paying particular attention to their rank. Other details are more curious to the modern reader – the number of candles on the chandeliers, the types of refreshments served and the rich clothing of the guests. All of these details reflected the social status of the occasions and suggest that such accounts were written with conspicuous consumption in mind. Although the situation was beginning to change elsewhere in Europe, the Russian court played a leading role in shaping elite tastes in clothing, accessories and even household furnishings during the eighteenth century.[176] By publicising such details – in effect, their 'highlights' – the *Vedomosti* played an important role in reflecting the wealth and splendour of these court events.

The regularity of its publication meant that the *SPV* provides a useful alternative source of information about the calendar of state celebrations. Such accounts were usually derived from the official court record, kept by the Chamber Stewards (*kamer-fur'ery*), but there were occasions when this information was not available or attention was focused on something else. Elizabeth's coronation on 25 April 1742 provides a good example of one such occasion. A proclamation announcing plans for her coronation appeared in the *SPV* at the start of the year to inform all subjects 'of every rank and dignity' to take part in public prayers for the health of their new ruler, to give thanks for her accession to the throne, and for a successful and peaceful reign.[177] The court left St Petersburg for Moscow on 22 February with the usual ceremony, involving cannon salutes from both of the city's fortresses.[178] With the departure of the court, the focus of the major official sources for this particular year naturally shifted to Moscow.[179] This leaves the *SPV* as one of the only sources of information about the coronation celebrations that took place in St Petersburg while the court was away. The reporting of the celebrations in St Petersburg was carried in a special supplement (*pribavlenie*) to the *Vedomosti*, with a brief note in the text of the main issue of the paper that directed the reader to the separate description of these events.[180]

The celebrations in St Petersburg began at 7 a.m. on 25 April, when a total of 10,000 troops were drawn up in parade in front of the Winter Palace, under the command of General-in-Chief Count Ulrich von Löwendahl. This parade included the Guards regiments, the Horse Guards and the field regiments garrisoned in the city. The troops garrisoned on Vasil'evskii Island conducted a separate parade under the command of Major-General Ivan S. Karaulov, since the ice on the river was not considered safe to cross. At 9 a.m. there was a service in churches throughout the city. The remaining members of the elite in St Petersburg, which included the heads of the two armed services Admiral Count Nikolai F. Golovin and General Field-Marshal Count Peter Lacy, attended mass in the large court church. They were joined by the senior officers of the Guards regiments and the navy, members of the *Generalitet* and the diplomats from Britain and the Holy Roman Empire, Edward Finch and Nickolaus-Sebastian von Hohenholzer. After the gospel, a rocket signalled a cannon salute from both fortresses (a total of 262 guns), followed by three musket volleys and cannon fire from the troops on Vasil'evskii Island and then the Admiralty side. Then all of the troops threw their hats in the air and gave the traditional three shouts of *Vivat!*

At 1 p.m., 250 invited guests joined spiritual, military and civil dignitaries to dine at specially prepared tables in the Winter Palace, with the SPV description noting the expensive silver and porcelain tableware used for the occasion. Captain Adrian I. Lopukhin and Lieutenant-Captain Stepan G. Miachkov of the Preobrazhenskii Guards were in charge of proceedings. These men proposed the usual toasts to the Empress and her future reign with cannon salutes accompanying each 'health'. Meanwhile, outside the palace, another traditional public aspect of such state celebrations was displayed: wine and beer were distributed to the people. Some wine was also given to the junior officers and soldiers of the regiments in order to drink the Empress's health, with more shouts of *Vivat!* alongside the more generic *Ura!* At 5pm, there was a ball in the palace, which lasted until midnight. On a pre-arranged signal, the Fireworks Theatre beside Vasil'evskii Island (27), the Sts Peter and Paul Fortress, the Cadet Corps and many of the city's palaces lit prepared illuminations, augmented by burning braziers on top of many ordinary houses, so that the whole city was 'decorated' that evening. In addition, at 10pm, there was a firework display on Tsaritsyn Meadow dominated by a central illumination with Elizabeth's initial letter, symbolic devices such as the imperial crown and representations of the three Russian chivalric orders, and allegorical figures representing Wisdom and Bravery. Finally, the account mentions that there were other popular celebrations elsewhere in the city to mark the occasion.[181]

Further celebrations continued for the rest of April and into the following month, albeit recorded in much less detail than the main event. Both Lacy and Golovin hosted banquets and balls at their residences, followed by similar events hosted by other leading officials in the fortnight after the coronation. These banquets were attended by all members of the *Generalitet* and other distinguished persons, and comprised the usual drinking of toasts, accompanied by drums, trumpets and multiple cannon salutes, and then a ball or similar entertainment until midnight.[182] No indication is given as to why these members of the elite were not in Moscow, participating in the main ceremony and celebrations, although practical administrative concerns gave sufficient reason to ensure that the capital should not be deserted by all of the high-ranking officials. All of the prominent figures mentioned in these reports, particularly those in charge of the different parts of the celebrations, were members of the military and naval hierarchy. As Russia was still at war with Sweden, their presence in St Petersburg, along with large numbers of troops, reflects the ongoing need for security, rather than for court attendance.

The major public celebrations in St Petersburg mirrored many of the events in Moscow, such as the military salutes, the elaborate fireworks and the traditional provision of food and drink for the people. However, it was important that, even in the absence of the ruler, St Petersburg hosted major public celebrations for the coronation, since they enabled members of the elite not present in Moscow to participate in activities that were traditionally displays of loyalty to the new ruler. The reports in the *SPV*, alongside the descriptions of the ceremonies at the Kremlin, not only allowed the readership to 'experience' the spectacle, but also represented it in ideal terms. In this sense, the *Vedomosti* performed a similar role to the text that accompanied the engravings in the coronation albums of Anna Ivanovna and Elizabeth, which explained their symbolism and helped to condition appropriate responses to them.[183] However, the *SPV* remained an official account and there was no latitude in its reporting akin to the editorials of other European newspapers. The court was quick to respond to any inaccuracies, particularly in the reporting of ranks or titles.[184] As a result, a *Vedomosti* 'expedition' was established in 1744 to oversee the production of the newspaper.[185] Descriptions of the imperial family's activities proved of particular concern and, in 1751, Elizabeth ordered that such content had to be approved before publication.[186] Since these descriptions were intended to emphasise the majesty of the ruler and their court, her response was understandable.

While the *SPV* reached a relatively broad audience, it was not a very large one. Until the 1750s, when it was joined by the *Moskovskie Vedomosti* printed in Moscow, it was the only Russian-language newspaper. By comparison, London itself published a dozen different newspapers and the various territories of the Holy Roman Empire were publishing around 100 titles in the same period. Although some of these newspapers were short-lived, the successful examples had circulation figures that dwarfed those of the *SPV* – by 1730, the *Hamburg Correspondent* had 1600 subscribers.[187] The rapid expansion of print media that developed elsewhere in Europe during this period required a familiarity and engagement with the periodical form that was not yet firmly established in Russia.[188] The *SPV* was important for providing information, in the form of court ceremonies, official proclamations and foreign news, on a regular basis for its readership amongst the urban population. However, its reach was limited by its small print run, its metropolitan focus and a relatively low literacy rate in Russia.

The importance of this period lies in the conscious efforts of successive rulers and their advisers to overhaul the Russian court as an institution. Contemporary European practice had a clear influence on the creation of new posts and on the first attempts to formalise the duties and responsibilities of court officials in the form of regulations. This 'Europeanised' court took some time to establish its role – new posts and titles did not always result in new attitudes. But, by the 1750s, it was clear that the court in St Petersburg had more in common with its other European contemporaries than its Muscovite predecessor, both physically and ideologically. The court's evolution can also be seen in the calendar of official celebrations, with the resulting events often representing the complex blend of influences – tradition, religion and the ruler's authority – apparent at other courts. The hosting of these events in St Petersburg was crucial in establishing the Russian court's relationship with the city and it was the stage for many important dynastic occasions that had previously been the reserve of Moscow. These ceremonies also made use of St Petersburg's spaces and architectural features, particularly its arterial routes, as a focus for public attention. The intention behind these ceremonies was to create an elaborate performance for an audience at several levels. For the guests, their participation and privileged access was part of an inclusive, but regulated courtly setting. For the population of St Petersburg, the spectacle presented by these major celebrations, with large-scale processions and illuminations, was a statement about the court's presence at the very heart of the city. At an international level, other contemporary courts – drawing on their diplomats in Russia or informed by the lavish commemorative volumes that they were sent, by way of reciprocity – were made aware of Russia's desire to be considered part of the courtly mainstream.

4
Interaction: the City's Social Life

By the end of the seventeenth century, most royal courts across Europe had an established and regular calendar of daily activities and entertainments, as well as the annual round of major feast days and anniversaries. This daily or weekly schedule focused on the various elements of the ruler's routine: rising (*lever*) and retiring (*coucher*) for the day, religious devotion (mass or religious service), dining, conducting state business, receiving guests and various pleasurable diversions, for example hunting, gambling and attending entertainments, like the theatre or masked balls. Individual courts placed different value on the symbolic importance of these events and, correspondingly, the amount of time, money and effort spent on them. Once again, the French court at Versailles represents a particularly regimented, representational example; the Habsburg court at the Hofburg in the middle of Vienna was a less extensive establishment in a different context, but had a similar approach to this daily routine.[1] The same basic outline can be seen in other examples across the continent during the eighteenth century, such as the Bavarian court in Munich.[2] However, the perceived extravagance of such court entertainments led to a reaction against them, principally at Frederick William I's court in Berlin.[3] Yet, even at otherwise financially conservative courts, like the Hanoverian court in London, these occasions were deemed important as a means to gather the court's prime movers and their participation was expected as a result.[4]

Although the introduction of new European-style social forums had naturally begun in Moscow, particularly in the aftermath of Peter I's return from his Grand Embassy in the late 1690s, the process was continued and consolidated in the 'new' setting of St Petersburg. Peter had ensured the transfer of many of the main state institutions and the relocation of leading noble and merchant families to the city. His successors, with the exception of the young Peter II, spent the majority of their reigns in or around St Petersburg, which meant that the social elite was primarily resident in the city during this period. The smaller size and planning of the city led to important differences between the space of St Petersburg and the traditional social settings for the

Russian elite, in other words, in Moscow and on their estates. The residences of the royal family and the elite were now generally closer to one another and were located beside the city's main arterial routes – the river and, later, Nevskii Prospekt. The new social forums introduced in St Petersburg, such as the *assamblei*, took advantage of these differences and established a new pattern of elite sociable interaction that increasingly resembled the practices of their contemporaries elsewhere in Europe.

There were naturally common elements between these social events and the public state celebrations, discussed in the previous chapter. The theatrical and musical performances for those occasions also became a firm fixture of the court's regular social calendar. The emphasis in this chapter is on the more select social spaces created initially by the court elite, but that were gradually extended to include members of other groups in Russian society. The theatre, musical entertainments and masquerades took place both in the royal palaces in St Petersburg and in the principal residences of the city's leading families. A related space, the Summer Gardens, was used for both court entertainments and regular sociable interaction during this period. As such, these events and entertainments highlight the influence of foreign trends and tastes on the social life of the Russian court and members of the elite. These social activities were established primarily through the court's patronage and, as a result, participation was initially restricted to its privileged personnel.

However, as elsewhere in Europe, this period saw a move towards granting access to a broader section of the upper strata of urban society, not only members of the nobility but other respectable social groups, like the city's wealthier merchants. This access was conditional and occasional, with a number of firm restrictions relating to status, wealth or appropriate dress. The foreign companies hired by the court often sought additional income and introduced performances for a paying public, whose membership was wider still. Finally, in common with many early modern cities, St Petersburg was the site of popular entertainments that were open to both the privileged and the ordinary inhabitants of the city. These events were often a mixture of traditional (often seasonal) Russian forms of entertainment and those provided by foreign entrepreneurs. Their popularity not only underlines a degree of continuity in St Petersburg's social life, but parallels the persistence of these activities in other cities across Europe.

Theatre audiences

The patronage of the theatre by royal courts across early modern Europe was a logical extension of their interests in ritual and representation. Plays, operas and other performances were used to both entertain and inform, using symbols, metaphors and situations to address their audience in a manner similar to that of the colourful spectacles created for the court's major festivities.[5] By the end of the seventeenth century, despite ongoing moral concerns about its content and conduct, attending the theatre was an established part of the regular round of entertainments at courts across Europe. However, at the same time, there were different approaches to the question of public access to the theatres patronised by the court. Royal patronage by successive dynasties had established a vibrant theatre tradition in England, and the court there regularly attended performances at the likes of Drury Lane or Covent Garden by the eighteenth century. These commercial theatres were preferred to any revival of an expensive court theatre, the last example of which was destroyed by the fire at Whitehall in 1698.[6] The three royal theatres in Paris, chief amongst them the *Comédie Française*, were patronised and subsidised by the court, but financial necessity meant that they also opened their doors to the paying public.[7]

By contrast, many German-speaking courts enjoyed such performances at private theatres, often built as an extension of their residences. These theatres were a symbol of the court's prestige and cultural sophistication, even at relatively minor courts.[8] Spectacular examples were constructed for Augustus II in Dresden (1719) and for Frederick II in Berlin (1743), both of which were for the sole use of the ruler and their invited guests.[9] However, from the 1740s, a number of these private court theatres began to admit paying patrons to offset the financial costs of maintaining such institutions.[10] This access was by no means unrestricted; ticket prices meant that attendance was restricted to those with disposable income. The paying public might also be restricted to certain parts of the theatre, as in the Mannheim Court Theatre in the 1750s, where they were only allowed to sit in the upper level.[11] This period saw similar developments at the Russian court. Although theatre, opera and ballet were still relatively new to Russia in this period, they were quickly adopted as part of the court's social calendar. Access was then granted to groups outside the court elite, thereby promoting a wider interest in these forms of entertainment.

The origins of theatre in Russia are generally considered to be in the religious plays performed on certain feast days during the Orthodox calendar. Their secular equivalents, which focused on rather more earthy concerns, were denounced as immoral by the Orthodox Church.[12] Consequently, European-style theatrical performances as a form of entertainment only appeared in Russia during the reign of Tsar Aleksei Mikhailovich, who expressed an interest in hiring performers from England through one of his agents, John Hebdon, in 1660.[13] Performances in private houses in Moscow began in the same period, such as the comedy performed at the residence of Charles Howard, the English ambassador, in 1664. Patrons included not only foreigners, but also a number of Russians, most notably Artamon S. Matveev (1625–82), a close associate of the Tsar. In 1672, Aleksei Mikhailovich appointed Matveev to organise theatrical performances at court. The first of these plays, *The Play of Ahasuerus* (*Artakserksovo deistvo*), was performed at Preobrazhenskoe in October of the same year using hired foreign actors and musicians. However, since the audience consisted only of the Tsar, his family and other members of the court elite, these performances were essentially private. This innovation was relatively short-lived; after Aleksei Mikhailovich's death in 1676, it was closed by his successor Fedor, probably acting on the advice of conservative advisers. The theatre's materials were disposed of and such performances ceased until the reign of Peter I.[14]

Peter attended a number of theatrical performances during the Grand Embassy. Indeed, he was rumoured to have gained a more intimate perspective on the charms of the theatre while in London through the actress Letitia Cross.[15] Drawing on this experience, in 1702, he opened Russia's first public theatre – i.e., open to a paying audience – on Red Square. A German comedy troupe was hired at considerable expense to perform there, initially under Johann-Christian Kunst, until his death in 1703, and subsequently under Otto Fürst. However, the theatre was not a success. The unfamiliar German repertoire and the language barrier for the Russian members of the audience were problematic, while the location of the theatre did not help either, as patrons had to pay a toll to enter the Kremlin, as well as the price of a seat (between three and ten kopecks). Consequently audiences were small, often as little as 50 people, and the theatre finally closed in 1713.[16] However, there was continued interest within the royal family from Peter's sister, Tsarevna Natal'ia Alekseevna, who ran a personal theatre at Preobrazhenskoe between 1707 and 1710, which moved with her to St Petersburg in 1711.[17] Initially located in her palace on Krestovskii Island, on the northern outskirts of the city, the theatre was later given its own building close to her new residence on Liteinyi Prospekt (15) near the Neva River.[18] This theatre was open to the public – Weber noted that 'every body was admitted' to ensure a sizeable audience. However, unlike its Moscow predecessor, patrons did not have to pay for their seats.[19]

The theatre did not last beyond Natal'ia's death in 1716, although the building continued to be used by visiting troupes, such as that of Johann Mann in mid-1723, prior to the construction of a new 'comedy house' on the Moika later that year.[20] Bergholz attended a performance by Mann's troupe in August 1723 and was singularly unimpressed, noting that Peter's daughters left early and the rest of the small audience were clearly not used to attending the theatre.[21] In part, this may have reflected the attitude of the ruler since, while Peter attended such performances, he appears to have been frustrated by the passive nature of theatre, where one was required to sit and listen, rather than join in.[22] He issued instructions to visiting troupes about the length and nature of their plays; they had to be no longer than three acts, the plot should not involve complicated love affairs, and it should be neither too serious nor too happy.[23] Nevertheless, Peter's reign had established theatre as an acceptable form of social entertainment amongst the elite and the construction of the 'comedy house' in St Petersburg gave it a permanent presence, albeit one that remained underused until the 1730s. But despite the public nature of these theatres, they failed to attract a regular paying audience in either Moscow or St Petersburg. Bergholz tellingly commented that Mann's troupe would have starved, had it not been for the income from their performances for court audiences.[24]

As with many aspects of court social life in this period, the ruler's personal tastes governed those of the court as a whole and the theatre was no exception. Anna Ivanovna had enjoyed the performances of foreign comedy troupes whilst in Mitau and, when she became Empress, she ordered that suitable troupes should be invited to come to St Petersburg to perform at her court. The first to arrive was a company of German and Italian comic actors, sent from Dresden by Augustus II in January 1731.[25] While not all members of this group stayed in Russia in the long term, there was a steady stream of both individuals and companies that followed over the coming years. The next major innovation came with the arrival of Francesco Araja's opera troupe in late 1735, following considerable success in a number of major Italian cities. In January 1736, Araja organised the first Italian opera performance in Russia, *La forza dell'amore e dell'odio*, a work of his own composition. The troupe included Antonio Rinaldi, a renowned Italian ballet-master who was instrumental in developing that art at the Russian court.[26] Ballets were often performed alongside one-act comic *intermezzi* in the build-up to or between the acts of the main theatrical or operatic performance. Anna's enthusiasm for these forms of entertainment was reflected in the considerable amount of money spent on them during her reign. Figures compiled in 1741 revealed that just over 191,000 rubles had been spent on supporting theatre, opera and music over the previous decade.[27]

In the same period, Tsarevna Elizabeth was also a keen supporter of the theatre and music, holding private performances in her palace at Smol'nyi.[28] When she came to power, her coronation celebrations featured the opera *La Clemenza di Tito*, composed by Adolf Hasse with a libretto by Pietro Metastasio. Such performances were a consistent feature of her court calendar.[29] Elizabeth was evidently keen to ensure that these performances enjoyed a sizeable audience and issued a number of decrees to this effect throughout her reign. In particular, non-attendance of the theatre by members of her court annoyed her. At a French comedy in September 1752, she noted that her court ladies were not in their usual place – the first row of the stalls – and sent a court servant to enquire if they had forgotten that there was a performance that evening.[30] Unsurprisingly in view of the Orthodox attitude to the theatre, members of the Holy Synod were given more latitude in this respect, since their absence from a performance only the week before had been noted, but no action was taken.[31] In addition to the personal pressure that the Empress could undoubtedly bring to bear on absentees, Elizabeth was said to have enforced a fine of 50 rubles on members of the court and other invited guests who failed to attend the theatre without an adequate excuse.[32] Some historians suggest the influence of her father in adopting this approach to 'shirkers'.[33]

Another response to the question of audience size was to widen access to these events beyond the court elite. A court journal entry in late June 1751 records the performance of a French comedy for the Empress in the opera house. However, the small numbers present in the stalls and in the circle prompted Elizabeth to order that 'distinguished' (*znatnye*) merchants and their wives should be allowed free entry to tragedies, comedies and inter-mezzos, providing that their clothing was not 'objectionable' (*gnusno*).[34] The Court Office then issued a decree by the Empress to this effect two days later, which confirmed the extension of this privileged access to Russian and foreign merchants. The decree further specified where they were to be allowed to sit: in the upper circle, in the stalls (if there was room) or in the rear boxes (if they were empty). The details of this order were to be sent to the Police Chancellery, who were responsible for notifying these people about these events.[35] Performances for these wider audiences were indicated by the use of terms like 'open' (*vol'noi*) in contemporary official documents.[36] The practice continued for the rest of this period. For example, the opera house in the Summer Gardens staged an 'open' comic opera in mid-January 1758, which was attended by the Empress.[37] Later the same year, in mid-May, the Empress attended another such performance, this time of an unnamed Russian comedy in the wooden Winter Palace's small theatre.[38]

These performances took place in spaces previously reserved for the privileged few, since the major venues were in or beside royal palaces. The 'new' Winter Palace, built for Anna Ivanovna by Rastrelli between 1732 and 1737, housed the main court theatre and a second small theatre was added to it in 1749 on Elizabeth's orders. Rastrelli also designed the opera house that was constructed for Elizabeth in the Summer Gardens, beside the 'old' Summer Palace, in 1750 (**29**). Even the temporary, wooden Winter Palace on Nevskii Prospekt, which housed the court during the renovation and extension of the Winter Palace in the late 1750s, had two theatres, with the larger one (referred to as the 'new opera house') occupying its own building.[39] Beyond the royal palaces, St Petersburg had other venues during this period. Although the existing 'comedy house' on the Moika was in a poor state by Anna's reign and was demolished in 1733, another one was built beside the Lutheran church on Nevskii Prospekt in 1743 using a former stable as a foundation (**24**). It hosted regular performances for the court throughout the 1740s, including the opera *Scipio* for the wedding of the Grand Duke and Duchess in 1745.[40] This building burned down in October 1749 and Rastrelli was commissioned to build a replacement venue on Tsaritsyn Meadow in 1750.[41]

The performances given by these foreign troupes in the court theatres provided the mainstay of their income. Enterprising individuals tried to supplement this income by providing additional performances to a paying audience, but the response from Russian punters remained decidedly mixed. The example of Giovanni-Battista Locatelli's company reveals the extent to which foreign impresarios continued to rely on the court's financial support, even after the theatre had become an established part of the city's social calendar.[42] The troupe was first mentioned in the court journal in early December 1757 although, given the Russian climate and travelling conditions, it had probably arrived slightly earlier in the year. The entry notes the troupe's rehearsal of an opera, which was to be part of the Empress's ongoing celebrations for the anniversary of her accession to the throne, on 25 November. The rehearsal took place in the opera house and was open to anyone wishing to attend, reflected in the lack of a sentry detachment. The entry noted the attendance of the imperial ambassador, several of the Empress's court ladies and other dignitaries.[43]

The performance of this opera, *Sanctuary of the Gods* (*Ubezhishche bogov*), took place the following evening at the opera house and the court journal entry provides an overview of the considerable security for such an occasion. The usual guard detail outside the theatre consisted of a senior officer with 60 troops, whilst another senior officer with a further 40 troops was stationed inside the theatre itself to take action in the event of a fire. In addition, there was an unspecified number of court footmen in charge of admission and seating. The first five ranks were seated in the boxes of the first circle and on benches in the stalls, which carried an inscription or small notice (*po nadpisiam*) to further differentiate rank. The officers of the Guards regiments and the 'Life' Company stood along the sides of the stalls and in the space in front of the orchestra, whilst their families (i.e., wives and older children) were in the boxes on the upper level, if there was not sufficient room in the gallery and the stalls. Merchants were to be admitted only if there was space to accommodate them. Intentional overcrowding in the theatre was specifically prohibited to avoid discomfort and the risk of spoiling the Empress's enjoyment of the performance.[44] An order sent to the Police Chancellery about the same event adds that members of the civil administration were allowed to sit or stand in the same areas as their equivalent military rank.[45]

It is hardly surprising that the merchants were the first to be excluded when space was lacking at such court events. However, they were able to attend other performances of the same material. For example, on 8 December, Grand Duke Peter attended another performance of *Sanctuary of the Gods* at the opera house by the same company, but this time the intended audience was composed of paying patrons (*za den'gi*).[46] The advertisement for this performance in the *Sanktpeterburgskie Vedomosti* also reflects this aspect: 'On 8 December, there will be a performance of a comic opera for the public in the Large Theatre near the Summer Palace by the newly-arrived director Locatelli, a dramatic play in the Italian language called "Sanctuary of the Gods", which is being sold in an unbound Russian translation in the Academic bookshop for 12 kopecks; and Locatelli will announce the way to purchase a ticket on a specially-printed sheet.'[47] This performance was repeated on 23 December.[48] Grand Duke Peter was in attendance, perhaps seeking a respite from his domestic life following the birth of 'his' daughter Anna on 9 December.[49] Again, an announcement was published in the *Sanktpeterburgskie Vedomosti* several days beforehand.[50] However, the popularity and indeed the desirability of these occasions for a paying audience is difficult to gauge without reliable information on the number of attendees.

The Empress attended an operatic performance by Locatelli's troupe at Ekateringof on 27 May 1758.[51] Ekateringof was very rarely mentioned as a venue for such performances and so this was probably a private viewing for the Empress in a temporary theatre. She attended two further opera performances in St Petersburg, on successive Mondays.[52] Finally, there was a performance by two *castrati* from Locatelli's company, singing excerpts from a comic opera for Elizabeth, her court ladies and gentlemen in Monplaisir at Petergof.[53] Locatelli subsequently moved to Moscow in 1759, where he opened his own theatre with a state subsidy. However, he suffered ongoing financial problems and, despite a contract with Moscow University to have a group of students translate contemporary European drama, Locatelli was forced to declare himself bankrupt in 1762.[54] This failure was not the result of a lack of interest in the theatre in this period, but rather a reflection of the need for ongoing court subsidy. This relationship was embodied in the establishment of the 'Russian Theatre for the Presentation of Tragedies and Comedies' in late August 1756, under the directorship of the playwright Aleksandr P. Sumarokov.[55] Although its budget was modest, at 500 rubles per year, this institution was very important in providing a stage (quite literally) for Russian actors and actresses. Its company included members of Fedor Volkov's successful theatre in Iaroslavl', who had been summoned to St Petersburg in 1752.[56] The Russian Theatre was to become one of St Petersburg's leading venues during the reign of Catherine II.

As a fairly recent innovation, the Russian audience required some guidance on the more unfamiliar elements of these new theatrical entertainments. Jakob von Stählin wrote extensively on the subject in the supplementary *Primechaniia* to the *Sanktpeterburgskie Vedomosti* during the 1730s, particularly his 18-part overview of opera in 1738.[57] In the same vein, the practice of printing opera libretti for audiences had been introduced along with the form itself in the mid 1730s. These libretti were published in the original language and in Russian translation, with a typical print run of only 100 copies, and sold at the Academy bookshop in St Petersburg from the late 1740s.[58] They usually contained an introductory comment of the work's themes and a summary of each act, in order to facilitate the audience's engagement with it, especially if it had an allegorical message that might be lost amidst the on-stage action or uncertainty about the words being sung. A similar approach was taken in the materials produced for other theatrical performances; Sumarokov's plays *Khorev* (1747) and *Sinav i Truvor* (1750) dealt with the theme of the ruler's duty to the people and to God. The moral tone of such plays, exposing the folly of vice and emphasising the need for civic responsibility and proper conduct, was reflected in eighteenth-century Russian literature of all kinds and addressed themes with which the predominantly noble audience could identify.[59]

Overall, during this period, the theatre became an important forum for both entertainment and interaction. Attendance of the court theatre was a mark of social distinction and it could serve as an introduction to society for the younger members of the nobility. Aleksandr R. Vorontsov briefly mentions his visits to the court theatre in the 1750s in his autobiographical notes; his father hired a box in the theatre, from which his family watched French comedies twice a week.[60] The theatre provided a suitable occasion to display one's wealth – through clothing or jewellery – or status – from one's position in the theatre, seated or standing. The foyer of a theatre, as much as a *kurtag* or the earlier 'assemblies', provided an opportunity and a space in which to interact.[61] However, it was a privilege that was subsequently extended to other prominent social groups in St Petersburg, principally military officers and wealthy merchants, together with their families. Initially, the access to the court theatres was by invitation but, by the 1750s, performances for paying patrons were becoming an established part of St Petersburg's social life. The court remained essential to the financial support of both domestic and foreign theatre troupes, but there was undoubtedly a paying audience amongst those who could afford it and who sought the cultural capital of attending such events.

Musical entertainments

Music was an ever-present feature of court life throughout the early modern period. Major court celebrations, whether sacral or secular, were augmented by a combination of aural components, from bell-ringing to specially composed choral and instrumental pieces.[62] As with other art forms deployed by the royal courts of this period, such music was intended to praise and glorify its subject matter. The overlapping nature of religious and courtly influences on such compositions meant that for both royal patrons and individual composers, music in praise of God could serve equally well for his earthly representative. As a result, many courts spent considerable sums on their musical establishment, which was typically organised around the institution of the Court or Royal Chapel.[63] Music also served as an accompaniment to the everyday life of the court, during services in the court church, during meals and as part of other entertainments, like balls and masquerades. With such an important role in court life, leading composers and musicians became prized assets and were rewarded accordingly, as with Louis XIV's director of music Jean-Baptiste Lully. Similarly, the flautist and composer Johann Quantz was employed by Augustus II of Poland–Saxony before moving to the court of Frederick II, his former student.[64] However, not all of their counterparts were as privileged and their freedom of movement was limited by the attitude of their royal patrons, who exercised strict control over their musical personnel.[65]

The choral tradition of the Orthodox Church was the dominant form of music at the ceremonies of the early modern Muscovite court. Although its origins lay in the Eastern Byzantine tradition, by this period it also had a relationship with its Latin counterpart, particularly in the development of polyphonic forms in the sixteenth century. However, Orthodox Church music retained its distinctiveness throughout this period, such as the absence of any instruments.[66] At the same time, the existing folk tradition was a common element in popular festivities. In particular, this type of entertainment was provided by groups of 'minstrels' (*skomorokhi*), whose origins lay in the medieval period. Although their performance incorporated elements of theatre and mime, often with bawdy intent, they were primarily musical entertainers, with popular folk songs at the heart of their act.[67] With regard to foreign music, visitors to the Muscovite court from the late sixteenth century onward noted that there was considerable interest shown in both instruments and performances.[68] As the foreign community in Moscow grew, musicians and instruments began to appear more regularly in Russia, particularly during the reign of Tsar Aleksei Mikhailovich.[69] However, the strict official attitude toward such music, as with many other foreign cultural forms, meant that, with a handful of exceptions, it remained uncommon by the end of the seventeenth century.

As with theatrical performances, including opera and ballet, musical performances were gradually introduced to a wider Russian audience through the use of foreign musicians to perform at court celebrations and other social events by both the Tsar and other members of the elite. The new components of the Petrine social calendar, notably the 'assemblies', usually featured music for dancing, and Peter's reign was an important period for establishing the regular performance of foreign music at the Russian court. Peter himself was not a music-lover, despite being an enthusiastic singer, but his wife Catherine maintained a sizeable orchestra of German musicians that performed regularly at court celebrations during the 1720s.[70] For contemporaries like Menshikov, owning a private orchestra and choir was as much a symbol of wealth and status as it was to entertain his guests.[71] However, Bergholz – a self-professed music-lover – noted a considerable enthusiasm for music amongst other members of the Petrine elite, including Princess Maria Iu. Cherkasskaia, who also had her own orchestra, and Pavel Iaguzhinskii, who regularly attended musical evenings organised by the city's foreign diplomats, particularly the Duke of Holstein.[72]

This pattern of patronage continued in the decades following Peter's death. The court and its leading figures invested strongly in musical personnel, both foreign and domestic, in order to provide a suitably impressive accompaniment to its social activities and entertainments. As with theatre in this period, a number of foreign singers and musicians took the opportunity to supplement their court salaries by organising performances for paying audiences beyond the environs of the court. By the end of the seventeenth century, these concerts were an established fixture in the musical life of London and, by the mid-eighteenth century, it was possible for entrepreneurs to make a lot of money by staging these events.[73] Public performances of music appeared in other European cities during the same period. In a number of German cities, they emerged out of the periodic gatherings of musicians in taverns and coffee-houses, known as a *collegium musicum*, and involved high profile names, such as Georg-Philipp Telemann and Johann-Sebastian Bach.[74] Prior to the eighteenth century, Russia lacked the required personnel and setting for this kind of venture to develop out of the existing musical context. Although the term 'concert' appeared during the reign of Peter I, it was initially used to refer to agreements (i.e., *soglasie*); it was applied to musical performances during the reign of Anna Ivanovna and then only to musical performances at court.[75]

Musical concerts for a paying public first appeared during the reign of Elizabeth. The first recorded instance of a public concert appeared in the notices section of the *Sanktpeterburgskie Vedomosti* in early July 1746. It announced that, in two days' time, there was to be a performance by an unnamed foreign bass singer with musical accompaniment at 7pm in the house of General Artemii G. Zagriazskii, on Bol'shaia Morskaia Ulitsa. Tickets were on sale at this house at one rouble per person.[76] For the potential entrepreneur who moved beyond the immediate surroundings of the court, and consequently the resources and support that it afforded him, there were a number of practical concerns. A concert required a venue, usually a large room in a private residence that was hired for the occasion. The organiser then had to approach the owner of an appropriately sized premises and propose holding a 'public' concert in his (or her) house, in other words, opening it to a paying public. The fact that many of these early concerts took place near, but not in the major theatres in St Petersburg indicates the practicalities of such ventures. In addition to the problems of permission, the organiser had to make enough money to cover the hiring of premises and musicians – a smaller venue reduced costs.[77]

If the potential host agreed, then the next step was to get permission to hold the event from the Police Chancellery. Failure to do so could result in arrest and a sizeable fine. For example, following a complaint from the Empress's Cabinet, the Police Chancellery reprimanded a German comic actor – referred to only as Pantalon – for trying to organise performances by the court's Italian violinist Giuseppe Passerini without permission in February 1748.[78] After the event had been approved by the police, a flyer or poster (*afisha* or *letuchka*) was printed and distributed in public areas, such as the city's main squares and markets, giving details of the intended performance and where it would take place. Significantly, these notices also contained details of which groups of people were allowed to attend and what they would be asked to pay for a ticket. Important exceptions to the ticketing arrangement were the 'distinguished' (*znatnye*) patrons, who could pay at their own discretion, rather than any fixed fee. The elevated social status of such individuals was certainly one factor, since organisers were keen to attract members of the elite to 'raise the tone'. This status also meant that such 'distinguished' people did not expect to have to pay in the first place – indeed, a request to pay would not only cause considerable offence, but also carried the possibility of a beating from the noble's servants. On the other hand, by making any contribution purely discretionary, the organisers could use the desire of members of the elite to appear generous and cultured to their advantage, whilst benefiting from the honour of their attendance.[79]

Two examples of musical performances that took place outside the setting of a theatre illustrate a number of these points. The first instance was a series of concerts, conducted according to the Italian, English and Dutch manner, which were to take place at 7 p.m. on Wednesdays, beginning in early October 1748, in the house of Prince Sergei V. Gagarin on Bol'shaia Morskaia Ulitsa. The notice mentions that these concerts had been organised at the request of several music 'enthusiasts'. Tickets were available for one rouble per person, and an invitation was extended to all 'distinguished' persons, merchants and townsmen. There was also a note that the singing would be in Italian, Russian, English and German. On the other hand, drunken servants and 'unsuitable' (*bezdel'nye*) women, probably referring to prostitutes, would not be allowed to enter.[80] The second example was a concert at 9 p.m. on 28 June 1750, performed in the house of Madame Kern, opposite the Admiralty meadow. The notice stated that this location had been used previously to stage performances by Passerini. Again, tickets cost one rouble per person and servants were not allowed to attend.[81] Both cases suggest the existence of a paying, not to say enthusiastic audience for such performances in St Petersburg, and explicitly state which undesirable elements of society were excluded from these social occasions.

Music was also important for other aspects of St Petersburg's social life beyond the confines of the court during this period. During the extensive investigation of the 'Dresdensha' prostitution scandal, discussed in Chapter 2, the Police Chancellery collected information about the types of entertainment available to paying patrons, some of which were being used to cover illicit activities. They were generally referred to as 'evening parties' (*vecherinki*) in official reports, although they covered a range of activities, including music, dancing and gambling. As with other entertainments, these events required permission from the Police Chancellery. This requirement was reinforced after a large fight amongst military officers outside one such gathering on Millionnaia Ulitsa in November 1744.[82] These events were typically organised by foreigners and, in a number of cases, by married couples. The host(s) hired a suitably sized room in the house of a noble or a merchant for the occasion. Musicians – usually from the city's regiments – were hired to provide accompaniment for the dancing. The host also provided refreshments, including tea and coffee, for the paying patrons and usually some other amenities, such as tables for playing cards.

Maria Vintsler and her husband held such events in hired rooms in the houses of Admiral Golovin on the Admiralty side in 1746 and Veselovskaia on Vasil'evskii Island in 1747. They paid for soldiers to ensure orderly conduct, costing one ruble fifty kopecks, and for regimental musicians to accompany the dancing, costing three rubles. Their clientele included army officers, merchants, ship captains and administrative officials, who each paid one ruble to attend – women did not pay an entry fee. Patrons were provided with drinks, both alcoholic and non-alcoholic, during the evening.[83] With the emphasis squarely on profit, some entrepreneurs sought to circumvent the usual procedure for obtaining permission for these events. Johann Forster, a tavern-keeper by trade, and his wife organised a dance evening in the house of Vice-Admiral Korsakov in July 1750. Their patrons were from a lower social background than those who attended Vintsler's events – military ensigns and non-commissioned officers, tradesmen and low-level administrative staff, like clerks – and they paid only fifty kopecks for entry. As with Vintsler's events, women were not charged anything. The musicians came from the navy and were again paid three rubles.[84] However, under interrogation, Forster admitted that he had bribed police officials, particularly secretary Matvei Fadeev, to help him get permission for the event. He was instructed to plead poverty and that the event was necessary to make money.[85] The St Petersburg authorities were mainly concerned with the maintenance of good order – musical entertainments only became an issue for them if they were linked to irregular or inappropriate activities.

By the end of this period, music had become an established part of St Petersburg's social life. The court had played the most significant role in this process through its patronage of foreign and domestic musicians throughout this period. According to one contemporary, the Russian court had joined its other European contemporaries, like Vienna, Dresden, Berlin and Mannheim, as a major patron of music.[86] St Petersburg became a destination for aspiring composers and musicians, who sought opportunities not only in the main court, but also in that of the Grand Duke and Duchess. Grand Duke Peter was a violinist of (admittedly limited) ability and held regular concerts in his apartments during Elizabeth's reign.[87] The steady stream of Italian and German performers that had flowed since the 1730s continued unabated during the 1760s, with established names such as Baldassare Galuppi coming to St Petersburg under Catherine II.[88] Interest in music also flourished amongst the court elite, as it had done earlier in the century. For example, Semen K. Naryshkin maintained an extensive horn orchestra, drawn from his hunting retinue, and hired Johann Maresch, an acclaimed Bohemian horn-player, to oversee its further development in the early 1750s.[89] These personal musical ventures would later develop further with the emergence of serf orchestras and choirs on the estates of leading families like the Sheremetevs from the 1770s onward.[90]

There was also interest in such musical performances beyond the court. As with theatre, although such events were initially restricted to members of the elite who could afford to pay for and host them in their homes, the potential of a paying public, similar to those in other European cities, encouraged entrepreneurs to organise their own performances. While the frequency and audience size of these events was not on the same scale as London or even the smaller German cities, like Leipzig, their introduction nevertheless widened access to this type of entertainment and the sociability associated with it. The increasing frequency of these performances in St Petersburg during the second half of the eighteenth century suggests that they proved sufficiently popular to merit continued efforts. However, as with the other aspects of St Petersburg's social life, such events were subject to official scrutiny if they were suspected of an impropriety, not least due to the implications of mixed company interaction. Although this period represented an important step toward establishing St Petersburg as a leading venue for musical talent, it was very much at the beginning of its journey.

Masquerades

As with several other elements of the court's social life during the first half of the eighteenth century, the masquerade was a foreign import. It developed out of the traditions of public pageantry during the Renaissance, with the use of costumes, music and scenery to create an allegorical scene. These celebrations gradually evolved into elaborate masques that presented a colourful, symbolic scene in praise of the ruler. These masques were a prominent part of court celebrations across Europe during the seventeenth century, with their emphasis on the absolute and divine nature of royal authority. The English court masques under Charles I, designed by Inigo Jones, were a prominent example and played a similar representational role to the *ballet de cour* at Versailles under Louis XIV, albeit with a less successful political outcome.[91] A further development came with the emergence of public masquerades in England in the early eighteenth century. The Swiss theatrical entrepreneur, Johann Jacob Heidegger, introduced weekly masquerades for a paying public in 1717, using his position as manager of the Haymarket Theatre in London to provide a suitable venue.[92] These events proved very successful and attracted royal support in the form of the early Hanoverian rulers, George I and II, despite vocal opposition from the Church, the legal profession and other concerned parties, like William Hogarth who criticised them in his print *The Bad Taste of the Town, or Masquerades and Operas* (1724).[93] Similar events were organised in other European cities, like the *bals publics* in Paris that emerged in the same period.[94]

There was no secular precedent for these 'masques' at the Russian court, although the use of costume and allegorical settings bore some resemblance to the Christmas and Easter play cycles that also influenced other early Russian theatrical entertainments. Unsurprisingly in view of its attitude to dancing and music, the Orthodox Church disapproved of these occasions; in Orthodox tradition, masks were associated with possession by a spirit.[95] Instead, costumed entertainments were introduced to Russia as part of the court's celebrations only during Peter I's reign. Spectacular examples of these public masquerades were used in the week-long celebrations for the signing of the Peace of Nystadt in September 1721 (which also incorporated the wedding of the third 'Prince-Pope' of the 'All-Drunken Synod' Petr I. Buturlin) and its anniversary in 1723.[96] However, with the exception of Peter himself, transgressive behaviour was not encouraged on these occasions, unlike in other European examples.[97] Rather, these celebrations were planned under Peter's supervision, with stipulations about costumes, attendance, the order of floats in processions, and other details. The wider purpose of these entertainments has been compared to a form of theatre, in which the participants (in other words, members of the Petrine elite) celebrated the ruler's authority.[98] This interpretation puts these early Russian examples at odds with the carnivalesque and hierarchy-challenging nature of similar festivities in other contexts.[99] Whilst Peter I's elaborate parodies of traditional forms of religious and cultural authority, for example the 'All-Drunken Assembly', often resembled the tone and content of such masquerades, participation was restricted to members of the Tsar's circle. The 'world turned upside down' was still very much under Peter's control.[100]

While the carnivalesque aspect of the masquerade may be difficult to apply to the Russian court in this period, masquerades or masked balls as a form of entertainment became an established part of the court social calendar. Masquerades were organised for Anna Ivanovna although, with the exception of two masquerades held near the end of the Persian embassy to St Petersburg in July 1739, they do not feature regularly in the accounts of her court entertainments.[101] However, near the end of Anna's reign, her court organised an elaborate masquerade to celebrate the mock wedding of her courtier Mikhail A. Golitsyn to a (much older) Kalmyk maid Avdot'ia I. Buzheninova in February 1740.[102] Various ethnicities from across the Empire were gathered in St Petersburg to form the wedding procession and the event culminated in a spectacular 'ice house', designed by Eropkin, where the 'happy couple' had to spend their wedding night, under armed guard.[103] Shortly after taking power, Elizabeth used the costumes from this event, and from those of the disgraced Count Heinrich Ostermann, to stage her own masquerades that served to parody the reign of Anna.[104]

This type of celebration remained very much the domain of the ruler and the elite but, during Elizabeth's reign, there was a conscious effort to widen access to court masquerades or masked balls through the creation of 'public' (*publichnyi* or *vol'noi*) versions. These terms were used to describe such events in both official court accounts and contemporary personal accounts. However, in several cases, the terms appear to be used interchangeably, so in order to examine the question of who these occasions were intended for, we must study the specified groups of invited guests. Catherine II noted this development in her *Mémoires*, stating that two masquerades (or masked balls) were held each week during the autumn and winter following her marriage in 1745, one at court and the other hosted in the residences of St Petersburg's leading families. She added that, although the participants appeared to be enjoying themselves, these events were in fact quite boring affairs because of the rather formal atmosphere and the small number of guests. This modest level of participation created a problem of space since the court masquerades, when held in the royal palaces, seemed empty, whereas the 'principal houses' chosen to host them were not quite large enough.[105]

While her memory may have accentuated the negatives, Catherine's description of these masquerades at least suggests that they were a regular feature of court life, even if she provides very little detail on their conduct or content. In the period discussed by Catherine, the court journal entry for 15 September 1745 included a note to the Chamber Steward Sergei Nesterov, which set out the weekly schedule for entertainments at court over the coming months. It began with a *kurtag* on Sunday evenings, followed by an Italian *intermezzo* (presumably in the court opera house) on Mondays. Court masquerades would be held on Tuesdays and French comedies were to be performed on Thursdays.[106] There is no mention of any other weekly masquerade. The same information was repeated in an order sent from the Court Office to the Police Chancellery on the following day.[107] Subsequent entries list the Summer Palace as the focus for the court's social life – the seasonal move to the Winter Palace took place on 30 September.[108]

Unusually, the entry named a number of women who were invited to these court masquerades. This list, along with a contemporary register of the first five ranks and their families residing in St Petersburg, reveals some details about these guests.[109] The list included: Ekaterina Mikhailovna (aged 19), the daughter of the Chief Stewardess Princess Tat'iana B. Golitsyna; Princess Aleksandra I. Kurakina (aged 35) and her daughters, Anna (aged 14) and Tat'iana (aged 13); Mar'ia A. Naryshkina (aged 15), daughter of the Empress's cousin Aleksandr L'vovich (who had died in January of the same year); Mar'ia A. Rumiantseva's eldest daughter, Praskov'ia Aleksandrovna (aged 15); and Princess Natal'ia G. Belosel'skaia (aged 35).[110] The reason for the specific mention of these women is not known. In overall numbers, the court remained a largely male environment. Consequently, when arranging social events where dancing was a prominent feature, the desire to ensure a reasonable of women in attendance is understandable. Likewise, the court was an important social forum at which young women gained valuable experience of social interaction and decorum when they were considered to have reached a suitable age. Such experience was just as important for young men, and members of the Cadet Corps were encouraged to attend court masquerades, as discussed in the next chapter. These events therefore served as an important means for young noblemen and women to meet and interact with one another.

The second type of masquerade described by Catherine only appeared in the official court records at the beginning of the following year. In early January 1746, Elizabeth ordered that masquerades were to be held in the houses of prominent nobles in St Petersburg on Mondays, Wednesdays and Thursdays, beginning on 13 January and lasting until Shrovetide.[111] Attendance was extended to the *Generalitet* and to others living in St Petersburg, presumably meaning the nobility. The guests were to gather at the intended venue at 5pm, although no indication was given as to the exact starting time – in practice, proceedings would only get under way upon the Empress's arrival. The decree stated that the hosts for the evening had to be present and in appropriate masquerade dress, but there was no requirement for them to formally greet their guests. Similarly, it stipulated that the host had to provide tables for playing cards and music for dancing. Both sections are reminiscent of the list of requirements in Peter I's law on 'assemblies' of 1718, which stated that the owner of the house in which they were held did not have to be present for the occasion, but instead had simply to make the arrangements for his guests' refreshment and entertainment.[112]

On 12 January 1746, the Police Chancellery issued the decree, together with the register that contained the names of the dignitaries chosen by the Empress to host the masquerades and the dates on which they were to be held. This programme began with members of the first rank, General-Fieldmarshal Ivan Iu. Trubetskoi (13 January) and Chancellor Aleksei P. Bestuzhev-Riumin (16 January), followed by members of the second rank. It continued with prominent court officials, such as Chief Marshal of the Court Dmitrii A. Shepelev (6 February) and Chief Master of the Hunt Aleksei G. Razumovskii (4 February), and leading civil officials, such as Prince Nikita Iu. Trubetskoi, the Senate General-Procurator (27 January) and Prince Boris G. Iusupov, president of the Commerce College (8 February). The diminished role of the host was reinforced by the inclusion of the late Aleksandr L. Naryshkin (29 January).[113] A contemporary view of these masquerades can be found in a letter from Chancellor Bestuzhev-Riumin to Count Mikhail I. Vorontsov on 23 January 1746. He describes the court's masquerades as following the pattern for entertainments established by Peter I (i.e. the 'assemblies') in that they are held in the houses of the city's elite on the Empress's orders. He adds that, in addition to the Empress, members of the royal family and her courtiers, the invited guests included the *Generalitet* and the 'distinguished' nobility, with a total attendance of between three and four hundred people.[114] Since the host had to provide at least three rooms – one for dancing, another for dining and a third (probably smaller) for playing cards – these events required a lot of space and Catherine's previous comment on their rather cramped nature comes to mind.

Catherine also mentioned the court's penchant for masquerades slightly later in her *Mémoires*, when discussing its social calendar around 1750. She noted that two evenings a week were set aside for masquerades. One of these evenings was only for members of the court and specially invited guests of the Empress, with a total attendance of around 150 people. The other event was intended for all persons of rank from colonel (equivalent to rank VI in the Table of Ranks) upwards, as well as officers from the Guards regiments. She added that these occasions were sometimes opened to other members of the nobility and the most distinguished merchants. She estimates the attendance for this event at around 800 people.[115] Early in 1748, the court journals noted that a number of 'public' (using the terms *vol'noi* and *publichnyi*) masquerades would be held in the opera house, with the Empress's approval. These events were organised by Charles Sérigny, the head of the French theatre company that had been invited to St Petersburg from Paris in 1742.[116] Sérigny may have been drawing on a knowledge of the *bals publics* in Paris when setting up this type of event in Russia – certainly, there are similarities between the two.

The masquerade was open to anyone who paid two roubles for a ticket and was wearing a mask, although prominent noble families (described as *liudi boiarskie*[117]) did not have to worry about the latter requirement. Tickets could be bought either in advance from Sérigny or at the door on the evening itself. It further stated that Sérigny had to provide the necessary tickets and promotional materials in Russian and French at his own cost, and these were to be printed by the Academy of Sciences. The production of printed announcements was already used to advertise theatrical performances, and the journal entry makes clear that they were intended to publicise the event. Although the word *vol'noi* is used to describe these masquerades, suggesting a more informal atmosphere than similar court events, there were clearly several social restraints in place. For example, there were two entrances to the opera house: one was for the 'distinguished' guests and other members of the nobility, while the other was for everyone else. Similarly, during the masquerade, members of these two groups were not permitted to dance together.[118]

Several precautions were taken against any potential 'quarrels' and 'impoliteness'. Two senior court servants were assigned to collect tickets and a detachment of Guards, consisting of a sergeant, three corporals and 30 soldiers, was detailed to ensure orderly conduct, especially near the two entrances.[119] As refreshment for the patrons, Sérigny had to provide (again, at his own expense) tea, coffee, lemonade, chocolate, *orshad* (an almond-flavoured milk drink) and confectionery. The order specifically stated that vodka and wine were not to be served, indicating some concern about the effect of alcohol on the behaviour and conduct of the patrons. There was no formal meal, unlike at court masquerades, when a banquet typically followed the end of the dancing. However the Empress, Grand Duke and Grand Duchess were able to dine in their boxes, with their meals prepared in the court kitchens and then brought to the opera house.[120] The event was also listed, as a *vol'noi* masquerade, in the daily sentry journals because of the involvement of the Guards regiments. The Guards' preliminary instructions were issued by the Marshal of the Court Semen K. Naryshkin; on the evening, the troops were under the command of Captain Ivan A. Shubin of the Izmailovskii Guards regiment. The Empress left the palace to attend this masquerade at 8 p.m. and returned at 1 a.m.[121]

The event appears to have been successful, since the Empress, the Grand Duke and Duchess attended another such masquerade at the opera house on 16 February, and then, whilst the Empress spent a night at Tsarskoe Selo, the Grand Duke and Duchess attended two further masquerades on consecutive evenings, all organised by Sérigny. In each case, they were simply referred to as *vol'noi* masquerades.[122] When the Empress returned, she ordered another masquerade to be organised in the opera house, on an evening that the Grand Duke and Grand Duchess dined with Chancellor Bestuzhev-Riumin. The distinction between this event and the preceding Sérigny masquerades is made clear by the groups invited to participate: 'distinguished' persons, senior officers of the Guards regiments and the field regiments stationed in St Petersburg, other military and civil 'officers' (no mention of rank) and all distinguished nobles. The masks of these guests were inspected at the doors of the opera house by a Court Steward (*gof-fur'er*) and a Guards officer.[123] There was an evening meal as part of the event, which was served on the stage of the opera house, while dancing was confined to the main hall. The table was set for 100 people, allowing a rough estimate of the number of guests involved.[124]

The fact that such a meal was served at this masquerade and not at the others, which were open to a paying public, again highlights the limited interaction between the two groups of guests. The light refreshments at the 'public' masquerade made prolonged interaction between guests from the two broad social groups much less likely than at a proper meal. However, the latter masquerade was attended by the nobility, thus the meal was no longer a potential source of controversy. The stage was used because of the practical problems of accommodating a meal for so many guests in a space like the opera house. However, such a setting also highlights the theatrical elements of the masquerade as an entertainment, not merely for its participants, but also as a spectacle. This interpretation is reinforced by the Empress, Grand Duke and Grand Duchess sitting in their boxes during the first masquerade and watching the event as if it was a play or an opera. Although this innovation was short-lived – there were no further references to Sérigny holding similar events after 1748 – it signalled an intention to introduce this type of entertainment for paying patrons in St Petersburg.

A similar process was at work for the masquerades held at court during this period. On 1 January 1751, the sentry journal contained a report on a law issued on 12 December, in which the Empress had ordered a 'public' masquerade as part of her birthday celebrations on 18 December. The birthday masquerade had to be postponed until 2 January, hence the inclusion of the *ukaz* in the sentry journal. For this masquerade, access was granted to all court and 'distinguished' persons, foreign ministers, and all members of the nobility with their families (except very young children), providing they were wearing suitable masks and dressed appropriately. Entry was controlled by tickets, distributed through the Court Office – military officers wishing to attend had to apply through their regiments. Two senior officers and six junior officers were in charge of admission.[125] The masquerade began at 8.30 pm and lasted until 7.30 a.m. During the masquerade, pages circulated with a selection of drinks – including tea, coffee, lemonade and the enticing 'various' category – and confectionery for the guests. In between the dancing, there was a (cold) evening meal at 1 a.m. The guests were divided into two main groups for this meal. The first and second ranks of the *Generalitet*, the ladies and gentlemen of the court, and the foreign guests joined the Grand Duke and Duchess at two specially prepared tables set up in their dining room. The rest of the guests dined at three tables in the second and third ceremonial rooms from the main hall, where the dancing was held. A total of 665 people attended this event.[126]

An order from the Court Office in 1751 on the weekly court masquerades reveals three important areas for comparison with this 'public' masquerade: day, guests and dress code. The court masquerades would take place on the Tuesday of every week. Invitations were to be sent to members of the first two classes of the *Generalitet*, with their wives (but not their children), and the court ladies and gentlemen. A side-note mentioned that the wife of the Saxon ambassador was to be included as well. The order detailed what these guests should wear, i.e. masquerade dress. The Court Staff Quartermaster (*gofshtap-kvartirmeister*) and the Chamber Steward (*kamer-fur'er*) were responsible for sending out notifications (*povestki*) to the relevant people on the eve of the masquerade. Then the Chief Marshal of the Court and his deputy were given a register of guests, which could be checked at the masquerade itself.[127] Later in the same month, another order dealt with 'public' masquerades at court, which would be held weekly from Friday 18 January until Lent.[128] The precedent of the masquerade held on 2 January 1751 is directly referenced in the order. Access was granted to the whole nobility, both Russian and foreign, along with their families (although not very young children) for these events. Non-nobles were not allowed (literally, would not dare) to attend.

The court journal entry for the first masquerade on 18 January distinguished two main groups amongst the prospective guests: 'distinguished' persons, which included the foreign ministers at court, and the nobility with their families. Entry was controlled by tickets, which had to be ordered from the Court Office. This stipulation served two purposes: it ensured that the court knew the number of people attending for organisational purposes and it enabled the composition of a register, similar to that of the court masquerades. The latter is particularly significant, since the order stressed that those who ordered tickets and then did not use them would be fined, using the register to check names.[129] The court journal entry bears this point out as it notes that, although 867 tickets were issued by the Court Office, only 637 people attended the masquerade.[130] The dress requirements for this masquerade were 'appropriate' (*prilichnyi*) or 'decent' (*pristoinyi*) masks, and attending in pilgrim, harlequin or 'indecent' (*nepristoinyi*) rural costumes was specifically prohibited. Similarly, cheap or tawdry trinkets and glass jewellery were not allowed, and those bringing weapons (presumably swords) would be punished by a fine. Finally, the order ends with an instruction to Chamber Steward Nesterov to amend the list of those who were to be admitted, which was to be given to the Court Stewards on the doors, who were responsible for checking the guests and their masks. These amendments were based on an order given to Nesterov by the Empress on 31 December, likely relating to the masquerade held on 2 January.[131]

A further order about a 'public' masquerade on 8 February contains many of the same details as the one issued on 15 January, but differs in several important ways. In the list of permitted attendees, all 'distinguished' ranks were included alongside the Russian and foreign nobility, with their families. In this context, the term likely refers to the top ranks of the *Generalitet*, who were mentioned in the court masquerade order of 9 January, and were reflected in the description of the event in the court journal for 1751.[132] The punishment for non-nobles attempting to attend the masquerade was made more specific in the form of a fine. Finally, the importance of the numbers of people intending to attend was given a practical explanation with the inclusion of an evening meal after the masquerade, at 1 a.m. Whereas in the earlier order, the concern revolved primarily around the provision of drinks and confectionery, in this case, a meat course had to be provided.[133] The distinction to be made between the two groups at a public masquerade is more explicit in another *ukaz* from later in the same year, as part of the celebrations for the anniversary of Elizabeth's coronation. The masquerade was to take place in the gallery and ceremonial chambers of the Winter Palace, and there was to be a meal afterwards. However, the 'distinguished' guests were to dine in the hall, whereas the rest of the guests were to dine in the newly built entrance chambers, situated opposite the hall.[134] Therefore, a physical and descriptive distinction was drawn between these two groups, despite the fact that they were both drawn from the ranks of the nobility.

This form of 'public' masquerade proved much more long-lived at Elizabeth's court. Alongside their more select court equivalents, they were a regular feature of her social calendar, until her health took a turn for the worse in the late 1750s and she preferred more sedentary forms of entertainment. As with theatre and music, the enthusiasm for the masquerade also extended to members of the court elite, such as Ivan I. Shuvalov and Petr B. Sheremetev, who staged such events for the Empress and her family during this period.[135] They continued under Elizabeth's successors. Despite Catherine II's negative opinion of the 'public' masquerades, she was an enthusiastic participant in other masked entertainments at court and paid for the spectacular three-day 'Minerva Triumphant' masquerade on the streets of Moscow in 1763.[136] The examples from this period highlight that the Russian court adopted masquerades in their various forms as part of its courtly spectacle. St Petersburg hosted extensive, planned masquerades as part of the court's celebrations, akin to those of its European contemporaries. By the 1750s, they were a regular feature of the court's social life. The developments of this period are another example of an entertainment that was initially restricted to members of the court elite, but was subsequently extended to include the wider nobility and other distinguished members of St Petersburg's population. This access was still regulated, as embodied in the instructions issued by the Court Office about the guests' appearance. The emergence of masquerades for a paying audience, similar to the provision of public theatre and music performances, was significant, insofar as it mirrored similar commercial ventures elsewhere in Europe, but it proved less successful in Russia during this period.

The Summer Gardens[137]

During the late seventeenth and early eighteenth centuries, royal courts across Europe created and maintained extensive gardens as part of their palace estates. The creation of these gardens and their features, including purpose-built lodgings and fountain arrays, required considerable investment and they were therefore an important symbol of the ruler's wealth and status. These gardens were also of symbolic importance for the courts as they served to embody the inherent hierarchy of nature and, through its regulation, reflected the authority of the ruler over their earthly domain.[138] The elaborate gardens at Versailles were a glorious reflection of these ideals and their design inspired both imitators and competitors across Europe throughout this period.[139] For example, Augustus II of Poland-Saxony visited Versailles in 1687 and applied this influence to his development of Dresden's principal gardens during his reign. The gardens at the Zwinger complex and the Grossergarten were important sites for the court's major celebrations thereafter.[140] Similarly, Nicodemus Tessin, the Swedish architect, visited the designer of the gardens at Versailles, André le Nôtre, in the

1680s before redesigning the palace gardens in Stockholm and on the royal estate at Drottningholm.[141] This trend was also apparent amongst leading members of these courts. The gardens of Prince Eugene of Savoy's palace at Belvedere were designed by Dominique Girard, one of Le Nôtre's pupils who had also worked on the Bavarian court's gardens at Nympenburg.[142] Belvedere's gardens were at least as impressive as those of the Schönbrunn palace, the Habsburg summer residence, whose design was extended by Johann Bernhard Fischer von Erlach in the early 1720s.

These palace gardens were also an important social and festive space for the courts. Gardens provided a suitable forum for the sociable activities, such as strolling and polite conversation, that were increasingly an established part of European social interaction by the late seventeenth century. However, in providing a space for these activities, one must consider the location of these gardens. Several of the examples cited were on royal estates at some distance from the royal seat – Versailles (Paris) and Drottningholm (Stockholm) – and there were similar cases elsewhere – Hampton Court (London). The Summer Gardens were very close to the centre of St Petersburg. As such, they bear comparison in their use to the centrally located gardens of other European cities, whether owned by the ruler or leading noble families, like Dresden's Palais Garten and Grossergarten or the gardens of the Tuileries Palace and the Palais-Royale in Paris, or urban green spaces, such as Hyde Park or St James's Park in London.[143] Importantly, for the developments that took place in St Petersburg, access was granted to these gardens either on an occasional or regular basis during the eighteenth century and they formed important social spaces within the city as a result.[144]

The Summer Gardens in St Petersburg were an important feature of the city's landscape, as discussed in Chapter 1. During their early decades, however, they were largely reserved for use by the royal family and the members of their courts. Other individuals or groups were granted access to them, particularly if the gardens were used to host celebrations. For example, in late June 1721, Karl Friedrich, Duke of Holstein, attended a celebration in the Summer Gardens after a military presentation by the two Guards regiments to the Tsar on Tsaritsyn Meadow. Bergholz describes strolling along the garden's alleys and conducting polite conversation with women by the garden's fountains. He also notes that the other invited guests, including the royal family, members of the elite and foreign dignitaries, also participated in these activities. The sociable atmosphere was dampened by a sudden shower that forced participants to take shelter in one of the galleries in the garden.[145] The Summer Gardens also hosted the celebrations for the wedding of Anna Petrovna to Karl Friedrich in late May 1725. For the occasion, the wedding party and other invited guests – Russian and foreign dignitaries – were in the first Summer Garden, while access to the rest of the gardens was granted to other social groups.[146] No further details are given and the presence of a wider group at these celebrations is not mentioned by Bergholz, who was himself a guest.[147]

The Summer Gardens continued to play a role in court events during the reign of Anna Ivanovna. Although they are generally mentioned much less frequently in the official court journals than during either Peter or Elizabeth's reigns, the limited nature of these sources for Anna's reign should not be taken as an indication of declining use or interest. The Empress continued to use the Summer Palace as her main residence in St Petersburg from early May until mid-October each year and the gardens were thus used to host several important celebrations that occurred during these months. For example, in late June 1734, a banquet was held under the covered sections near the 'Grotto' in the first Summer Garden to celebrate the capture of Danzig during the War of Polish Succession, as noted by Mrs Jane Vigor, then wife to the English resident, Claudius Rondeau.[148] A similar banquet was held to celebrate the capture of the Ottoman fortress of Ochakov in late August 1737.[149] At the same time, the gardens continued to be used to host elements of the more regular social events of the court calendar, as with the banquet held in front of the 'Grotto' for the Empress and some distinguished guests, after a court masquerade in the Summer Palace in July 1739.[150]

This pattern of use continued during Elizabeth's reign, although the court generally spent more time at the royal estates of Petergof, Tsarskoe Selo and Oranienbaum during the summer months than previously and the gardens were not used quite as regularly for court celebrations. Perhaps to encourage their use, Elizabeth introduced a series of orders that permitted access to the Summer Gardens for a number of different groups within St Petersburg society. This legislation provides another example of the participation of a broader group of people in the spaces of the court's social life that had previously been accessible only by a small elite. As with the theatre and other entertainments in the royal palaces, this access was mediated by a number of strict criteria, which were used to exclude unsuitable or inappropriate groups from this privileged space.

In May 1750, the court journal noted that a written communication was sent to the Office for Ceremonial Affairs stating that the Imperial ambassador was to be allowed to stroll in the Empress's garden (the specific garden is not named), adding that this access had been granted to previous ambassadors.[151] However, an entry in the sentry journals in July of the same year throws an interesting light on the issue of access to the gardens. An order from the Empress's Cabinet to Major Gur'ev of the Life Guards stated that the Empress had been made aware that foreign ministers and members of the *Generalitet* were not being allowed to access the imperial gardens. As a result, the Empress ordered that any foreign minister, member of the *Generalitet* or other 'distinguished' person wishing to stroll in the Summer Gardens should be allowed to do so, but that 'commoners' (*podlye*) should be firmly excluded.[152] Both orders suggest that certain privileged groups had previously been allowed to make use of the Summer Gardens for strolling but that this practice had lapsed, either through a lack of use or by mistake. The relative dates of the two entries and the fact that the case of the Imperial ambassador was dealt with by written communication suggests that an error had occurred; one which, when discovered, was then corrected. In the light of the subsequent legislation on the gardens, it is also significant that the second order was issued when Elizabeth and her court were resident at Petergof and thus not making regular use of the Summer Gardens.

Access to the gardens was further extended in late May 1752, a month after the Empress had made her annual move from the Winter Palace to her 'new' Summer Palace.[153] The Court Office sent an order to the Police Chancellery that select groups from the Empress's 'loyal subjects', with their families, and foreign dignitaries were to be allowed access to the first and second gardens by the Neva River on Sundays and holidays in order to 'stroll' (*guliat'*). The various groups were listed in some detail, beginning with the junior officers, corporals and grenadiers of the Life Company, followed by the staff officers and senior officers of the Life Guards and army regiments, the Cadet Corps, the Artillery and Engineering Corps, and the Navy. The list continued with civil ranks, equivalent to military officers, and all of the nobility, without exception. The list then moved on to non-noble social groups, principally Russian and foreign merchants and, perhaps reflecting Elizabeth's social experiences during the reign of her father, foreign naval personnel. Foreign ship captains were included, as were other senior members of the crew, but common sailors were specifically excluded.

The decree required these people to be appropriately dressed, according to their rank or status, in order to be allowed into the gardens. Ladies were not allowed to enter if they wore clothing considered inappropriate for the setting, such as domestic headwear or dresses without the 'hoops' or crinolines (*v fizhmennykh iupkakh*). Merchants were not to have beards or 'untidy' hair, where the latter may refer to the lack of a wig or similar styling for one's natural hair. Under no circumstances were liveried servants or any kind of serfs to be allowed into the gardens, nor were they allowed to accompany any member of the permitted groups mentioned above, under the threat of severe punishment, rather than the fines mentioned in connection with transgressions at court events. The decree was to be published and the Police Chancellery would also notify those groups concerned.[154] This decree suggests a desire to increase the number of people who were granted access to the gardens in comparison with the earlier period, when access tended to be either on an occasional basis or in response to an individual query, as with the Imperial minister. From 1752, the gardens were open on a weekly basis for use by both the city's elite – including foreign ambassadors, the top ranks of the administration and senior military officers – and members of the wider nobility with their families, as well as select non-noble groups, like the merchantry.

Following this decree, this question of access to the imperial gardens does not feature in either the court journals or in the orders issued by the Court Office, although the sentry journal continued to list instructions to sentries when the Empress was resident in the 'new' Summer Palace and if there was an event in either the Summer Palace or the Gardens. However, in May 1755, again shortly after the Empress's move from the Winter Palace to her 'new' Summer Palace, the Empress issued an order to the Court Office to inform the Guards captain in charge of the sentries that on Thursday of every week, foreign ministers, members of the *Generalitet* (resident in St Petersburg) and other persons of 'every rank/status' were to be allowed to 'stroll' in the first and second gardens. As above, they were required to dress in a clean and tidy manner. The order then goes on to define what was considered an untidy, and therefore unsuitable, appearance – undressed hair, work boots (*sapogi*), grey (undyed, coarse cloth) kaftans for men, 'simple' (*prostoi*) and traditional Russian dresses for women.[155] Liveried servants were still forbidden from the gardens. A special mention was made of the Imperial ambassador, who was permitted to make use of these two gardens whenever he wished. This privilege was also extended to the members of his entourage, namely his gentlemen and their attendant pages, although it still did not include their liveried servants. All of these groups were required to enter the gardens by means of the canal bridge by the opera house, which had a permanent sentry post.[156]

The same information was also sent to the ladies and gentlemen of the court, the Police Chancellery and the Office of Ceremonial Affairs; the latter was made responsible for informing the various foreign diplomats, especially the Imperial ambassador in this case.[157] A more specific order was sent on the same day to the Guards Captain in charge of the court's sentries. This order was virtually identical to the Court Office notification, but included more detail in the clothing regulations. It included a note about merchants with beards, as in the 1752 order, and the prohibited 'simple' dresses were described as those without a 'hoop' or crinoline.[158] Merchants were mentioned in this order, although not in the original, which suggests that they were still considered to be part of the general group of people of 'every rank/status'. A similar order was issued from the Court Office the following month in which the same people, with the same dress stipulations, were granted access to the first, second and third Summer Gardens on both Thursdays and Sundays.[159] Again, the entry in the court journal, listing details of the permitted groups and their required appearance, was the basis of the notification sent to court ladies and gentlemen, the Police Chancellery and the Office of Ceremonial Affairs, as on 10 May.[160]

The inclusion of the third imperial gardens in this order coincided with the departure of the Empress and the court for Petergof on the following day, while the Grand Duke and Duchess had already left St Petersburg to stay at Oranienbaum. When Elizabeth returned to St Petersburg early on 3 August, a *prikaz* was sent to Guards Captain Ashcherin, then head of the sentries, by which access to the third imperial gardens was no longer allowed on Thursdays and Sundays (although the first and second gardens were still open on those days).[161] This exclusion of the third imperial gardens upon the court's return suggests that they were still largely the domain of the Empress and her family. The effect of Elizabeth's presence in St Petersburg was given a more explicit form in 1756. An order issued by the Court Office to the Police Chancellery in May 1756 stated that access to the first and second imperial gardens was granted on Thursdays of every week when the Empress was present in St Petersburg, and on Thursdays and Sundays of every week when she was not present. The order included the noble and non-noble groups previously mentioned in the decree from May 1752, while the prohibited groups were listed as ordinary sailors, personal serfs and commoners. The dress stipulations were the same as those from 1755.[162]

The decree further stated that the first two ranks of the *Generalitet* and foreign ambassadors, especially those of the Holy Roman Empire, England and Sweden, along with their entourage, were permitted to make use of the first and second gardens on the above days whenever they wished. Finally, it is noted that the ladies and gentlemen of the Empress's court would continue to have their usual privileged access, a detail that had not previously been noted in such orders.[163] The privileged nature of this smaller group was confirmed by a further order in June 1756, when the Empress ordered that foreign ministers and members of the *Generalitet* from the rank of brigadier upwards were allowed access to the third imperial garden on Thursdays and Sundays.[164] These *ukazy* created a divide between the social groups who had access to the first and second imperial gardens, depending on Elizabeth's presence in St Petersburg, and those who could access any of the three imperial gardens on both days. The inclusion of the third imperial gardens, previously open only to the Empress's family when they were in St Petersburg, was an important step towards creating this smaller and more select group, which consisted of the same group that attended other closed court events, such as the *kurtagi*.

Alongside the question of access, security was an obvious concern for such an open location. In May 1748, Captain Shubin of the Semenovskii Guards entered a register of the positions of and instructions to sentries in the daily sentry journals on the eve of the court's transfer to the Summer Palace. There were the standard sentry posts at both the 'new' Rastrelli Summer Palace, beside the Moika River, and the 'old' Petrine Summer Palace, to restrict access to the apartments of the royal family and service areas, such as the kitchens. Guards were posted at the entrances to the gardens, like the gates by the 'Private Quay' (*Partikuliarnyi verf'*) on the Fontanka River, and at certain places in the gardens, such as the 'grotto' where the Empress often dined with her guests.[165] The bridge across the canal separating the Summer Gardens from Tsaritsyn Meadow was permanently manned by a corporal and two soldiers from the Guards regiments, since it also controlled access to the opera house. The Guards regiments also provided a sentry patrol for the gardens themselves, consisting of a junior officer, two corporals and 20 soldiers.[166] The instructions issued to these sentries depended on the occasion and the register included in this entry sets out the standard procedure. Those who had official business at court were issued with a special ticket or seal to allow them to pass the sentries. In 1748, such tickets were issued to the priests, deacons and psalm-readers serving at the 'old' and 'new' Summer Palaces.[167]

Further orders were issued for court events at the Summer Palace or involving the gardens. In May 1755, the *Generalitet*, foreign ministers and the nobility with their families (excluding young children) were invited to attend a 'public' masquerade in the 'new' Summer Palace. However, whilst the members of the *Generalitet* were instructed to enter the Summer Palace in the usual manner, the other guests were instructed to come through the Summer Gardens. From Tsaritsyn Meadow, they were to enter the Summer Gardens using the bridge across the canal by the opera house, where they would have their tickets checked by one of the Empress's chamber servants (*kamer-lakei*) and a detachment of troops from the Guards regiments. They were then to proceed through the gardens as far as the Moika River and use the lower entrance, on the left-hand side of the Summer Palace.[168] For this particular event, the information contained in the notification sent to members of the court was also entered in the sentry journals. This entry meant that it was passed on to the officers in charge of the Guards detachment at the bridge by the opera house and to the sentries patrolling the gardens, in order to avoid any confusion about the invited guests.[169]

The granting of access to the Summer Gardens for a number of social groups was an important step in the development of gardens as social spaces within St Petersburg. The restrictions placed on this access are entirely in keeping with their contemporaries elsewhere in Europe. Visitors to Kensington Gardens in this period noted the importance of dress to gain entrance and it was also a requisite for access to Hyde Park's 'Rotten Row'.[170] Similarly, guards enforced a strict appearance policy to keep 'domestics' and the lower ranks from both the gardens of the Tuileries Palace and the Palais-Royale.[171] At the same time, the Summer Gardens did not become a space for paying patrons, akin to the pleasure gardens like Vauxhall, Marylebone or Ranelagh in contemporary London.[172] The idea for these pleasure gardens, known as 'vauxhalls' after the English model, was introduced in St Petersburg by foreign entrepreneurs only from the 1780s onwards.[173] Instead, the desire to access gardens amongst the city's population found expression in the gradual opening of other, previously private gardens. For example, in June 1759, the journal *Prazdnoe vremia v pol'zu upotreblennoe* carried an announcement that the gardens of the Cadet Corps were to be opened on certain days of the week to people of all ranks, with the established exception of liveried servants and poorly dressed individuals.[174] This sociable use of gardens was consolidated during Catherine II's reign, although St Petersburg's weather continued to prove a problem for promenading in the city, as noted by at least one observer.[175]

Popular entertainments

Although the focus thus far has been on the gradual introduction of some broader participation in the court's social spaces, there were other, more established forms of entertainment open to all groups within society. Traditional recreations took a number of forms across Europe, although they often had common elements: consumption of food and drink, musical and theatrical entertainments, competitions (whether displays of physical prowess or sporting events) and blood-sports (bear-baiting, cock-fighting or similar), with the latter two providing an opportunity for gambling.[176] These recreations were the bedrock of the popular festivities traditionally held for religious feasts, like Shrovetide or Christmas, on traditional feast days, like the first day of May (the start of spring), and for official celebrations, such as coronations. Rather than simply being the preserve of the common man, these entertainments attracted patrons from across the social spectrum and the wealthy elite enjoyed many traditional forms of entertainment throughout this period, albeit not necessarily in the same forums.[177] As so often with any form of public enjoyment, these festivities also came under repeated scrutiny from disapproving official bodies, particularly from a moralising standpoint, but such popular culture proved typically resilient, and flourished by the eighteenth century.[178]

These fairs or fêtes (*gulian'e*) were the most common site of public entertainments in Russia as well. Such fairs were held throughout the early modern period and naturally transitioned to St Petersburg along with the population of the city. A distinctive feature of festivities in St Petersburg is that they typically made use of the Neva River during the winter months when it was frozen solid. The ice provided an essential part of several traditional winter forms of entertainment, such as large ice-slides, and the section of the river alongside the Admiralty and the Winter Palace was a popular location for such events.[179]As well as their strong connection with peasant tradition, these events provided a source of additional revenue for the wide variety of foreign entertainers who began to come to Russia during the eighteenth century. Elements of rural, traditional, and generally popular entertainments made the transition to the urban setting, which is hardly surprising given the large migrant population for much of the city's early history.

Sideshow booths (*balagany*) provide a good example of how rural traditions could be assimilated into the urban festive space. These were covered wooden booths, with a small stage and rough benches for their patrons set out in front of it, in which short plays (usually 30 to 40 minutes in length) were performed. The repertoire usually included elements drawn from Russian folk tales (*skazki*) and broad, physical comedy. These performances featured popular and familiar characters, to ensure sufficient recognition for enjoyment amongst the paying Russian audience, despite the fact that many of the early booth owners were foreign. Another means of attracting Russian patrons was the use of Russian 'jesters' (*balagury*) to draw a crowd to them by telling anecdotes and jokes, while encouraging them into their particular booth.[180] The *balagany* represent a relationship between a traditional form of entertainment in Russia and the emerging theatrical entertainments in St Petersburg and Russia's other urban centres. This relationship was pushed forward by the influx of foreign entrepreneurs and theatrical troupes, who adapted to the Russian context to generate interest and profit.

A related form of entertainment – puppet theatre – was also considered accessible by a broad audience because of its familiar stories and popular characters from folk tales, such as Petrushka the buffoonish hero. These elements also provided a link to an older rural entertainment tradition, much in the same manner as the *balagany*.[181] This form of theatre had a royal enthusiast in the form of Grand Duke Peter, who owned and operated his own puppet theatre in the mid-1740s, although it was derided by his spouse as 'the most insipid thing in the world'.[182] Performances for a paying public were provided by the likes of Martin Nierenbach and Johann Friedrich Schütz in the same period.[183] In a similar vein, Johann Hilverding, manager of the German Theatre in St Petersburg, brought the conjurer Fritz Anton Sarger, whose act used very life-like marionettes, to St Petersburg from Riga in 1759.[184] Automata were a more sophisticated, mechanical form of puppetry and they also appeared in Russia during this period. For example, in December 1756, the French 'engineer' (*mekhanik*) Pierre du Moulin displayed a number of different curiosities in Count Petr Sheremetev's house on Millionnaia Ulitsa. His collection included a small, moving Dutch woman, who could sew 18 inches of ribbon every minute, and a mechanical canary, that could sing various songs 'as if it was alive'. The display was open every day between 2 and 9 p.m. and the room in which these automata were displayed could hold up to eight visitors at a time, who were charged the considerable sum of two roubles and fifty kopecks for the privilege.[185]

Two particularly popular forms of entertainment gave the authorities cause for concern. Both bear-baiting and performing bears were popular at Russian fairs throughout this period.[186] However the presence of such dangerous animals in urban areas was potentially hazardous for inhabitants, which led Elizabeth to personally ban them from St Petersburg and Moscow in 1752.[187] However, their popularity as a source of entertainment ensured the continuation of these practices into the following century. Catherine and Martha Wilmot, Anglo-Irish visitors to Russia in 1805, attended a bear fight in Moscow, albeit much to their chagrin.[188] Drinking was another common feature of these popular festivities across Europe and there were repeated attempts to regulate drinking establishments and drunkenness, as discussed in Chapter 2. However, drinking on feast days was part of the Carnival tradition in many states, and it was arguably celebrated as much as it was vilified.[189] The British traveller William Richardson visited St Petersburg in the 1760s and described a number of popular festivities that he witnessed in the city. In common with other early visitors to Russia, he believed that the peasants, when not working, spent most of their time drinking in 'cabecks' (i.e. taverns), especially on holidays.[190] Refreshments, liquid and otherwise, could be bought from a variety of kiosks, stalls and wandering vendors on these occasions. 'The Bell' was one such area; a large, colourful tent serving drinks that was located in the midst of proceedings, usually marked out by the symbol of a flag and fir tree.[191]

Ice hills (*ledianye gory*) were a popular form of entertainment in St Petersburg during the winter months and particularly during the Shrovetide celebrations. They are usually mentioned in most foreign accounts of the city's festive calendar. In the 1730s, Mrs Vigor describes these ice slides, although she was not a fan of this pursuit, as she was 'terrified out of my wits' by the speed and danger of the descent.[192] In the same period, the Danish traveller Peder von Haven gives a fuller description of them in his account of St Petersburg. The slides were essentially large wooden structures, with steps on one side and a long, steep slope on the other descending to the frozen river. Patrons were charged one kopeck per descent and Haven noted the ice hills attracted both men and women. As a result, three such hills were built in St Petersburg during his stay and functioned every day until the late evening during Shrovetide.[193] In the 1760s, Richardson describes the process of constructing these ice hills (or 'glissades', as he calls them). The wooden slope was packed with snow and then sprayed with water, to ensure an appropriately icy surface. Patrons would slide down this slope on special wooden seats, with foreigners usually accompanied by a Russian, who sat behind them to guide their descent. Two such structures could be built opposite one another, making it possible to slide down one slope and up the other, thereby avoiding having to climb the steps.[194]

Pavel Svin'in, writing an account of St Petersburg in the early nineteenth century, noted that such ice hills were traditionally set up on the Neva, especially the section between the Strelka and the Palace Embankment, on the Okhta River and on Krestovskii Island. The frames of the hills were often decorated with coloured lanterns that, in the dark St Petersburg winters, created an impressive spectacle on the ice of the frozen rivers at night.[195] They also provided a convenient focus for purveyors of other forms of entertainment, such as puppet shows, and various types of refreshment, no doubt relying on the long queues for the ice hills to provide a 'captive' clientele.[196] Interestingly, the ice hills are an example of a popular entertainment that was enjoyed by the elite as well, although this is not to suggest the two groups were necessarily concurrent on the slopes.[197]

Catherine II experienced this sledding during a visit to Count Nikolai Choglokov's island retreat at the mouth of the Neva in early 1752. A 'sleigh run' had been constructed on the nearby river for Choglokov and his guests. Catherine shared her sledge with Count Mikhail Vorontsov; another sledge contained Princess Dar'ia Gagarina and Count Ivan Chernyshev.[198] The risky nature of this pastime was highlighted when Catherine's sledge overturned and her arm was injured, a danger that had also been noted by foreign visitors.[199] The treacherous nature of the icy surface and the considerable height of the hills meant that they were prone to cause accidents, and the Police Chancellery were charged with ensuring that there were safety railings along the upper sections.[200] There was also a summer equivalent, usually referred to as 'rolling mountains' (*katal'nye gory*), whose name came from the wheeled carts used to provide momentum in the absence of ice. Two prominent examples were constructed for court use in this period. The Russian engineer Andrei K. Nartov built one such structure for Elizabeth at Tsarskoe Selo in the 1740s, although it was subsequently rebuilt with a pavilion by Bartolomeo Rastrelli in 1757. At Oranienbaum, a permanent set was incorporated into the *Pavil'on katal'noi gorki* for use by Grand Duke Peter and Grand Duchess Catherine in the 1750s, which was renovated by Antonio Rinaldi between 1762 and 1774.[201] The pavilion still survives, although now in a rather dilapidated condition.

Naturally, these popular entertainments tended to appeal more to the lower levels of society due to their rather unrefined and uncomplicated nature, and their relative inexpensiveness. For a large proportion of the population who, unlike the elite, had very few other social distractions, they played an important role in Russian festive life.[202] However, the lasting popularity of these popular forms of entertainment across the social spectrum demonstrates that many traditional elements of festive life endured in the new city, alongside the more fashionable innovations introduced through the court. Their repeated appearance in the descriptions of St Petersburg by foreigners, particularly those associated with the court, suggests that there was little stigma attached to elite enjoyment of traditional festivities, like the ice hills.

By the middle of the eighteenth century, the Russian elite socialised in different spaces and enjoyed different entertainments from their Muscovite predecessors. With the exceptions of the important, but isolated developments under Tsar Aleksei Mikhailovich, theatre, opera and ballet were largely unfamiliar to the majority of early-eighteenth-century Russian audiences. In other areas, there were elements in common with folk traditions, as with musical entertainments and aspects of the masquerade, but they occurred in new social spaces, not least St Petersburg itself, and required some degree of engagement with the form and content. The efforts made to widen the degree of access to each of these areas, which had previously been reserved for members of the elite, reflect the desire to create a suitable audience for these events. However, the privileged court setting in which they took place meant that access was strictly regulated – guests had to be suitably presented for such an occasion, and the issuing of tickets allowed for a degree of planning. There was also a clear sense of hierarchy reflected in the use of a different entrance for each group. However this extension of access, combined with the patronage of the court for foreign theatre troupes and other entertainers, contributed to the emergence of entertainment aimed at attracting paying patrons, with money as the principal means of access. These events incorporated traditional elements within Russian festive life and were enjoyed by both the elite and the ordinary populace of the city, since the 'new' context of St Petersburg did not fundamentally change their nature or accessibility.

5
Instruction: Fashioning an Audience

The introduction of social gatherings in the houses of prominent nobles, and the other developments which this entailed, such as new forms of inter-action (most notably dancing) and the conspicuous inclusion of women in social events for the first time in Russia, placed the Russian elite in unfamiliar territory. This social disorientation was compounded by the enforced changes in everyday clothing and personal grooming for the urban population, which altered the process of personal interaction, not only between men and women, but also between different social groups. As a result of these changes, the Russian elite had to adapt to the requirements of the new social situation and this chapter examines some of the key elements in this process. Education was central to many of Peter I's plans for the Russian nobility, particularly in relation to their envisaged role as a service elite. Although Peter's main educational interests were practical, stressing skills that were of interest to him personally and were considered 'useful' for the state, social skills were an important part of noble education in order to promote Russian interests in the diplomatic and commercial spheres. This approach further developed under his successors, with the establishment of specialist academies like the Cadet Corps which, although intended to pro-vide a mainly military education for young noblemen, provided instruction in dancing and other skills useful in a social setting.

An important element of noble education in this period was to learn about the behaviour and social roles associated with the new social spaces present in St Petersburg. The type of formal behaviour associated with the Muscovite elite, particularly in relation to ceremonial court occasions but also reflected in more commonplace social practices, such as receiving and entertaining guests, was not immediately applicable in the new social gatherings introduced in St Petersburg. The first Russian work on social conduct, *The Honourable Mirror of Youth*, was published in 1717 to deal with this *naïveté* amongst the Russian elite. Another aspect of noble education, dancing, was a prominent feature of court entertainments. Its significance lay not only in its encouragement of interaction between the sexes, thereby helping to overcome social reticence at such gatherings, but it also helped to inform and control the movements of the body. When considered alongside the contemporary reforms of clothing and personal appearance, dancing provided defined roles for its participants. At the same time, this set of skills allowed for graceful movement in the newly introduced European fashions for members of the nobility and other urban social groups. The new clothing not only altered physical appearance, but also affected concepts of beauty and propriety. All of these reforms required St Petersburg's inhabitants, as they did Russian society as a whole, to behave and dress in an unfamiliar manner and the results enjoyed varying degrees of success.

Education

Education has often been used to contrast Muscovite Russia and its European neighbours during the early modern period. The Church maintained the dominant position that it had held in education and scholarship during the medieval period across Europe, but there were important differences between the Western and Eastern Christian traditions. The rise of Latin Humanism during the Renaissance and the intense ideological struggle of the Reformation both had a major influence on the extent and nature of education across Western Christendom. Orthodox Christianity derived many of its traditions from its Byzantine heritage and the Reformation debate was largely irrelevant to the Orthodox, who viewed their Western counterparts as heretical in the first place. Similarly, the Orthodox worldview did not encourage the tradition of intellectual enquiry that prompted the philosophical and scientific work across Europe in the sixteenth and seventeenth centuries. In contrast to the medieval foundations of England, France, Italy and Germany, Russia did not establish its first full university until the mid-1750s.[1] Instead, the leading educational centres in Muscovite Russia were the Kiev Academy, which came under Russian authority with the annexation of Left-Bank Ukraine in the 1650s, and the Slavo-Greco-Latin Academy in Moscow, founded in 1687.[2] While both institutions were aware of and engaged with the ideas and methods of Latin Christianity, their primary purpose was to train members of the Orthodox clergy.

Education came in many forms across early modern Europe. The lower groups in society sent their children to local schools, where they were taught basic literacy and some practical skills by the parish priest or, in some cases, anyone willing to teach. One such example was the *Winkelschulen* that existed in many German towns, although the difficulty of regulating these meant that they often faced censure.[3] At the upper end of society, there were many more options, both informal and formal. For the nobility, there was an established tradition of household education using tutors, which was supported by writers on education like John Locke.[4] However, for both these children and for those of the middling social groups, there was a move toward the formal, Classical education, which was offered at institutions like English grammar schools, French *collèges* and German *Fürstenschulen* during the seventeenth century.[5] During the same period, there was also a move to establish specialist institutions that were intended primarily for the nobility, such as the *Ritterakademien* in several German states. These elite academies taught both academic subjects and practical skills, including riding, fencing and dancing, that were considered appropriate to prepare young noblemen for their future roles as state servants and military officers.[6] By the eighteenth century, there were prominent examples in Berlin (1717), Woolwich (1741) and Vienna (1752).

For much of the early modern period, Russia lacked a formal, institutional framework for conducting education beyond the household, with the exception of the schools to train the clergy. Instead, for most Russians, education was conducted largely on an individual basis under the supervision of a household or parish priest, using the traditional methods of the psalter, the breviary and the abecediary (*azbuka*), or an apprenticeship with an established craftsman to learn a trade.[7] Peter I had personally experienced some of the limitations of a traditional education during the 1670s, although his well-documented character traits suggest that he was not a willing or easy pupil to teach.[8] Yet Peter was convinced that some measure of educational reform was essential to more effective service from certain groups within Russian society, as well as altering some of their cultural attitudes. The intensive and often technical nature of Petrine education required more time, and this meant separating parents from children for longer periods, especially if it involved travel, whether within Russia or abroad.[9] In common with contemporaries elsewhere, Peter and his successors were keen to reform and regulate education, particularly that of the future leaders of its armies and administration.

Since the rest of Europe provided important examples for many of Peter's reforms, it is hardly surprising that he sought foreign tutelage in several key areas. The 61 noblemen who accompanied Peter during his 'Grand Embassy' were the beginning of his policy of sending Russian men to countries like England, Holland, Germany, Italy and Spain to study subjects that could not be taught within Russia.[10] The initial emphasis was on acquiring skills that Peter considered useful, so priority was given to areas relating to the military and navy. One example, Ivan I. Nepliuev, subsequently wrote about his experiences. He was one of 30 young men sent to Venice in 1716 to train as a midshipman (*gardemarin*). They were then ordered to serve with the Spanish navy in 1719. Their formal training included studying military theory, fencing and dancing, while they also travelled extensively through the major ports of the western Mediterranean. However, Nepliuev's account reveals the difficulties faced by these young men. They struggled with the local language, they did not see the point of their lessons and they were frequently short of money. To make matters worse, several members of the group died or went mad. The remainder returned to Russia in May 1720 and were inspected by Peter, before being deployed to serve in the navy.[11] Young noblemen were by no means the only social group involved in this process. For example, 40 clerks were sent to Königsberg in March 1716 to train in administrative practice and learn German, sons of Moscow merchants studied commercial practices in Holland in June 1716, and other students studied fine art and architecture in Italy during this period.[12]

This foreign education did not prove a popular measure. The prospect of sending one's heir to a foreign country while being asked to contribute financially to their upkeep cannot have appealed to many noble families. It was also daunting for the young men involved, since not only were they being asked to spend a long time apart from their families – Nepliuev had a wife and two children by the time he left Russia – but they were also being sent to non-Orthodox countries, of which they had no experience.[13] Nevertheless, it was inadvisable to attempt to avoid Peter's orders; Vasilii P. Sheremetev was punished for allowing his son to get married in 1709 after he had been ordered to study abroad, which delayed his departure.[14] However, there were some objections that it proved difficult to overcome. When describing Russian women during his visit to Moscow in 1716, Weber noted an abortive plan proposed around 1711 to send young women abroad 'in order to learn foreign customs and languages'. He believed that this plan failed because of the moral objections of their parents, who feared the malign influence of foreign interaction, but a more practical explanation was that the families of the young women were expected to provide most of the funding for it and refused to pay.[15] The situation was also altered by the development of suitable educational institutions in Russia. A Petrine decree of 1715 required all noble families to send children over the age of 10 to be educated in St Petersburg, but included an assurance that they would not be sent abroad.[16]

The young noblemen sent abroad to study were only part of a wider engagement with Europe during Peter's reign. Another element in this process was the transformation of Russian diplomatic policy and practice at the start of the eighteenth century. Peter took the important step of establishing permanent embassies at other leading European courts, like London, Paris, Vienna and Berlin.[17] Whether those involved were sent to a foreign country to study or to represent Russia, the experience imparted a number of very important cultural lessons. Reading and instruction gave some knowledge of appropriate behaviour in certain social situations, but practical experience was more important. Living in a foreign country provided many opportunities both to observe and participate in European social life, such as attending the theatre or a ball, walking around European cities or visiting someone's house.[18] Similarly, both Petr Tolstoi and Andrei Matveev were struck by the differences in the dress and behaviour of foreign women when visiting Italy and France, respectively, albeit with the former generally adopting a moralistic, rather than inquisitive tone.[19]

Domestically, the ongoing process of reform under Peter meant that education at both central and local level was an important means to cultivate useful members of a 'well-ordered' state and society. Although Peter was naturally keen to overhaul the existing system in pursuit of his goals, he did not dismiss it. The Church's existing role in education and its extensive network of personnel mean that they held the key to any reform of the system. The Church's official role in education was defined in the Spiritual Regulation in 1721, in which its financial and regulatory responsibilities were detailed.[20] The essential tools – the psalter, the breviary and the abecediary – also remained the basis for teaching basic literacy. As with other Petrine measures, the results were mixed. The creation of the provincial 'cipher' schools in 1714 used the existing network of schools attached to parish churches, monasteries or individual clerics that had previously been only for boys intended for the vocation.[21] These schools were now instructed to allow attendance for boys from various social backgrounds in order to teach them literacy and numeracy.[22] This innovation proved largely unsuccessful for several reasons. The requirement for prospective pupils to have some degree of literacy before admission favoured the children of local officials and clergy, although the latter were allowed to leave and attend new ecclesiastical schools in 1722.[23] Other families were reluctant to send their children to these schools, since they were of an age to be put to work instead. As a result, of the 2000 students who attended these schools in the decade after their creation, only around 300 completed their studies, while around twice that number either ran away or were dismissed.[24] In 1744, the surviving schools were amalgamated with the garrison schools, which had been established in the early 1730s for each army regiment in order to teach soldier's children.[25]

Another strand of this educational reform was the creation of new specialist institutions, a considerable number of which were founded in St Petersburg. The Naval Academy, founded in St Petersburg in late 1715, was a further development of the model established by the Moscow School of Mathematics and Navigation in 1701.[26] The latter had been inspired by the Royal Mathematical School at Christ's Hospital in London, which Peter encountered during his visit in 1698, and had an intake of 200 students when it opened.[27] The new academy, inspired by the example of the French naval schools in Toulon and Brest, provided a broader range of subjects for prospective members of the Petrine service elite.[28] Building on the technical education provided by the Moscow School, the students were taught civil law, heraldry and other 'noble sciences' (*shliakhetnye nauki*). Foreign languages featured strongly, with instruction available in English, French, Italian, German, Swedish, Danish and Latin.[29] Ivan Kirilov's overview of the Russian Empire, which was compiled in the late 1720s, contained figures for the composition of classes at the Naval Academy. The list reveals that certain subjects were only taught to noble children, namely geometry, trigonometry, astronomy and geography, as well as the aforementioned 'noble sciences'. Other general subjects, such as drawing and dancing, had a much more even distribution of pupils, suggesting that they were considered useful skills for all young men to learn. The only classes in which children from other social backgrounds outnumbered the nobility were those teaching literacy.[30] The shifting emphasis in the type of subjects being taught to the two groups of pupils has been linked to the future roles envisaged for them. The nobility were intended to become naval officers, whilst the others would likely either enter government service as land surveyors, train in a specialist field – like architecture – or be sent to teach in the new 'cipher' schools.[31]

Alongside the Naval Academy, other specialist institutions were founded in St Petersburg during this period. The Engineers' School, founded in 1719, and a school attached to the St Petersburg Artillery laboratory, founded in 1721, were both related to similar establishments founded earlier in the century in Moscow. The Engineers' School in St Petersburg subsequently absorbed its Moscow equivalent in 1723.[32] At a lower level, plans were made to open school for other social groups. The 'Statute to the General Magistracy', issued to the new body responsible for urban administration in early 1721, was instructed to found schools in towns to teach literacy and numeracy.[33] Peter also established schools attached to the Admiralty to teach literacy and numeracy to the various craftsmen and sailors, with the aim of improving their general performance. The 'Regulation for the Administration of the Admiralty and Quays' (1722) allowed for the education of the sons of the Admiralty's carpenters, and other craftsmen, in basic literacy and geometry.[34] The teachers in these schools were mainly clergy, although a survey of the teaching staff by the Holy Synod in 1722 included government clerks, former soldiers, and even house-serfs. They were paid an allowance by the government and they taught in the traditional manner, using the abecediary, breviary and psalter.[35] In both cases, financial constraints meant that plans were often not realised. The individual projects pursued by some leading figures in this period were somewhat more successful. Archbishop Feofan Prokopovich established a school for orphans and other needy children from a variety of social backgrounds at his house on the Karpovka River in St Petersburg in 1721. Although it enjoyed a good reputation – Prokopovich had been well educated at the Kiev Academy and he wrote a primer specifically for his students – the school closed shortly after his death in 1736.[36]

This period saw an increasing use of foreigners as teachers within Russia. The practice of hiring foreign tutors was becoming more common amongst the Muscovite elite towards the end of the seventeenth century, but it became established at the start of the eighteenth century, with members of the royal family leading the way. For example, despite the reticence of Tsaritsa

Praskov'ia Fedorovna towards several of her brother-in-law's reforms, she took a different stance on education. She ensured that her three daughters – Ekaterina, Anna and Praskov'ia – were educated both in a traditional manner, using the primer (*bukvar'*), and in new subjects, including foreign languages (French and German) and dancing. For the latter purpose, she employed Dietrich Ostermann, a Westphalian and brother of Heinrich, a leading member of Peter's administration, and Etienne Rambour, a Frenchman who later taught Peter's own daughters, Anna and Elizabeth.[37] Natal'ia B. Dolgorukaia (*née* Sheremeteva) and her brothers were taught by a Swiss governess, Maria Schtauden, who was employed by their family.[38]

In spite of the challenges facing the educational reforms, the younger generation soon began to show signs of their influence, particularly in the acquisition of foreign languages. In 1721, the French ambassador, Jacques de Campredon, noted the grace and charm of Andrei Matveev's daughter, Mariia (the future wife of Field-Marshal Aleksandr I. Rumiantsev), which he saw as evidence of a good education.[39] Bergholz made similar comments on the young Princess Cherkasskaia, adding that she could easily have been educated in France.[40] The experience of foreign service could also influence decisions about the education of one's children, as in the case of Count Nikolai F. Golovin, who spoke good English and French after serving on an English ship between 1708 and 1716. He then ensured that both his sons and daughters learned foreign languages as part of their education.[41] Bergholz noted on several occasions that both men and women of the Russian elite were conversant with French, German and Italian, although he provides few details on their actual conversational ability.[42] The stress placed on the study and practice of foreign languages, both in formal education and in the advice literature of this period, reflects their importance as an aid to social interaction. By the mid-eighteenth century, French was de rigueur amongst the Russian elite, as at many other European courts.[43]

This changing attitude toward noble education resulted in the foundation of specific institutions to cater to the needs of the elite, similar to the academies for young noblemen in other European states. The 'Noble Cadet Corps' was founded in St Petersburg in mid-1731 by General Burkhard C. von Münnich, the governor of St Petersburg and President of the War College.[44] An earlier draft plan for this institution notes the model of the Berlin 'Royal Cadet Corps', founded in 1717.[45] The Cadet Corps was more than simply a functional military training school. Although the focus remained on producing young men who could usefully serve the state in the military or in the civil administration, it reflected the demand for a Europeanised noble education. Cadets were instructed in both academic subjects, such as arithmetic, history and jurisprudence, and in skills thought appropriate for a nobleman, such as horse-riding, fencing, dancing and foreign languages. Annual enrolment was limited to 150 Russians and 50 Baltic Germans, and between 1732 and 1762, the Corps had around 2000 students, of which

1557 graduated.[46] In 1752, a second 'Naval' Cadet Corps was established in St Petersburg (26), which superseded the existing Naval Academy and several other smaller naval schools. Its curriculum was a similar blend of vocational, academic and practical subjects to its 'land' equivalent and its intake was largely from noble families.[47]

In addition to the military and academic skills taught to the young noblemen, the cadets were encouraged to make use of their education in the new social settings, and consequently they were invited to attend the court's regular calendar of evening entertainments, such as masqued balls.[48] Cadets put their foreign language training into practice by providing translations, not only of technical and academic works, but also literature and history, and these endeavours later found a publishing outlet in the presses opened by the Cadet Corps in the late 1750s.[49] These activities also prompted the formation of literary discussion groups amongst the cadets, one of which ('Society of Lovers of Russian Literature') was founded by Aleksandr P. Sumarokov, later a leading playwright and director of the Russian Theatre. Other pupils from this period included Mikhail M. Kheraskov, Petr A. Rumiantsev-Zadunaiskii and Ivan P. Elagin, all prominent figures in Russia's cultural and political life during Catherine II's reign.[50] Theatre was another area where the cadets could use their education to participate in a social forum, not least due to the role of their teachers in helping to organise performances for the court. As a result, they provided the performers for a number of comedies, tragedies and ballets performed at court throughout this period, as directed by Sumarokov in the 1750s and 1760s.[51]

An alternative to the state educational institutions, particularly for the nobility, was to send children to a *pansion* (from the French *pension*), a private school that offered instruction in literacy, foreign languages, dancing and 'proper behaviour' (*pristoinoe obkhozhedenie*). Advertisements for these schools, and for foreign tutors for both boys and girls appeared in the *Sanktpeterburgskie Vedomosti* throughout the first half of the eighteenth century.[52] The educational qualifications and value of these tutors were difficult to assess, since many Russians were relatively inexperienced in dealing with foreigners. It was entirely possible for any Frenchman to get a post as a foreign tutor, providing he could convince his potential employers of his credentials, genuine or otherwise.[53] In response, Elizabeth issued a decree in 1757 that required all foreign tutors to pass an examination, organised by either the Academy of Sciences or the new Moscow University, before they could be hired. Unqualified tutors could be deported and their employers risked a fine, if they ignored this requirement.[54] Tutors who passed the examination then noted the qualification as part of the advertisement of their services in the *Vedomosti*.[55]

Two contemporary accounts help to reveal some of the issues in education during the first half of the eighteenth century. Mikhail V. Danilov (1722–90) recalled his early education with his two cousins, Elisei and Boris, by a local sexton, Brudasti, and his wife, who taught him how to read from around the age of seven. In the mid-1730s, he attended the Moscow Artillery School, although the poor quality or serious personal problems of the teaching staff greatly diminished the school's educational value. Danilov mentioned the examples of Gunnery-Cadet Alabushev, who was a violent drunk – the school had to retrieve him from prison on at least three occasions – and Captain Grin'kov, who was a diligent teacher but was missing an arm below the elbow and (perhaps as a result) suffered from a bad stutter. Unsurprisingly, many pupils either ran away or sought to be excused on health grounds. Danilov moved to the St Petersburg Artillery School in the 1740s, where his brother Vasilii had preceded him and which had a better standard of staff.[56] He became a skilled draughtsman and was subsequently employed by the school's artillery laboratory to work on new designs for both artillery pieces and fireworks.[57]

Andrei T. Bolotov (1738–1833) described his childhood education in his *Memoirs*; this began at the age of six when he studied the Gospels with other local children under a Ukrainian teacher. When Bolotov was eight, his father (a colonel) employed one of his German junior officers to teach him German and arithmetic, although the teacher's military mentality was all too apparent in his frequent recourse to the birch. His third tutor had enjoyed the benefit of a university education and taught German, French, drawing and some basic geography.[58] After this, Bolotov was sent to study at a private *pension* in St Petersburg, run by Daniel Féray, a teacher at the Cadet Corps. The lessons centred on studying a French translation of Aesop's Fables and articles taken from Russian newspapers. Bolotov seems to have encountered the usual problems that Russian eighteenth-century writers describe in relation to their school days. Ferre was more interested in turning a profit from his young charges than in their welfare and consequently fed them very badly.[59] Bolotov also described a later visit to his uncle, General-in-Chief Iakov A. Maslov, who lived in St Petersburg, during which he observed the lessons of his young cousins with their tutor, Monsieur Lapis. Although clearly educated, the Frenchman chose to teach using the dictionary of the *Académie Française*, from which he would read articles on the etymology of certain French words. This teaching method proved both confusing and of little practical use to his pupils.[60]

By the late 1750s, St Petersburg housed a number of significant educational institutions. For the nobility, the two Cadet Corps and the amalgamated Artillery and Engineers School (1758) provided an important foundation for a future service career, with a particular emphasis on the military. The new Corps of Pages, founded in 1759, was used to educate and socialise young noblemen within the court environment. The status and connections proved very valuable to the pages in their subsequent careers.[61] Each of these institutions focused on the acquisition of new skills, particularly those considered suitable for a young nobleman, which could then be used in one's career and, importantly, in the new social circumstances at court or in everyday life. The Cadet Corps also played an important role in the development of Russia's cultural life, as their students took part in theatrical performances for the court and the translation of foreign works. Beyond the official institutions, foreign tutors and governesses continued to provide lessons in a range of subjects, again with a definite role for social skills. However, St Petersburg was not the only element in this development. The foundation of Moscow University in 1755 created a more consistent institution for higher education within Russia than its small St Petersburg predecessor, attached to the Academy of Sciences, and there still remained the possibility of studying at prestigious foreign universities, like Leipzig or Halle.[62]

Two areas of educational provision that had proven problematic during this period were tackled during the reign of Catherine II. She encouraged the establishment of a specific institution for the education of young noblewomen at Smol'nyi, under the directorship of Ivan I. Betskoi, in 1764.[63] These young women were given a wide-ranging curriculum and, as with the members of the Cadet Corps, they were encouraged to participate in the court's social life, with privileged access to the court theatres and the Summer Gardens.[64] At a wider level, Catherine also established a national school system in 1786, influenced by the Austrian model introduced by Joseph II.[65] The attitude toward education throughout this period was similar across Europe, whether for members of the elite or other social groups – an educated populace was more useful to the ruler and to the state. Although the results of these reforms were decidedly mixed – Russian literacy rates outside the urban centres remained very low in comparison to its contemporary neighbours – they provided a foundation for educational reformers in the nineteenth century to build on.[66]

Conduct literature

Alongside formal instruction, improving literature provided another source of information about proper conduct and appropriate behaviour in a social setting for young people. The work of Norbert Elias linked the emergence of these texts with his theory of the 'civilising process', wherein the refinement of manners as part of the transition from the medieval to the early modern world was a means for the ruler to regulate and 'civilise' the aristocracy. For Elias, this process was encapsulated in the rise of 'civility', with the publication of Erasmus of Rotterdam's *De civilitate morum puerilium* in 1530 representing a key moment in this process.[67] An increasing number of works provided this type of advice, with notable examples including Baldassare Castiglione's *Il libro del cortegiano* (1528), Giovanni della Casa's *Il Galateo* (1558), Eustache de Refuge's *Traicté de la cour, ou instruction des courtisans* (1616) and Antoine de Courtin's *Nouveau traité de civilité* (1671). These works were sold in considerable numbers, translated into other languages and helped to inspire other works dealing with this theme. The rise of this type of literature reflected the increased complexity of life at the early modern court and offered advice to the aspiring courtier on how best to flourish in that environment.[68]

While acknowledging the importance of Elias's interpretation, subsequent scholarship has challenged his analysis in a number of ways. For example, the emphasis on early modern texts has often overshadowed the extent of continuity from the medieval 'courtesy' texts, from the twelfth century onward, which covered similar themes with reference to their contemporary social setting.[69] Similarly, his 'progressive' (not to say Whiggish) model of the refinement of manners during this period has been criticised for adopting an overly simplistic approach to the complex discourse of the 'appropriate'. The absence of guidance on governing one's bodily functions, a common feature of the early modern texts, in eighteenth-century advice literature is taken by Elias as evidence of the progress of their refinement, but it had also been absent from their preceding medieval courtesy texts, meaning that Elias's assumed trajectory of manners appears overly straightforward.[70] Moreover, there was an ongoing tension between the influence of these works, and contemporary moral criticism of this courtly behaviour with its perceived cynicism and associated vices – deceit, corruption and even degeneracy.[71]

Early modern Russia did not develop this type of advice literature, since the Muscovite court setting and its forms of social interaction were quite different to other European contemporaries. There were, of course, common elements between the edifying religious texts that informed the behaviour of good Christians, both Latin and Orthodox, such as religious primers to teach literacy and the lives of saints. These texts were produced in very large numbers across Europe throughout the early modern period.[72] However, before the late seventeenth century, Muscovite Russia had no equivalent to the type of sociable gatherings that populated the social calendars of other European courts, particularly those that involved the active participation of women. As a result of the Petrine reforms at the start of the eighteenth century, the social experience of the early-eighteenth-century Russian elite was very different from that of their Muscovite predecessors. The 'formal' setting of state celebrations was closely related to the traditional Muscovite ritual setting, even with the addition of new elements, and could be dealt with by specific instructions to participants, like the order of a procession or specific ceremonial roles. However, in an 'informal' social setting where an individual was free to choose their activities, such as at a Petrine 'assembly', Russian participants lacked guidance about appropriate behaviour of the type offered by education and advice literature.

In response to the need to provide a new basis for personal comportment and social interaction, the *Honourable Mirror of Youth or a guide to social conduct, compiled from various authors (Iunosti chestnoe zertsalo ili pokazanie*

k zhiteiskomu obkhozhdeniiu, sobrannoe ot raznykh avtorov) was published in
St Petersburg on 4 February 1717.[73] Although the initial print run was only
100 copies, it was subsequently republished in 1719 (600 copies), 1723
(1200 copies, in Moscow), 1740 (578 copies), 1745 and 1767.[74] The book
was divided into a number of sections, with the first part closely resembling
other primers of this period. It consisted of the Cyrillic alphabet, using the
old Slavonic script alongside the new 'civil' typeface, sample phrases to aid
pronunciation, and a list of Slavonic, Arabic and Latin numbers to teach
numeracy. The second part – the *Honourable Mirror* proper – was compiled by
Gavriil Buzhinskii, Iakov Bruce and Johann Werner Paus, a German scholar
and translator employed by the Russian state.[75] The main source for this section was Erasmus of Rotterdam's *De civilitate morum puerilium* (Amsterdam,
1530), although it also drew on Mathurin Cordier's *Miroir de la jeunesse pour
le former à bonnes moeurs et civilité de vie* (Poitiers, 1559), particularly for its
translated title.[76]

   This part of the book dealt with the appropriate conduct of young people
and was divided roughly into two halves, broadly along gender lines. The
first half was intended for young men and consisted of 63 pieces of advice,
followed by separate sections that dealt with the specifics of behaviour when
in the company of strangers. The numbered paragraphs of advice covered
a considerable range of topics and they had elements in common with the
traditional Slavic primers – the need to respect one's parents, the appropriate
way to deal with servants, and the importance of virtuous personal qualities
like honesty, humility and a love of hard work.[77] However, the *Honourable
Mirror* was the first official Russian publication to set these virtues in the
context of social interaction in order to help prepare young noblemen for
both 'polite' society and their service career. The paragraph on education
(No. 18) listed the skills considered important for a young nobleman. Horse-
riding and fencing were parts of a traditional noble upbringing, with one
eye on military service, and this aspect translated easily to Russia. However,
the inclusion of dancing was a new element for Russians and was to become
an important part of a noble education for their bearing and movement,
discussed below. Several passages emphasised the importance of learning
foreign languages (No. 30), since it reflected refinement and education.
Conversational skills were also discussed, with advice on expressing oneself
in a considered, respectful manner (Nos. 4 and 6), judging the tone of a
conversation (No. 7) and allowing others to express their views (No. 8).

   Other paragraphs provided advice on the nature of nobility, for example
the assertion that noble status was not merely the result of one's family
background, but should be borne out by one's words and actions (No. 15).
Similarly, space was devoted to the personal qualities that should be displayed
by an honourable 'gentleman' (No. 16), the importance of keeping one's
word (No. 43), and the proper way to deal with one's servants (Nos. 49–52).
The court was identified as an important part of the young nobleman's life

and presented a complex setting with various ceremonies that required care-ful study and a particular array of skills in order to negotiate successfully (Nos. 19 and 37). There was also general advice on how to conduct oneself in the less familiar social gatherings, like banquets, wedding celebrations and other occasions where dancing and other sorts of interaction could take place (Nos. 32 and 39). The practical tone of this advice – it warned against excessive drinking or fighting and provided guidance on the correct way to ask someone to dance – fits quite naturally with other paragraphs that dealt with the governing of one's bodily emissions whilst in the presence of others (Nos. 55–9). There were also two separate sections, after the 63 paragraphs, which covered table manners and body posture.

The second half of the *Honourable Mirror*, subtitled 'The Crown of Maidenly Honour and Virtue', was intended for young women. It consisted of 20 para-graphs devoted to the individual virtues, such as fear of God, cleanliness, honesty and charity, followed by two separate and more detailed essays on 'Maidenly Chastity' and 'Maidenly Modesty'.[78] Despite the change in social circumstances for women of the Russian elite and their newly visible role in Petrine social gatherings, the focus was very much on the virtues which young noblewomen should try to embody.[79] The tone of this sec-tion originated in the more traditional realm of religious authority, with the numerous biblical quotations and references further complemented by the writings of the Church Fathers on the appropriate role and behaviour of women.[80] While this emphasis on female virtue was no doubt familiar to its readers because of its religious roots and resonance with traditional Russian attitudes to women, this section contained little affirmative advice to young women on their conduct in social situations. There was no discus-sion of appropriate posture and movement in 'polite company' – the focus remained instead on the need for modest behaviour in women and warned against dressing or acting provocatively.[81] This emphasis was not unusual in such works, notably in the pronouncements of the influential 'On the Education of a Christian Woman', written by Juan Luis Vives in 1524 and dedicated to Catherine of Aragon.[82]

Although the *Honourable Mirror* was printed and sold in considerable numbers, for a secular work in this period at least, its impact on the Russian elite is difficult to assess.[83] It was, after all, a compilation of various trans-lated sources, notably Erasmus, by people who were unsure both of what they were trying to provide and for whom they were providing it. This uncertainty perhaps explains the varied and wide-ranging nature of some sections, particularly the 'Crown of Maidenly Honour and Virtue'. However, there was at least some recognition of its readership in the translation proc-ess. Unlike the translated technical works of this period, the language of the *Honourable Mirror* did not involve a large numbers of foreign loan words, but instead used existing Russian terms to describe the new social forums and practices, like *beseda* to refer to a social evening.[84] Therefore, although the situations and types of behaviour were largely unfamiliar to the Russian readership, they were described in such a way as to make them accessible, with the aim of bridging any potential cultural divide. Only a few foreign accounts from this period discuss Russian social habits in much detail, notably Bergholz's diary and de Campredon's diplomatic correspondence. In these two cases, the authors commented favourably, and with some surprise, on the social and cultural development of the Russian elite, but made no reference to conduct literature.

Although, in some respects, the *Honourable Mirror* addressed the lack of advice literature in the Russian language, it remained the sole example until the mid-1730s. The nature of the advice that it offered to the Russian elite surely proved of interest because it was reprinted on four more occasions in the 50 years following Peter I's death. In the same period, the development and consolidation of the Russian court as an institution comparable with its European contemporaries meant there was an increased interest in reading such literature. As one might expect, the emphasis on foreign languages in education meant that it was possible to read such books in their original languages or in other European translations, which was in itself a mark of sophistication. For example, Baltasar Gracián y Morales' famous *Oráculo manual y arte de prudentia* (1647) was published in French, translated by Amelot de la Houssaie, as *L'Homme de Court* in Rotterdam in 1728. Tsarevna Elizabeth had a copy of this French translation in her personal library in the 1730s.[85] The work was subsequently translated from the French by Sergei Volchkov, later a translator for the Academy of Sciences, in 1734. This manuscript translation (*Gratsian pridvornyi chelovek*) was produced at the behest of Anna Ivanovna's favourite, Biron, according to a preface dated 14 June 1735 in a bound copy preserved in the Vorontsov family archive.[86]

Volchkov's Russian translation was subsequently published by the Academy of Sciences in St Petersburg in 1741 and it was dedicated to the infant Tsar Ivan VI and his mother, the regent Anna Leopoldovna. Significantly, the print run for this edition – 1250 copies – was very high for a secular work.[87] There are also indications that the printing may have been spread over several years, since part of the print run for this edition featured a replacement title page with a dedication to Elizabeth, after her successful coup against Ivan VI in November 1741, and a revised publication date of 1742, even though the order relating to this rededication was issued on 23 January 1743. A second edition was produced in 1760, also by the Academy of Sciences, with an increased print run of 1433 copies, reflecting some measure of demand for the book.[88] The only major changes in this edition were the smaller format used for the book and the addition of a new section at the end, entitled 'Recapitulation' (*Rekapitulatsiia ili Kratkoe povtorenie glav*), which provided an index of the major topics and the major figures quoted in the text. The book consisted of numbered paragraphs that gave advice on how to succeed at court, with Gracián's comments on this advice.

The type of advice was not dissimilar to that offered by the relevant sections of the *Honourable Mirror*, with emphasis on the skills and characteristics of the ideal courtier, albeit with a worldly, rather than worthy tone. Given the length of the book and the number of topics that it addressed, the inclusion of the 'Recapitulation' was a practical measure, allowing the reader to quickly navigate to relevant paragraphs or quotations.

Another example from the same period was Vasilii K. Trediakovskii's translation of Nicolas Rémond des Cours's *La véritable politique des personnes de qualité* (Paris, 1692), published as *The True Policy of Distinguished and Well-Born Persons* (*Istinnaia politika znatnykh i blagorodnykh osob*) by the Academy of Sciences in 1737. The initial print run was 1200 copies and a second edition was subsequently printed in 1745.[89] This work consisted of 80 'rules' or pieces of advice on certain subjects. The list began with the duty to respect one's parents and then ranged from the need to serve one's ruler faithfully to appreciating the value of true friendship and using one's time usefully. In common with the earlier *Honourable Mirror*, *True Policy* devoted several paragraphs to education and the useful subjects for young 'well-born' people to study, as well as stressing the importance of personal appearance and bearing, especially at court. Similarly, at the end of the book, there was a series of short 'maxims', which carried simple messages such as 'Fear God' or 'Read books', which the young person could read and memorise easily.[90] *True Policy* can be seen as a transitional work, between the basic, wide-ranging approach of the *Honourable Mirror* and the worldlier themes of the translation of Gracián's work, since it began with a young person's development before moving on to specific areas like the court.

The intricacies of good conversation were not neglected in this period either. The aptly-titled *Domestic Conversations* (*Domashnie razgovory*) was published by the Academy of Sciences Press in 1749 in a quadrilingual edition, with French, German, Russian and Latin in parallel columns.[91] Although no details are given about the text (there is no preface), recent scholarship has shown that it was based on a Franco-German original by Georgio Philippo Plats, with the Russian and Latin translations added by Vasilii I. Lebedev and Christian Crusius for the 1749 edition.[92] It consisted of 96 conversations on a range of topics, from small talk while strolling or sitting in company to the correct way to ask for something. The value of these 'model' conversations lay in important details such as respectful forms of address, compliments, appropriate ways to express an opinion, and short anecdotes, all of which could then be incorporated into the reader's conversational repertoire.[93] Although there are no details on the initial print runs, the fact that this book went through eight editions in total before 1800, including three reprints in this quadrilingual format and four using only the Russian and German translations, demonstrates its enduring utility.[94]

Most of this literature was written with young men in mind. With the exception of 'The Maidenly Crown of Honour and Virtue', the subject of

appropriate behaviour and education for young women received little attention. There were, however, some exceptions. Andrei F. Khrushchev, a contemporary of Vasilii N. Tatishchev, had been educated in Holland between
1712 and 1720. He produced Russian translations of François de Fénelon's
L'Education des Filles (1687) and Joachim de la Chétardie's *Instruction pour une
jeune Princesse* (1697) in manuscript form in 1738, according to hand-written
notes inside his manuscript copy of both works.[95] However, these translations were never published, perhaps as a consequence of his involvement
with Artemii P. Volynskii's circles, which led to his execution for treason in
1740. Instead, the first publication of Fénelon's work in Russian (*O vospi-
tanii devits*) appeared in 1763 and used a translation by Ivan Tumanskii.[96]
Nevertheless, the existence of such manuscripts demonstrates that the
material was at the very least being read in Russia. This development was
particularly important in view of Fénelon's central assertion that education
was vital if women were to overcome their natural 'frailties'.[97] The subject
of female education, at least for noblewomen, was addressed in an institutional form the following year, with the opening of the Smol'nyi Institute
in 1764.

Overall, although the *Honourable Mirror* was in many ways an unsatisfac-
tory publication, compared with its more sophisticated foreign equivalents,
it was only one of a number of options for the discerning reader from the
1730s onward. Other forms of literature were considered useful for a young
person's education. For example, Fénelon's inspirational and moral work
Les Aventures de Télémaque was translated by Trediakovskii in 1736 and presented another model for noble upbringing. It was not a particularly flow-
ing translation because of the archaic tone of its prose, to the extent that
Catherine II made reading passages from it a forfeit for anyone breaking one
of her 'Hermitage' rules.[98] Nevertheless, judging by the growing number of
translated works available, there was an established interest in and use of
conduct literature for educational purposes during this period. It is difficult
to draw firm conclusions about the impact of this advice literature, since
the prescriptive model presents an ideal, rather than the reality of social
behaviour. Contemporary accounts usually focus on occasions when an
individual crossed the boundary of acceptable behaviour.[99] Rather, the significance of this literature lies in its introduction to Russia during a period of
considerable social and cultural change. These works were contemporary to
the growing importance of the court and the development of its associated
social forums in St Petersburg, mirroring a process that, for other European
states, occurred during the sixteenth and seventeenth centuries.[100]

Dance

Dancing was an important element in noble education throughout the early
modern period, and contemporary conduct literature often referred to its

role in providing discipline and control to the body's physical movement. Dancing and its instruction focused on two related areas: the physical skill of learning the movements associated with the different types of dances; and the various forms of social interaction that surrounded the act of dancing. For many members of the elite across Europe, this type of education began at a young age, with dance playing a fundamental role in teaching correct movement, improving posture and helping to develop physical strength. For young men, these aspects were further complemented by fencing lessons.[101] This discipline was embodied in the young Louis XIV who, like his father, was a gifted, natural dancer. He was trained by a succession of dancing masters, including Pierre Beauchamp who later choreographed the court ballets composed by Lully. The young king opened his first court ball in 1645, aged only seven.[102] This aspect of royal and noble education was common across Europe for both genders. For example, a French dancing master, Antoine de Beaulieu, was appointed to teach Queen Christina of Sweden and young noblemen at court in the 1630s – he later coordinated the first ballets for the court.[103]

Dancing at court had two related forms. Firstly, there were the elaborately choreographed dance spectacles, which had their origins in Italian Renaissance festivities and subsequently became an established feature at the French court, in the form of the *ballet de cour*, from the late sixteenth century onward.[104] These spectacles prompted a range of similar events at other European courts in the early seventeenth century, like the masques of the early Stuart court, discussed in the last chapter, and the ballets performed at the Württemberg court in Stuttgart.[105] Such occasions often featured the ruler as a performer. Louis XIV performed in a total of 18 ballets between 1651 and 1669, often with overt political symbolism, as with his role as the Rising Sun (royal authority) banishing the darkness (political dissension and uncertainty) at the climax of the *Ballet de la nuit* in 1653.[106] The *Académie Royale de Danse*, founded in 1661, provided a steady supply of skilled dancers for such court performances. From the mid-seventeenth century, the influences of these developments led to the hiring of French dancing masters to oversee the choreography of such celebrations at other European courts. The Saxon court at Dresden hired French dancing masters, including Charles du Mesniel, to oversee a number of *grand-ballets* for major dynastic celebrations in the 1660s and 1670s.[107]

Secondly, social dancing was an established and regular feature of the court calendar across Europe throughout the early modern period. The French *grand bal* at court in the late seventeenth and early eighteenth centuries served to reflect the glory of the monarch, who was at the centre of the spectacle. The court elite served as both participants in, and the primary audience for, this court celebration. The audience was then extended further by publishing a list of the dancers and a commentary on these ballets in the *Mercure galant*.[108] The popularity of this form of dancing can be seen at many contemporary courts, such as that of Charles II in England, who had spent time in exile in France. The English court represented a blend of continental and domestic styles, as it hosted a mixture of formal and 'ordinary' balls, with the latter featuring popular, traditional English country dances.[109] Even at the supposedly more restrained courts of Anne and the early Hanoverian rulers, dancing continued to be a frequent and popular part of court entertainment.[110] Dancing masters, particularly but not exclusively French, became a common feature of many courts across Europe and, while primarily responsible for teaching members of the royal family, they would often hold other classes that were open to members of the court elite and other leading families.[111]

As befitted a visible element of the court repertoire, dancing became an important symbol of refinement and education, which was reflected in one's ability to perform certain types of dances. For example, the minuet was an integral part of dancing at court during this period and, despite the relative simplicity of its various component movements, it required an assured and balanced dancer to be performed elegantly.[112] The mastery of such physical movement was not only reflected on the dance floor, but in other areas, like personal comportment. Pierre Rameau's *Le maître à danser* (1725), one of the leading dance manuals of the period, provided considerable detail on certain dances, like the minuet, but also covered the correct manner to enter a room and genteel behaviour at a court ball for both men and women. It contained 57 plates to illustrate the position of the limbs and the relationship between the dance partners for each of the featured dances.[113] The influence of dancing instruction, albeit through the prism of artistic representation, can be seen in the position of the feet and hands in the portraiture of this period, particularly when figures are pictured interacting with one another.[114]

By comparison, this type of social dancing was not an organic development at the Russian court. Popular folk dances faced the twin disapproval of the Church, which considered such activities as promoting sinful, lascivious behaviour until well into the eighteenth century, and of the elite, who considered it beneath their dignity.[115] Some aspects of Polish and Ukrainian dancing were familiar to the Muscovite elite, particularly during the reign of Tsar Aleksei Mikhailovich, but they were restricted to the privacy of individual residences and the royal theatre.[116] The impact of such dancing was strictly limited, particularly in the theatre context since it was presented as a spectacle, rather than a participatory activity. The segregated nature of elite Muscovite social events meant that women were not allowed to participate in this kind of activity, which precluded any further development during this period. The lack of familiarity with a sociable form of dancing was reflected in the introduction of new terminology to describe it in Russian. From the late seventeenth century, traditional forms of dancing, including the popular folk dances, were described as *pliaski*, whereas the foreign styles were referred to as *tantsy*, from either the Polish *taniec* or the German *tanz*.[117]

This distinction was reflected in both official legislation and contemporary accounts throughout the eighteenth century.

Instead, according to Stählin, dancing as a form of secular elite entertainment emerged only during Peter's reign, influenced by his encounters with it during the Grand Embassy.[118] The social interaction and physical skill involved in courtly dancing was evidently a surprise to Peter's retinue, demonstrated by their puzzled reactions to it at a reception organised by Sophia-Charlotte, wife of Frederick III, Elector of Brandenburg, in June 1697.[119] Nevertheless it was precisely occasions such as this that influenced Peter to create similar forums for this type of interaction upon his return to Russia the following year. A ball was held at Franz Lefort's palace outside Moscow after an audience for the ambassador of Brandenburg-Prussia on 19 February 1699, at which Russian ladies took part in the dancing. This event was unusual enough to draw a comment to that effect from the secretary of the Austrian Legation, Johann-Georg Korb.[120] The presence of armed guards to ensure participation and prevent the guests from leaving was a characteristic Petrine response to the understandable reticence on the part of most guests.

An unusual but nevertheless instructive recent analysis of this subject has highlighted two aspects of the altered 'dance paradigm' that emerged during Peter's reign. Firstly, dancing provided an entertainment within an ordered space, similar to the military or ceremonial parade, with dancers performing in symmetrical, set patterns.[121] It is therefore possible to interpret the function of dancing at Petrine entertainments as a sociocultural adjunct to the parade ground because of the considerable degree of personal control that Peter wielded when he was present.[122] Indeed, the military context of much of Peter's reign suggests that the encouragement of dancing as part of court entertainments reflected a practical function, since the ability to move in time with music and execute manoeuvres in formation was a useful and relevant skill, as also seen in the education of other European elites.[123] Secondly, with the deliberate introduction of European dance styles during Peter's reign, there is a question about whether such dancing brought with it the symbolic connotations that it had at other European courts.[124] While the elaborate symbolism of power of Louis XIV's court ballets can be linked to the large-scale celebrations of the Petrine court, like the public masquerades organised in 1715 and 1721, it was not a regular feature of the court dances under Peter I, which were intended primarily as a means to encourage sociable interaction in the new mixed-company social forums.

Such occasions were nevertheless dominated by the Tsar's personal authority, as the participants were expected to follow his lead. Since Peter had never been formally taught to dance, court dancing in this period could be rather haphazard. If he decided on a new dance figure, a change of tempo or style, or indeed how long they would dance for, then they had to obey or face a penalty, frequently a large measure of alcohol. By the same token,

Peter appears to have found considerable amusement in compelling the older members of his court to dance with the very young.[125] In addition, the process of organising large-scale, allegorical dances was complicated by a lack of practical expertise at the Russian court. This style of dancing was a recent introduction to Russia and it lacked a codex of dancing literature in this period akin to the works available in French or English during this period.[126] The first Russian works on dancing appeared only later in the century.[127] There were also no formal institutions to teach dancing and foreign dancing masters, who were hired by members of the royal family and other members of the elite, instead provided instruction on an individual basis. Etienne Rambour taught several members of the royal family, including the future Empresses Anna Ivanovna and Elizabeth.[128] Other leading families followed suit, including the Romanodanovskii, Golovkin and Cherkasskii households.[129] These efforts were not always successful. Menshikov's (unnamed) German dancing master complained to Bergholz in March 1722 that he was punished for failing to interest the prince's son in his studies.[130]

Nevertheless, from a hesitant start, dancing had become an important part of elite social life in St Petersburg by the early 1720s, as the numerous mentions in Bergholz's diary make clear, with positive comments about the proper conduct of different dance styles – including English, French and Polish – featuring in a number of his descriptions.[131] This consolidation continued under Peter's successors, with the reign of Anna Ivanovna being particularly important for the formal adoption of European dance styles as part of the regular round of court entertainments. Although she was taught dancing from an early age and, from her days as Dowager-Duchess in Mitau onward, ensured that her entourage had a large number of musicians and singers to entertain her, Anna was not an enthusiastic dancer. Instead, she preferred to pull the strings and then watch the spectacle unfold, as Berch noted in the mid-1730s with reference to her role at the regular court balls.[132] Her behaviour on these occasions sometimes resembled that of her late uncle, Peter I, with the refined atmosphere presented by the dancing then undercut by Anna slapping anyone who was not performing to her satisfaction, according to Shubinskii.[133] Nevertheless, her enthusiasm for music and dancing led to the introduction of opera and ballet through foreign troupes, as discussed in Chapter 4.

Her reign witnessed the rise of the most significant of the early dancing masters at the Russian court – the Frenchman Jean-Baptiste Landé. He had come to Russia during Peter I's reign to teach dancing, like his fellow countryman Rambour. Although initially employed by noble families, Landé was subsequently hired to instruct several members of the royal family, notably Tsarevna Elizabeth. He joined the staff at the Cadet Corps in August 1734, initially for three years, on an annual salary of 300 rubles (later 500 rubles) and he was provided with a set of rooms in the old Petrine Winter Palace.[134]

As with dancing masters at other European courts, Landé also ran a private dance class from his rooms for his more able cadets and other children, including girls, who subsequently appeared in court ballet performances.[135] The Cadet Corps became an important centre for providing this kind of instruction to young noblemen in this period, although it proved difficult to find and keep talented staff. For example, the Swedish dancing master Carl Conrad Menck came to St Petersburg with his family in August 1733 and was appointed to a post at the Cadet Corps, but died early in the following year. The Cadet Corps advertised for a replacement in the *Sanktpeterburgskie vedomosti* in March 1734, shortly before losing another dancing master, Johann Schmidt, who was forced to return to his native Berlin in July because of his ill health.[136]

Landé's position at the Cadet Corps was also short-lived, although for different reasons. His cadets performed three ballets, devised by Landé himself, for the Empress during the performance of the opera *La forza dell'amore e dell'odio* in March 1736, and another ballet was performed by his pupil Thomas Lebrun and other cadets in the theatre at the Summer Palace in 1737. On the basis of this success, Landé petitioned the Empress in September 1737 to establish a dance school under his supervision. He requested that the school should consist of twelve students, six boys and six girls, drawn from his existing pupils, whose food and clothing would be provided by the Court Office, and that it should be given a permanent home. In response, the Empress ordered that Landé receive a salary of 1000 roubles per year from the state income from the salt monopoly, and provided two rooms in the upper apartments of the old Petrine Winter Palace to house the school's pupils, since Landé's quarters were in the same palace.[137] His work as a choreographer and an instructor continued under Elizabeth and Landé taught dancing to the young Grand Duke and Duchess in the mid-1740s. However, Antonio Rinaldi increasingly took the lead role in devising the court's major ballets and he was made head of the ballet school in 1747. Landé died the following year.

Ballet and social dancing continued to play an important role in court entertainments during the reign of Elizabeth, not least because the Empress was an enthusiastic and capable dancer herself, as noted by several contemporaries.[138] A total of 21 different ballets were devised (or adapted) and performed for Elizabeth's court, with repeat performances of those that the Empress enjoyed at later dates. The repertoire drew on both the French classical style, exemplified by Landé, and the comic or burlesque Italian style, provided by Rinaldi and his troupe.[139] The latter left for Italy in 1751, following his wife's illness, but he subsequently returned to St Petersburg with new dancers in 1753.[140] In 1758, the Russian court was able to lure the Viennese court's *maître de ballet*, Franz Anton Hilverding, to St Petersburg, where he oversaw the production of court ballets for the next seven years – his pupil and successor, Gasparo Angiolini, was later similarly employed in St Petersburg.[141]

Elizabeth's court also hosted regular events that featured dancing as the centrepiece, such as the masquerades discussed in Chapter 4, and weekly court balls.[142] Although dismissive of some aspects of court entertainments in her *Mémoires*, Catherine's account reflects the colourful, refined atmosphere of these occasions, with the importance of appearance and behaviour very much to the fore.[143] Beyond the court, private tutors advertised dance instruction alongside tuition in other desirable skills for young men and women in the *Sanktpeterburgskie vedomosti* throughout this period.[144]

Overall, this period was crucial for the establishment of social dancing as part of the canon of court and elite entertainments. The ability to dance in the contemporary European fashion, which was related to but made distinct from the existing Russian folk tradition, became a symbol of education and refinement from the 1720s onwards. This development hinged on the introduction of a system for teaching dancing in educational institutions, principally the Cadet Corps, and in private homes by trained dancing masters and, occasionally, foreign opportunists. The regular performance of ballets in the court theatres led to the establishment of Landé's dancing school in St Petersburg, which has been credited with establishing the Russian ballet tradition that flourished in the late nineteenth and early twentieth centuries.[145] The nature of court dancing gradually moved away from the personal whim of the ruler toward a more refined, informed style that generally followed the practices of court dancing elsewhere, although royal taste still played an influential role in proceedings. That several of the rulers in this period had been tutored by dancing masters like Landé and that many of the elite by the 1740s had enjoyed the benefits of a similar education helped to consolidate these rules. The encouragement of wider participation in some of the court's social events in St Petersburg, discussed in the last chapter, contributed to the growing awareness and acceptance of this form of sociable entertainment in urban Russian society, where it co-existed with folk dance traditions at popular festivities.

Clothing[146]

The importance of being properly dressed had ancient origins, with most societies developing moral and practical concerns about the manner of their dress over the centuries.[147] With the emergence of courtly society, rulers and their elites used clothing to reflect their values or ambitions. The enlargement and increasing sophistication of these courts during the Renaissance was mirrored in their appearance, with the emphasis on magnificence.[148] Early modern historians have increasingly sought to analyse the symbolic value of fashion, alongside the existing scholarship on the economic value and consumption of clothing.[149] The manner of dress made an important statement about an individual or group's self-perception, as well as their perception of other groups in society. Appearance was an important qualifier for access to the corridors of power around the ruler.[150] Courts and rulers throughout the early modern period repeatedly emphasised the importance of being 'properly dressed' through official regulations, both for formal state occasions and also for the regular round of court entertainments. As with the court's residences, their patronages and their celebrations, the appearance of the ruler, their family and leading courtiers was judged by their contemporaries across Europe.[151]

Court fashions followed the currents of political and cultural life in early modern Europe, as with the prominence of Italian fashions in the sixteenth century, the contrast between Bourbon and Habsburg court dress during the seventeenth century and the English's court's various stylistic relationships with its Continental contacts – Spain, Denmark and France.[152] By the late seventeenth century, Louis XIV's court was the established leader of courtly taste across Europe, leading to a transmission of designs, terminology and materials (like silk and lace) to both allies and rivals. His court clearly embodied the principle of conspicuous consumption, with the wealthy and aspirational using expensive materials and decorative details, such as buttons, lacing and embroidery, to stake their claim to status.[153] The cost of these outfits and a desire to limit their use to members of the elite led to the introduction of sumptuary laws in a number of states during this period, including Elizabeth I's England, Philip IV's Spain and Louis XIII's France.[154] For many states, these official regulations were difficult to enforce and were often repealed. Instead, during the eighteenth century, court fashion gradually incorporated military aspects, as embodied by Frederick-William I of Prussia or Charles XII of Sweden, while retaining many of the hallmarks of status and wealth of the previous centuries.[155] The combination of functional and symbolic presented an appealing model to a young ruler seeking to establish himself on the European stage: Peter I of Russia.

Although sometimes regarded as relatively isolated during the early modern period, the Russian elite was already familiar with some elements of European dress from the mid-seventeenth century onwards. The Kremlin library contained illustrated books showing foreign clothing. A number of foreign craftsmen and tailors resided in the Foreign Quarter in Moscow, who later supplied costumes for the court theatre between 1672 and 1675.[156] However, the expensive foreign fabrics like silks and velvets purchased for the Tsar and members of the elite originated in the Ottoman and Persian Empires, rather than European markets, since Russia had existing trade links with these regions.[157] Adopting foreign fashions was linked to the influence of foreign ideas, which clashed with the conservative elements in the Muscovite hierarchy. Tsar Aleksei Mikhailovich issued a decree in 1675 that prohibited dressing in foreign clothes and shaving off one's beard.[158] Nevertheless, some prominent nobles began to purchase and dress in this manner. Prince Vasilii V. Golitsyn, the regent Sophia Alekseevna's favourite, wore Polish-style clothing in his house, particularly when entertaining foreign guests, and also occasionally in public.[159] A portrait of Tsar Fedor Alekseevich's wife, Marfa M. Apraksina, from the very late seventeenth century highlights some of the developments taking place within the Muscovite elite. She is dressed in traditional manner, in long formal robes and with a covered head. However, in her hands, she holds a small dog and a closed fan. Although these features are typical of elite female portraits elsewhere in Europe, this is their first appearance in a Russian portrait.[160]

Peter I experienced foreign attire in the Foreign Quarter in Moscow as a young man and during his travels through Germany, the Netherlands and England during the Grand Embassy in the late 1690s. It is no coincidence that one of his first actions after returning to Moscow in 1698 was to shave members of the leading *boyar* families.[161] This was not only an assertion of power by Peter over the Muscovite elite, with the Tsar himself wielding the razor on this occasion, but also part of a wider plan to reduce the symbolic 'distance' between Russia and its potential allies in the rest of Europe, starting with appearance. The reform of everyday clothing began on 4 January 1700 and was subsequently extended to include ceremonial clothing on 28 February 1702, requiring members of the elite and Russia's urban population to adopt initially 'Hungarian' and subsequently 'German' dress for both everyday and ceremonial occasions.[162] In mid-January 1705, the same groups were ordered to shave their beards off or pay a fine of between 30 and 100 rubles per year. Only the clergy and rural peasants were exempted from these reforms, and even the latter had to pay a 'beard tax' of one kopeck if they wished to enter towns.[163] Ivan Zheliabuzhskii describes how dummies (*chuchely*) were set up by the gates of Moscow to display the new manner of dress, thereby ensuring that ignorance or illiteracy was no excuse for disobedience.[164]

The very visible change created by Peter's laws on required dress is illustrated by the comparison between the traditional and often hereditary ceremonial robes of the *boyar* elite, made from expensive materials and adorned with precious stones, and the less ornate European-style clothing that took its place. However, this is not to suggest that important distinctions did not still exist between the clothing of different social groups, particularly in the use of expensive materials in one's outfit. Weber experienced this distinction when he was invited to a social event in St Petersburg but was refused entry. He was subsequently advised by 'a certain minister' that he should dress 'all trimmed over with Gold and Silver', with the implication that this would distinguish him from the average man on the street.[165] The desire of the wealthy to purchase clothing and accessories of sufficient quality to reflect their status made this transition a potentially expensive process.[166] One of Peter's advisers, Ivan Pososhkov, sought to minimise this expense for certain groups, particularly the merchantry, by proposing a new system for regulating dress on the basis of income and seniority. This system applied to all levels of urban society, from the lowest urban peasantry (who could only wear undyed Russian cloth), through the various groups of crafts-men and merchants, to the nobility (who were entitled to wear expensive, imported materials). Anyone who dressed above or below their means was to be reported, assessed and punished accordingly.[167] Although Pososhkov's proposals were not introduced, alongside, they reflect a concern about the socio-economic impact of the clothing reforms that was mirrored by later Russian writers.

The new clothing also presented certain issues related to gender and moral-ity. For men, the shaving of their long beards was an attack on several impor-tant parts of their identity. A beard was a symbol of masculinity – indeed, in the Orthodox tradition, the beardless were sometimes identified as homosexuals. The beard represented a man's attainment of adulthood and was a visual link to the image of God.[168] For women, traditional elite dress was multi-layered and used expensive materials, such as furs and imported cloth like silk, to reflect the wealth and status of either their husbands or their families. This style of dress concealed the outline of the female figure and covered her limbs, thereby upholding the Orthodox ideal of modesty. By contrast, the new foreign styles had a defined waistline, visible *décolletage* and bare forearms.[169] Another aspect that caused discomfort was the use of stays or corsets, essentially a cloth bodice, with strips of metal or whalebone sewn in it to shape the woman's figure. Such corsets were the product of the fashion of the sixteenth-century Spanish court, which sought to sup-press the chest. However, a woman with a large bust – as with both Anna Ivanovna and Elizabeth – would find it squeezed upwards by the pressure of the corset, so an additional bodice was worn under the dress and was laced at the side to ensure that the ideal shape was maintained. The two common types of corsets found in Russia in the eighteenth century were the English style – laced down the front – and the French style – laced down the back and generally tighter, which allowed for a waist of only 40 centimetres.[170]

The process of transition was complicated further still with the emergence of the English-style hoop (*paniers* in French) after 1718, although this was more commonly referred to in Russian as a *fizhma* or *fizhbein* (from the German *fischbein*). It was a common part of the female wardrobe at courts across Europe and consisted of a round (and later oval) birch-strip or whale-bone framework worn around the waist over an underskirt, with the dress then worn over the top. Its circumference gradually increased, reaching its height (or should that be width?) in the 1730s.[171] Its introduction had a number of consequences for the wearer's posture and movement. It was no longer possible to stand with one's hands by one's sides, meaning that they were usually bent at the elbow and held in front. Also, the sheer size of the frame (which varied according to the social occasion) made any lateral movement difficult and previously simple manoeuvres, such as walking around a room, sitting down or passing through a doorway, became an exer-cise in their own right.[172] For Russian women accustomed to the relatively loose Muscovite robes, the transition was uncomfortable to say the least, since it was difficult to both move and breathe in such clothing without practice. Since Petrine women were ordered to dress in a manner that was considered unseemly and caused them physical discomfort, it is not difficult to understand why it was that some elite women preferred to revert to their old style of dress in the privacy of their homes or estates (see below).

Muscovite fashion persisted in some areas of female fashion, as with make-up. In the sixteenth and seventeenth centuries, make-up was used to ensure that a lady had the requisite pale skin and red cheeks, traditional signs of feminine beauty. Georg Schleissing, a German visitor to Russia in the 1680s, noted that such make-up was amongst the first gifts that a husband would buy his new wife.[173] But a delicate glow was not what the Russian ladies aspired to. Samuel Collins, Tsar Aleksei Mikhailovich's personal physician, compared the mixture of rouge and Spanish cerise applied by Russian ladies to the consistency of the paint that the English used to protect their house pipes![174] Its heavy application often drew comment from foreign observers, though not all were as blunt as Peter Henry Bruce when he dismissed it as 'that preposterous custom of painting their faces'.[175] Several contemporaries compared this to the English fashion for beauty spots (or patches) – small pieces of silk or velvet used to cover skin blemishes on the face, the shoulders, the chest or the arms.[176] They became popular in Russia too, a means of attracting attention to a particular part of the wearer's body and, just as with fans, there was a 'language' to these beauty spots, whose names were linked to their location.[177] The popularity of their use can be seen in a mid-eighteenth-century woodcut engraving (*lubok*), which set out their various forms, names and meanings.[178]

The process of enforcing these reforms proved challenging. For practical reasons, there was little that the government could do when the local authorities in Siberia petitioned to keep their existing clothing, since they simply could not afford to obey the new laws.[179] On the other hand, an informant's assertion that noblewomen in Moscow were dressing in the traditional manner and laughing at ladies in 'German' dress was more serious, since such women were amongst the main targets of Peter's reforms and the names included in the letter – the wives of Petr Dolgorukii and Ivan Musin-Pushkin – were from leading noble families.[180] There were several reasons why the reforms took hold, despite the attendant discomfort and resentment. There was the usual Petrine blend of financial and physical coercion, along with an element of shame. Those who failed to comply with Peter's reforms faced the prospect of fines, such as the 'beard tax', at the very least and risked a physical assault from the Tsar, as in several cases involving reluctant members of the elite.[181] Kurakin recalled how officials would stand by the gates of Moscow to collect fines from those wearing old-style clothing – those who were unable to pay were humiliated by having their *kaftan* trimmed to an appropriate length on the spot.[182] Adherence to the new style of dress and grooming was also important because of the continued importance of proximity to the Tsar for those seeking to have influence at court or its patronage. During Peter's reign, the leading noble families were often willing to undergo the humiliation of shaving and dressing in a foreign manner to ensure that another family did not take their privileged position.[183]

As a result, there were visible signs of success by the 1720s, particularly amongst the younger women at court. Bergholz commented on the young Russian noblewomen that he encountered at court events, comparing them favourably with their French contemporaries in their demeanour and bearing.[184] Prominent members of the court were expected to aid this transition by ensuring that their children were dressed and tutored in the appropriate European manner. Members of the royal family were expected to participate as well. Thus, although Tsaritsa Praskov'ia Fedorovna was allowed to continue to dress in the old Muscovite manner, her three daughters (including future Empress Anna Ivanovna) dressed in German fashion 'in public', as noted by the Dutch artist Cornelius de Bruyn, who painted their portraits during his visit to Moscow in 1702.[185] Peter I's half-sister, Natal'ia Alekseevna, provides a useful example of the blend of traditional and 'new' elements in the lifestyle of a female member of the Russian elite. The inventory of her considerable collection of material possessions, compiled after her death in 1716, shows a sizeable collection of European clothing and accessories. She owned no less than eleven corsets, four *fontanges* and seven fans, as well as a large number of mirrors. This was no doubt aided by the generosity of her brother, Peter, who was believed to have given her an annual sum of 20,000 roubles. However, she also possessed a large number of icons and religious texts.[186]

The transition was never going to be as rapid or complete as Peter wanted, as demonstrated by the issuing of nine different *ukazy* on clothing and grooming during his reign and again, with specific reference to St Petersburg's inhabitants, under Catherine I.[187] However, by the end of Peter's reign, European-style dress and grooming was irrevocably established as the norm amongst the groups who had regular dealings with the ruler and the court in St Petersburg and Moscow. During the reigns that followed, there was a gradual refinement of male and female elite dress at court, as clothing styles began to more closely follow current European fashions. For example, Russian elite women quickly adopted the mantua, from the French *manteuil*, which was the dominant style of formal court dress at many courts in the late seventeenth century.[188] During Anna Ivanovna's reign, it was superseded by the *samara* – from the Dutch word *samaar* (dress) – which became the standard dress required for women attending court celebrations.[189] This style was based on the French *contouche* and consisted of a loose overdress with a pleated back that was worn over a corset and decorated underskirt, supported by a 'hoop'.[190] Later, it was replaced by the more refined and formal *robe à la française* (*roba* in Russian), with a more defined waistline, which became the dominant style of dress for formal court occasions during Elizabeth's reign.[191] From the mid-1740s, her court ladies were allowed to attend *kurtagi* in a variant of the informal style of morning dresses worn in England (referred to as *shlafroki*, from the German *schlafrock*).[192]

As the contemporary Rococo style began to make its presence felt in Russia, the colour palate of the court brightened, with female court dress increasingly using lighter, pastel shades – rose, light blue, pale green and yellow. Although male court dress still favoured darker colours, there were exceptions, like the flamboyant Danish envoy, Count Rochus Friedrich zu Lynar.[193] As with their contemporaries elsewhere in Europe, Russian court clothing was frequently embellished with silk embroidery, decorative buttons or gold and silver braid. Expensive accessories, like fans, snuff-boxes, watches and walking canes, became a regular feature of elite purchases. Elizabeth's court spent very large sums on these items, which were imported by both domestic and foreign merchants. For the years 1753 and 1754 alone, the total cost was around 230,000 rubles.[194] The Empress gave such items as gifts to members of her close circle, as reflected in the wedding inventories of several of her court ladies during this period.[195] Elizabeth also gave gifts of money that helped to pay off any requisite debts from the extravagant lifestyle at her court, as Catherine herself discovered on several occasions.[196] As at the contemporary German courts, the Russian court introduced sumptuary laws during this period in an attempt to curb such excesses.[197] Two such laws were issued in the early 1740s, but most of the evidence from Elizabeth's reign suggests that elite spending remained undeterred.[198]

Certain occasions required particular types of clothing, whether for occasional events, like major state celebrations – the royal weddings discussed in Chapter 3 – or regular entertainments, like the court masquerades discussed in Chapter 4. This period witnessed the formal adoption of court mourning as the Russian court marked the passing of members of fellow European dynasties, in accordance with protocol at other courts.[199] Elizabeth famously disliked the colour black, naturally associating it with death, but her court assiduously recorded and observed (with a few breaks) the appropriate mourning period for the leading royal deaths of the period. In 1751, for example, the court marked the deaths of the dowager Holy Roman Empress, Elisabeth Christine, Frederick I of Sweden, Frederick, Prince of Wales, and William IV, Prince of Orange.[200] Required dress also varied according to the court's location. Members of both the main court and the 'young' court of the Grand Duke and Duchess were given specific instructions about the required clothing, colour scheme and style which they were expected to wear when at Petergof and Oranienbaum during the summer months.[201]

Although appropriate dress was increasingly important at court during this period, there were still occasions when the ruler's taste trumped convention. During Elizabeth's reign, she held several cross-dressing masquerades (*metamorfozy*), where male participants wore female clothing and vice versa. By undermining the acceptable forms of dress, these events help to highlight the extent of the changes in appearance and the necessary skills needed to interact properly in the new social environment. These masquerades were first mentioned, briefly, in the official court journals during the court's stay in Moscow in 1744 and the transgender nature of the costumes worn for these events was made clear in these entries. Catherine, who attended these events shortly after arriving in Russia, noted in her *Mémoires* that Elizabeth only invited 'those whom she herself selected' – this was clearly not an entertainment that could be widely imposed.[202] The court then held these masquerades again in 1750, this time at its more usual residence in St Petersburg.[203] The description in the court journal provided a bit more detail on the required appearance of the male participants: 'large hoop skirts', dresses and feminine court hairstyles.[204]

Although the 15-year-old Catherine enjoyed these occasions, it was not a widespread feeling. She described how the court gentlemen strongly disliked them because they were ashamed of their appearance and unsure of how to manoeuvre in such unaccustomed clothing. Court ladies were only slightly better off, as the cut of their masculine clothing plainly did not suit them, with the older women described as having 'short, fat legs'.[205] Catherine mentioned an incident from one such masquerade when Countess Anna A. Gendrikova knocked her over while dancing so that she fell under Karl E. Sievers's 'hoop'. Although it is recounted as a humorous episode, it highlights the very real practical difficulty that both genders encountered in swapping their clothing, since the latter occupied a different space than they were accustomed to. The fact that this occurred when Catherine and Sievers were dancing a polonaise, in which the man usually takes the lead, can only have added to the confusion, since the gender roles had been effectively reversed. At their heart, these occasions were dominated by the central figure of Elizabeth, who apparently had the build (specifically, the legs) and the poise from her dance instruction to carry male dress convincingly.[206]

The 'cross-dressing' masquerades were an unusual occurrence at the Russian court and did not become a feature of their entertainments as a result. This type of activity was known, as it was a common part of masquerade culture elsewhere in Europe and a famous contemporary cross-dresser, the Chevalier d'Éon, was part of a French diplomatic mission to the court of St Petersburg in the 1750s.[207] But such gender reversal was very rare in Russian culture since, like its Latin counterparts, the Orthodox Church strongly disapproved of such deviant behaviour, which was linked to homosexuality and licentiousness.[208] The reversal of clothing also encapsulates some of the trials faced by successive generations of the Russian elite in adapting to the demands of their new physical and social environment at court, albeit in reverse. Men and women at the masquerades had to very quickly adapt to the new mode of dress and successfully negotiate its associated difficulties.

For women, this transition was certainly uncomfortable and embarrassing, but this paled in comparison to the prospect faced by their male counterparts, who had to learn how to walk, dance and otherwise conduct themselves in their wide dresses. In short, men were expected to learn the same difficult lessons as Russian women had done during the two preceding decades.

Overall, clothing provided a very visible sign of the process of change in Russian society during this period. European styles and accessories were initially introduced by state legislation but were soon assimilated by members of both the elite and other groups in urban society. A comparison has been drawn between the role of the new fashions in shaping the bodies of the Russian elite and the way in which St Petersburg's buildings and spaces were designed to regulate and embellish the city's appearance. This view also highlights the contemporary Russian practice of describing clothes as being 'built' (*stroit'*), rather than 'sewn'.[209] However, this change came at a cost. Prince Mikhail M. Shcherbatov, writing in the 1780s, described this period as responsible for the growth of excessive luxury at the Russian court and its harmful effects on morality, principally amongst the nobility. This development was explicitly linked to the impact of female rulers in Russia, since they did not have the self-discipline of Peter I. Clothing was clearly identified as a symbol of these problems, with the nobility forced to invest heavily in expensive clothing and accessories by the court.[210] Leaving aside the issue of Shcherbatov's conservative views on female monarchs, there is no denying the very large sums that the court and the elite spent on clothing and accessories during this period. Catherine II's more balanced approach, while no less magnificent in its appearance, was in keeping with the contemporary move toward restraining court expenditure in many states.[211]

By the early 1760s, the maturing development of the Russian court and its attendant elite was clearly visible. The reforms of the social and cultural milieu that Peter I had introduced, forcibly in many cases, were now a commonplace in noble lifestyle and were also a recognisable feature of life in St Petersburg, as they also were in Moscow and other large towns, for other social groups. This social phenomenon was founded on a blend of education and experience. New institutions were founded throughout this period, such as the Naval Academy and the Cadet Corps, to teach young people the requisite skills – academic, practical and sociable – to play a useful role in service to the state and at court. This development was complemented by the use of foreign tutors in the private household setting, a more traditional approach to elite education that was important for young women until the foundation of the Smol'nyi Institute. The introduction of conduct literature in Russian translation encouraged self-education and refinement, and also provided guidance on behaviour in the altered social setting at court and in everyday life. These skills were particularly important in the aftermath of the clothing and grooming reforms, which affected group interaction and interpersonal space. While the court actively promoted these processes as the leading exemplar and patron of such pursuits, it was their adoption by the members of the nobility and, increasingly during the second half of the century, by other urban social groups, that was crucial in ensuring their longevity.

Conclusion

There can be little doubt about the significance of St Petersburg's foundation in 1703. The city is a striking physical embodiment of one ruler's desire to create a 'new' city and then use it as a platform for other projects, be they commercial, naval or cultural. However, the city was barely two decades old when its founder died. Its subsequent rise to prominence, both within Russia and more importantly on the European (later world) stage, owed more to the continued efforts of his successors. The legacy of Peter I was of major symbolic importance – his interment at the heart of his creation, in the Sts Peter and Paul Cathedral in 1725, could hardly be more representative of this relationship. While the brief return to Moscow under the young Peter II threatened to relegate St Petersburg to a provincial port, Anna Ivanovna's symbolic return to the northern city in 1732 signalled the intention to cultivate St Petersburg as the principal court residence and her successors continued this process. The continued presence of the court and the elite revived St Petersburg's role as a testing ground for the 'Europeanisation' project in Russia from the 1730s onwards. This book has explored different aspects of Russia's relationship with the rest of Europe in this period through institutions and practices that were introduced in St Petersburg.

The city's creation, discussed in the first chapter, was a major undertaking, particularly in the difficult physical environment of the Baltic coast. Despite the various plans and regulations issued during the first decades of its existence, St Petersburg almost inevitably bore the marks of the rapid and patchy nature of its construction. The physical limitations of St Petersburg's appearance were arguably less significant than what the city had come to represent by the end of its founder's life in 1725. The deliberate creation and fostering of certain spaces within the city – from the palaces of the royal family and leading nobles to the shipyards of the Admiralty, from the creation of a new exemplary scientific institution to the promotion of St Petersburg as a site of established religious rituals – all reflected a mixture of traditional and new influences. Most significantly, the city was a physical embodiment of Russia's engagement with the rest of Europe, which largely set the tone

156

for this relationship over the course of the next 100 years. St Petersburg's appearance, its institutions, and its social and cultural life all bore relation to contemporary courts and cities elsewhere in Europe, but they were given a distinctive Russian flavour in this context.

The planning and construction of St Petersburg reflected the contemporary interest in regularity in states across Europe. The second chapter examined the application of these ideas to St Petersburg through the creation of a new institution, the Police Chancellery. This body was made responsible for the promotion of 'good order' through the attempt to regulate many aspects of the city's everyday life. Much of this police legislation dealt with similar areas of concern to their equivalents elsewhere in northern and central Europe, with an emphasis on safeguarding the health and safety of the city's population. Certain areas of regulation, like the attempts to limit excessive alcohol consumption or punish immoral behaviour, had precedents in the Russian context, although the setting of St Petersburg raised their profile, as with the prosecution of the 'Dresdensha' affair. Other areas of legislation, like gambling, were relatively new and owed something to the 'Europeanised' social life at court. The legislation makes clear the division between excessive or inappropriate behaviour and sociable pursuits with these new elements, as the latter were increasingly expected of the elite, but were only gradually spreading to other social groups.

The third chapter focused on another institution, the court, which played a crucial role in asserting St Petersburg's claims to legitimacy and, at the same time, was responding to a similar process of 'Europeanisation' as the city itself. The transfer of the court to St Petersburg, although piecemeal at first and only consolidated under Anna Ivanovna, was nevertheless an important statement about the city's status and intended role. From the 1730s onward, St Petersburg was the official *Residenz* of the Russian court and its attendant elite. As an institution, the Russian court gradually adopted offices, titles and practices drawn from the example of other contemporary European states. Its major celebrations similarly reflected an interest in observing and equalling, if not surpassing, the practices of other courts in terms of the appropriate form, expense and spectacle of these occasions. The Russian court's desire to engage with this courtly milieu can also be seen in the publication of commemorative volumes for major court occasions, which were then sent to embassies at other European courts. However, the Russian court retained a distinctive character and Orthodoxy continued to play a central role in its ritual culture, thereby ensuring a solid foundation for the other innovations. During this period, St Petersburg became a stage on which the court could present itself and its activities to both a domestic and international audience.

The fourth chapter looked at the spaces for sociable interaction created in St Petersburg by the court. The court again took the lead role in creating and fostering new sociable activities. This patronage initially restricted access to members of the elite, although there were exceptions during Peter I's reign, notably the assemblies. However, from the late 1740s, there was a conscious move to widen access to particular events ('public' masquerades and theatrical performances) and spaces (the opera house and the Summer Gardens) to the wider nobility and certain other groups in St Petersburg society. This access was still subject to certain strictures, principally relating to appearance and behaviour, but the desire for wider participation played an important role in developing the social life of the city. These events and the skilled personnel hired by the court, such as theatrical troupes and musicians, also led to the organisation of these forms of entertainment for a paying public from a number of different social backgrounds. As a result, by the 1760s, there were a number of well-established sociable forums in St Petersburg utilised by the court, the nobility and other selected social groups on a regular basis.

The final chapter stressed that the activities and appearance of the members of St Petersburg's elite reflected the 'Europeanisation' process in its most visible form; both in the introduction of new social spaces and the various elements required for participation in those spaces – European fashions and social skills, like dancing. These skills became an increasingly common part of education throughout this period and their message was reinforced by the introduction of conduct literature, which encouraged the reader to regulate their own behaviour. These areas were then enforced as the means for other social groups to access the social events that emerged toward the end of this period. The court played a leading role in shaping tastes and fashions within St Petersburg society. This influence was reflected in the purchase of the goods associated with a European elite, including clothes, wigs and other accessories, and the hiring of specialist service personnel for maintenance purposes, such as dressmakers, hair-stylists and a range of specialist craftsmen. This period was crucial in the consolidation of these trends at the Russian court and St Petersburg, as seat of the court and an important point of contact with the rest of Europe, acted as a stage on which these changes could be practised and highlighted.

The importance of these areas is reflected in their continuing significance in the years immediately following Elizabeth's death in 1761. The court played a key role as her successors sought to establish themselves in a position of authority and legitimacy. Peter III's rather dismissive attitude toward appropriate decorum at court ceremonies and his withdrawal into a clique of Holsteiner officers stood in stark contrast to his assiduous, devout and well-connected wife, Catherine. Following her seizure of power in 1762, Catherine ensured that all of the appropriate ceremonial trappings of power were present, with elaborate celebrations for her coronation in Moscow then followed by a triumphal return to St Petersburg.[1] Catherine was clear in her preference for St Petersburg to be the principal seat of her power, writing in her personal papers of her dislike for Moscow, and she immediately took steps to further promote its suitability as a ruling city. A new 'Commission for Masonry Construction' was established in late 1762 to oversee and extend the building programmes within the city. The existing police legislation was also extended to deal with a variety of ongoing concerns, such as fires, disease and vagrancy.[2] In both respects, St Petersburg served as an important model for the newly established provincial towns, later in Catherine's reign.[3]

Catherine also continued the established practice of using the court as a focal point for St Petersburg's vibrant social life, even if she ensured that she had an exclusive retreat, the Hermitage, within that sphere.[4] Paying audiences had a greater range of options in the second half of the eighteenth century as foreign entrepreneurs visited St Petersburg in increasing numbers.[5] The city also continued in its role as an important cultural centre, with Catherine and her court's patronage of the arts and literature combined with a new generation of writers, musicians and artists trained at Russian and foreign educational institutions.[6] One of Peter III's enduring legacies, the 'emancipation' of the nobility from compulsory service that was subsequently confirmed by Catherine, gave the nobility the freedom to undertake education and other opportunities, such as foreign travel. While the results were mixed at best, with some contemporaries scathing in their assessment of the ill-mannered and narrow-minded young nobles that 'benefited' from this experience, this was hardly unique to Russia.[7]

Russia enjoyed a much more established relationship with the rest of Europe than in the previous century. Russia's involvement in the alliance against Prussia in the Seven Years War reflected a recognition of its relevance in such a major continental conflict by Europe's leading powers. However, Russia's position remained a process of negotiation, rather than a generally accepted fact. In particular, its political nature and cultural diversity continued to be a source of considerable debate amongst the period's writers, including Montesquieu, Voltaire and Diderot.[8] However, Russia was contributing its own views in this debate, as scholars and writers in Russia began to explore the historical and ethnographical nature of their situation, relative to Europe and Asia.[9] The intended position was famously stated by Catherine II herself in her 'Instruction to the Legislative Commission' (*Nakaz*), subsequently published in French, German and Latin: 'Russia is a European state'.[10] The increasing number of foreign visitors to St Petersburg during the second half of the eighteenth century frequently commented positively on the city's development in such a short space of time, albeit a project still very much in progress.[11]

Returning to the comments made by Algarotti in the 1730s about St Petersburg's shortcomings, the English merchant Jonas Hanway noted similar characteristics in his account of 1753, but instead stressed the achievement that St Petersburg represents. 'St Petersburg, which was founded by Peter the Great in the beginning of this century, may at present be considered as the modern and polite metropolis, and the chief residence of the Russian empire; and though so lately a morass, it is now an elegant and superb city.'[12] In its first half-century of existence, St Petersburg had become the established seat of the Russian ruler's court and a recognised presence on the map of Europe. The next half-century would see it become Russia's largest city and the capital of one of Europe's leading military powers.

Notes

Introduction

1. Francesco Algarotti, *Letters from Count Algarotti to Lord Hervey and the Marquis Scipio Maffei...* (London, 1769), vol. 1, p. 70.
2. See, for example, Naum A. Sindalovskii, *Legendy i mify Sankt-Peterburga* (St Petersburg, 1994).
3. On Peter's presence, see Aleksandr M. Sharymov, *Predystoriia Sankt-Peterburga. 1703 god. Kniga issledovanii* (St Petersburg, 2004), pp. 520–41; more generally, see Saulo Kepsu, *Peterburg do Peterburga: istoriia ust'ia Nevy do osnovaniia goroda Petra* (St Petersburg, 2000).
4. Lev V. Pumpianskii, 'Mednyi vsadnik i poeticheskaia traditsiia XVIII veka', *Pushkin: Vremennik Pushkinskoi komissii*, 4–5 (1939), pp. 94–100.
5. A popular modern example is Robert Massie, *Peter the Great: His Life and World* (New York, 1981), which first introduced me to both the ruler and the period.
6. Unsurprisingly, Peter featured prominently in the debate between 'Westernisers' and 'Slavophiles' in the nineteenth century: Nicholas Riasanovsky, *Russian Identities: a Historical Survey* (Oxford, 2005), pp. 151–60.
7. For an overview of the Soviet stance on Peter, see Nicholas Riasanovsky, *The Image of Peter the Great in Russian History and Thought* (Oxford, 1985), pp. 234–302.
8. James Cracraft, *The Petrine Revolution in Russian Culture* (Cambridge, MA, 2004), pp. 1–12. One such critique of the Petrine reforms is presented in Evgenii V. Anisimov, *The Reforms of Peter the Great: Progress through Coercion in Russia*, transl. John Alexander (Armonk, NY, 1993).
9. Two exemplary studies are: Lindsey Hughes, *Russia in the Age of Peter the Great* (New Haven, CT, 1998) and Paul Bushkovitch, *Peter the Great: the Struggle for Power, 1671–1725* (Cambridge, 2001).
10. See, for example, Jarmo Kotilaine and Marshall Poe (eds), *Modernizing Muscovy: Reform and Social Change in Seventeenth-Century Russia* (London, 2005).
11. Michael Florinsky, *Russia: a History and an Interpretation* (London, 1953), vol. 1, p. 432.
12. Examples that remain relevant contributions on the period include: Alexander Lipski, 'A Re-Examination of the "Dark Era" of Anna Ioannovna', *American Slavic and East European Review*, 15 (1956), pp. 477–88 and Evgenii V. Anisimov, *Rossiia v seredine XVIII veka: bor'ba za nasledie Petra* (Moscow, 1986), published in English as *Empress Elizabeth: Her Reign and Her Russia, 1741–1761*, transl. John Alexander (Gulf Breeze, FL, 1995).
13. See, in particular, Igor' V. Kurukin, *Epokha 'dvorskikh bur': ocherki politicheskoi istorii poslepetrovskoi Rossii, 1725–1762 gg.* (Riazan', 2003).
14. Aleksandr B. Kamenskii, *The Russian Empire in the Eighteenth Century: Searching for a Place in the World*, ed. and transl. David Griffiths (Armonk, NY, 1997), pp. 128–9.
15. Robert Jones, 'Why St Petersburg?', in Lindsey Hughes (ed.), *Peter the Great and the West: New Perspectives* (Basingstoke, 2001), pp. 189–205.
16. James Cracraft, *The Revolution of Peter the Great* (Cambridge, MA, 2003), pp. 135–56.

17. On the Russian fascination with St Petersburg, see: Emily D. Johnson, *How St. Petersburg Learned to Study Itself: the Russian Idea of Kraevedenie* (University Park, PA, 2006).
18. See, for example, W. Bruce Lincoln, *Sunlight at Midnight: St Petersburg and the Rise of Modern Russia* (Oxford, 2001).
19. Riccardo Nicolosi, *Peterburgskii panegirik XVIII veka: mif – ideologiia – ritorika*, transl. M. N. Zharova (Moscow, 2009); Julie Buckler, *Mapping St. Petersburg: Imperial Text and Cityshape* (Princeton, NJ, 2005).
20. Petr N. Petrov, *Istoriia Sankt-Peterburga s osnovaniia goroda do vvedeniia v deistvie vybornogo gorodskogo upravleniia po uchrezhdeniiam o guberniiakh, 1703–1782* (St Petersburg, 1884).
21. Sergei P. Luppov, *Istoriia stroitel'stva Peterburga* (Moscow, 1957).
22. Ol'ga G. Ageeva, *'Velichaishii i slavneishii bolee vsekh gradov v svete' – grad sviatogo Petra: Peterburg v russkom obshchestvennom soznanii nachala XVIII veka* (St Petersburg, 1999); Evgenii V. Anisimov, *Iunyi grad: Peterburg vremen Petra Velilkogo* (St Petersburg, 2003).
23. Aleksandr A. Kizevetter, *Posadskie obshchina v Rossii XVIII stoletiia* (Moscow, 1903), p. 113.
24. Catherine II's policies toward the city are discussed extensively in George Munro, *The Most Intentional City: St. Petersburg in the Reign of Catherine the Great* (Madison Cranbury, NJ, 2008).
25. Peter Burke, 'Did Europe Exist before 1700?', *History of European Ideas*, 1 (1980), pp. 1–29.
26. J. G. A. Pocock, 'Some Europes in their History', in Anthony Pagden (ed.), *The Idea of Europe: From Antiquity to the European Union* (Cambridge, 2002), pp. 55–71.
27. Christian Raffensberger, *Reimagining Europe: Kievan Rus' in the Medieval World* (Cambridge, MA, 2012).
28. George Majeska, 'Rus' and the Byzantine Empire', in Abbot Gleason (ed.), *A Companion to Russian History* (Oxford, 2009), pp. 61–2.
29. Marshall Poe, *A People Born to Slavery: Russia in Early Modern European Ethnography, 1476–1748* (Ithaca, NY, 2000).
30. See, for example, Dmitrii Shvidkovsky, *Russian Architecture and the West* (New Haven, CT, 2007), pp. 73–104.
31. Samuel Baron, 'The Origins of Seventeenth-Century Moscow's Nemeckaja Sloboda', *California Slavic Studies*, 5 (1970), pp. 1–17.
32. Geoffrey Hosking, *Russia and the Russians* (Cambridge, MA, 2001), pp. 181–2.
33. W. H. Parker, 'Europe: How Far?', *The Geographical Journal*, 126/3 (1960), pp. 278–86.
34. Mark Bassin, 'Russia between Europe and Asia: the Ideological Construction of Geographical Space', *SR*, 50/1 (1991), pp. 6–7.
35. See the contributions by Wortman and Allman in Cynthia Whittaker (ed.), *Russia Engages the World, 1453–1825* (Cambridge, MA, 2003), pp. 91–117 and 139–61.
36. For example, on the debate surrounding 'modernisation' and the question of its applicability to eighteenth-century Russia, see Simon Dixon, *The Modernisation of Russia, 1676–1825* (Cambridge, 1999), pp. 1–24.
37. See, for example, the discussion on these issues between Raeff, de Madariaga and Cracraft in *SR*, 41/4 (1982), pp. 611–38.
38. Paul Bushkovitch, 'Cultural Change among the Russian Boyars, 1650–1680: New Sources and Old Problems', *Forschungen zur osteuropaischen Geschichte*, 56 (2000), pp. 92–94.

39. Cracraft, *Petrine Revolution in Russian Culture*, p. 308.
40. Norbert Elias, *The Court Society*, transl. Stephen Mennell (Dublin, 2006). For a useful overview of court historiography and a balanced critique of Elias's work on the court, see Jeroen Duindam, *Myths of Power: Norbert Elias and the Early Modern European Court* (Amsterdam, 1994).
41. An important collection that explores these questions is Ronald Asch and Adolf Birke (eds), *Princes, Patronage, and the Nobility: the Court at the Beginning of the Modern Age, c. 1450–1650* (Oxford, 1991).
42. See, for example, the essays presented in John Adamson (ed.), *The Princely Courts of Europe: Ritual, Politics and Culture under the Ancien Régime, 1500–1750* (London, 1999).
43. See, for example, Nikolai E. Volkov, *Dvor russkikh imperatorov v ego proshlom i nastoiashchem, v 4-kh chastiakh* (St Petersburg, 1900).
44. Simon Dixon, 'Catherine the Great and the Romanov Dynasty: the Case of the Grand Duchess Mariia Pavlovna (1854–1920)', in Roger Bartlett and Lindsey Hughes (eds), *Russian Society and Culture and the Long Eighteenth Century* (Münster, 2004), pp. 200–9.
45. A fundamental study on this area is Sergei M. Troitskii, *Finansovaia politika russkogo absoliutizma v XVIII veke* (Moscow, 1966).
46. For an excellent overview of some leading contributions, see Ernest Zitser, 'New Histories of the Late Muscovite and Early Imperial Russian Court', *Kritika: Explorations in Russian and Eurasian History*, 6/2 (2005), pp. 375–92.
47. See, for example, Paul Bushkovitch, *Religion and Society in Russia: the Sixteenth and Seventeenth Centuries* (Oxford, 1992); Isolde Thyret, *Between God and Tsar: Religious Symbolism and the Royal Women of Muscovite Russia* (DeKalb, IL, 2001); Elise Kimerling Wirtschafter, *Social Identity in Imperial Russia* (DeKalb, IL, 1997).
48. For example, a version of this view is expressed in Matthew Anderson, 'Peter the Great: Imperial Revolutionary?', in Arthur Dickens (ed.), *The Courts of Europe: Politics, Patronage and Royalty, 1400–1800* (London, 1977), pp. 263–81.
49. Elena Pogosian, *Petr I – arkhitektor rossiiskoi istorii* (St Petersburg, 2001).
50. Viktor M. Zhivov, 'Kul'turnye reformy v sisteme preobrazovanii Petra I', in A. D. Koshelev (ed.) *Iz istorii russkoi kul'tury* (Moscow, 1996), vol. 3, pp. 528–83; Ernest Zitser, *The Transfigured Kingdom: Sacred Parody and Charismatic Authority at the Court of Peter the Great* (Ithaca, NY, 2004).
51. Gary Marker, *Imperial Saint: the Cult of St Catherine and the Dawn of Female Rule in Russia* (DeKalb, IL, 2007).
52. Ol'ga G. Ageeva, *Evropeizatsiia russkogo dvora, 1700–1796 gg.* (Moscow, 2006).
53. Ol'ga G. Ageeva, *Imperatorskii dvor Rossii, 1700–1796 gody* (Moscow, 2008).
54. Konstantin A. Pisarenko, *Povsednevnaia zhizn' russkogo dvora v tsarstvovanie Elizavety Petrovny* (Moscow, 2003).
55. See, for example, John Alexander, 'Petersburg and Moscow in Early Urban Policy', *Journal of Urban History*, 8/2 (1982), pp. 146–8.
56. Peter Wilson, *Absolutism in Central Europe* (London, 2000), pp. 65–6.
57. The classic, if idiosyncratic, treatment of this subject is: Lewis Mumford, *The Culture of Cities* (London, 1938), Chapter 2, esp. pp. 78–82 and 108–13.
58. See, for example, Kurt Andermann (ed.), *Residenz – Aspekte hauptstädtischer Zentralität von der frühen Neuzeit bis zum Ende der Monarchie* (Sigmaringen, 1992).
59. Mia Rodríguez-Salgado, 'The Court of Philip II of Spain', in Asch and Birke (eds), *Princes*, pp. 207–44.

60. T. C. W. Blanning, *The Culture of Power and the Power of Culture* (Oxford, 2002), pp. 29–33.
61. John Spielman, *The City and Crown: Vienna and the Imperial Court, 1600–1740* (West Lafayette, IN, 1992).
62. Thomas DaCosta Kauffmann, *Court, Cloister, and City: the Art and Culture of Central Europe, 1450–1800* (Chicago, IL, 1995), pp. 270–9.
63. For a useful overview, see Joachim Whaley, *Germany and the Holy Roman Empire* (Oxford, 2012), vol. 2, pp. 228–9.
64. Samuel Klingensmith, *The Utility of Splendor: Ceremony, Social Life, and Architecture At the Court of Bavaria, 1600–1800* (Chicago, IL, 1993), pp. 19–64; Helen Watanabe-O'Kelly, *Court Culture in Dresden: From Renaissance to Baroque* (Basingstoke, 2002), pp. 193–212.
65. Karin Friedrich and Sara Smart (eds), *The Cultivation of Monarchy and the Rise of Berlin: Brandenburg-Prussia, 1700* (Farnham, 2010); Christopher Clark, *Iron Kingdom: the Rise and Downfall of Prussia, 1600–1947* (London, 2007), pp. 67–114.
66. Anisimov, *Iunyi grad*, pp. 71–2.
67. See, for example, Mikhail M. Shcherbatov, 'Proshenie Moskvy o zabvenii eia', in Konstantin G. Isupov (comp.), *Moskva-Peterburg: pro et contra* (St Petersburg, 2000), pp. 81–7.
68. James Cracraft, *The Petrine Revolution in Russian Architecture* (Chicago, IL, 1988), pp. 111–31.
69. Dixon, *Modernisation*, p. 170.
70. Aleksandr V. Postnikov, *Russia in Maps: a History of the Geographical Study and Cartography of the Country* (Moscow, 1996), pp. 42–9.
71. Algarotti, *Letters*, pp. 76–7.

1   Location: Situating the City

1. For one such view, see Friedrich Christian Weber, *The Present State of Russia* (London, 1968), vol. 1, p. 190. More critical views are discussed in Maria di Salvo, 'A Venice of the North? Italian Views of St Petersburg', in Anthony Cross (ed.), *St Petersburg, 1703–1825* (Basingstoke, 2004), pp. 71–9.
2. See, for example, Charles Whitworth, *An Account of Russia as it was in the Year 1710* (London, 1758), p. 126.
3. Iurii A. Egorov, *The Architectural Planning of St. Petersburg*, transl. Eric Dluhosch (Athens, GA, 1969), pp. 23–5.
4. Lindsey Hughes, 'Western European Graphic Material as a Source for Moscow Baroque Architecture', *SEER*, 55/4 (1977), pp. 433–43.
5. James Cracraft, *The Petrine Revolution in Russian Architecture* (Chicago, IL, 1988), pp. 150–2.
6. Sergei P. Luppov, *Istoriia stroitel'stva Peterburga* (Moscow, 1957), pp. 62–6.
7. Cracraft, *Petrine Revolution in Russian Architecture*, p. 175, fn. 77.
8. 'Letter to Fedor M. Apraksin, 27 June 1709', *PiBIPV*, vol. 9, part 1, p. 231.
9. Cracraft, *Petrine Revolution in Russian Architecture*, pp. 158–9.
10. These sketches are reproduced in: Irina I. Lisaevich, *Pervyi arkhitektor Peterburga* (Leningrad, 1971), p. 48.
11. *PSZ*, 5, 2850 (12 October 1714), pp. 126–7.
12. *PSZ*, 4, 2540 (6 June 1712), pp. 840–1.
13. *PSZ*, 5, 2748 (4 December 1713), p. 74.

14. Lindsey Hughes, *Russia in the Age of Peter the Great* (New Haven, CT, 1998), pp. 215–17.
15. Friedrich W. von Bergholz, 'Dnevnik kamer-iunkera Fridrikha-Vil'gel'ma Berkhgol'tsa, 1721–1725 (ch. 3 and 4)', in Viktor P. Naumov (ed.), *Iunost' derzhavy* (Moscow, 2000), p. 272.
16. Sir Francis Dashwood, 'Sir Francis Dashwood's Diary of his Visit to St Petersburg in 1733', ed. Betty Kemp, *SEER*, 38 (1959), pp. 202 and 206.
17. *PSZ*, 10, 7323, (10 July 1737), pp. 216–17.
18. 'Petr Eropkin', *Zodchie Sankt-Peterburga. XVIII vek* (St Petersburg, 1997), pp. 156–90.
19. Although this work was influential in the period after Eropkin's death – it was completed by Eropkin's colleagues Mikhail Zemtsov and Ivan Korobov, who then promoted it during the reign of Elizabeth – it remained unpublished until appearing in *Arkhitekturnyi arkhiv*, 1 (Moscow, 1946), pp. 21–100.
20. An overview of these plans can be found in: Sergei V. Sementsov et al., *Sankt-Peterburg na kartakh i planakh pervoi poloviny XVIII veka* (St Petersburg, 2004), pp. 186–7.
21. Konstantin V. Malinovskii, *Sankt-Peterburg XVIII veka* (St Petersburg, 2008), pp. 310–16.
22. Sementsov et al., *Sankt-Peterburg*, pp. 190–1.
23. Petr N. Petrov, *Istoriia Sankt-Peterburga s osnovaniia goroda do vvedeniia v deistvie vybornogo gorodskogo upravleniia po uchrezhdeniiam o guberniiakh: 1703–1782* (St Petersburg, 1884), pp. 57–61.
24. Mikhail V. Klochkov, *Naselenie Rossii pri Petre Velikom po perepisiam togo vremeni* (St Petersburg, 1911), pp. 141–9.
25. For the various accounts of foreign visitors to St Petersburg during Peter I's reign and the number of deaths they give for the city's construction, see the excellent overview provided in the notes for the Russian translation of Sir Francis Dashwood's diary in: Iurii N. Bespiatykh (ed.), *Peterburg Anny Ioannovny v inostrannykh opisaniiakh* (St Petersburg, 1997), pp. 73–4. For example, by the time of Dashwood's visit in 1733, the rumoured figure had risen to 300,000 (!) deaths: Dashwood, 'Diary', p. 203.
26. Luppov, *Istoriia*, p. 94.
27. For a detailed discussion of the subject, see Ol'ga G. Ageeva, '*Velichaishii i slavneishii bolee vsekh gradov v svete' – grad sviatogo Petra: Peterburg v russkom obshchestvennom soznanii nachala XVIII veka* (St Petersburg, 1999), pp. 78–81 and Evgenii V. Anisimov, *Iunyi grad: Peterburg vremen Petra Velilkogo* (St Petersburg, 2003), pp. 105–11.
28. Luppov, *Istoriia*, p. 23.
29. *SIRIO*, vol. 61, pp. 205–6 (Whitworth to St-John: St Petersburg, 26 May 1712).
30. Hughes, *Russia*, p. 215.
31. Luppov, *Istoriia*, pp. 25–6.
32. *PSZ*, 7, 4405 (5 January 1724), pp. 196–7.
33. Hughes, *Russia*, pp. 175–6.
34. Weber, *Present State*, vol. 1, p. 191.
35. Dashwood, 'Diary', p. 205.
36. Robert E. Jones, 'Getting the Goods to St. Petersburg: Water Transport from the Interior, 1703–1811', *SR*, vol. 43 (1984), pp. 413–17.
37. *PSZ*, 5, 3339 (23 March 1719), pp. 686–87.
38. Svetlana R. Dolgova, '"... ekhat' i perepisat' imianno bez medleniia": Pervye zhiteli Peterburga. 1717 g.', *Istoricheskii arkhiv*, 2 (2003), pp. 7–20.

39. Ageeva, *"Velichaishii"*, pp. 113–15.
40. Lidiia N. Semenova, *Byt i naselenie Sankt-Peterburga (XVIII vek)* (St Petersburg, 1998), pp. 6–7.
41. *RGADA*, f. 16, d. 459, ll. 1–4 ('O chisle zhitelei v Peterburge', 6 July 1750).
42. *RGADA*, f. 16, d. 459, ll. 5–5ob (18 July 1750).
43. *RGADA*, f. 16, d. 459, l. 11 (n.d.).
44. Johann G. Georgi, *Opisanie rossiisko-imperatorskogo stolichnogo goroda Sankt Peterburga i dostopamiatnostei v okrestnostiakh onogo* (St Petersburg, 1794), vol. 1, p. 168.
45. Munro, *Most Intentional City*, pp. 49–51.
46. All figures are taken from: Jan de Vries, *European Urbanization, 1500–1800* (Cambridge, MA, 1984), pp. 270–8.
47. Hughes, *Russia*, p. 265.
48. *PSZ*, 5, 3193 (12 April 1712), pp. 559–60.
49. A subsequent report from 1 September indicates that fines were collected from Admiral Fedor M. Apraksin, Iakov Bruce and Cornelius Cruys: *SIRIO*, vol. 11, pp. 519–21 ('Ukazy, pis'ma, bumagi i rezoliutsii imperatora Petra I').
50. Mikhail S. Bunin, *Mosty Leningrada: ocherki istorii i arkhitektury mostov Peterburga – Petrograda – Leningrada* (Leningrad, 1986), pp. 10–11.
51. Andrei I. Bogdanov, *Opisanie Sanktpeterburga, 1749–1751* (St Petersburg, 1997), p. 259.
52. Dashwood, 'Diary', p. 203. These establishments will be discussed in Chapter 3.
53. *Ob"iavlenie nyneshnego triumfalnogo vkhoda, ego tsarskago velichestva v Sankt Piterburkh* (St Petersburg, 1714). The event was also commemorated in an engraving by Aleksei Zubov, produced the following year.
54. *PoZh*, 1714 (9 September), p. 47. A brief description of events is also provided in Weber, *Present State*, vol. 1, pp. 35–40.
55. *PoZh*, 1720 (8 September), p. 50. Zubov again commemorated the event in an engraving, albeit later in the 1720s (the exact date is not confirmed). It is rather more detailed than the one produced for Hangöudd, depicting the triumphal procession route from the river to the Sts Peter and Paul Fortress. Both of the aforementioned images are reproduced in: Mikhail S. Lebedianskii, *Graver Petrovskoi epokhi Aleksei Zubov* (Moscow, 1973).
56. Hughes, *Russia*, p. 255.
57. *KfZh*, 1737, p. 23–5 (13 and 21 June).
58. Simon Dixon, '30 July 1752: the Opening of the Peter the Great Canal', in Anthony Cross (ed.), *Days from the Reigns of Eighteenth-Century Russian Rulers* (Cambridge, 2007), vol. 1, pp. 93–108.
59. See, for example, the following entries in the court journals for 1745, wherein river transport is used: *KfZh*, 1745, pp. 37 (24 July), 43 (26 July), 84–92 (30 August), 155 (26 May) and 158–9 (1 and 3 June).
60. 'Letter to Tikhon N. Streshnev, 24/25 March 1704', *PiBIPV*, vol. 3, p. 42.
61. Anisimov, *Iunyi grad*, p. 242.
62. For details on the design and construction of the grotto, see Tat'iana B. Dubiago, *Russkie reguliarnye sady i parki* (Leningrad, 1963), p. 71.
63. Semenova, *Byt i naselenie*, pp. 145–7.
64. See, for example, Friedrich W. von Bergholz, 'Dnevnik kamer-iunkera Fridrikha-Vil'gel'ma Berkhgol'tsa, 1721–1725 (ch. 1 and 2)', in Viktor P. Naumov (ed.), *Neistovyi reformator* (Moscow, 2000), pp. 135–42.

65. Erik Jong, *Nature and Art: Dutch Garden and Landscape Architecture, 1650–1740* (Philadelphia, PA, 2000), p. 18.
66. Hughes, *Russia*, p. 218.
67. Grigorii Kaganov, '"As in the Ship of Peter"', *SR*, 50 (1991), pp. 762–4.
68. Grigorii Kaganov, *Sankt-Peterburg: Obrazy prostranstva* (Moscow, 1995), pp. 22–5.
69. The engravings are beautifully reproduced in: Galina N. Komelova, *Vidy Peterburga i ego okrestnostei serediny XVIII veka. Graviury po risunkam M. Makhaeva* (Leningrad, 1968).
70. Petr N. Stolpianskii, *Peterburg: kak voznik, osnovalsia i ros Sankt-Piterburkh* (St Petersburg, 1995), pp. 173–4.
71. Semenova, *Byt i naselenie*, pp. 141–2.
72. Ageeva, 'Velichaishii', pp. 230–1.
73. Carolyn Pouncy, *The 'Domostroi': Rules for Russian Households in the time of Ivan the Terrible* (Ithaca, NY, 1994), pp. 84–5, 132–3 and 138–9.
74. Ol'ga G. Ageeva, 'Assamblei petrovskogo vremeni v russkoi dorevoliutsionnoi istoriografii', in Lev N. Pushkarev et al. (eds), *Istoriograficheskie i istoricheskie problemy russkoi kultury: sbornik statei* (Moscow, 1983), pp. 47–8.
75. On the origins of the term, see James Cracraft, *The Petrine Revolution in Russian Culture* (Cambridge, MA, 2004), p. 433.
76. Lidiia N. Semenova, *Ocherki istorii byta i kul'turnoi zhizni Rossii: pervaia polovina XVIII v.* (Leningrad, 1982), p. 200.
77. *PSZ*, 5, 3246 (26 November 1718), pp. 597–8.
78. Hughes, *Russia*, pp. 268–9.
79. Bergholz, 'Dnevnik', 'Neistovyi reformator', pp. 337–9.
80. Nikolai I. Pavlenko, *Ekaterina I* (Moscow, 2004), p. 64.
81. Max Vasmer, *Etimologicheskii slovar' russkogo iazyka*, ed. Boris A. Larin, transl. Oleg N. Trubachev (Moscow, 1986), vol. 2, p. 429.
82. Viktor I. Buganov, 'Ekaterina I', *Voprosy istorii*, 11 (1994), p. 48.
83. *SIRIO*, vol. 3, p. 439 (Lefort to Augustus II: St Petersburg, 25 May 1726).
84. Bergholz, 'Dnevnik', *Iunost' derzhavy*, p. 251.
85. Jane Vigor, *Letters From a Lady, Who Resided Some Years in Russia, to Her Friend in England* (London, 1775), pp. 71–5.
86. Karl Reinhold Berch, 'Putevye zametki o Rossii', in Bespiatykh (ed.), *Peterburg Anny Ioannovny*, p. 166.
87. *PSZ*, 8, 5963 (18 February 1732), p. 632; *PSZ*, 13, 9951 (3 March 1752), p. 611.
88. Richard Wortman, *Scenarios of Power: Myth and Ceremony in Russian Monarchy* (Princeton, NJ, 1995), vol. 1, p. 70.
89. *Slovar' russkogo iazyka XVIII veka* (St Petersburg, 1984–), vol. 8, p. 212.
90. RGIA, f. 1329, op. 2, d. 40, l. 42 (Order from the Empress's Cabinet to the Police Chancellery).
91. See, for example, the listing in the court journal for a *kurtag* in March 1756 – *KFZh*, 1756, pp. 24–5 (10 March) – and an example of a typical notification sent to the Police Chancellery from the following month – RGIA, f. 1329, op. 2, d. 48, l. 12 (Order sent by *Kamer-fur'er* Ivan Skobeltsyn to the Police Chancellery, 15 April 1756).
92. See, for example, the order noted in the sentry logs for 4 June 1750: *ZhDGA*, p. 205.
93. Nikolai N. Petrukhintsev, 'Stanovlenie Kadetskogo korpusa pri Anne Ioannovne, 1731–1741 gg.', *Trudy Gosudarstvennogo Ermitazha. Tom XXXVII. Pervyi Kadetskii Korpus vo dvortse Menshikova: K 275-letiiu osnovanie* (St Petersburg, 2007), pp. 132–44.

94. For this correspondence, see: V. Ger'e (ed.), *Sbornik pisem i memorialov Leibnitsa, otnosiashchkhsia k Rossii i Petru Velikomu* (St Petersburg, 1873).
95. James E. McClellan, *Science Reorganized: Scientific Societies in the Eighteenth Century* (New York, 1985).
96. See, for example, the views of: Petr P. Pekarskii, *Istoriia Imperatorskoi Akademii Nauk v Peterburge* (St Petersburg, 1870), vol. 1, pp. xvii–xxxi; Alexander Vucinich, *Science in Russian Culture* (London, 1965), vol. 1, pp. 65–74.
97. Simon Werrett, *Fireworks: Pyrotechnic Arts and Sciences in European History* (Chicago, IL, 2010), pp. 109–10.
98. *PSZ*, 7, 4443 (28 January 1724), pp. 220–4.
99. Michael Gordin, 'The Importance of Being Earnest: the Early St Petersburg Academy of Sciences', *Isis*, 91 (2000), pp. 15–16.
100. *PSZ*, 7, 4443 (28 January 1724), p. 223.
101. Gary Marker, *Publishing, Printing, and the Origins of Intellectual Life in Russia, 1700–1800* (Princeton, NJ, 1985), p. 46.
102. On the successes and failures of these two subsidiary bodies, see Ludmilla Schulze, 'The Russification of the St Petersburg Academy of Sciences and Arts in the Eighteenth Century', *British Journal for the History of Science*, 18 (1985), pp. 310–11.
103. N. I. Nevskaia (ed.), *Letopis' Rossiiskoi Akademii Nauk. Tom I: 1724–1802* (St Petersburg, 2000), p. 43.
104. *Protokoly zasedanii konferentsii Imperatorkoi Akademii nauk s 1725 po 1803 goda* (St Petersburg, 1897), vol. 1, p. 1–2.
105. Details of his election can be found in: John Appleby, 'James Spilman, F.R.S. (1680–1763), and Anglo-Russian Commerce', *Notes and Records of the Royal Society of London*, 48 (1994), pp. 17–29.
106. The speeches were printed in: *Sermones in primo solenni Academiae scientiarum imperialis conventu die XXVII decembris anni 1725 publice recitati* (St Petersburg, 1725).
107. *Protokoly*, vol. 1, p. 5.
108. Simon Werrett, *Fireworks: Pyrotechnic Arts and Sciences in European History* (Chicago, IL, 2010), p. 111.
109. Nevskaia (ed.), *Letopis'*, pp. 111 and 367.
110. 500 copies of this volume were printed: *SK*, vol. 3, p. 231.
111. *SK*, vol. 3, p. 232. For an example of their coverage of the public assemblies, see: *SPV*, 1755, no. 73 (12 September), p. 5.
112. *MIIAN*, vol. 6, pp. 105–8 and 155.
113. Petr P. Pekarskii, *Nauka i literatura v Rossii pri Petre Velikom* (St Petersburg, 1862), vol. 1, pp. 46–58.
114. Thomas DaCosta Kaufmann, *Court, Cloister, and City: the Art and Culture of Central Europe, 1450–1800* (Chicago, IL, 1995), pp. 167–83.
115. Beket Bukovinska, 'The *Kunstkammer* of Rudolph II', in Eliška Fučíková (ed.), *Rudolph II and Prague: the Court and the City* (London, 1997), pp. 199–208.
116. Helen Watanabe-O'Kelly, *Court Culture in Dresden: From Renaissance to Baroque* (Basingstoke, 2002), pp. 212–20.
117. Oleg Neverov, '"His Majesty's Cabinet" and Peter I's Kunstkammer', in Oliver Impey and Arthur McGregor (ed.), *The Origins of Museums: the Cabinet of Curiosities in Sixteenth- and Seventeenth-Century Europe* (Oxford, 1985), pp. 54–61.

118. Anthony Anemone, 'The Monsters of Peter the Great: the Culture of the St Petersburg *Kunstkamera* in the Eighteenth Century', *Slavic and East European Journal*, 44 (2000), p. 586.
119. The Globe was a gift to the Tsar from Karl Friedrich, Duke of Holstein-Gottorp. On its arduous journey to Russia, see: Bergholz, 'Dnevnik', *Neistovyi reformator*, pp. 207–8.
120. *PSZ*, 5, 3159 (13 February 1718).
121. Anemone, 'Monsters', pp. 588–90.
122. Jakob von Stählin, *Original Anecdotes of Peter the Great* (London, 1788), pp. 94–7.
123. Sergei P. Luppov and M. S. Fillipov (eds), *Istoriia Biblioteki Akademii nauk SSSR, 1714–1964* (Leningrad, 1964), pp. 15–16.
124. I. N. Lebedeva, 'Leib-medik Petra I i Robert Areskin i ego biblioteka', in Sergei P. Luppov and Boris B. Piotrovskii (eds), *Russkie biblioteki i ikh chitatel'* (Leningrad, 1983), pp. 98–105.
125. Luppov and Fillipov, *Istoriia Biblioteki Akademii nauk*, p. 31.
126. Johann D. Schumacher, *Palaty Sanktpeterburgskoi imperatorskoi Akademii nauk biblioteki i kunstkamery* (St Petersburg, 1741).
127. For a very comprehensive study of these catalogues and their meanings, see: Barbara Balsiger, 'The *Kunst- und Wunderkammern*: a catalogue raisonné of collecting in Germany, France and England, 1565–1750', unpublished PhD thesis (Pittsburgh, PA, 1970).
128. See, for example, Aubry de la Mottraye, *Travels through Europe, Asia, and into part of Africa...* (London, 1732), vol. 3, pp. 174–6; Peder von Haven, 'Puteshestvie v Rossiiu', in Bespiatykh (ed.), *Peterburg Anny Ioannovny*, p. 356; Dashwood, 'Diary', p. 205; Berch, 'Putevye zametki', pp. 177–97.
129. Simon Dixon, 'Religious Ritual at the Eighteenth-Century Russian Court', in Michael Schaich (ed.), *Monarchy and Religion: the Transformation of Royal Culture on Eighteenth-Century Europe* (Oxford, 2007), pp. 217–48.
130. Ernest Zitser, *The Transfigured Kingdom: Sacred Parody and Charismatic Authority at the Court of Peter the Great* (Ithaca, NY, 2004), pp. 12–15.
131. Anatolii I. Mazaev, *Prazdnik kak sotsial'no-khudozhestvennoe iavlenie: opyt istoriko-teoreticheskogo issledovaniia* (Moscow, 1978), p. 106.
132. Elena E. Keller, *Prazdnichnaia kul'tura Peterburga: ocherki istorii* (St Petersburg, 2001), pp. 41 and 51–2.
133. Kaganov, *Sankt-Peterburg*, pp. 34–5.
134. Martha Pollak, *Cities at War in Early Modern Europe* (Cambridge, 2010), pp. 244–65.
135. Dmitrii D. Zelov, *Ofitsial'nye svetskie prazdniki kak iavlenie russkoi kul'tury kontsa XVII - pervoi poloviny XVIII veka* (Moscow, 2002), pp. 132–3 and 259–64.
136. Keller, *Prazdnichnaia kul'tura*, p. 58.
137. Peter Burke, *Popular Culture in Early Modern Europe*, 3rd ed. (Farnham, 2009), p. 261.
138. Details of the city's various churches for this period can be found in Bogdanov, *Opisanie*, pp. 292–308 (for Orthodox) and 315–16 (for non-Orthodox).
139. Irina A. Chudinova, *Penie, zvony, ritual* (St Petersburg, 1994), pp. 27–36.
140. 'Reliatsiia o zakliuchenii mira so Shvetsii... 30 October 1721', in Nikolai A. Voskresenskii, *Zakonodatel'nye akty Petra I* (Moscow–Leningrad, 1945), vol. 1, pp. 157–62.
141. Bogdanov, *Opisanie*, p. 302.
142. Dixon, 'Religious Ritual', pp. 222–3.

2 Regulation: Policing the City

1. Marc Raeff, *The Well-Ordered Police State: Social and Institutional Change through Law in the Germanies and Russia, 1600–1800* (New Haven, CT, 1983), p. 5.
2. Evgenii V. Anisimov, *The Reforms of Peter the Great: Progress through Coercion in Russia*, transl. John Alexander (Armonk, NY, 1993), p. 217.
3. Ol'ga E. Kosheleva, *Liudi Sankt-Peterburgskogo ostrova petrovskogo vremeni* (Moscow, 2004).
4. A classic presentation of this argument is Vasilii O. Kliuchevskii, *Peter the Great*, transl. Liliana Archibald (London, 1968), pp. 57, 84 and 157.
5. Joachim Whaley, *Germany and the Holy Roman Empire* (Oxford, 2012), vol. 1, pp. 386 and 493.
6. Thomas Munck, *Seventeenth-Century Europe: State, Conflict and the Social Order in Europe, 1598–1700* (Basingstoke, 1990), pp. 349–50.
7. Christopher Clark, *Iron Kingdom: the Rise and Downfall of Prussia, 1600–1947* (London, 2007), pp. 38–66.
8. Marc Raeff, 'The Well-Ordered Police State and the Development of Modernity in Seventeenth- and Eighteenth-Century Europe: An Attempt at a Comparative Approach', *American Historical Review*, 80 (1975), pp. 1223–4. On the 'fiscal-military state', see Christopher Storrs (ed.), *The Fiscal-Military State in Eighteenth-Century Europe: Essays in Honour of P. G. M. Dickson* (Farnham, 2009).
9. Raeff, *Well-Ordered Police State*, pp. 188–94.
10. Lars Behrisch, 'Social Discipline in Early Modern Russia, Seventeenth to Nineteenth Centuries', in Heinz Schilling (ed.), *Institutionen, Instrumente und Akteure sozialer Kontrolle und Disziplinierung im frühneuzeitlichen Europa* (Frankfurt am Main, 1999), p. 325.
11. Peter Wilson, *Absolutism in Central Europe* (London, 2000), pp. 100–5. For a more cynical take on the intentions of the Cameralists, see Andre Wakefield, *The Disordered Police State: German Cameralism as Science and Practice* (Chicago, IL, 2009), pp. 1–25.
12. Behrisch, 'Social Discipline', pp. 338–9.
13. James Cracraft, *The Church Reform of Peter the Great* (London, 1971).
14. Anisimov, *Reforms*, p. 217.
15. For example, the Swedish model was an influence on the central administrative reforms: see Claes Peterson, *Peter the Great's Administrative and Judicial Reforms: Swedish Antecedents and the Process of Reception* (Stockholm, 1979), pp. 67–76.
16. Keith Tribe, 'Cameralism and the Science of Government', *Journal of Modern History*, 56 (1984), pp. 263–84; Raeff, *Well-Ordered Police State*, pp. 222–46.
17. Anisimov, *Reforms*, pp. 225–6.
18. Sergei M. Troitskii, *Finansovaia politika russkogo absoliutizma v XVIII veke* (Moscow, 1966), pp. 114–44.
19. James Cracraft, *The Petrine Revolution in Russian Culture* (Cambridge, MA, 2004), pp. 157–63.
20. *PSZ*, 5, 3006 (30 March 1716), pp. 203–453; *PSZ*, 6, 3485 (13 January 1720), pp. 2–116.
21. *PSZ*, 6, 3534 (28 February 1720), pp. 141–60.
22. *PSZ*, 6, 3890 (24 January 1722), pp. 486–93. On the drafting and implementation of this reform, see: Sergei M. Troitskii, *Russkii absoliutizm i dvorianstvo v XVIII v.: formirovanie biurokratii* (Moscow, 1974), pp. 47–140.
23. Lindsey Hughes, *Russia in the Age of Peter the Great* (New Haven, CT, 1998), p. 181.

24. James Hassell, 'Implementation of the Russian Table of Ranks during the Eighteenth Century', *SR*, 29/2 (1970), p. 283.
25. Raeff, 'Well-Ordered Police State', pp. 1231–3.
26. *PSZ*, 6, 3890 (24 January 1722), p. 490.
27. Brenda Meehan-Waters, *Autocracy and Aristocracy: the Russian Service Elite of 1730* (New Brunswick, NJ, 1982), pp. 37–48.
28. John LeDonne, *Absolutism and Ruling Class: the Formation of the Russian Political Order, 1700–1825* (Oxford, 1991), pp. 19–21.
29. See, for example, C. B. A. Behrens, *Society, Government and the Enlightenment: the Experiences of Eighteenth-Century France and Prussia* (London, 1985), pp. 47–67.
30. Raeff, 'Well-Ordered Police State', p. 1238.
31. *PSZ*, 1, (6 April 1649), pp. 164–6.
32. *PSZ*, 3, 1181 (19 March 1686), pp. 760–6.
33. *PSZ*, 5, 3203 (25 May 1718), pp. 569–70.
34. *PSZ*, 5, 3203 (25 May 1718), pp. 570–1.
35. *PSZ*, 5, 3420 (31 August 1719), p. 732.
36. For more detail, see Alan Williams, *The Police of Paris, 1718–1789* (Baton Rouge, LA, 1979).
37. William Rougle, 'António Manuel de Vieira and the Russian Court, 1697–1745', in Roger Bartlett, Anthony Cross and Karen Rasmussen (eds), *Russia and the World of the Eighteenth Century* (Bloomington, IN, 1988), pp. 577–90.
38. *PSZ*, 12, 9219 (21 October 1745), p. 472; *PSZ*, 12, 9283 (1 May 1746), p. 545.
39. Ol'ga E. Kosheleva, *Liudi Sankt-Peterburgskogo ostrova petrovskogo vremeni* (Moscow, 2004), p. 45.
40. Ivan K. Kirilov, *Tsvetushchee sostoianie vserossiiskogo gosudarstva*, ed. Boris A. Rybakov, Leonid A. Gol'denberg, and Sergei M. Troitskii (Moscow, 1977), p. 44.
41. *PSZ*, 8, 6190 (22 September 1732), p. 930.
42. *PSZ*, 6, 3494 (24 January 1720), p. 121.
43. Kosheleva, *Liudi*, pp. 44–5.
44. *PSZ*, 6, 3777 (29 April 1721), p. 381.
45. See, for example, *PSZ*, 3, 1420 (22 November 1691), p. 116–17.
46. Hughes, *Russia*, p. 164.
47. *PSZ*, 6, 3676 (16 November 1720), p. 264.
48. Feofan Prokopovich, *The Spiritual Regulation of Peter the Great*, ed. and transl. Alexander Muller (Seattle, WA, 1972), pp. 54–5.
49. *PSZ*, 13, 10095 (29 April 1753), pp. 828–9.
50. Friedrich Christian Weber, *The Present State of Russia* (London, 1968) vol. 1, pp. 128 and 277–8.
51. Whaley, *Germany and the Holy Roman Empire*, vol. 2, pp. 260–1.
52. *The Russian Primary Chronicle*, transl. Samuel Cross and Olgerd Shobowitz-Wetzor (New York, 1953), p. 97.
53. Adam Olearius, *The Travels of Olearius in Seventeenth-Century Russia*, transl. Samuel H. Baron (Stanford, CA, 1967), pp. 143–5 and 270.
54. John Burnett, *Liquid Pleasures: a Social History of Drinks in Modern Britain* (London, 1999), p. 114.
55. Robert Smith and David Christian, *Bread and Salt: a Social and Economic History of Food and Drink in Russia* (Cambridge, 1984), pp. 200–1.
56. A typical example of the legislation on the alcohol duty is: *PSZ*, 8, 5706 (19 February 1731), p. 387.

57. Arcadius Kahan, *The Plow, the Hammer, and the Knout: An Economic History of Eighteenth-Century Russia* (Chicago, IL, 1985), pp. 322–4.
58. See, for example, Richard Unger, *Beer in the Middle Ages and the Renaissance* (Philadelphia, PA, 2007), pp. 207–30.
59. Boris I. Kurakin, 'Gistoriia o Petre I i blizhnikh k nemu liudiakh, 1682–95', *Russkaia starina*, 68/10 (1890), p. 249.
60. Clark, *Iron Kingdom*, pp. 79–80. A typically damning verdict on drinking at several German courts is provided by Adrien Fauchier-Magnan, *The Small German Courts of the Eighteenth Century* (London, 1958), pp. 81–3.
61. Marshall Poe, *A People Born to Slavery: Russia in Early Modern European Ethnography, 1476–1748* (Ithaca, NY, 2000), pp. 149–50.
62. Quoted in Eugene Schuyler, *Peter the Great, Emperor of Russia: a Study of Historical Biography* (New York, 1967), vol. 1, p. 286.
63. Hughes, *Russia*, pp. 250–7.
64. Ernest Zitser, *The Transfigured Kingdom: Sacred Parody and Charismatic Authority at the Court of Peter the Great* (Ithaca, NY, 2004), p. 12.
65. Juel, 'Zapiski', p. 211.
66. Anisimov, *Reforms*, p. 208.
67. Friedrich W. von Bergholz, 'Dnevnik kamer-iunkera Fridrikha-Vil'gel'ma Berkhgol'tsa, 1721–1725 (ch. 3 and 4)', in Viktor P. Naumov (ed.), *Iunost' derzhavy* (Moscow, 2000), pp. 124–5.
68. See, for example, de Campredon's experience at a reception in Aleksandr Rumiantsev's house in March 1721: *SIRIO*, vol. 40, pp. 166–8 (De Campredon to the Archbishop of Cambrai: St Petersburg, 14 March 1721).
69. Friedrich W. von Bergholz, 'Dnevnik kamer-iunkera Fridrikha-Vil'gel'ma Berkhgol'tsa, 1721–1725 (ch. 1 and 2)', in Viktor P. Naumov (ed.), *Neistovyi reformator* (Moscow, 2000), p. 238.
70. Hughes, *Russia*, p. 419.
71. 'Letter to Fedor M. Golovin, September 1694', *PiBIPV*, vol. 1, pp. 26–7.
72. Susan Pinkard, *A Revolution in Taste: the Rise of French Cuisine, 1650–1800* (Cambridge, 2010), pp. 222–35.
73. Smith and Christian, *Bread and Salt*, p. 176.
74. See, for example, Bergholz, 'Dnevnik', *Neistovyi reformator*, pp. 188, 382 and 484.
75. Smith and Christian, *Bread and Salt*, p. 215.
76. *PSZ*, 9, 6566 (5 April 1734), pp. 301–3.
77. *PSZ*, 10, 7233 (19 April 1737), p. 130.
78. Smith and Christian, *Bread and Salt*, p. 216.
79. Weber, *Present State*, vol. 1, pp. 179–80.
80. *PSZ*, 9, 6786 (12 August 1735), pp. 558–9.
81. *PSZ*, 10, 8260 (17 October 1740), p. 275.
82. *PSZ*, 11, 8759 (11 July 1743), p. 847.
83. *PSZ*, 12, 9365 (26 January 1747), pp. 642–5.
84. *PSZ*, 11, 8674 (1 December 1742), p. 728.
85. *PSZ*, 12, 9278 (11 April 1746), p. 543.
86. *PSZ*, 13, 10030 (14 October 1752), pp. 707–8.
87. *PSZ*, 15, 10904, (11 December 1758), pp. 288–9.
88. Smith and Christian, *Bread and Salt*, p. 216.
89. *PSZ*, 15, 11050 (16 April 1760), p. 466.
90. Jerry White, *London in the Eighteenth Century: a Great and Monstrous Thing* (London, 2012), pp. 327–32.

91. For two different case studies, see B. Ann Tlusty, *Bacchus and Civic Order: the Culture of Drink in Early Modern Germany* (London, 2001), pp. 80–101 and Thomas Brennan, 'Social Drinking in Paris', in Susanna Barrows and Robin Room (ed.), *Drinking: Behaviour and Belief in Modern History* (Berkeley, CA, 1991), pp. 68–77.

92. An expanded version of this section has been published as: 'Card-playing and Gambling in Eighteenth-Century Russia', *European History Quarterly*, 42/3 (2012), pp. 385–402.

93. David S. Parlett, *A History of Card Games* (Oxford, 1991), pp. 45–60.

94. David Miers, *Regulating Commercial Gambling: Past, Present, and Future* (Oxford, 2004), pp. 19–38.

95. See, for example, Olivier Grussi, *La vie quotidienne des joueurs sous l'Ancien Régime à Paris et à la cour* (Paris, 1985).

96. Robert Malcolmson, *Popular Recreations in English Society, 1700–1850* (Cambridge, 1973), pp. 5–14 and 34–51.

97. Roy Porter, *English Society in the Eighteenth Century* (London, 1991), pp. 237–9.

98. Isaak M. Linder, *Shakhmaty na Rusi*, 2nd edition (Moscow, 1975).

99. Mikhail I. Pyliaev, *Staroe zhit'e: ocherki i razskazy* (Moscow, 1990), p. 23.

100. On this theme, see Thomas Kavanagh, *Dice, Cards, Wheels: a Different History of French Culture* (Philadelphia, PN, 2005).

101. See, for example, Iurii M. Lotman, *Besedy o russkoi kul'ture: Byt i traditsii russkogo dvorianstva (XVIII – nachalo XIX veka)* (St Petersburg, 2002), pp. 136–63; Georgii F. Parchevskii, *Karty i kartezhniki* (St Petersburg, 1998).

102. Ian Helfant, *The High Stakes of Identity: Gambling in the Life and Literature of Nineteenth-Century Russia* (Evanston, IL, 2002).

103. See, for example, Pyliaev, *Staroe zhit'e*, pp. 22–59.

104. Vladimir O. Mikhnevich, 'Istoriia kartochnoi igry na Rusi', *Istoricheskii vestnik*, vol. 83, no. 1 (1901), pp. 141–61 and no. 2. (1901), pp. 559–87.

105. *Stoglav*, ed. Dmitrii E. Kozhanchikov (St Petersburg, 1863), ch. 92, p. 263.

106. *The Muscovite Law Code (Ulozhenie) of 1649*, ed. and transl. Richard Hellie (Irvine, CA, 1988), 21:15, p. 197.

107. Patrick Gordon, *Diary of General Patrick Gordon of Auchleuchries, 1635–1699. Volume II: 1659–1667*, ed. Dmitri Fedosov (Aberdeen, 2010), p. 143.

108. Petr Tolstoi, *The Travel Diary of Peter Tolstoi: a Muscovite in Early Modern Europe*, ed. and transl. Samuel H. Baron (DeKalb, IL, 1987), pp. 155–7.

109. Bergholz, 'Dnevnik', *Neistovyi reformator*, pp. 284–5.

110. *PSZ*, 13, 9737 (13 April 1750), p. 253.

111. Weber, *Present State*, vol. 1, p. 188.

112. Bergholz, 'Dnevnik', *Neistovyi reformator*, pp. 338–9.

113. See, for example, the references to gambling in 1726 in Menshikov's work diary – *Trudy i dni Aleksandra Danilovicha Menshikova: povsednevnye zapiski delam kniazia A. D. Menshikova, 1716–1720, 1726–1727 gg.*, ed. S. R. Dolgova and T. A. Lapteva (Moscow 2004), p. 389 – and the anonymous Polish diary from the same period – Iurii N. Bespiatykh (ed.), *Peterburg Petra I v inostrannykh opisaniiakh* (Leningrad, 1991), p. 199.

114. See, for example, the distinguished treatment of the French and Imperial ambassadors during the Seven Years War: *KfZh*, 1758, p. 148 (23 November) and *KfZh*, 1761, p. 116 (26 August).

115. Pisarenko, *Povsednevnaia zhizn'*, pp. 159–60.

116. Christoph von Manstein, *Contemporary Memoirs of Russia, from the Year 1727 to 1744* (London, 1968), p. 257.

117. John Dunkley, *Gambling: a Social and Moral Problem in France, 1685–1792* (Oxford, 1985), p. 22.
118. *PSZ*, 15, 11275 (16 June 1761), p. 731.
119. Miers, *Regulating*, pp. 25–6.
120. The banker could exercise a strong influence on proceedings in such games, which may explain Anna Ivanovna's preference for the role, as noted by Manstein. On faro and its derivations, see Parlett, *History*, pp. 75–8.
121. For example, Manstein claimed to have seen losses of 20,000 rubles in a single sitting of quinze or faro at court: Manstein, *Contemporary Memoirs*, p. 257. Likewise, Catherine II recalled stakes of 40–50,000 rubles being gambled by members of the court in the 1740s: Catherine II, 'Mémoires I', *Sochineniia imperatritsy Ekateriny II, na osnovanii podlinnykh rukopisei*, ed. A. N. Pypin (St Petersburg 1901–7), p. 52.
122. Dunkley, *Gambling*, pp. 21 and 25.
123. White, *London*, pp. 339–42.
124. *PSZ*, 9, 6313 (23 January 1733), p. 20.
125. *PSZ*, 9, 6703 (5 March 1735), p. 489.
126. *PSZ*, 12, 9380 (11 March 1747), pp. 670–1.
127. *PSZ*, 15, 11275 (16 June 1761), p. 731.
128. *PSZ*, 15, 11275 (16 June 1761), p. 732
129. Dunkley, *Gambling*, pp. 38–9.
130. Miers, *Regulating*, pp. 27–34.
131. John Spielman, 'Status as Commodity: the Habsburg Economy of Privilege', in Charles Ingrao (ed.), *State and Society in Early Modern Austria* (West Lafayette, IN, 1994), pp. 116–17.
132. Roger Munting, *An Economic and Social History of Gambling in Britain and the USA* (Manchester, 1996), p. 14.
133. *PSZ*, 15, 11083 (15 July 1760), pp. 489–93; *PSZ*, 16, 12098 (20 March 1764), pp. 656–7.
134. See, for example, Johanna Rickman, *Love, Lust, and License in Early Modern England: Illicit Sex and the Nobility* (Aldershot, 2008), pp. 27–9 and 69–73; Jennifer Jones, *Sexing La Mode: Gender, Fashion and Commercial Culture in Old Regime France* (London, 2004), pp. 54–9.
135. See, for example, the rumours about Louis XVI later in the century: T. C. W. Blanning, *The Culture of Power and the Power of Culture: Old Regime Europe, 1660–1789* (Oxford, 2002), pp. 410–14.
136. Merry E. Wiesner, *Women and Gender in Early Modern Europe*, 2nd edition (Cambridge, 2000), pp. 122–3.
137. John K. Brackett, 'The Florentine *Onesta* and the Control of Prostitution, 1403–1680', *Sixteenth-Century Journal*, 24/2 (1993), pp. 273–300.
138. Estimates vary, due to the unreliability of data, but London was thought to have had between 3000 and 7000 prostitutes (White, *London*, p. 347), while Paris had an estimated 20,000 prostitutes in the same period (Colin Jones, *Paris: the Biography of a City* (London, 2006), p. 206).
139. The best of these studies remains Laurie Bernstein, *Sonia's Daughters: Prostitutes and their Regulation in Imperial Russia* (Berkeley, CA, 1995).
140. The classic study of the subject is Mikhail Kuznetsov, *Prostitutsiia i sifilis v Rossii: istoriko-statisticheskiia izsledovaniia* (St Petersburg, 1871). The new approach is exemplified by Marianna Muravyeva, 'Forms and Methods of Violence against Women in Eighteenth-Century Russia: Law against Morality', *SGECRN*, 26 (2008), pp. 15–19.

141. *PSZ*, 3, 1612 (26 December 1697), p. 418.
142. Eve Levin, *Sex and Society in the World of the Orthodox Slavs, 900–1700* (Ithaca, NY, 1989), pp. 74–6.
143. *PSZ*, 1, 1 (*Ulozhenie*, 1649, ch. 22), p. 156.
144. See, for example, Olearius, *Travels*, pp. 142–3. For other examples, see Marshall Poe, 'The Sexual Life of Muscovites: Evidence from the Foreign Accounts', *Russian History/Histoire Russe*, 35 (2008), pp. 408–27.
145. Johann-Georg Korb, *Diary of an Austrian Secretary of Legation at the Court of Czar Peter the Great*, transl. Count MacDonnell (London, 1968) vol. 1, p. 152.
146. Korb, *Diary*, vol. 2, p. 200.
147. *PSZ*, 5, 3006 (30 March 1716), pp. 370–3.
148. *PSZ*, 6, 3485 (13 January 1720), p. 78.
149. Lidiia N. Semenova, *Byt i naselenie Sankt-Peterburga (XVIII vek)* (St Petersburg, 1998), pp. 128–9.
150. *PSZ*, 9, 6947 (6 May 1736), p. 805.
151. Mikhail I. Pyliaev, *Staryi Peterburg: razskazy iz byloi zhizni stolitsy* (St Petersburg, 1889), pp. 155–6.
152. *RGADA*, f. 8, op. 1, d. 2, l. 1 (Letter from the Cabinet to Vasilii I. Demidov, 28 June 1750).
153. *RGADA*, f. 8, op. 1, d. 2, l. 2 (Letter from the Cabinet to Police Assessor Beketov, 29 June 1750).
154. *RGADA*, f. 8, op. 1, d. 2, l. 8 (Report by Vasilii I. Demidov, 5 July 1750).
155. *RGADA*, f. 8, op. 1, d. 12, ll. 1–3ob (Anna Felker's responses to questioning, 11–13 July 1750).
156. *RGADA*, f. 8. op. 1, d. 10, ll. 22–23 (Deposition by Anna Dresdensha about the contents of her parties, 25 September 1750).
157. *RGADA*, f. 8, op. 1, d. 12, l. 6.
158. *PSZ*, 13, 9789 (1 August 1750), pp. 340–1.
159. *RGADA*, f. 8, op. 1, d. 2, l. 133 (Report by Vasilii I. Demidov, 19 November 1750).
160. Semenova, *Byt i naselenie*, pp. 125–7.
161. *Proekty ugolovnago ulozheniia 1754–1766 godov*, ed. Aleksandr A. Vostokov (St Petersburg, 1882), pp. 169–70.
162. Andrei I. Bogdanov, *Opisanie Sanktpeterburga, 1749–1751* (St Petersburg, 1997), pp. 201–2.
163. Olearius, *Travels*, pp. 142 and 161; Korb, *Diary*, vol. 2, pp. 199–200.
164. Anthony Cross, 'The Russian *Banya* in the Descriptions of Foreign Travellers and in the Depictions of Foreign and Russian Artists', *Oxford Slavonic Papers*, 24 (1991), pp. 35–9.
165. *PSZ*, 11, 8842 (21 December 1743), p. 984.
166. *PSZ*, 15, 11094 (31 August 1760), p. 499.
167. *PSZ*, 17, 13664 (30 September 1771), pp. 318–19.
168. *PSZ*, 21, 15379 (8 April 1782), p. 468.

3 Organisation: the Court and its Celebrations

1. An excellent study of the complexities involved in this process is provided by Peter Burke, *The Fabrication of Louis XIV* (New Haven, CT, 1992).
2. See, for example, the range of case studies presented in Arthur Dickens (ed.), *The Courts of Europe: Politics, Patronage and Royalty, 1400–1800* (London, 1977), and

John Adamson (ed.), *The Princely Courts of Europe: Ritual, Politics and Culture under the Ancien Régime, 1500–1750* (London, 1999).

3. The French and German examples are explored in T. C. W. Blanning, *The Culture of Power and the Power of Culture* (Oxford, 2002), pp. 29–77.

4. Jeroen Duindam, 'Versailles, Vienna and Beyond: Changing Views of Household and Government in Early Modern Europe', in Jeroen Duindam, Tülay Artan and Metin Kunt (eds), *Royal Courts in Dynastic States and Empires: a Global Perspective* (Boston, MA, 2011), pp. 401–31.

5. For more detail on these two examples, see Jeroen Duindam, *Vienna and Versailles: the Courts of Europe's Major Dynastic Rivals, 1550–1780* (Cambridge, 2003), pp. 45–89.

6. A useful overview, including the overall number of chancelleries for each task, is provided by Peter Brown, 'Bureaucratic Administration in Seventeenth-Century Russia', in Jarmo Kotilaine and Marshall Poe (eds), *Modernizing Muscovy: Reform and Social Change in Seventeenth-Century Russia* (London, 2005), especially pp. 62–5.

7. Lindsey Hughes, *Russia in the Age of Peter the Great* (New Haven, CT, 1998), pp. 112–13.

8. Ol'ga G. Ageeva, *Imperatorskii dvor Rossii, 1700–1796 gody* (Moscow, 2008), pp. 45–6.

9. *PoZh*, 1711 (7 March), p. 4.

10. Volkov, Nikolai E., *Dvor russkikh imperatorov v ego proshlom i nastoiashchem, v 4–kh chastiakh* (St Petersburg, 1900), p. 159.

11. John Alexander, 'Catherine I, Her Court and Courtiers', in Lindsey Hughes (ed.), *Peter the Great* (Basingstoke, 2001), p. 234.

12. Mikhail I. Semevskii, *Tsaritsa Katerina Alekseevna, Anna i Villem Mons, 1692–1724* (Leningrad, 1990), pp. 91–3.

13. Evgenii V. Anisimov, *Gosudarstvennye preobrazovaniia i samoderzhavie Petra Velikogo v pervoi chetverti XVIII veka* (St Petersburg, 1997), p. 144.

14. Ageeva, *Imperatorskii dvor*, p. 48.

15. Ol'ga G. Ageeva, *Evropeizatsiia russkogo dvora, 1700–1796 gg.* (Moscow, 2006), pp. 68–74.

16. Sergei M. Troitskii, *Russkii absoliutizm i dvorianstvo v XVIII v.: formirovanie biurokratii* (Moscow, 1974), pp. 83–104.

17. Ageeva, *Imperatorskii dvor*, pp. 83–4.

18. Nikolai E. Volkov, *Dvor russkikh imperatorov v ego proshlom i nastoiashchem, v 4–kh chastiakh* (St Petersburg, 1900), pp. 19–21.

19. These regulations are published in Volkov, *Dvor*, pp. 52–8 and 58–64 respectively.

20. Leonid E. Shepelev, *Chinovnyi mir Rossii: XVIII – nachalo XX v.* (St Petersburg, 1999), pp. 403–4.

21. Volkov, *Dvor*, pp. 22–3.

22. Volkov, *Dvor*, p. 150.

23. Konstantin A. Pisarenko, *Povsednevnaia zhizn' russkogo dvora v tsarstvovanie Elizavety Petrovny* (Moscow, 2003), p. 48.

24. Volkov, *Dvor*, pp. 25–6.

25. *PSZ*, 8, 5877 (13 November 1731), pp. 555–6.

26. A balanced overview of the role of favourites in this period is provided by John Alexander, 'Favourites, Favouritism and Female Rule in Russia, 1725–1796', in Roger Bartlett and Janet Hartley (eds), *Russia in the Age of Enlightenment: Essays for Isabel de Madariaga* (London, 1990), pp. 106–24.

27. Pisarenko, *Povsednevnaia zhizn'*, pp. 49–50; Volkov, *Dvor*, p. 172.

28. See, for example, John LeDonne, 'Ruling Families in the Russian Political Order, 1689–1825', *Cahiers du Monde russe et sovietique* (1987), pp. 233–322.
29. For their roles at the contemporary Habsburg court, see Duindam, *Vienna and Versailles*, pp. 157 and 176.
30. Grigorii A. Miloradovich, *Materialy dlia istorii pazheskago Ego Imperatorskago Velichestva korpusa, 1711–1875* (Kiev, 1876), pp. 10–11.
31. *RGIA*, f. 466, op. 1, d. 87, ll. 44–45ob (Order from the Court Office, 28 February 1752).
32. Otto von Freymann (comp.), *Pazhi za 183 goda (1711–1894): biografii byvshikh pazhei, s portretami* (Fredrikshavn, 1894), pp. 1–33.
33. Miloradovich, *Materialy*, pp. 23–30.
34. See, for example, Duindam, *Vienna and Versailles*, pp. 48–9.
35. Mikhail I. Semevskii, *Tsaritsa Praskov'ia, 1664–1723* (Leningrad, 1991), pp. 27–8.
36. Mikhail M. Bogoslovskii, *Petr Velikii: materialy dlia biografii* (Moscow, 2005), vol. 1, pp. 49–52.
37. D, *Dvor*, p. 22.
38. Ageeva, *Imperatorskii dvor*, pp. 126–27.
39. *AKV*, vol. 2, pp. 98–111.
40. See, for example, the faction that emerged around the young Duc de Bourgogne in France during the late stages of Louis XIV's reign: Emmanuel LeRoy Ladurie, *Saint-Simon and the Court of Louis XIV* (Chicago, IL, 2001), ch. 4, esp. pp. 144–8. Likewise, Frederick William I of Prussia and Prince Frederick had a very problematic relationship: Theodor Schieder, *Frederick the Great*, ed. and transl. Sabina Berkeley and Hamish Scott (London, 2000), pp. 10–12.
41. The best discussion of this affair is Paul Bushkovitch, *Peter the Great: the Struggle for Power, 1671–1725* (Cambridge, 2001), pp. 339–425.
42. On the Secret Chancellery, see Evgenii V. Anisimov, *Dyba i knut: Politicheskii sysk i russkoe obshchestvo v XVIII veke* (Moscow, 1999).
43. See, for example, Catherine II, 'Mémoires IV (2)', *Sochineniia imperatritsy Ekateriny II, na osnovanii podlinnykh rukopisei*, ed. A. N. Pypin (St Petersburg 1901–7), p. 385.
44. Ageeva, *Imperatorskii dvor*, pp. 76 and 134–5.
45. A classic overview of the Muscovite court calendar is provided in: Ivan E. Zabelin, *Domashnii byt russkago tsarei v XVI I XVII stoletiiakh*, 3rd edition (Moscow, 1895), part 1, pp. 376–435.
46. See, for example, Adam Olearius, *The Travels of Olearius in Seventeenth-Century Russia*, transl. Samuel H. Baron (Stanford, CA, 1967), pp. 99–100.
47. Robert Crummey, 'Court Spectacles in Seventeenth-Century Russia: Illusion and Reality', in Daniel Clarke Waugh (ed.), *Essays in Honour of A. A. Zimin* (Columbus, OH, 1985), pp. 132 and 136.
48. Paul Bushkovitch, 'The Epiphany Ceremony of the Russian Court in the Sixteenth and Seventeenth Centuries', *Russian Review*, 49/1 (1990), pp. 1–18.
49. Hughes, *Russia*, pp. 274–5.
50. Irina A. Chudinova, Irina A., *Penie, zvony, ritual: Topografiia tserkovno–muzykal'noi kul'tury Peterburga* (St Petersburg, 1994), pp. 39–40.
51. Elena Pogosian, Elena, *Petr I – arkhitektor rossiiskoi istorii* (St Petersburg, 2001), pp. 29–41.
52. Just Juel, 'Zapiski datskogo poslannika v Rossii pri Petre Velikom', in Viktor P. Naumov (ed.), *Lavry Poltavy* (St Petersburg, 2001), pp. 188–9.
53. Hughes, *Russia*, p. 273.

54. For a detailed description, see Friedrich W. von. Bergholz, 'Dnevnik kamer-iunkera Fridrikha-Vil'gel'ma Berkhgol'tsa, 1721–1725 (chs 1 and 2)', in Viktor P. Naumov (ed.), *Neistovyi reformator* (Moscow, 2000), pp. 225–32.
55. *PoZh*, 1723 (30 May), p. 15.
56. *PoZh*, 1724 (25 and 29 June), pp. 9–10.
57. See, for example, *KfZh*, 1734 (29 June), p. 4.
58. See, for example, the description of its celebration in *KfZh*, 1744 (29 June), pp. 59–67.
59. For Anna Ivanovna, this anniversary was celebrated on 19 January; for Elizabeth, it was on 25 November.
60. Hughes, *Russia*, p. 275.
61. The court journal for 1750 provides typical examples for the celebration of these feast days: *KfZh*, 1750, pp. 5–6 (6 January), 13–15 (2 February), 34 (25 March), 37–40 (8–15 April), 60 (24 May), 88 (15 August) and 103 (8 September).
62. *PSZ*, 9, 6832 (29 October 1735), pp. 598–600.
63. Simon Dixon, 'Religious Ritual at the Eighteenth-Century Russian Court', in Michael Schaich (ed.), *Monarchy and Religion: the Transformation of Royal Culture in Eighteenth-Century Europe* (Oxford, 2007), pp. 245–7.
64. Another celebration of the dynasty's future – royal births – is covered by Ol'ga G. Ageeva, 'Tseremonialy rozhdeniia tsarskikh detei v vek evropeizatsii: ot Petra I do Ekateriny II', in Ol'ga A. Prutskova (ed.), *Rossiiskaia real'nost' kontsa XVII – pervoi poloviny XIX v. Sbornik statei k 80–leiiu Iu. A. Tikhonova* (Moscow, 2007), pp. 210–39.
65. See, for example, János Bak (ed.), *Coronations: Medieval and Early Modern Monarchic Ritual* (Berkeley, CA, 1990).
66. Richard Wortman, 'The Russian Coronation: Rite and Representation', *The Court Historian*, 9/1 (2004), pp. 15–32.
67. Roy Strong, *Art and Power: Renaissance Festivals, 1450–1650* (Woodbridge, 1984), pp. 44–50
68. Edward Muir, *Ritual in Early Modern Europe*, 2nd edition (Cambridge, 2005), pp. 265–71.
69. R. Malcolm Smuts, 'Public Ceremony and Royal Charisma: the English Royal Entry in London, 1485–1621', in A. Lee Beier, David Cannadine and James M. Rosenheim (eds), *The First Modern Society: Essays in English History in Honour of Lawrence Stone* (Cambridge, 1989), pp. 83–5.
70. Lawrence Bryant, *The King and the City in the Parisian Royal Entry Ceremony: Politics, Ritual and Art in the Renaissance* (Geneva, 1986), pp. 208–12.
71. Christopher Clark, *Iron Kingdom: the Rise and Downfall of Prussia, 1600–1947* (London, 2007), p. 68.
72. The details of the entry plans can be found in Karin Friedrich, Karin and Sara Smart (eds), *The Cultivation of Monarchy and the Rise of Berlin: Brandenburg-Prussia, 1700* (Farnham, 2010), pp. 247–60.
73. Richard Wortman, *Scenarios of Power: Myth and Ceremony in Russian Monarchy* (Princeton, NJ, 1995), vol. 1, p. 90.
74. Peter I was distracted by upcoming Baltic fleet manoeuvres and recurrent illness, so there was no ceremony to mark his return to St Petersburg with the newly crowned Catherine I in 1724. Peter II did not return to St Petersburg before his death in 1730.
75. See, for example, the opinion of James FitzJames Stuart, the Spanish envoy to Russia, in 1728: 'Zapiski gertsoga De–Liria–Bervika, byvshego ispanskim poslom pri rossiisko dvore, s 1727 po 1731 god', *Syn otechestva*, 7/2 (1839), pp. 144–5.

76. Simon Werrett, *Fireworks: Pyrotechnic Arts and Sciences in European History* (Chicago, IL, 2010), pp. 112–14.
77. Burkhard C. von Münnich, 'Dispozitsiia i tseremoniial torzhestvennogo v"ezda imperatritsy Anny Ivanovny v S.-Peterburg 16 genvaria 1732', comp. M. D. Khmyrov, *Russkii arkhiv*, 2 (1867), pp. 332–41.
78. *Pribavleniia k Vedomostiam*, no. 6 (18 January 1732), pp. 27–8.
79. Münnich, 'Dispozitsiia', pp. 339–40.
80. Münnich, 'Dispozitsiia', pp. 333–7.
81. *Primechaniia na Vedomosti*, no. 21 (6 March 1732), pp. 81–8.
82. Anna N. Voronikhina, 'Triumfal'nye vorota 1742 g. v Sankt–Peterburge', in Tat'iana V. Alekseeva (ed.), *Russkoe iskusstvo barokko: materialy i issledovaniia* (Moscow, 1977), pp. 159–72; Zelov, *Ofitsial'nye*, pp. 261–3.
83. *MIIAN*, vol. 5, pp. 346–7.
84. *RGIA*, f. 473, op. 1, d. 246, ll. 74–75ob (Disposition de l'entrée de S. M. I. Elizabeth Petrovna à St. Petersbourg, 21 December 1742) and ll. 81–86ob (Dispozitsiia vo vremia shestviia Eia Imp. Vel. vsemil. gdrni imperatritsy Elisavety Petrovny v Sankt Piterburkh, December 1742).
85. *RGIA*, f. 473, op. 1, d. 246, l. 87 (O torzhestvennom v"ezde Eia Imperatorskogo Velichestva v Sankt Pitersburg, 23 December 1742).
86. Natal'ia A. Ogarkova, *Tseremonii, prazdnestva, muzyka russkogo dvora* (St Petersburg, 2004), pp. 45 and 264.
87. *RGIA*, f. 473, op. 1, d. 246, ll. 81–5ob.
88. Chudinova, *Penie*, pp. 21–4.
89. *RGIA*, f. 473, op. 1, d. 246, ll. 82ob–83.
90. *TZhREP*, vol. 2, part 2, p. 520.
91. *SIRIO*, vol. 99, pp. 195–7 (Wyche to Carteret: Moscow, 20 December 1742) and 200 (Wyche to Carteret: St Petersburg, 28 December 1742).
92. *SIRIO*, vol. 100, p. 465 (D'Alion to Amelot: Moscow, 27 December, 1742).
93. *SIRIO*, vol. 100, p. 465 (L'Estocq to de la Chétardie: Moscow, 28 December, 1742).
94. However, the supplies required for the fireworks and illuminations are mentioned: *SPV*, no. 100 (13 December 1742), p. 813 concerns the quantity of animal fat, pitch and 'Venetian turpentine' required by the Admiralty; *SPV*, no. 101 (16 December 1742), p. 820 deals with a consignment of mica for the Artillery Office.
95. *RGIA*, f. 473, op. 1, d. 246, ll. 77–78ob (Account by *ober-tseremoniimeister* Franz Santi, n.d.).
96. *RGIA*, f. 473, op. 1, d. 246, l. 77ob.
97. *RGIA*, f. 473, op. 1, d. 246, ll. 78–78ob.
98. Andrei I. Bogdanov, *Opisanie Sanktpeterburga, 1749–1751* (St Petersburg, 1997), p. 343.
99. *SK*, vol. 2, p. 97.
100. Voronikhina 'Triumfal'nye vorota', p. 169.
101. Clark, *Iron Kingdom*, p. 75.
102. Simon Dixon, *Catherine the Great* (London, 2009), p. 127.
103. Russell Martin, *A Bride for the Tsar: Bride-Shows and Marriage Politics in Early Modern Russia* (DeKalb, IL, 2012), pp. 43–56 and 76–87.
104. Lindsey Hughes, 'Peter the Great's Two Weddings: Changing Images of Women in a Transitional Age', in Rosalind Marsh (ed.), *Women in Russia and Ukraine* (Cambridge, 1996), pp. 32–5.

105. On Louis XIV's wedding, see Abby Zanger, *Scenes From the Marriage of Louis XIV: Nuptial Fictions and the Making of Absolutist Power* (Stanford, CA, 1997); on Leopold I's weddings, see Maria Goloubeva, *The Glorification of Emperor Leopold I in Image, Spectacle and Text* (Mainz, 2000), pp. 103–20.
106. 'Tochnoe izvestie o... kreposti i gorode Sankt–Peterburg, o kreposttse Kronshlot i ikh okresknostiakh...', in Iurii N. Bespiatykh (ed.), *Peterburg Petra I v inostrannykh opisaniiakh* (Leningrad, 1991), pp. 72–5.
107. Juel, 'Zapiski', p. 216.
108. Ol'ga G. Ageeva, 'Novye iavleniia v obshchestvennoi zhizni i bytu Peterburga pervoi chetverti XVIII v.: na primere tsarskikh svadeb', in A. N. Kopylov, Ol'ga G. Ageeva and Lev N. Pushkarev (eds), *Russkaia kul'tura v perekhodnyi period ot srednevekov'ia k novomu vremeni: sbornik statei* (Moscow, 1992), p. 98.
109. Ernest Zitser, *The Transfigured Kingdom: Sacred Parody and Charismatic Authority at the Court of Peter the Great* (Ithaca, NY, 2004), pp. 119–21.
110. *PoZh*, 1712, pp. 1–7. The engraving is analysed in Grigorii V. Mikhailov, 'Graviura A. Zubova "Svad-ba Petra I": realnost' i vymysel', *Panorama iskusstv*, 11 (1988), pp. 25–38.
111. The wedding celebrations are described in: *Opisanie o brake mezhdu Eia Vysochestvom Annoiu Petrovnoiu, Tsesarevnoiu Vserossiikoiu, i Ego Korolevskim Vysochestvom Karlom Fridrikhom, Gertsogom Golshteinogottorpskim* (St Petersburg, 1725); Jane Vigor, *Letters from a Lady, Who Resided Some Years in Russia, to her Friend in England* (London, 1775), pp. 189–207.
112. *PSZ*, 11, 8658 (7 November 1742), pp. 712–13.
113. See, for example, the concerns of the English court in the 1730s in choosing suitable matches for George II's children: Hannah Smith, *Georgian Monarchy: Politics and Culture, 1714–1760* (Cambridge, 2006), pp. 46–7.
114. Catherine II, 'Mémoires I', *Sochineniia*, vol. 12, p. 63.
115. This seems an odd decision, given the published account of the wedding (as noted above).
116. *RGIA*, f. 473, op. 3, d. 15, ll. 2–2ob (Notes du Comte de Santi, Grand-Maître des Cérémonies sous le règne de l'Impératrice Elisabeth I, 1745).
117. *RGIA*, f. 473, op. 3, d. 15, ll. 3–5ob (Points préables qui demandaient la résolution de Sa Majesté Impériale à fin de pouvoir arranger le Cérémonial des Noces de Leurs Altesses Impériales, 4 March 1745).
118. *RGIA*, f. 473, op. 3, d. 15, ll. 3ob–4ob.
119. *RGIA*, f. 473, op. 3, d. 15, ll. 5ob–6.
120. *PSZ*, 12, 9123 (16 March 1745), p. 346.
121. *PSZ*, 12, 9124 (16 March 1745), pp. 346–7.
122. *SPV*, no. 63 (9 August 1745), p. 543.
123. *KfZh*, 1745 (14 and 16 August), p. 50.
124. For example, in Santi's notes, the date of the wedding is listed as 18 August ('le mariage de les Altesses Impériales s'effectua le 18 d'août 1745'): *RGIA*, f. 473, op. 3, d. 15, l. 13. Similarly, a planning document by Rastrelli contained a footnote giving the date of the wedding as 18 August: *RGIA*, f. 473, op. 3, d. 14, l. 2 (Description des bals et fêtes données au palais d'hyver au mariage de Pierre III, 1745).
125. Catherine II, 'Mémoires I', *Sochineniia*, p. 67.
126. *SIRIO*, vol. 102, p. 320 (Hyndford to Harrington, 20 August 1745).
127. Catherine II, 'Mémoires I', *Sochineniia*, p. 67 and *KfZh*, 1745 (17 August), p. 51.
128. *ZhDGA*, 1745 (21 August), p. 35.

129. Catherine II, 'Mémoires I', *Sochineniia*, p. 69.
130. *KfZh*, 1745 (22 August), pp. 69–70.
131. The programme is reprinted in: *TZhREP*, vol. 2, part 1, pp. 89–96.
132. *KfZh*, 1745 (26 August), pp. 75–81.
133. *KfZh*, 1745 (26 August), p. 80.
134. Catherine II, 'Mémoires II', *Sochineniia*, pp. 73–74.
135. *RGADA*, f. 16, op. 1, d. 443, ll. 177 and 178–178ob (Vedomost' obretaiushchiisia v Sankt–Peterburge ot pervago do piatogo klassu personam zhenam ikh i detiam, c.1747).
136. See, for example, the expense lavished on the wedding of Joseph II to Isabella of Parma in late 1760, which linked the Habsburg and Bourbon dynasties: Derek Beales, *Joseph II. Volume I: In the Shadow of Maria Theresa, 1741–1780* (Cambridge, 1987), pp. 69–72.
137. For (brief) comments on its magnificence, see: *SIRIO*, vol. 102, p. 321 (Hyndford to Harrington: St Petersburg, 24 August 1745) and *SIRIO*, vol. 105, p. 546 (D'Allion to d'Argenson: St Petersburg, 24 August 1745). For a press description, see *Westminster Journal, or New Weekly Miscellany*, no. 200 (28 September 1745), p. 2.
138. Michael Schaich, 'Introduction', in Schaich (ed.), *Monarchy and Religion*, pp. 33–4. For a recent European-wide study, see Juliusz Chroscicki, Mark Hengerer and Gérard Sabatier (eds), *Les funérailles princières en Europe, XVIe–XVIIIe siècle* (Versailles, 2012).
139. Mark Hengerer, 'The Funerals of the Habsburg Emperors in the Eighteenth Century', in Schaich (ed.), *Monarchy and Religion*, pp. 376–8.
140. Paul Fritz, 'The Trade in Death: the Royal Funerals in England', *Eighteenth Century Studies*, 15/3 (1982), pp. 291–316.
141. Marina Logunova, *Pechal'nye ritualy imperatorskoi Rossii* (Moscow, 2011), pp. 16–17 and 22–6.
142. Lindsey Hughes, 'The Funerals of the Russian Emperors and Empresses', in Schaich (ed.), *Monarchy and Religion*, pp. 395–7.
143. Logunova, *Pechal'nye ritualy*, pp. 58–63.
144. Ol'ga G. Ageeva, 'Peterburgskii traurnyi tseremonial doma Romanovykh v nachale XVIII v.', in Iurii N. Bespiatykh (ed.), *Fenomenon Peterburga* (St Petersburg, 2001), pp. 491 and 496–7.
145. Friedrich Christian Weber, *The Present State of Russia* (London, 1968), vol. 1, pp. 110–11.
146. Ageeva, 'Peterburgskii traurnyi tseremonial', pp. 503–4.
147. Wortman, *Scenarios*, vol. 1, p. 75.
148. Hughes, 'Funerals', pp. 400–2.
149. For a detailed description of the 'chamber of mourning', see 'Opisanie pogrebeniia Ego Imperatorskogo Velichestva i gosudaryni tsesarevny', in Feofan Prokopovich, *Kratkaia povest' o smerti Petra Velikago...* (St Petersburg, 1831), pp. 39–63. This is a reprint of the official account published in 1725.
150. Prokopovich, *Kratkaia povest'*, p. 12. Again, this is a reprint of the 1726 original.
151. 'Opisanie pogrebeniia', pp. 67–71.
152. Friedrich W. von Bergholz, 'Dnevnik kamer–iunkera Fridrikha–Vil'gel'ma Berkhgol'tsa, 1721–1725 (ch. 3 and 4)', in Viktor P. Naumov (ed.), *Iunost' derzhavy* (Moscow, 2000), p. 267.
153. Hughes, 'Funerals', pp. 406–7.

154. For more details, see *Vnutrennii byt russkago gosudarstva s 17-go oktiabria 1740 goda po 25-e noiabria 1741 goda* (Moscow, 1880), vol. 1, pp. 432–40.

155. Petr N. Petrov, *Istoriia Sankt-Peterburga s osnovaniia goroda do vvedeniia v deistvie vybornogo gorodskogo upravleniia po uchrezhdeniiam o guberniiakh: 1703–1782* (St Petersburg, 1884), pp. 429–30.

156. Dixon, *Catherine*, pp. 115–16.

157. Petr N. Trubetskoi, 'Zametki na kalendare v 1762 godu', *Russkaia starina*, 73/2 (1892), p. 444.

158. Catherine II, 'Zapiska na rossiiskom iazyke I', *Sochineniia*, vol. 12, p. 508.

159. Dixon, *Catherine*, p. 117.

160. Eckhart Hellmuth, 'The Funerals of the Prussian Kings in the Eighteenth Century', in Schaich (ed.), *Monarchy and Religion*, pp. 453–6.

161. John Adamson, 'The Making of the Ancien-Régime Court 1500–1700', in Adamson (ed). *Princely Courts*, pp. 32–3.

162. Helen Watanabe-O'Kelly, 'The Early Modern Festival Book: Function and Form', in James Mulryne, Helen Watanabe-O'Kelly and Margaret Shewring (eds), *Europa triumphans: Court and Civic Festival in Early Modern Europe* (Aldershot, 2004), vol. 1, pp. 6–12.

163. Ute Daniel, 'The Baroque Court Festival: the Example of German Courts around 1700', in Mulryne, Watanabe-O'Kelly and Shewring (eds), *Europa triumphans*, vol. 1, pp. 34–5.

164. On the Prussian *Krönungs-Geschichte* of 1702, see Friedrich and Smart (eds), *Cultivation of Monarchy*, pp. 177–79.

165. *Opisanie koronatsii Eia Velichestva Imperatritsy i Samoderzhitsy Vserossiiskoi Anny Ioannovny torzhestvenno otpravlennoi v tsarstviushchem grade Moskve, 28 aprelia, 1730 g.* (Moscow, 1730); *Obstoiatel'noe opisanie torzhestvennykh poriadkov blagopoluchnogo vshestviia v tsarstvuiushchii grad Moskvu i sviashchenneishei koronovaniia eia Avgusteishago imperatorskogo velichestva... Elisavety Petrovny* (St Petersburg, 1744).

166. *SK*, vol. 2, pp. 330–2 and 356–7. For a detailed discussion of Elizabeth's coronation album, see Wortman, *Scenarios*, vol. 1, p. 91–106.

167. Werrett, *Fireworks*, pp. 118–19.

168. For some examples, see Nikolai A. Kopanev, 'Repertuar priozvedenii F. M. Vol'tera v Peterburgskoi akademicheskoi knizhnoi lavke v seredine XVIII v. (1731–61 gg.)', in G. V. Bakhareva and Sergei P. Luppov (eds), *Kniga i knigotorgovlia v Rossii v XVI–XVIII vv.* (Leningrad, 1984), pp. 87–93.

169. Burke, *Fabrication*, p. 17.

170. For more details, see Stepan M. Shamin, *Kuranty XVII stoletiia: evropeiskaia pressa v Rossii i vozniknovenie russkoi periodicheskoi pechati* (Moscow, 2011).

171. *SK*, vol. 4, pp. 51–52. On Müller's appointment, see Pekarskii, *Istoriia*, vol. 1, pp. 310–11.

172. *SK*, vol. 4, pp. 63–66 and Gary Marker, *Publishing, Printing, and the Origins of Intellectual Life in Russia, 1700–1800* (Princeton, NJ, 1985), p. 48.

173. Dmitrii V. Tiulichev, 'Sotsial'nyi sostav podpischikov "Sanktpeterburgskikh vedomostei" (seredina XVIII v.)', in A. A. Zaitseva (ed.), *Kniga v Rossii. XVI – seredina XIX veka: knigarasprostranenie, biblioteka, chitatel'* (Leningrad, 1987), p. 62.

174. Gary Marker, 'Russian Journals and their Readers in the Late Eighteenth Century', *Oxford Slavonic Papers*, 19 (1986), pp. 89–90.

175. Tiulichev, 'Sotsial'nyi sostav', pp. 64 and 66.

176. On the consumption debate, see John Brewer and Roy Porter (eds), *Consumption and the World of Goods* (London, 1993), pp. 1–4.

177. *SPV*, no. 3 (8 January 1742), pp. 22–23. See also *PSZ*, 11, 8495 (1 January 1742), p. 557.
178. *SPV*, no. 17 (26 February 1742), p. 134. See also *PridZh*, p. 14 ((22 February 1742).
179. *KfZh*, 1742, passim and *PridZh*, pp. 15–40 (28 February – 15 December 1742).
180. *SPV*, no. 35 (29 April 1742), p. 278.
181. *Pribavlenie k Vedomostiam*, no. 35 (29 April 1742), pp. 281–84.
182. *SPV*, no. 38 (10 May 1742), pp. 306–7.
183. Wortman, *Scenarios*, vol. 1, pp. 90–91.
184. *PSZ*, 11, 8529 (18 March 1742), p. 588.
185. *SK*, vol. 4, p. 51.
186. *PSZ*, 11, 9903 (3 November 1751), pp. 534–35.
187. Thomas Munck, *The Enlightenment: a Comparative Social History, 1721–1794* (London, 2000), pp. 112–14.
188. The appearance of Aleksandr P. Sumarokov's journal, *Trudoliubovaia pchela*, in 1759 was a signal of the direction that this area would take during Catherine II's reign: *SK*, vol. 4, p. 196.

4 Interaction: the City's Social Life

1. For a detailed comparison, see Jeroen Duindam, *Vienna and Versailles: the Courts of Europe's Major Dynastic Rivals, 1550–1780* (Cambridge, 2003), pp. 151–80.
2. Samuel Klingensmith, *The Utility of Splendor: Ceremony, Social Life, and Architecture at the Court of Bavaria, 1600–1800* (Chicago, IL, 1993), pp. 145–76.
3. Markus Volkel, 'The Hohenzollern Court, 1535–1740', in John Adamson (ed.), *The Princely Courts of Europe: Ritual, Politics and Culture under the Ancien Régime, 1500–1750* (London, 1999), pp. 225–7.
4. Hannah Smith, *Georgian Monarchy: Politics and Culture, 1714–1760* (Cambridge, 2006), pp. 218–23.
5. Burke, *Fabrication*, pp. 7–8.
6. Smith, *Georgian Monarchy*, pp. 68–69.
7. Jeffrey Ravel, *The Contested Parterre: Public Theater and French Political Culture, 1680–1791* (Ithaca, NY, 1999), pp. 13–14.
8. See, for example, the range of courts covered in Samantha Owens, Barbara Reul and Janice Stockigt (eds), *Music at German Courts, 1715–1760: Changing Artistic Priorities* (Woodbridge, 2011).
9. T. C. W. Blanning, *The Culture of Power and the Power of Culture* (Oxford, 2002), pp. 63–4 and 93.
10. James van Horn Melton, *The Rise of the Public in Enlightenment Europe* (Cambridge, 2001), p. 187.
11. Bärbel Pelker, 'The Palatine Court in Mannheim', in Owens, Reul, and Stockigt (eds), *Music at German Courts*, p. 148.
12. Catriona Kelly, 'The Origins of Russian Theatre', in Robert Leach and Victor Borovsky (eds), *A History of Russian Theatre* (Cambridge, 1999), pp. 24–7.
13. Claudia Jensen, *Musical Cultures in Seventeenth-Century Russia* (Bloomington, IN, 2009), pp. 168–9.
14. Jensen, *Musical Cultures*, pp. 180–210.
15. Anthony Cross, *Peter the Great through British Eyes: Perceptions and Representations of the Tsar since 1698* (Cambridge, 2000), pp. 22–4.

16. Lindsey Hughes, *Russia in the Age of Peter the Great* (New Haven, CT, 1998), pp. 241–2.
17. For further discussion, see Il'ia S. Shliapkin, *Tsarevna Natal'ia Alekseevna i teatr ee vremeni* (St Petersburg, 1898).
18. V. N. Vsevolodskii-Gerngross, *Teatral'nye zdaniia v Sankt-Peterburge v XVIII stoletii* (St Petersburg, 1910), p. 4.
19. Friedrich Christian Weber, *The Present State of Russia* (London, 1968), vol. 1, p. 189.
20. Vsevolodskii-Gerngross, *Teatral'nye zdaniia*, p. 5.
21. Bergholz, 'Dnevnik', *Iunost' derzhavy*, p. 131.
22. Hughes, *Russia*, p. 241.
23. Friedrich W. von Bergholz, 'Dnevnik kamer–iunkera Fridrikha–Vil'gel'ma Berkhgol'tsa, 1721–1725 (chs 3 and 4)', in Viktor P. Naumov (ed.), *Iunost' derzhavy* (Moscow, 2000), p. 199.
24. Bergholz, 'Dnevnik', *Iunost' derzhavy*, p. 131.
25. For details on this company, see V. N. Vsevolodskii-Gerngross, *Teatr v Rossii pri imperatritse Anne Ioannovne i imperatore Ioanne Antonoviche* (St Petersburg, 1914), pp. 3–15.
26. On Araja, see *MP*, vol. 1, pp. 49–61. On Rinaldi, see *MP*, vol. 3, pp. 15–19.
27. *TZhRAI*, pp. 15–75.
28. *MP*, vol. 1, pp. 335–36.
29. For a list of the operas and ballets performed on the major anniversaries during Elizabeth's reign, see Natal'ia A. Ogarkova, *Tseremonii, prazdnestva, muzyka russkogo dvora* (St Petersburg, 2004), pp. 240–3.
30. *KfZh*, 1752, p. 66 (15 September).
31. *KfZh*, 1752, p. 65 (7 September).
32. See, for example, Iakov K. Grot (ed.), *Zhizn' Derzhavina, po ego sochineniiam i pis'mam i po istoricheskim dokumentam* (Moscow, 1880), vol. 1, p. 103.
33. See, for example, V. N. Vsevolodskii-Gerngross, *Istoriia russkogo teatra* (Moscow, 1929), vol. 1, p. 462.
34. *KfZh*, 1751, pp. 67–8 (25 June).
35. *RGIA*, f. 466, op. 1, d. 84, l. 76 (Order from the Court Office to the Police Chancellery, 27 June 1751).
36. This term carried a number of meanings in this period: *Slovar'*, vol. 4, pp. 53–5.
37. *KfZh*, 1758, pp. 13–14 (17 January).
38. A footnote by the journals' nineteenth-century editors defines 'vol'noi' as 's platoiu dlia publiki' (with paying for the public): *KfZh*, 1758, p. 72 (14 May).
39. Vsevolodskii-Gerngross, *Teatral'nye zdaniia*, pp. 7–20.
40. *MP*, vol. 2, pp. 297–98.
41. Vsevolodskii-Gerngross, *Teatral'nye zdaniia*, pp. 16–17.
42. For more details on Locatelli and his theatrical troupe, see V. N. Vsevolodskii-Gerngross, *Teatr v Rossii po imperatritse Elisavete Petrovne* (St Petersburg, 2003), pp. 100–32.
43. *KfZh*, 1757, p. 109 (2 December).
44. *KfZh*, 1757, pp. 109–10 (3 December).
45. *RGIA*, f. 1329, op. 2. d. 49, l. 5 (Order from the Court Office to the Police Chancellery, 2 December 1757).
46. *KfZh*, 1757, p. 111 (8 December).
47. *SPV*, no. 97 (5 December 1757), p. 7.
48. *KfZh*, 1757, p. 122 (23 December).

49. *KfZh*, 1757, p. 112 (9 December). The paternity of Anna Petrovna, who died in infancy, was the subject of speculation, with the likeliest candidate being Stanislaw-August Poniatowski, secretary to the English envoy Sir Charles Hanbury-Williams.
50. *SPV*, no. 101 (19 December 1757), p. 8.
51. *KfZh*, 1758, p. 75 (27 May).
52. *KfZh*, 1758, pp. 77–78 (1 and 8 June).
53. *KfZh*, 1758, p. 106 (4 July).
54. *MP*, vol. 2, pp. 141–3.
55. *PSZ*, vol. 14, no. 10599 (30 August 1756), p. 613.
56. Vsevolodskii-Gerngross, *Teatr v Rossii po imperatritse Elizavete*, pp. 202–42
57. Stählin's articles are collected in: *TZhRAI*, pp. 532–76.
58. Sergei P. Luppov, *Kniga v Rossii v poslepetrovskoe vremia: 1725–1740* (Leningrad, 1976), p. 82.
59. Elise Kimerling Wirtschafter, *The Play of Ideas in Russian Enlightenment Theatre* (DeKalb, IL, 2003), pp. 29–31.
60. *AKV*, vol. 5, p. 12.
61. Blanning, *Culture of Power*, pp. 120.
62. Iain Fenlon, 'Music and Festival', in James Mulryne, Helen Watanabe-O'Kelly and Margaret Shewring (eds), *Europa triumphans: Court and Civic Festival in Early Modern Europe* (Aldershot, 2004), vol. 1, p. 47.
63. Samantha Owens and Barbara Reul, 'An Introduction to German *Hofkapellen*', in Owens, Reul, and Stockigt (eds), *Music at German Courts*, pp. 1–16.
64. Blanning, *Culture of Power*, pp. 84–5 and 97.
65. T. C. W. Blanning, *The Triumph of Music* (London, 2008), pp. 13–14.
66. Nikolai F. Findeizen, *History of Music in Russia from Antiquity to 1800*, transl. Samuel William Pring, ed. Milo Velimirovic and Claudia Jensen (Bloomington, IN, 2008), vol. 1, pp. 97–9 and 188–9.
67. On the *skomorokhi*, see Russell Zguta, *Russian Minstrels: a History of the Skomorokhi* (Philadelphia, PA, 1978).
68. See, for example, Jerome Horsey, 'The Travels of Sir Jerome Horsey, Knt.' in Edward Bond (ed.), *Russia at the Close of the Sixteenth Century* (London, 1856), p. 222.
69. Jensen, *Musical Cultures*, pp. 89–98.
70. Friedrich W. von Bergholz, 'Dnevnik kamer-iunkera Fridrikha-Vil'gel'ma Berkhgol'tsa, 1721–1725 (chs 1 and 2)', in Viktor P. Naumov (ed.), *Neistovyi reformator* (Moscow, 2000), pp. 138 and 177.
71. *MP*, vol. 2, pp. 204–8.
72. Bergholz, 'Dnevnik', *Neistovyi reformator*, pp. 178 and 449; Bergholz, 'Dnevnik kamer-iunkera Fridrikha-Vil'gel'ma Berkhgol'tsa, 1721–1725 (chs 3 and 4)', in Viktor P. Naumov (ed.), *Iunost' derzhavy* (Moscow, 2000), 11–324, p. 136.
73. Blanning, *Culture of Power*, pp. 163–4.
74. Christoph Wolff, *Bach: Essays on His Life and Music* (Cambridge, MA, 1991), pp. 226–7.
75. *Slovar'*, vol. 10, p. 155.
76. *SPV*, no. 54 (8 July 1746), p. 334.
77. Petr N. Stolpianskii, *Muzyka i muzitsirovanie v starom Peterburge* (Leningrad, 1989), p. 15.
78. 'Pis'mo Spb. ober-politsiimeistera Tatishcheva k kabinet-sekretariu Bakhirevu', *Istoricheskii vestnik*, 5 (1881), p. 681.

79. Stolpianskii, *Muzyka*, p. 22.
80. *SPV*, no. 81 (4 October 1748), p. 698. This notice was published again at the end of the month, in no. 87.
81. *SPV*, no. 51 (26 June 1750), p. 406.
82. *RGIA*, f. 8, op. 1, d. 10, ll. 21–21ob (Copy of a report by General-Policemaster Antonio de Vieira, 29 January 1745).
83. *RGIA*, f. 8, op. 1, d. 10, ll. 7–7ob (Deposition by Maria Vintsler, 30 August 1750).
84. *RGIA*, f. 8, op. 1, d. 10, ll. 1–2 (Deposition by Johann Forster, 22 August 1750).
85. *RGIA*, f. 8, op. 1, d. 10, ll. 12–13 (Further questioning of the *vecherinki* organisers, 12 September 1750).
86. Jakob von Stählin, *Muzyka i balet v Rossii XVIII veka* (St Petersburg, 2002), p. 148.
87. Catherine II, 'Mémoires IV (1)', *Sochineniia*, pp. 239 and 250; Stählin, *Muzyka*, pp. 141–3.
88. *MP*, vol. 1, pp. 226–32.
89. Stählin, *Muzyka*, pp. 150–9; Findeizen, *History of Music*, vol. 2, pp. 55–7.
90. Richard Stites, *Serfdom, Society, and the Arts in Imperial Russia* (New Haven, CN and London, 2005), pp. 71–9.
91. Strong, *Art and Power*, pp. 153–70; Georgia Cowart, *The Triumph of Pleasure: Louis XIV and the Politics of Spectacle* (Chicago, IL, 2008), pp. 5–6.
92. Terry Castle, *Masquerade and Civilisation: the Carnivalesque in Eighteenth-Century English Culture and Fiction* (Stanford, CA, 1986), pp. 9–11.
93. Smith, *Georgian Monarchy*, pp. 237–8.
94. Richard Semmens, *The Bals Publics at the Paris Opéra in the Eighteenth Century* (Hillsdale, NY, 2004), pp. 2–6 and 10–21.
95. Iurii M. Lotman, *Besedy o russkoi kul'ture: Byt i traditsii russkogo dvorianstva (XVIII – nachalo XIX veka)* (St Petersburg, 2002), p. 100.
96. Bergholz, 'Dnevnik', *Neistovyi reformator*, pp. 208–16; Bergholz, 'Dnevnik', *Iunost' derzhavy*, pp. 136–45.
97. Castle, *Masquerade*, p. 6.
98. Richard Wortman, *Scenarios of Power: Myth and Ceremony in Russian Monarchy* (Princeton, NJ, 1995), vol. 1, p. 5.
99. Burke, *Popular Culture*, pp. 281–6.
100. Hughes, *Russia*, pp. 256–57.
101. *KfZh*, 1739 (7 and 9 July), p. 38.
102. Elena Pogosian, '"I nevozmozhnoe vozmozhno": svad'ba shutov v ledianom dome kak fakt ofitsial'noi kul'tury', *Trudy po russkoi i slavianskoi filologii. Literaturovedenie*, 4 (2001), pp. 80–109.
103. For the extensive planning documents, see *TZhRAI*, pp. 642–93.
104. Elena Pogosian, 'Masks and Masquerades at the Court of Elizaveta Petrovna (1741–42)', in Steven Usitalo and William Benton Whisenhurst (eds), *Russian and Soviet History: From the Time of Troubles to the Collapse of the Soviet Union* (Lanham, MD, 2008), pp. 39–41.
105. Catherine II, 'Mémoires II', *Sochineniia*, p. 79.
106. *KfZh*, 1745, p. 93 (15 September).
107. *RGIA*, f. 1329, op. 2, d. 39, l. 15 (Order from the Empress to the Police Chancellery, 16 September 1745).
108. *KfZh*, 1745, pp. 94–101 (17–30 September).
109. *RGADA*, f. 16, op. 1, d. 443, ll. 176–184ob (n.d.). NB. using the ages of the listed individuals, the likeliest year of compilation is 1747.

110. For more detail on these women, see V. P. Parkhomenko (comp.), *Siiatel'nye zheny: biografii i rodoslovnaia stats-dam i freilin russkogo dvora, po spiskam P. F. Karabanova* (St Petersburg, 1992), p. 23 and 52.
111. *RGIA*, f. 1329, op. 2, d. 40, l. 1 (Order issued by the Police Chancellery, 11 January 1746).
112. *PSZ*, vol. 5, no. 3241 (26 November 1718), p. 598. See also Chapter 1.
113. *RGADA*, f. 14, op. 1, d. 95, l. 1–1ob (Order concerning court masquerades in St Petersburg, 12 January 1746).
114. *AKV*, vol. 2, pp. 142–3.
115. Catherine II, 'Mémoires IV (1)', *Sochineniia*, p. 296.
116. On Sérigny and his company, see Vsevolodskii-Gerngross, *Teatr v Rossii pri Elizavete Petrovne*, pp. 136–49.
117. By this period, this term was a somewhat old-fashioned way to refer to the elite families of the Russian nobility: *Slovar'*, vol. 2, p. 119.
118. *KfZh*, 1748, p. 15 (11 February).
119. *KfZh*, 1748, pp. 15–16 (11 February).
120. *KfZh*, 1748, p. 15 (11 February).
121. *RGIA*, f. 439, op. 1, d. 2, ll. 24 and 25ob (Orders recorded in the daily sentry log, 10 and 11 February 1748).
122. *KfZh*, 1748, p. 19 (16, 18 and 19 February).
123. *KfZh*, 1748, p. 20 (20 February). The sentry logs added that foreign ministers were amongst the guests: *RGIA*, f. 439, op. 1, d. 2, l. 32 (Order recorded in the daily sentry log, 20 February 1748).
124. *KfZh*, 1748, p. 19 (20 February).
125. *ZhDGA*, 1751, p. 225 (1 January).
126. *KfZh*, 1751, pp. 7–8 (2 January).
127. *RGIA*, f. 466, op. 1, d. 84, l. 3 (Order issued by the Court Office, 9 January 1751).
128. *RGIA*, f. 466, op. 1, d. 84, l. 6–7 (Order issued by the Court Office, 15 January 1751).
129. *RGIA*, f. 466, op. 1, d. 84, l. 6–6ob.
130. *KfZh*, 1751, p. 15 (18 January).
131. *RGIA*, f. 466, op. 1, d. 84, l. 7.
132. *KfZh*, 1751, p. 31 (8 February).
133. *RGIA*, f. 466, op. 1, d. 84, l. 14 (Order issued by the Court Office, 5 February 1751).
134. *RGIA*, f. 466, op. 1, d. 84, l. 50 (Order issued by the Court Office, 23 April 1751).
135. See, for example, *KfZh*, 1755 (22 and 26 February), p. 23.
136. Wortman, *Scenarios*, vol. 1, pp. 119–20.
137. An extended version of this section is published as: 'The Summer Gardens in the Social Life of St Petersburg, 1725–61', *SEER*, 88/1–2 (2010), pp. 134–55.
138. Chandra Mukerji, *Territorial Ambitions and the Gardens of Versailles* (Cambridge, 1997), pp. 8–18 and 248–72.
139. Ian Thompson, *The Sun King's Garden: Louis XIV, André Le Nôtre and the Creation of the Gardens of Versailles* (London, 2006), esp. pp. 297–307.
140. Roland Puppe, 'Saxon Baroque Gardens (1694–1733): Nature's Entertainment Palaces', in Michel Conan (ed.), *Baroque Garden Cultures: Emulation, Sublimation, Subversion* (Washington DC, 2005), pp. 215–18 and 226–31.
141. Linda Hendriksson, 'Landscape Gardening', in Mårten Snickare (ed.), *Nicodemus Tessin the Younger: Royal Architect and Visionary* (Stockholm, 2002), pp. 151–65.

142. Thomas Baumgartner, 'Vienna Gloriosa and the Prince's Garden', in Agnes Husslein-Arco (ed.), *Prince Eugene: General-Philosopher and Art Lover* (Vienna, 2010), pp. 120–3.

143. On Paris, see Colin Jones, *Paris: the Biography of a City* (London, 2006), pp. 142–3 and 182–5. On London, see Lisa Picard, *Dr. Johnson's London: Life in London, 1740–1770* (London, 2000), pp. 35–40.

144. Melton, *Rise*, p. 169.

145. Bergholz, 'Dnevnik', *Neistovyi reformator*, pp. 135–42.

146. 'Opisanie o brake mezhdu Eia Vysochestvom Annoiu Petrovnoiu, Tsesarevnoiu Vserossiiskoiu, i Ego Korolevskim Vysochestvom Karlom Fridrikhom, gertsogom Golshteinogottorpskim', *Syn otechestva*, 8/3 (1839), pp. 268–9.

147. Bergholz, 'Dnevnik', *Iunost' derzhavy*, pp. 287–91.

148. Jane Vigor, *Letters from a Lady, Who Resided Some Years in Russia, to her Friend in England* (London, 1775), pp. 98–104.

149. *KfZh*, 1737 (28 August), pp. 33–5.

150. *KfZh*, 1739 (9 July), p. 38.

151. *KfZh*, 1750, pp. 58–59 (22 May).

152. *ZhDGA*, 1750, p. 208 (1 July).

153. *KfZh*, 1752, p. 34 (28 April).

154. *RGIA*, f. 1329, op. 2, d. 44, ll. 13–13ob (Order from Petr I. Shuvalov to the Police Chancellery, 25 May 1752).

155. *RGIA*, f. 439, op. 1, d. 10, l. 37ob (Order recorded in the daily sentry log, 10 May 1755).

156. *RGIA*, f. 439, op. 1, d. 10, l. 38 (Order to Guards Captain Fedor Vadkovskii, 10 May 1755).

157. *KfZh*, 1755, pp. 54–5 (10 May).

158. *RGIA*, f. 439, op. 1, d. 10, l. 38 (10 May 1755).

159. *RGIA*, f. 1329, op. 2, d. 47, l. 29 (Order recorded in the daily sentry log, 17 June 1755).

160. *KfZh*, 1755, p. 66 (16 June).

161. *KfZh*, 1755, p. 73 (3 August) and *RGIA*, f. 439, op. 1, d. 10, l. 64ob (Order to Guards Captain Mikhail Ashcherin, 3 August 1755).

162. *RGIA*, f. 1329, op. 2, d. 48, ll. 16–16ob (Order from Aleksandr B. Buturlin to the Police Chancellery, 24 May 1756).

163. *PSZ*, 14, 10560 (24 May 1756), pp. 573–4.

164. *RGIA*, f. 1329, op. 2, d. 48, l. 19 (Order from Aleksandr B. Buturlin to the Police Chancellery, 19 June 1756). See also *PSZ*, 14, 10573 (19 June 1756), p. 588.

165. *ZhDGA*, 1748, pp. 70–71 (1 May).

166. *RGIA*, f. 439, op. 1, d. 10, l. 38 (Order to Guards Captain Fedor Vadkovskii, 10 May 1755).

167. *ZhDGA*, 1748, p. 76 (19 May). This order notes that such tickets had already been issued on 4 and 18 May.

168. *KfZh*, 1755, pp. 56–58 (17 and 21 May).

169. *RGIA*, f. 439, op. 1, d. 10, ll. 43–43ob (Order recorded in the daily sentry log, 17 May 1755).

170. George Rudé, *Hanoverian London* (London, 1971), pp. 71–2.

171. David Garrioch, *The Making of Revolutionary Paris* (Berkeley, CA, 2002), pp. 99–101.

172. For more detail on these gardens, see the classic Warwick Wroth, *The London Pleasure Gardens of the Eighteenth Century* (London, 1896).

173. Mikhail I. Pyliaev, *Staryi Peterburg: razskazy iz byloi zhizni stolitsy* (St Petersburg, 1889), pp. 432–5.

174. *Prazdnoe vremia v pol'zu upotreblennoe*, part 1 (1759), pp. 365–6, cited in Douglas Smith, *Working the Rough Stone: Freemasonry and Society in Eighteenth-Century Russia* (DeKalb, IL, 1999), p. 68.

175. Heinrich Friedrich von Storch, *The Picture of Petersburg* (London, 1801), p. 430.

176. On the English context, see Robert Malcolmson, *Popular Recreations in English Society, 1700–1850* (Cambridge, 1973), pp. 5–14 and 34–51. On Paris, see Robert Isherwood, 'Entertainment in the Parisian Fairs in the Eighteenth Century', *Journal of Modern History*, 53/1 (1981), pp. 24–48.

177. Peter Burke, *Popular Culture in Early Modern Europe*, 3rd edition (Farnham, 2009), pp. 49–54.

178. Trevor Johnston, 'The Reformation and Popular Culture', in Andrew Pettigrew (ed.), *The Reformation World* (London, 2000), pp. 547–52.

179. Malcolm Burgess, 'Fairs and Entertainers in Eighteenth-Century Russia', *SEER*, 38 (1959), pp. 95–6.

180. Elena E. Keller, *Prazdnichnaia kul'tura Peterburga: ocherki istorii* (St Petersburg, 2001), p. 72–3.

181. Catriona Kelly, *Petrushka: the Russian Carnival Puppet Theatre* (Cambridge, 1990), pp. 46–58.

182. Catherine II, 'Mémoires IV (1)', in A. N. Pypin (ed.), *Sochineniia imperatritsy Ekateriny II, na osnovanii podlinnykh rukopisei* (St Petersburg 1901–7), p. 232.

183. *SPV*, no. 83 (17 October 1743), p. 682 and no. 1 (3 January 1745), p. 8.

184. Burgess, 'Fairs', pp. 101–2.

185. *SPV*, no. 101 (19 Dec. 1755), p. 8.

186. Anna F. Nekrylova, *Russkie narodnye gorodskie prazdniki, uveseleniia i zrelishcha: konets XVIII – nachalo XX veka* (St Petersburg, 2004), pp. 46–8.

187. *PSZ*, vol. 13, no. 9959 (13 March 1752), p. 620.

188. Martha and Catherine Wilmot, *The Russian Journals... 1803–1808* (London, 1934), pp. 192–93.

189. See, for example, Edward Muir, *Ritual in Early Modern Europe*, 2nd edition (Cambridge, 2005), pp. 89–92.

190. William Richardson, *Anecdotes of the Russian Empire in a Series of Letters Written, a Few Years Ago, from St Petersburg* (London, 1784), p. 216.

191. Burgess, 'Fairs', pp. 96–97.

192. Vigor, pp. 144–6.

193. Peder von Haven, 'Puteshestvie v Rossiiu', in Iurii N. Bespiatykh (ed.), *Peterburg Anny Ioannovny v inostrannykh opisaniiakh* (St Petersburg, 1997), p. 339.

194. Richardson, *Anecdotes*, pp. 212–13.

195. Pavel Svin'in, *Dostopamiatnosti Sanktpeterburga i ego okrestnostei* (St Petersburg, 1997), pp. 76–8.

196. Albin M. Konechnyi, 'Peterburgskie narodnye gulian'ia na maslenoi i paskhal'noi nedeliakh', in Natal'ia V. Iukhneva (ed.), *Peterburg i guberniia: istoriko-etnograficheskie issledovaniia* (Leningrad, 1989), p. 23.

197. Karl Reinhold Berch, 'Putevye zametki o Rossii', in Bespiatykh (ed.), *Peterburg Anny Ioannovny*, p. 121.

198. Catherine II, 'Mémoires IV (2)', *Sochineniia*, p. 309–10.

199. See, for example, Haven, 'Puteshestvie', p. 339.

200. Ivan P. Vysotskii, *Sankt-Peterburgskaia stolichnaia politsiia i gradonachal'stvo, 1703–1903* (St Petersburg, 1903), p. 41.

201. *Tri veka Sankt-Peterburga. Entsiklopediia. Tom I: Os'mnadtsatoe stoletie* (St Petersburg, 2003), part 1, pp. 448–9.
202. Burgess, 'Fairs', p. 98.

5   Instruction: Fashioning an Audience

1. For an overview of university foundations, see Willem Frijhofs, 'Patterns', in Hilde de Ridder-Symoens (ed.), *A History of the University in Europe* (Cambridge, 1996), vol. 2, pp. 74–94.
2. On these two institutions, see Liudmila Charipova, *Latin Books and the Eastern Orthodox Clerical Elite in Kiev, 1632–1780* (Manchester, 2006), esp. pp. 47–55 and Nikolaos Chrissidis, 'Creating the New Educated Elite: Learning and Faith in Moscow's Slavo-Greco-Latin Academy, 1685–1694', unpublished PhD thesis (Yale University, 2000).
3. Christopher Friedrichs, 'Whose House of Learning? Some Thoughts on German Schools in Post-Reformation Germany', *History of Education Quarterly*, 22 (1982), pp. 371–7.
4. Helen Jewell, *Education in Early Modern England* (Basingstoke, 1998), p. 104.
5. Robert Houston, *Literacy in Early Modern Europe: Culture and Education, 1500–1800* (London, 1988), pp. 23–6.
6. Maria Rose di Simone, 'Admission', in Hilde de Ridder-Symoens (ed.), *A History of the University in Europe* (Cambridge, 1996), vol. 2, pp. 317–18.
7. Joseph Black, *Citizens for the Fatherland: Education, Educators, and Pedagogical Ideals in Eighteenth-Century Russia* (New York, 1979), pp. 15–22.
8. On Peter's education, see Nikolai Astrov, 'Pervonachal'noe obrazovanie Petra velikago', *Russkii arkhiv*, 8 (1875), pp. 480–1.
9. Lidiia N. Semenova, *Ocherki istorii byta i kul'turnoi zhizni Rossii pervaia polovina XVIII v.* (Leningrad, 1982). p. 101.
10. Max Okenfuss, 'Russian Students in Europe in the Age of Peter the Great', in John Garrard (ed.), *The Eighteenth Century in Russia* (Oxford, 1973), pp. 131–45.
11. Ivan I. Nepliuev, 'Zapiski', in Viktor P. Naumov (ed.), *Imperia posle Petra, 1725–1765* (Moscow, 1998), pp. 389–420.
12. Lindsey Hughes, *Russia in the Age of Peter the Great* (New Haven, CT, 1998), p. 306.
13. Mikhail M. Bogoslovskii, *Byt i nravy russkogo dvorianstva v pervoi polovine XVIII veka*, 2nd edition (Petrograd, 1918), p. 11.
14. Hughes, *Russia*, p. 174.
15. Friedrich Christian Weber, *The Present State of Russia* (London, 1968), vol. 1, p. 149.
16. *PSZ*, 5, 2968 (20 December 1715), p. 186.
17. Nikolai N. Molchanov, *Diplomatiia Petra Velikogo* (Moscow, 1990).
18. Mikhail M. Bogoslovskii, *Byt i nravy russkogo dvorianstva v pervoi polovine XVIII veka*, 2nd edition (Petrograd, 1918), p. 12.
19. See, for example, Petr A. Tolstoi, *The Travel Diary of Peter Tolstoi: a Muscovite in Early Modern Europe*, ed. and transl. Max J. Okenfuss (DeKalb, IL, 1987), pp. 75–6 (Venice), 209 (Naples), 242 (Malta) and 298 (Rome); Andrei A. Matveev, *Russkii diplomat vo Frantsii: zapiski Andreia Matveeva* (Leningrad, 1972), p. 198.
20. Feofan Prokopovich, *The Spiritual Regulation of Peter the Great*, ed. and transl. Alexander Muller (Seattle, WA, 1972), pp. 20–1 and 30–9.

21. Georges Bissonnette, 'Peter the Great and the Church as an Educational Institution', in John Curtiss (ed.), *Essays on Russian and Soviet History in Honour of Geroid Tanquary Robinson* (Leiden, 1963), pp. 8–9.
22. *PSZ*, 5, 2762 (20 January 1714), p. 78.
23. *PSZ*, 6, 4021 (31 May 1722), pp. 697–9.
24. Max Okenfuss, 'Technical Training in Russia under Peter the Great', *History of Education Quarterly*, 13 (1973), pp. 338–39.
25. *PSZ*, 12, 9054 (26 October 1744), pp. 247–51; *PSZ*, 8, 6188 (21 September 1732), pp. 928–30.
26. *PSZ*, 5, 2937 (1 October 1715), pp. 173–6.
27. Nicholas Plumley, 'The Royal Mathematical School, Christ's Hospital', *History Today*, 23/8 (1973), pp. 581–7; Nicholas Hans, 'The Moscow School of Mathematics and Navigation (1701)', *SEER*, 29 (1951), pp. 532–36.
28. Okenfuss, 'Technical Training', pp. 334–5.
29. Feodosii F. Veselago, *Ocherk istorii morskago kadetskago korpusa* (St Petersburg, 1852), pp. 37–47.
30. Ivan K. Kirilov, *Tsvetushchee sostoianie vserossiiskogo gosudarstva*, ed. Boris A. Rybakov, Leonid A. Gol'denberg and Sergei M. Troitskii (Moscow, 1977), p. 51.
31. William Ryan, 'Navigation and the Modernisation of Petrine Russia: Teachers, Textbooks, Terminology', in Roger Bartlett and Janet Hartley (ed.), *Russia in the Age of the Enlightenment: Essays for Isabel de Madariaga* (London, 1990), p. 79.
32. Vladimir N. Benda, 'Pervye rossiiskie artilleriiskie i inzhenernye shkoly v kontse XVII – pervoi chetverti XVIII veka', *Voenno-istoricheskii zhurnal*, 9 (2009), pp. 23–8.
33. *PSZ*, 6, 3708 (16 January 1721), p. 302.
34. Okenfuss, 'Technical Training', p. 340; *PSZ*, 6, 3937 (5 April 1722), p. 535.
35. Semenova, *Ocherki*, pp. 94–5.
36. Joseph Black, *Citizens for the Fatherland: Education, Educators, and Pedagogical Ideals in Eighteenth-Century Russia* (New York, 1979), p. 28.
37. Mikhail I. Semevskii, *Tsaritsa Praskov'ia, 1664–1723* (Leningrad, 1991), p. 34.
38. D. Korsakov, 'Kniaginia Natal'ia Dolgorukaia', *Istoricheskii vestnik*, 23 (1886), p. 265.
39. *SIRIO*, vol. 40, p. 390 (De Campredon to Cardinal Dubois: St Petersburg, 12 December 1721).
40. Friedrich W. von Bergholz, 'Dnevnik kamer-iunkera Fridrikha-Vil'gel'ma Berkhgol'tsa, 1721–1725 (chs 1 and 2)', in Viktor P. Naumov (ed.), *Neistovyi reformator* (Moscow, 2000), p. 139.
41. Bogoslovskii, *Byt i nravy*, pp. 18–19. See also Bergholz, 'Dnevnik', *Neistovyi reformator*, p. 292.
42. See, for example, Bergholz, 'Dnevnik', *Neistovyi reformator*, pp. 160 and 248.
43. See, for example, Marc Fumaroli, *When the World Spoke French*, transl. Richard Howard (New York, 2011).
44. *PSZ*, 8, 5881 (29 July 1731), pp. 793–4.
45. *RGADA*, f. 16, op. 1, d. 76 (Proekt ob uchrezhdenii kadetskogo korpusa, naidennyi v bumagakh Verkhovnogo Tainogo soveta, c. 1726–30), ll. 1–4ob.
46. Black, *Citizens*, pp. 47–8.
47. Veselago, *Ocherk*, pp. 115–40; *PSZ*, 13, 10062 (15 December 1752) and 'Kniga shtatov', 2, pp. 45–53.
48. See, for example, *RGVIA*, f. 314, op. 1, vol. 1, d. 2637, ll. 1–23ob (O bytii pri vys. dvore maskaradov, 1753–4) and d. 2702, ll. 1–17ob (O byvshikh korpusnykh chinakh pri dvore na maskarade, 1755).

49. Gary Marker, *Publishing, Printing, and the Origins of Intellectual Life in Russia, 1700–1800* (Princeton, NJ, 1985), pp. 77–8. *RGVIA*, f. 314, op. 1, vol. 1, d. 2656, ll. 1–8 (O perevode frantsuzskikh knig na rossiiskoi iazyk, 1754–6).

50. Marc Raeff, *Origins of the Russian Intelligentsia: the Eighteenth-Century Nobility* (New York, 1966), p. 139.

51. V. N. Vsevolodskii-Gerngross, *Istoriia teatral'nago obrazovaniia v Rossii* (St Petersburg, 1913), vol. 1, pp. 201–15.

52. See, for example, *SPV*, no. 18 (3 March 1749), p. 7, no. 81 (9 October 1752), p. 7 and no. 59 (25 July 1755), p. 7.

53. This point was raised in the law that established Moscow University in 1755: *PSZ*, 14, 10346 (24 January 1755), p. 286.

54. *PSZ*, 14, 10724 (5 May 1757), p. 765.

55. See, for example, the advertisement for Saucerotte's school in: *SPV*, no. 70 (2 September 1757), pp. 7–8.

56. Mikhail V. Danilov, *Zapiski M. V. Danilova, artillerii maiora, napisannyia im v 1771 godu (1722–62)* (Kazan, 1913), pp. 27–47.

57. Simon Werrett, *Fireworks: Pyrotechnic Arts and Sciences in European History* (Chicago, IL, 2010), pp. 160–2.

58. Andrei T. Bolotov, *Zhizn' i prikliucheniia Andreia Bolotova* (Moscow, 1986), vol. 1, pp. 17 and 39–41.

59. Bolotov, *Zhizn'*, vol. 1, pp. 86–92.

60. Bolotov, *Zhizn'*, vol. 1, pp. 174–5.

61. Oleg A. Khazin, *Pazhi, kadety, iunkera: istoricheskii ocherk* (Moscow, 2002), pp. 19–28.

62. *PSZ*, 14, 10346 (24 January 1755), pp. 284–94. The freedom to choose where and how to educate one's children, whether in Russia or abroad, was included in the edict 'emancipating' the Russian nobility from compulsory service issued by Peter III in 1762: *PSZ*, 15, 11444 (18 February 1762), p. 914.

63. *PSZ*, 16, 12154 (5 May 1764), pp. 742–55.

64. Zinaida E. Mordvinova, 'Smol'nyi institut v epokhu imperatritsy Ekateriny II (1764–96), *Istoricheskii vestnik*, 136/6 (1914), pp. 996–7.

65. Janet Hartley, *A Social History of the Russian Empire, 1650–1825* (London, 1999), pp. 135–9; on the Austrian system, see James van Horn Melton, *Absolutism and the Eighteenth-Century Origins of Compulsory Schooling in Prussia and Austria* (Cambridge, 1988), esp. pp. 200–30.

66. Simon Dixon, *The Modernisation of Russia, 1676–1825* (Cambridge, 1999), pp. 156–7.

67. Norbert Elias, *The Civilizing Process*, revised edition, ed. and transl. Edmund Jephcott (London, 2000), 2 vols. pp. 47–172.

68. See, for example, Peter Burke, *The Fortunes of the 'Courtier': the European Reception of Castiglione's 'Cortegiano'* (Cambridge, 1995), pp. 62–5 and 158–62.

69. John Gillingham, 'From *Civilitas* to Civility: Codes of Manners in Medieval and Early Modern England', *Transactions of the Royal Historical Society*, 6th Series, 12 (2002), pp. 267–89.

70. Anna Bryson, *From Courtesy to Civility: Changing Codes of Conduct in Early Modern England* (Oxford, 1998), pp. 96–105.

71. Sydney Anglo, 'The Courtier: the Renaissance and Changing Ideals', in Arthur Dickens (ed.), *The Courts of Europe: Politics, Patronage and Royalty, 1400–1800* (London, 1977), pp. 44–53.

72. On early Slavic primers, see Max Okenfuss, *The Discovery of Childhood in Russia: the Evidence of the Slavic Primer* (Newtonville, MA, 1980), pp. 8–11.
73. *Iunosti chestnoe zertsalo ili pokazanie k zhiteiskomu obkhozhdeniiu, sobrannoe ot raznykh avtorov* (St Petersburg, 1717).
74. *SK*, vol. 3, pp. 452–3.
75. James Cracraft, *The Petrine Revolution in Russian Culture* (Cambridge, MA, 2004), pp. 370–1. The role of Paus as translator is also covered in Maria Cristina Bragone, 'K istorii vospriiatiia Erazma Rotterdamskogo v Rossii v XVIII veke', *SGECRN*, 34 (2006), pp. 44–8.
76. The title link was made by Isabel de Madariaga, acknowledged in Lindsey Hughes, '"The Crown of Maidenly Honour and Virtue": Redefining Femininity in Peter I's Russia', in Wendy Rosslyn (ed.), *Women and Gender in Eighteenth-Century Russia* (Aldershot, 2003), p. 39.
77. Okenfuss, *Discovery*, p. 47.
78. Hughes, '"The Crown"', pp. 39–40.
79. Catriona Kelly, *Refining Russia: Advice Literature, Polite Culture, and Gender from Catherine to Yeltsin* (Oxford, 2001), p. 20.
80. Cracraft, *Petrine Revolution in Culture*, pp. 375–6.
81. Hughes, '"The Crown"', p. 41.
82. Charles Fantazzi, 'Vives and the *emargenati*', in Charles Fantazzi (ed.), *A Companion to Juan Luis Vives* (Leiden, 2008), pp. 71–86.
83. Marker, *Publishing*, pp. 30 and 36–7.
84. Cracraft, *Petrine Revolution in Culture*, pp. 377–8.
85. Nikolai A. Kopanev, 'Frantsuzskie knigi v Letnem dome imperatritsy Elizavety Petrovny', in A. A. Zaitseva and Sergei P. Luppov (ed.), *Kniga i biblioteki v Rossii v XIV – pervoi polovine XIX veka* (Leningrad, 1982), p. 37.
86. *StPb IRI RAN*, f. 36, op. 1, d. 846, l. 2.
87. Marker, *Printing*, p. 61.
88. *SK*, vol. 1, p. 254.
89. *SK*, vol. 1, pp. 406–7.
90. *Istinnaia politika znatnykh i blagorodnykh osob*, transl. Vasilii K. Trediakovskii (St Petersburg, 1745), pp. 82–3, 119–21 and 164–5.
91. *Dialogues domestiques. Gespräche von Haussachen. Domashnye razgovory. Colloquia domestica* (St Petersburg, 1756).
92. Charles L. Drage, 'Russian Model Conversations, c. 1630–1773', in Roger Bartlett and Lindsey Hughes (eds), *Russian Society and Culture and the Long Eighteenth Century: Essays in Honour of Anthony G. Cross* (Münster, 2004), pp. 161–2.
93. *Domashnye razgovory*, pp. 23–41 (tea), 43–59 (tobacco and smoking), 59–77 (coffee), 77–87 (strolling), and 105–45 (being at or hosting a dinner).
94. *SK*, vol. 1, pp. 307–8.
95. Pavel I. Khoteev, 'Frantsuzskaia kniga v biblioteke Peterburgskoi Akademii nauk (1714–1742 gg.), in Sergei P. Luppov (ed.), *Frantsuzskaia kniga v Rossii v XVIII v. Ocherki istorii* (Leningrad, 1986), p. 38. For details on Khrushchev's background and book collection, see Sergei P. Luppov, *Kniga v Rossii v poslepetrovskoe vremia: 1725–1740* (Leningrad, 1976), pp. 227–34.
96. *SK*, vol. 3, p. 208.
97. Kelly, *Refining*, p. 19 and 25.
98. Kelly, *Refining*, p. 17.
99. See, for example, Catherine II, 'Mémoires II', *Sochineniia*, pp. 117–18 and 131.

100. On England, see Bryson, *From Courtesy to Civility*, pp. 122–41; on France, see Mark Motley, *Becoming a French Aristocrat: the Education of the Court Nobility, 1580–1715* (Princeton, NJ, 1990).

101. Kate van Orden, *Music, Discipline, and Arms in Early Modern France* (Chicago, IL, 2005), pp. 91–2.

102. Régine Astier, 'Louis XIV *Premier Danseur*', in David Lee Rubin (ed.), *Sun King: the Ascendancy of French Culture during the Reign of Louis XIV* (London, 1992), pp. 73–9.

103. Gunilla Dahlberg, 'Ballet in Sweden', in Pierre Béhar and Helen Watanabe-O'Kelly (eds), *Spectaculum Europæum: Theatre and Spectacle in Europe 1580–1750* (Wiesbaden, 1999), pp. 577–83.

104. Strong, *Art and Power*, pp. 57–60.

105. Sara Smart, 'The Württemberg Court and the Introduction of Ballet in the Empire', in Mulryne, Watanabe-O'Kelly and Shewring (eds), *Europa Triumphans*, vol. 2, pp. 35–45.

106. Julia Prest, 'The Politics of Ballet at the Court of Louis XIV', in Jennifer Nevile (ed.), *Dance, Spectacle, and the Body Politick, 1250–1750* (Bloomington, IN, 2008), p. 234.

107. Watanabe-O'Kelly, *Court Culture in Dresden*, pp. 183–5.

108. Rebecca Harris-Warrick, 'Ballroom Dancing at the Court of Louis XIV', *Early Music*, 14/1 (1986), pp. 41–50.

109. These dances are described in John Playford, *The English Dancing Master, or Plaine and Easie Rules for the Dancing of Country Dances* (London, 1651).

110. See, for example, the calendar present in Robert Bucholz, *The Augustan Court: Queen Anne and the Decline of Court Culture* (Stanford, CA, 1993), pp. 231–4 and Smith, *Georgian Monarchy*, pp. 200–2.

111. Jennifer Nevile, 'Dance in Europe, 1250–1750', in Nevile (ed.), *Dance*, pp. 22–3.

112. Meredith Little and Natalie Jenne, *Dance and the Music of J. S. Bach* (Bloomington, IN, 1991), pp. 62–6.

113. Pierre Rameau, *The Dancing Master*, transl. Cyril Beaumont (Brooklyn, NY, 1970), pp. 1–45 (on movement) and 52–74 (on the minuet).

114. See, for example, JoLynn Edwards, 'Watteau and the Dance', in François Moureau and Margaret Morgan Grasselli (ed.), *Antoine Watteau (1684–1721): le peintre, son temps et sa légende* (Paris, 1987), pp. 219–25.

115. Sergei N. Shubinskii, *Istoricheskie ocherki i rasskazy* (Moscow, 1995), p. 21.

116. Stählin, *Muzyka*, p. 256.

117. Vasmer, vol. 4, pp. 18–19.

118. Stählin, *Muzyka*, pp. 257–58.

119. Lindsey Hughes, *Peter the Great: a Biography* (New Haven, CT, 2002), pp. 42–3.

120. Korb, *Diary*, vol. 1, pp. 263–5.

121. Dmitri Zakharine, 'Tanz– und Körperverhalten im kommunikativen Alltagsverkehr des 17.–19. Jh. Russland und Westeuropa im Vergleich', *Wiener Slawistischer Almanach*, 47 (2001), p. 142.

122. Hughes, *Russia*, pp. 268–9.

123. William McNeill, *Keeping Together in Time: Dance and Drill in Human History* (Cambridge, MA, 1995), pp. 132–4.

124. Zakharine, 'Tanz– und Körperverhalten', pp. 149–50.

125. Bergholz, 'Dnevnik', *Neistovyi reformator*, pp. 253–4.

126. Moira Goff, '"The Art of Dancing, demonstrated by Characters and Figures": French and English Sources for Court and Theatre Dance, 1700–1750', *British Library Journal*, 21 (1995), pp. 202–31.

127. For example, Ivan Kuskov, a Cadet Corps instructor, published 'The Dance Teacher' (*Tantsoval'noi uchitel'*) in 1794: *SK*, vol. 2, pp. 108–9.
128. Vsevolodskii-Gerngross, *Teatr v Rossii pri Elizavete Petrovne*, p. 10.
129. See, for example, Mikhail D. Khmyrov, *Grafinia Ekaterina Ivanovna Golovkina i eia vremia, 1701–91 goda* (St Petersburg, 1867), p. 67.
130. Bergholz, 'Dnevnik', *Neistovyi reformator*, p. 355.
131. For a detailed study, see Elizabeth Clara Sander, *Social Dancing in Peter the Great's Russia* (Hildesheim, 2007).
132. Berch, 'Putevye zametki', p. 158.
133. Shubinskii, *Istoricheskie ocherki*, p. 64.
134. *MP*, vol. 2, p. 124.
135. Stählin, *Muzyka*, p. 264.
136. The documents are collected in: *TZhRAI*, pp. 359–61, 367 and 379–80.
137. Vsevolodskii-Gerngross, *Istoriia teatral'nogo obrazovaniia*, vol. 1, pp. 391–3.
138. See, for example, Vigor, *Letters*, p. 73 and Catherine II, 'Mémoires IV (1)', *Sochineniia*, p. 296.
139. For a useful overview of these ballets, see *MP*, vol. 1, pp. 99–102.
140. Stählin, *Muzyka*, pp. 269–70.
141. On Hilverding, see, *MP*, vol. 1, pp. 247–49; on Angiolini, see *MP*, vol. 1, pp. 40–2.
142. See, for example, *RGIA*, f. 466, op. 1, d. 84, l. 104 (Order from the Court Office, 6 October 1751).
143. Catherine II, 'Mémoires IV (1)', *Sochineniia*, pp. 301–2.
144. See, for example, *SPV*, no. 18 (3 March 1741), p. 6, no. 52 (29 June 1753), p. 8, and no. 14 (17 February 1758), p. 6.
145. Natal'ia P. Roslavleva, *Era of the Russian Ballet* (London, 1966), pp. 21–3.
146. An earlier version of this section appeared as: 'The Function of Fashion: Women and Clothing at the Russian Court, 1700–1762', in Wendy Rosslyn and Alessandra Tosi (eds), *Women in Eighteenth-Century Russian Culture and Society* (Basingstoke, 2007), pp. 125–43.
147. Aileen Ribeiro, *Dress and Morality*, 2nd edition (Oxford, 2003), pp. 12–14.
148. Strong, *Art and Power*, pp. 21–2.
149. Susan Vincent, *Dressing the Elite: Clothes in Early Modern England* (Oxford, 2003), pp. 2–5.
150. Daniel Roche, *The Culture of Clothing: Dress and Fashion in the Ancien Régime*, transl. Jean Birrell (Cambridge, 1994), pp. 185–6.
151. Philip Mansel, *Dressed to Rule: Royal and Court Costume from Louis XIV to Elizabeth II* (New Haven, CT, 2005), pp. xiv–xv.
152. For an overview of this period, see Christopher Breward, *The Culture of Fashion: a New History of Fashionable Dress* (Manchester, 1995), pp. 41–108.
153. Mansel, *Dressed*, pp. 1–15.
154. Alan Hunt, *Governance of the Consuming Passions: a History of Sumptuary Law* (Basingstoke, 1996).
155. Mansel, *Dressed*, pp. 22–3.
156. Hughes, *Russia*, pp. 280–1.
157. See, for example, Rudi Matthee, 'Anti-Ottoman Politics and Transit Rights: the Seventeenth-Century Trade in Silk between Safavid Iran and Muscovy', *Cahiers du Monde russe*, 35/4 (1994), pp. 739–61.
158. *PSZ*, 1, 607 (6 August 1675), pp. 1007–8.
159. Hughes, *Russia and the West*, p. 177.

160. Raisa M. Kirsanova, *Russkii kostium i byt XVIII – XIX vekov* (Moscow, 2002), pp. 36–8.
161. This event took place at Preobrazhenskoe on 26 August 1698: Korb, *Diary*, vol. 1, pp. 155–56.
162. *PSZ*, 4, 1741 (4 January 1700), p. 1 and 1898 (28 February 1702), p. 189.
163. *PSZ*, 4, 2015 (16 January 1705), p. 282–83.
164. Ivan A. Zheliabuzhskii, 'Dnevnye zapiski', in A. Liberman and S. Shokarev (eds), *Rozhdenie imperii* (Moscow, 1997), p. 325.
165. Weber, *Present State*, vol. 1, p. 4.
166. Arcadius Kahan, 'The Costs of "Westernisation" in Russia: the Gentry and the Economy in the Eighteenth Century', *SR*, 25 (1966), pp. 40–66.
167. Ivan T. Pososhkov, *The Book of Poverty and Wealth*, ed. and transl. A. P. Vlasto and L. R. Lewitter (London, 1987), pp. 262–4.
168. Lindsey Hughes, '"A Beard is an Unnecessary Burden": Peter I's Laws on Shaving and their Roots in Early Russia', in Bartlett and Hughes (ed.), *Russian Society and Culture*, pp. 21–34.
169. Lindsey Hughes, 'From Caftans to Corsets: the Sartorial Transformation of Women in the Reign of Peter the Great', in Peter Barta (ed.), *Gender and Sexuality in Russian Civilisation* (London, 2001), pp. 25–6.
170. Valerie Steele, *The Corset: a Cultural History* (New Haven, CT, 2001), pp. 6–13.
171. Aileen Ribeiro, *Dress in Eighteenth-Century Europe, 1715–1789*, 2nd ed. (New Haven, CT, 2002), pp. 42–5.
172. Kirsanova, *Russkii kostium*, p. 39.
173. Georg-Adam Schlessinger, 'Polnoe opisanie Rossii, nakhodiashcheisia nyne pod vlast'iu dvukh tsarei-sopravitelei Ivana Alekseevicha i Petra Alekseevicha', transl. Liudmila P. Lapteva, *Voprosy istorii*, 1 (1970), p. 115.
174. Samuel Collins, *The Present State of Russia, in a Letter to a Friend at London* (London, 1671), p. 69.
175. Peter Henry Bruce, *Memoirs of Peter Henry Bruce, Esq., a Military Officer in the Services of Prussia, Russia & Great Britain* (London, 1782), p. 85.
176. See, for example, Vigor, *Letters*, p. 20.
177. Pyliaev, *Staroe zhit'e*, p. 73.
178. 'Reestr mushek', *Lubok: russkie narodnye kartinki, XVII–XVIII vv. Al'bom*, ed. and comp. Iurii Ovsiannikov (Moscow, 1968), plate 46.
179. Hughes, *Russia*, p. 285.
180. Grigorii V. Esipov, *Raskol'nich'i dela XVIII stolietiia: izvlechennyia iz del Preobrazhenskago prikaza i tainoi rozysknykh del kantseliarii* (St Petersburg, 1863), vol. 2, p. 176.
181. Hughes, *Russia*, p. 281 and Korb, *Diary*, vol. 1, pp. 159–60.
182. Boris I. Kurakin, 'Zhizn' kniazia Borisa Ivanovicha Kurakina im samim opisannaia', in *Arkhiv kniazia F. A. Kurakina*, ed. Mikhail I. Semevskii (St Petersburg, 1890), vol. 1, p. 257.
183. Iurii M. Lotman, *Besedy o russkoi kul'ture: Byt i traditsii russkogo dvorianstva (XVIII – nachalo XIX veka)* (St Petersburg, 2002), p. 15.
184. Bergholz, 'Dnevnik', *Neistovyi reformator*, p. 168.
185. Cornelius de Bruyn, *Travels into Muscovy, Persia, and part of the East-Indies* (London, 1737), 1, p. 30.
186. Lindsey Hughes, 'Between Two Worlds: Tsarevna Natal'ia Alekseevna and the Emancipation of Petrine Women', in Maria di Salvo and Lindsey Hughes (eds), *A Window on Russia* (Rome, 1996), p. 31.
187. *PSZ*, 7, 4944 (5 July 1726) p. 684.

188. Ribeiro, *Dress in Eighteenth-Century Europe*, p. 34.
189. Pisarenko, *Povsednevnaia zhizn'*, p. 67. See, for example, *KfZh*, 1734 (30 August), p. 9; *KfZh*, 1736 (19 January), p. 6 and (3 February), p. 12.
190. Ribeiro, *Dress in Eighteenth-Century Europe*, p. 35.
191. Ribeiro, *Dress in Eighteenth-Century Europe*, pp. 136–8.
192. See, for example, *KfZh*, 1748 (25 October), p. 61; *KfZh*, 1755 (12 March), p. 26.
193. Catherine II, 'Mémoires IV (1)', *Sochineniia imperatritsy Ekateriny II, na osnovanii podlinnykh rukopisei*, ed. A. N. Pypin (St Petersburg 1901–7), pp. 288–9.
194. *RGADA*, f. 14, op. 1. d. 113 (Items ordered for the court of Elizaveta Petrovna, including cloth and accessories for a lady's toilette, 1748–55), ll. 41–4.
195. For example, Elizaveta O. Efimovskaia, one of Elizabeth's court ladies, married Ivan G. Chernyshev in 1749 and was given quantities of cloth, dresses and other items valued at 11,135 rubles: *RGADA*, f. 14, op. 1, d. 98 (Engagement gifts to ladies-in-waiting from the Empress, 1747–65), ll. 10–14ob.
196. Catherine II, 'Mémoires IV (1)', *Sochineniia*, p. 211; Catherine II, 'Mémoires IV (2)', *Sochineniia*, p. 345.
197. Ribeiro, *Dress in Eighteenth–Century Europe*, pp. 92–7.
198. *PSZ*, 9, 8301 (17 December 1740), pp. 320–21; *PSZ*, 9, 8680 (11 December 1742), pp. 832–34.
199. See, for example, Ribeiro, *Dress in Eighteenth-Century Europe*, pp. 202–5.
200. *KfZh*, 1751 (3 March), p. 40, (5 May), p. 61, (26 May), p. 63 and (8 December), p. 119.
201. *RGIA*, f. 466, op. 1, d. 87, l. 72 (Order from the Court Office, 26 May 1752); Catherine II, 'Mémoires IV (2)', *Sochineniia*, pp. 316–17.
202. Catherine II, 'Mémoires I', *Sochineniia*, p. 55.
203. *ZhDGA*, 1750 (23 October), p. 218.
204. *KfZh*, 1750 (23 October), p. 118.
205. Catherine II, 'Mémoires IV (1)', *Sochineniia*, p. 296.
206. Catherine II, 'Mémoires I', *Sochineniia*, p. 55.
207. Vern L. Bullough and Bonnie Bullough, *Cross Dressing, Sex, and Gender* (Philadelphia, PA, 1993), pp. 125–32.
208. *Stoglav*, ed. Dmitrii E. Kozhanchikov (St Petersburg, 1863), chapter 93, p. 265.
209. Grigorii Kaganov, *Sankt-Peterburg: Obrazy prostranstva* (Moscow, 1995), p. 27–8.
210. Mikhail M. Shcherbatov, *On the Corruption of Morals in Russia*, ed. and trans. Antony Lentin (Cambridge, 1969), pp. 159–61, 191–3 and 223–5.
211. France remained the exception: compare Jeroen Duindam, *Vienna and Versailles: the Courts of Europe's Major Dynastic Rivals, 1550–1780* (Cambridge, 2003), pp. 87–9; Derek Beales, *Joseph II. Volume I: In the Shadow of Maria Theresa, 1741–1780* (Cambridge, 1987), pp. 156–60; Theodor Schieder, *Frederick the Great*, ed. and transl. Sabina Berkeley and Hamish Scott (London, 2000), pp. 34–8.

Conclusion

1. Simon Dixon, *Catherine the Great* (London, 2009), pp. 3–22 and 114–28.
2. George Munro, *The Most Intentional City: St. Petersburg in the Reign of Catherine the Great* (Madison Cranbury, NJ, 2008), pp. 120–43.
3. Robert Jones, 'Urban Planning and the Development of Provincial Towns in Russia, 1762– 1796', in John Garrard (ed.), *The Eighteenth Century in Russia* (Oxford, 1973), pp. 321–44.

4. Dixon, *Catherine*, pp. 191–2.
5. Douglas Smith, *Working the Rough Stone: Freemasonry and Society in Eighteenth-Century Russia* (DeKalb, IL, 1999), pp. 64–72.
6. Lindsey Hughes, 'Russian Culture in the Eighteenth Century', in Dominic Lieven (ed.), *The Cambridge History of Russia* (Cambridge, 2006), vol. 2, pp. 81–8.
7. Simon Dixon, *The Modernisation of Russia, 1676–1825* (Cambridge, 1999), pp. 152–88.
8. Larry Wolff, *Inventing Eastern Europe: the Map of Civilisation in the Mind of the Enlightenment* (Stanford, CA, 1994).
9. Janet Hartley, 'Is Russia Part of Europe? Russian Perspectives on Europe in the Reign of Alexander I', *Cahiers du monde russe*, 33/4 (1992), pp. 369–85.
10. *The Nakaz of Catherine the Great: Collected Texts*, ed. William Butler and Vladimir A. Tomsinov (Clark, NJ, 2010).
11. See, for example, Anthony Cross, *St Petersburg and the British* (London, 2008), pp. 55–60.
12. Jonas Hanway, *An Historical Account of the British Trade over the Caspian Sea* (London, 1754), vol. 2, p. 135.

Bibliography

Archives

Archive of the St Petersburg Branch of the Institute of Russian History, Russian Academy of Sciences (StPb IRI RAN):
Fond 36 (Vorontsov Family)
State Archive of Ancient Acts, Moscow (RGADA):
Fond 8 (Kalinkin House and matters concerning crimes against morality)
Fond 14 (Court Affairs)
Fond 16 (Internal Governance)
State Historical Archive, St Petersburg (RGIA):
Fond 439 (Sentry Journals of the General-Adjutant, Orders and Passwords)
Fond 466 (Imperial Edicts of the Court Office)
Fond 473 (Ceremonial Affairs)
Fond 1329 (Imperial Edicts and Commands of the Senate)
State Military-Historical Archive, Moscow (RGVIA):
Fond 314 (First Cadet Corps)

Published Sources

Algarotti, Francesco, *Letters from Count Algarotti to Lord Hervey and the Marquis Scipio Maffei...* (London 1769), 2 vols.
Arkhiv kniazei Vorontsovykh, ed. Petr. I. Bartenev (Moscow, 1870–95), 40 vols.
Bergholz, Friedrich W. von, 'Dnevnik kamer-iunkera Fridrikha-Vil'gel'ma Berkhgol'tsa, 1721–1725 (chs 1 and 2)', in Viktor P. Naumov (ed.), *Neistovyi reformator* (Moscow, 2000), pp. 107–502.
Bergholz, Friedrich W. von, 'Dnevnik kamer-iunkera Fridrikha-Vil'gel'ma Berkhgol'tsa, 1721–1725 (chs 3 and 4)', in Viktor P. Naumov (ed.), *Iunost' derzhavy* (Moscow, 2000), pp. 11–324.
Bespiatykh, Iurii N. (ed.), *Peterburg Petra I v inostrannykh opisaniiakh* (Leningrad, 1991).
Bespiatykh, Iurii N. (ed.), *Peterburg Anny Ioannovny v inostrannykh opisaniiakh* (St Petersburg, 1997).
Bogdanov, Andrei I., *Opisanie Sanktpeterburga, 1749–1751* (St Petersburg, 1997).
Bolotov, Andrei T., *Zhizn' i prikliucheniia Andreia Bolotova* (Moscow, 1986), 4 vols.
Bruce, Peter Henry, *Memoirs of Peter Henry Bruce, Esq., a Military Officer in the Services of Prussia, Russia & Great Britain* (London, 1782).
Bruyn, Cornelius de, *Travels into Muscovy, Persia, and Part of the East-Indies* (London, 1737), 2 vols.
Catherine II, *Sochineniia imperatritsy Ekateriny II, na osnovanii podlinnykh rukopisei*, ed. A. N. Pypin (St Petersburg 1901–7), 12 vols.
Chteniia v Imperatorskom Obshchestve Istorii i Drevnostei Rossiiskikh pri Moskovskom universitete (Moscow, 1846–1918), 258 vols.
Collins, Samuel, *The Present State of Russia, in a Letter to a Friend at London* (London, 1671).

Danilov, Mikhail V., *Zapiski M. V. Danilova, artillerii maiora, napisannyia im v 1771 godu (1722–62)* (Kazan', 1913).

Dashwood, Francis, 'Sir Francis Dashwood's Diary of his Visit to St Petersburg in 1733', ed. Betty Kemp, *SEER*, 38 (1959), pp. 194–222.

Dialogues domestiques. Gespräche von Haussachen. Domashnye razgovory. Colloquia domestica (St Petersburg, 1756).

Georgi, Johann G., *Opisanie rossiisko-imperatorskogo stolichnogo goroda Sankt Peterburga i dostopamiatnostei v okrestnostiakh onogo* (St Petersburg, 1794), 2 vols.

Ger'e, V. (ed.), *Sbornik pisem i memorialov Leibnitsa, otnosiashchkhsia k Rossii i Petru Velikomu* (St Petersburg, 1873).

Gordon, Patrick, *Diary of General Patrick Gordon of Auchleuchries, 1635–1699. Volume II: 1659–1667*, ed. Dmitri Fedosov (Aberdeen, 2010).

Hanway, Jonas, *An Historical Account of the British Trade over the Caspian Sea* (London, 1754), 2 vols.

Horsey, Jerome, 'The Travels of Sir Jerome Horsey, Knt.' in Edward Bond (ed.), *Russia at the Close of the Sixteenth Century* (London, 1856).

Istinnaia politika znatnykh i blagorodnykh osob, transl. Vasilii K. Trediakovskii (St Petersburg, 1745).

Iunosti chestnoe zertsalo ili pokazanie k zhiteiskomu obkhozhdeniiu, sobrannoe ot raznykh avtorov (St Petersburg, 1717).

Juel, Just, 'Zapiski datskogo poslannika v Rossii pri Petre Velikom', in Viktor P. Naumov (ed.), *Lavry Poltavy* (St Petersburg, 2001).

Kamer-fur'erskie zhurnaly, 1726–1771 goda (St Petersburg, 1853–5), 40 vols.

Kirilov, Ivan K., *Tsvetushchee sostoianie vserossiiskogo gosudarstva*, ed. Boris A. Rybakov, Leonid A. Gol'denberg and Sergei M. Troitskii (Moscow, 1977).

Korb, Johann-Georg, *Diary of an Austrian Secretary of Legation at the Court of Czar Peter the Great*, transl. Count MacDonnell (London, 1968), 2 vols.

Kurakin, Boris I., 'Zhizn' kniazia Borisa Ivanovicha Kurakina im samim opisannaia', in Mikhail I. Semevskii, *Arkhiv kniazia F. A. Kurakina*, ed. (St Petersburg, 1890), vol. 1.

Kurakin, Boris I., 'Gistoriia o Petre I i blizhnikh k nemu liudiakh, 1682–95', *Russkaia starina*, 68/10 (1890), pp. 238–60.

Lubok. Russkie narodnye kartinki, XVII–XVIII vv. Al'bom, ed. and comp. Iurii Ovsiannikov (Moscow, 1968).

Manstein, Christoph H. von, *Contemporary Memoirs of Russia, From the Year 1727 to 1744* (London, 1968).

Materialy dlia istorii Imperatorskogo Akademii nauk, ed. Mikhail V. Sukhomlinov (St Petersburg, 1890–1900), 10 vols.

Matveev, Andrei A., *Russkii diplomat vo Frantsii (Zapiski Andreia Matveeva)* (Leningrad, 1972).

Menshikov, Aleksandr D., *Trudy i dni Aleksandra Danilovicha Menshikova: povsednevnye zapiski delam kniazia A. D. Menshikova, 1716–1720, 1726–1727 gg.*, ed. S. R. Dolgova and T. A. Lapteva (Moscow 2004).

Mottraye, Aubry de la, *Travels through Europe, Asia, and into part of Africa...* (London, 1723–32), 3 vols.

Münnich, Burkhard-Christophor von, 'Dispozitsiia i tseremoniial torzhestvennogo v''ezda imperatritsy Anny Ivanovny v S.–Peterburg 16 genvaria 1732', comp. M. D. Khmyrov, *Russkii arkhiv*, 2 (1867), pp. 332–41.

Münnich, Burkhard-Christophor von, 'Ocherk upravleniia rossiiskoi imperii', in Viktor P. Naumov (ed.), *Perevoroty i voiny* (Moscow, 1997), pp. 275–318.

Nepliuev, Ivan I., 'Zapiski', in Viktor P. Naumov (ed.), *Imperia posle Petra, 1725–1765* (Moscow, 1998).

Ob''iavlenie nyneshnego triumfalnogo vkhoda, ego tsarskago velichestva v Sankt Piterburkh (St Petersburg, 1714).

Obstoiatel'noe opisanie torzhestvennykh poriadkov blagopoluchnogo vshestviia v tsarstvui-ushchii grad Moskvu i sviashchenneishei koronovaniia eia Avgusteishago imperatorskogo velichestva... Elisavety Petrovny (St Petersburg, 1744).

Olearius, Adam, *The Travels of Olearius in Seventeenth-Century Russia*, transl. Samuel H. Baron (Stanford, CA, 1967).

Opisanie koronatsii Eia Velichestva Imperatritsy i Samoderzhitsy Vserossiiskoi Anny Ioannovny torzhestvenno otpravlennoi v tsarstviushchem grade Moskve, 28 aprelia, 1730 g. (Moscow, 1730).

Opisanie o brake mezhdu Eia Vysochestvom Annoiu Petrovnoiu, Tsesarevnoiu Vserossiikoiu, i Ego Korolevskim Vysochestvom Karlom Fridrikhom, Gertsogom Golshteinogottorpskim (St Petersburg, 1725).

Pis'ma i bumagi imperatora Petra Velikogo (Moscow, 1887–), 13 vols to date.

'Pismo Spb. ober-politsiimeistera Tatishcheva k kabinet-sekretariu Bakhirevu', *Istoricheskii vestnik*, 5 (1881), 681.

Playford, John, *The English Dancing Master, or Plaine and Easie Rules for the Dancing of Country Dances* (London, 1651).

Pokhodnye i putevye zhurnaly imperatora Petra I-go, 1695–1726 (St Petersburg, 1853–5), 32 vols.

Polnoe sobranie zakonov rossiiskoi imperii... 1649–1825 (St Petersburg, 1830), 40 vols.

Pososhkov, Ivan T., *The Book of Poverty and Wealth*, ed. and transl. A. P. Vlasto and L. R. Lewitter (London, 1987).

Pouncy, Carolyn, *The 'Domostroi': Rules for Russian Households in the time of Ivan the Terrible* (Ithaca, NY, 1994).

Pridvornye zhurnaly... 1741–42, 1743–48, ed. Ivan A. Cherkasov (St Petersburg, 1883 and 1913).

Proekty ugolovnago ulozheniia 1754–1766 godov, ed. Aleksandr A. Vostokov (St Petersburg, 1882).

Prokopovich, Feofan, *O smerti Petra Velikago Imperatora Rossiiskogo. Kratkaia povest'* (St Petersburg, 1831).

Prokopovich, Feofan, *The Spiritual Regulation of Peter the Great*, ed. and transl. Alexander Muller (Seattle, WA, 1972).

Protokoly zasedanii konferentsii Imperatorkoi Akademii nauk s 1725 po 1803 goda (St Petersburg, 1897–1911), 4 vols.

Rameau, Pierre, *The Dancing Master*, transl. Cyril Beaumont (New York, 1970).

Richardson, William, *Anecdotes of the Russian Empire in a Series of Letters Written, a Few Years Ago, from St Petersburg* (London, 1968).

Sbornik Imperatorskogo Rossiiskogo Istoricheskogo Obshchestva (St Petersburg, 1867–1926), 148 vols.

Schlessinger, Georg-Adam, 'Polnoe opisanie Rossii, nakhodiashcheisia nyne pod vlast'iu dvukh tsarei-sopravitelei Ivana Alekseevicha i Petra Alekseevicha', transl. Liudmila P. Lapteva, *Voprosy istorii*, 1 (1970), 104–24.

Schumacher, Johann D., *Palaty Sanktpeterburgskoi imperatorskoi Akademii nauk biblioteki i kunstkamery s kratkim pokazaniem vsekh nakhodiashchikhsia v nikh khudozhest-vennykh i natural'nykh veshchei soochinennoe dlia okhotnikov onyia veshchi smotret' zhelaiushchikh* (St Petersburg, 1741).

Sermones in primo solenni Academiae scientiarum imperialis conventu die XXVII decembris anni 1725 publice recitati (St Petersburg, 1725).

Shcherbatov, Mikhail M., *On the Corruption of Morals in Russia*, ed. and transl. Antony Lentin (Cambridge, 1969).

Shcherbatov, Mikhail M., 'Proshenie Moskvy o zabvenii eia', in Konstantin G. Isupov (comp.), *Moskva-Peterburg: pro et contra* (St Petersburg, 2000), 81–7.

Stählin, Jakob von, *Original Anecdotes of Peter the Great* (London, 1788).

Stählin, Jakob von, *Muzyka i balet v Rossii XVIII veka* (St Petersburg, 2002).

Starikova, Liudmila M. (ed.), *Teatral'naia zhizn' Rossii v epokhu Anny Ioannovny. Dokumental'naia khronika, 1730–1740* (Moscow, 1995).

Starikova, Liudmila M. (ed.), *Teatral'naia zhizn' Rossii v epokhu Elizavety Petrovny. Dokumental'naia khronika* (Moscow, 2003–), 3 parts to date.

Stoglav, ed. Dmitrii E. Kozhanchikov (St Petersburg, 1863).

Storch, Heinrich Friedrich von, *The Picture of Petersburg* (London, 1801), 2 vols.

Stuart, James FitzJames, 'Zapiski gertsoga De-Liria-Bervika, byvshego ispanskim poslom pri rossiyskom dvore, s 1727 po 1731 god', *Syn otechestva*, 7/2 (1839), 125–76.

Svin'in, Pavel, *Dostopamiatnosti Sanktpeterburga i ego okrestnostei* (St Petersburg, 1997).

Tolstoi, Petr A., *The Travel Diary of Peter Tolstoi: a Muscovite in Early Modern Europe*, ed. and transl. Max J. Okenfuss (DeKalb, IL, 1987).

The Muscovite Law Code (Ulozhenie) of 1649, ed. and transl. Richard Hellie (Irvine, CA, 1988).

The Nakaz of Catherine the Great: Collected Texts, ed. William Butler and Vladimir A. Tomsinov (Clark, NJ, 2010).

The Russian Primary Chronicle, transl. Samuel Cross and Olgerd Shobowitz-Wetzor (New York, 1953).

Trubetskoi, Petr N., 'Zametki na kalendare v 1762 godu', *Russkaia starina*, 73/2 (1892), 443–8.

Vigor, Jane, *Letters from a Lady, Who Resided Some Years in Russia, to her Friend in England* (London, 1775).

Voskresenskii, Nikolai A., *Zakonodatel'nye akty Petra I* (Moscow-Leningrad, 1945), vol. 1.

Weber, Friedrich Christian, *The Present State of Russia* (London, 1968), 2 vols.

Whitworth, Charles, *An Account of Russia as it was in the Year 1710* (London, 1758).

Wilmot, Martha and Catherine, *The Russian Journals... 1803–1808* (London, 1934).

Zheliabuzhskii, Ivan A., 'Dnevnye zapiski', in A. Liberman and S. Shokarev (eds), *Rozhdenie imperii* (Moscow, 1997), 261–358.

Zhurnaly dezhurnykh general-ad''iuntantov: tsarstvovanie imperatritsy Elizavety Petrovny, comp. Leonid V. Evdokimov (St Petersburg, 1897).

Scholarly Works

Adamson, John (ed.), *The Princely Courts of Europe: Ritual, Politics and Culture under the Ancien Régime, 1500–1750* (London, 1999).

Ageeva, Ol'ga G., 'Assamblei petrovskogo vremeni v russkoi dorevoliutsionnoi isto-riografii', in Lev N. Pushkarev et al. (eds), *Istoriograficheskie i istoricheskie problemy russkoi kultury* (Moscow, 1983), 47–66.

Ageeva, Ol'ga G., 'Novye iavleniia v obshchestvennoi zhizni i bytu Peterburga pervoi chetverti XVIII v.: na primere tsarskikh svadeb', in A. N. Kopylov, Olga G. Ageeva and Lev N. Pushkarev (eds), *Russkaia kul'tura v perekhodnyi period ot srednevekov'ia k novomu vremeni* (Moscow, 1992), 89–103.

Ageeva, Ol'ga G., *'Velichaishii i slavneishii bolee vsekh gradov v svete' – grad sviatogo Petra: Peterburg v russkom obshchestvennom soznanii nachala XVIII veka* (St Petersburg, 1999).

Ageeva, Ol'ga G., 'Peterburgskii traurnyi tseremonial Doma Romanovykh v nachale XVIII v.', in Iurii N. Bespiatykh (ed.), *Fenomenon Peterburga* (St Petersburg, 2001), 491–505.

Ageeva, Ol'ga G., *Evropeizatsiia russkogo dvora, 1700–1796 gg.* (Moscow, 2006).

Ageeva, Ol'ga G., 'Tseremonialy rozhdeniia tsarskikh detei v vek evropeizatsii: ot Petra I do Ekateriny II', in Ol'ga A. Prutskova (ed.), *Rossiiskaia real'nost' kontsa XVII – pervoi poloviny XIX v. Ekonomika, obshchestvennoi stroi, kul'tura* (Moscow, 2007), 210–39.

Ageeva, Ol'ga G., *Imperatorskii dvor Rossii, 1700–1796 gody* (Moscow, 2008).

Alexander, John, 'Petersburg and Moscow in Early Urban Policy', *Journal of Urban History*, 8/2 (1982), 145–69.

Andermann, Kurt (ed.), *Residenz – Aspekte hauptstädtischer Zentralität von der frühen Neuzeit bis zum Ende der Monarchie* (Sigmaringen, 1992).

Anemone, Anthony, 'The Monsters of Peter the Great: the Culture of the St Petersburg Kunstkamera in the Eighteenth Century', *Slavic and East European Journal*, 44 (2000), 583–602.

Anisimov, Evgenii V., *Rossiia v seredine XVIII veka: bor'ba za nasledie Petra* (Moscow, 1986).

Anisimov, Evgenii V., *The Reforms of Peter the Great: Progress through Coercion in Russia*, transl. John Alexander (Armonk, NY, 1993).

Anisimov, Evgenii V., *Empress Elizabeth: Her Reign and Her Russia, 1741–1761*, transl. John Alexander (Gulf Breeze, FL, 1995).

Anisimov, Evgenii V., *Gosudarstvennye preobrazovaniia i samoderzhavie Petra Velikogo v pervoi chetverti XVIII veka* (St Peterburg, 1997).

Anisimov, Evgenii V., *Dyba i knut: Politicheskii sysk i russkoe obshchestvo v XVIII veke* (Moscow, 1999).

Anisimov, Evgenii V., *Iunyi grad: Peterburg vremen Petra Velilkogo* (St Petersburg, 2003).

Appleby, John, 'James Spilman, F.R.S. (1680–1763), and Anglo-Russian Commerce', *Notes and Records of the Royal Society of London*, 48 (1994), 17–29.

Asch, Ronald and Adolf Birke (eds), *Princes, Patronage, and the Nobility: the Court at the Beginning of the Modern Age, c. 1450–1650* (Oxford, 1991).

Astier, Régine, 'Louis XIV *Premier Danseur*', in David Lee Rubin (ed.), *Sun King: the Ascendancy of French Culture during the Reign of Louis XIV* (London, 1992), 73–102.

Astrov, Nikolai, 'Pervonachal'noe obrazovanie Petra velikago', *Russkii arkhiv*, 2/8 (1875), 470–88.

Baehr, Stephen, *The Paradise Myth in Eighteenth-Century Russia: Utopian Patterns in Early Secular Russian Literature and Culture* (Stanford, CA, 1991).

Bak, János (ed.), *Coronations: Medieval and Early Modern Monarchic Ritual* (Berkeley, CA, 1990).

Balsiger, Barbara, 'The *Kunst- und Wunderkammern*: a Catalogue raisonné of Collecting in Germany, France and England, 1565–1750', unpublished PhD thesis (Pittsburgh, PA, 1970).

Baron, Samuel, 'The Origins of Seventeenth-Century Moscow's Nemeckaja Sloboda', *California Slavic Studies*, 5 (1970), 1–17.

Barta, Peter (ed.), *Gender and Sexuality in Russian Civilisation* (London, 2001).

Bartlett, Roger and Janet Hartley (eds), *Russia in the Age of Enlightenment: Essays for Isabel de Madariaga* (London, 1990).

Bartlett, Roger and Lindsey Hughes (eds), *Russian Society and Culture and the Long Eighteenth Century: Essays in Honour of Anthony G. Cross* (Münster, 2004).

Bassin, Mark, 'Russia between Europe and Asia: the Ideological Construction of Geographical Space', SR, 50/1 (1991), 1–17.

Baumgartner, Thomas, 'Vienna Gloriosa and the Prince's Garden', in Agnes Husslein-Arco (ed.), *Prince Eugene: General-Philosopher and Art Lover* (Vienna, 2010), 119–26.

Beales, Derek, *Joseph II. Volume I: In the Shadow of Maria Theresa, 1741–1780* (Cambridge, 1987).

Béhar, Pierre and Helen Watanabe-O'Kelly (eds), *Spectaculum Europæum: Theatre and Spectacle in Europe 1580–1750* (Wiesbaden, 1999).

Behrens, C. B. A., *Society, Government and the Enlightenment: the Experiences of Eighteenth-Century France and Prussia* (London, 1985).

Behrisch, Lars, 'Social Discipline in Early Modern Russia, Seventeenth to Nineteenth Centuries', in Heinz Schilling (ed.), *Institutionen, Instrumente und Akteure sozialer Kontrolle und Disziplinierung im frühneuzeitlichen Europa* (Frankfurt am Main, 1999), 325–57.

Benda, Vladimir N., 'Pervye rossiiskie artilleriiskie i inzhenernye shkoly v kontse XVII – pervoi chetverti XVIII veka', *Voenno-istoricheskii zhurnal*, 9 (2009), 23–8.

Bernstein, Laurie, *Sonia's Daughters: Prostitutes and their Regulation in Imperial Russia* (Berkeley, CA, 1995).

Bissonnette, Georges, 'Peter the Great and the Church as an Educational Institution', in John Curtiss (ed.), *Essays on Russian and Soviet History in Honour of Geroid Tanquary Robinson* (Leiden, 1963), 3–19.

Black, Joseph, *Citizens for the Fatherland: Education, Educators, and Pedagogical Ideals in Eighteenth-Century Russia* (New York, 1979).

Blanning, T. C. W., *The Culture of Power and the Power of Culture* (Oxford, 2002).

Blanning, T. C. W., *The Triumph of Music* (London, 2008).

Bogoiavlenskii, Sergei K., 'Moskovskii teatr pri tsariakh Aleksee i Petre', *ChIOIDR*, 249/2 (1914), 1–192.

Bogoslovskii, Mikhail M., *Byt i nravy russkogo dvorianstva v pervoi polovine XVIII veka*, 2nd edition (Petrograd, 1918).

Bogoslovskii, Mikhail M., *Petr Velikii: materialy dlia biografii* (Moscow, 2005), vol. 1.

Brackett, John, 'The Florentine *Onesta* and the Control of Prostitution, 1403–1680', *Sixteenth-Century Journal*, 24/2 (1993), 273–300.

Bragone, Maria Cristina, 'K istorii vospriiatiia Erazma Rotterdamskogo v Rossii v XVIII veke', *SGECRN*, 34 (2006), 44–8.

Brennan, Thomas, 'Social Drinking in Paris', in Susanna Barrows and Robin Room (ed.), *Drinking: Behaviour and Belief in Modern History* (Berkeley, CA, 1991), 68–77.

Breward, Christopher, *The Culture of Fashion: a New History of Fashionable Dress* (Manchester, 1995).

Brewer, John and Roy Porter (eds), *Consumption and the World of Goods* (London, 1993).

Bryant, Lawrence, *The King and the City in the Parisian Royal Entry Ceremony: Politics, Ritual and Art in the Renaissance* (Geneva, 1986).

Bryson, Anna, *From Courtesy to Civility: Changing Codes of Conduct in Early Modern England* (Oxford, 1998).

Bucholz, Robert, *The Augustan Court: Queen Anne and the Decline of Court Culture* (Stanford, CA, 1993).

Buckler, Julie, *Mapping St. Petersburg: Imperial Text and Cityshape* (Princeton, NJ, 2005).

Buganov, Viktor I., 'Ekaterina I', *Voprosy istorii*, 11 (1994), 39–49.

Bukovinska, Beket, 'The Kunstkammer of Rudolph II', in Eliška Fučíková (ed.), *Rudolph II and Prague: the Court and the City* (London, 1997), 199–208.

Bullough, Vern L. and Bonnie Bullough, *Cross Dressing, Sex, and Gender* (Philadelphia, PA, 1993).

Bunin, Mikhail S., *Mosty Leningrada: ocherki istorii i arkhitektury mostov Peterburga – Petrograda – Leningrada* (Leningrad, 1986).

Burgess, Malcolm, 'Fairs and Entertainers in Eighteenth-Century Russia', *SEER*, 38 (1959), 95–113.

Burke, Peter, 'Did Europe Exist before 1700?', *History of European Ideas*, 1/1 (1980), 21–9.

Burke, Peter, *The Fabrication of Louis XIV* (New Haven, CN and London, 1994).

Burke, Peter, *The Fortunes of the 'Courtier': the European Reception of Castiglione's 'Cortegiano'* (Cambridge, 1995).

Burke, Peter, *Popular Culture in Early Modern Europe*, 3rd edition (Farnham, 2009).

Burnett, John, *Liquid Pleasures: a Social History of Drinks in Modern Britain* (London, 1999).

Bushkovitch, Paul, 'The Epiphany Ceremony of the Russian Court in the Sixteenth and Seventeenth Centuries', *Russian Review*, 49/1 (1990), 1–18.

Bushkovitch, Paul, *Religion and Society in Russia: the Sixteenth and Seventeenth Centuries* (Oxford, 1992).

Bushkovitch, Paul, 'Cultural Change among the Russian Boyars, 1650–1680: New Sources and Old Problems', *Forschungen zur osteuropaischen Geschichte*, 56 (2000), 91–111.

Bushkovitch, Paul, *Peter the Great: the Struggle for Power, 1671–1725* (Cambridge, 2001).

Castle, Terry, *Masquerade and Civilisation: the Carnivalesque in Eighteenth-Century English Culture and Fiction* (Stanford, CA, 1986).

Charipova, Liudmila, *Latin Books and the Eastern Orthodox Clerical Elite in Kiev, 1632–1780* (Manchester, 2006).

Chrissidis, Nikolaos, 'Creating the New Educated Elite: Learning and Faith in Moscow's Slavo-Greco-Latin Academy, 1685–1694', unpublished PhD thesis (Yale University, 2000).

Chroscicki, Juliusz, Mark Hengerer and Gérard Sabatier (eds), *Les funérailles princières en Europe, XVIe–XVIIIe siècle* (Versailles, 2012).

Chudinova, Irina A., *Penie, zvony, ritual: Topografiia tserkovno-muzykal'noi kul'tury Peterburga* (St Petersburg, 1994).

Clark, Christopher, *Iron Kingdom: the Rise and Downfall of Prussia, 1600–1947* (London, 2007).

Cowart, Georgia, *The Triumph of Pleasure: Louis XIV and the Politics of Spectacle* (Chicago, IL, 2008).

Cracraft, James, *The Church Reform of Peter the Great* (London, 1971).

Cracraft, James, *The Petrine Revolution in Russian Architecture* (Chicago, IL, 1988).

Cracraft, James, *The Revolution of Peter the Great* (Cambridge, MA, 2003).

Cracraft, James, *The Petrine Revolution in Russian Culture* (Cambridge, MA, 2004).

Cross, Anthony, 'The Russian *Banya* in the Descriptions of Foreign Travellers and in the Depictions of Foreign and Russian Artists', *OSP*, 24 (1991), 34–59.

Cross, Anthony, *Peter the Great through British Eyes: Perceptions and Representations of the Tsar since 1698* (Cambridge, 2000).

Cross, Anthony (ed.), *St Petersburg, 1703–1825* (Basingstoke, 2003).

Cross, Anthony (ed.), *Days from the Reigns of Eighteenth-Century Russian Rulers* (Cambridge, 2007), 2 vols.

Cross, Anthony, *St Petersburg and the British* (London, 2008).

Crummey, Robert, 'Court Spectacles in Seventeenth-Century Russia: Illusion and Reality', in Daniel Clarke Waugh (ed.), *Essays in Honour of A. A. Zimin* (Columbus, OH, 1985), 130–58.

De Vries, Jan, *European Urbanization, 1500–1800* (Cambridge, MA, 1984).

Dickens, Arthur (ed.), *The Courts of Europe: Politics, Patronage and Royalty, 1400–1800* (London, 1977).

Dixon, Simon, *The Modernisation of Russia, 1676–1825* (Cambridge, 1999).

Dixon, Simon, *Catherine the Great* (London, 2009).

Dolgova, Svetlana R., '"… ekhat' i perepisat' imianno bez medleniia": Pervye zhiteli Peterburga. 1717 g.', *Istoricheskii arkhiv*, 2 (2003), 7–20.

Dubiago, Tat'iana B., *Russkie reguliarnye sady i parki* (Leningrad, 1963).

Duindam, Jeroen, *Myths of Power: Norbert Elias and the Early Modern European Court* (Amsterdam, 1994).

Duindam, Jeroen, *Vienna and Versailles: the Courts of Europe's Major Dynastic Rivals, 1550–1780* (Cambridge, 2003).

Duindam, Jeroen, Tülay Artan and Metin Kunt (eds), *Royal Courts in Dynastic States and Empires: a Global Perspective* (Boston, MA, 2011).

Dunkley, John, *Gambling: a Social and Moral Problem in France, 1685–1792* (Oxford, 1985).

Edwards, JoLynn, 'Watteau and the Dance', in François Moureau and Margaret Morgan Grasselli (eds), *Antoine Watteau (1684–1721): le peintre, son temps et sa légende* (Paris, 1987), 219–25.

Egorov, Igor, *The Architectural Planning of St. Petersburg*, transl. Eric Dluhosch (Athens, GA, 1969).

Elias, Norbert, *The Civilizing Process*, revised edition, ed. and transl. Edmund Jephcott (London, 2000), 2 vols.

Elias, Norbert, *The Court Society*, transl. Stephen Mennell (Dublin, 2006).

Esipov, Grigorii V., *Raskol'nich'i dela XVIII stolietiia: izvlechennyia iz del Preobrazhenskago Prikaza i tainoi rozysknykh del kantseliarii* (St Petersburg, 1861–3), 2 vols.

Fantazzi, Charles, 'Vives and the *emargenati*', in Charles Fantazzi (ed.), *A Companion to Juan Luis Vives* (Leiden, 2008), 71–86.

Fauchier-Magnan, Adrien, *The Small German Courts of the Eighteenth Century* (London, 1958).

Fennell, John, *A History of the Russian Church to 1448* (London, 1995).

Findeizen, Nikolai F., *History of Music in Russia From Antiquity to 1800*, transl. Samuel William Pring, ed. Milo Velimirovic and Claudia Jensen (Bloomington, IN, 2008), 2 vols.

Florinsky, Michael, *Russia: a History and an Interpretation* (London, 1953), 2 vols.

Freymann, Otto von (comp.), *Pazhi za 183 goda (1711–1894): biografii byvshikh pazhei, s portretami* (Fredrikshavn, 1894).

Friedrich, Karin and Sara Smart (eds), *The Cultivation of Monarchy and the Rise of Berlin: Brandenburg-Prussia, 1700* (Farnham, 2010).

Friedrichs, Christopher, 'Whose House of Learning? Some Thoughts on German Schools in Post-Reformation Germany', *History of Education Quarterly*, 22 (1982), 371–7.

Fritz, Paul, 'The Trade in Death: the Royal Funerals in England', *Eighteenth Century Studies*, 15/3 (1982), 291–316.

Fumaroli, Marc, *When the World Spoke French*, transl. Richard Howard (New York, 2011).

Garrard, John (ed.), *The Eighteenth Century in Russia* (Oxford, 1973).

Garrioch, David, *The Making of Revolutionary Paris* (Berkeley, CA, 2002).

Gillingham, John, 'From *Civilitas* to Civility: Codes of Manners in Medieval and Early Modern England', *Transactions of the Royal Historical Society*, 6th Series, 12 (2002), 267–89.

Gleason, Abbot (ed.), *A Companion to Russian History* (Oxford, 2009).

Goff, Moira, '"The Art of Dancing, demonstrated Characters and Figures": French and English Sources for Court and Theatre Dance, 1700–1750', *British Library Journal*, 21 (1995), 202–31.

Goloubeva, Maria, *The Glorification of Emperor Leopold I in Image, Spectacle and Text* (Mainz, 2000).

Gordin, Michael, 'The Importance of Being Earnest: the Early St. Petersburg Academy of Sciences', *Isis*, 91 (2000), 1–31.

Grot, Iakov K. (ed.), *Zhizn' Derzhavina, po ego sochineniiam i pis'mam i po istoricheskim dokumentam* (Moscow, 1880–83), 2 vols.

Grussi, Olivier, *La vie quotidienne des joueurs sous l'Ancien Régime à Paris et à la cour* (Paris, 1985).

Hans, Nicholas, 'The Moscow School of Mathematics and Navigation (1701)', *SEER*, 29 (1951), 532–6.

Harris-Warrick, Rebecca, 'Ballroom Dancing at the Court of Louis XIV', *Early Music*, 14/1 (1986), 41–50.

Hartley, Janet, 'Is Russia Part of Europe? Russian Perspectives on Europe in the Reign of Alexander I', *Cahiers du monde russe*, 33/4 (1992), 369–85.

Hartley, Janet, *A Social History of the Russian Empire, 1650–1825* (London, 1999).

Hassell, James, 'Implementation of the Russian Table of Ranks during the Eighteenth Century', *SR*, 29/2 (1970), 283–99.

Helfant, Ian, *The High Stakes of Identity: Gambling in the Life and Literature of Nineteenth-Century Russia* (Evanston, IL, 2002).

Hendriksson, Linda, 'Landscape Gardening', in Mårten Snickare (ed.), *Nicodemus Tessin the Younger: Royal Architect and Visionary* (Stockholm, 2002), 151–65.

Hosking, Geoffrey, *Russia and the Russians* (Cambridge, MA, 2001).

Houston, Robert, *Literacy in Early Modern Europe: Culture and Education, 1500–1800* (London, 1988).

Hughes, Lindsey, 'Western European Graphic Material as a Source for Moscow Baroque Architecture', *SEER*, 55/4 (1977), 433–43.

Hughes, Lindsey, *Russia and the West: the Life of a Seventeenth-Century Westerniser, Prince Vasily Vasil'evich Golitsyn (1643–1714)* (Cambridge, MA, 1984).

Hughes, Lindsey, *Sophia, Regent of Russia, 1657–1704* (New Haven, CT, 1990).

Hughes, Lindsey, 'Between Two Worlds: Tsarevna Natal'ia Alekseevna and the Emancipation of Petrine Women', in Maria di Salvo and Lindsey Hughes (eds), *A Window on Russia* (Rome, 1996), 29–36.

Hughes, Lindsey, 'Peter the Great's Two Weddings: Changing Images of Women in a Transitional Age', in Rosalind Marsh (ed.), *Women in Russia and Ukraine* (Cambridge, 1996), 31–44.

Hughes, Lindsey, *Russia in the Age of Peter the Great* (New Haven, CT, 1998).

Hughes, Lindsey (ed.), *Peter the Great and the West: New Perspectives* (Basingstoke, 2001).

Hughes, Lindsey, *Peter the Great: a Biography* (New Haven, CT, 2002).

Hughes, Lindsey, '"The Crown of Maidenly Honour and Virtue": Redefining Femininity in Peter I's Russia', in Wendy Rosslyn (ed.), *Women and Gender in Eighteenth-Century Russia* (Aldershot, 2003), 35–59.

Hughes, Lindsey, 'Russian Culture in the Eighteenth Century', in Dominic Lieven (ed.), *The Cambridge History of Russia* (Cambridge, 2006), vol. 2, 67–91.

Hunt, Alan, *Governance of the Consuming Passions: a History of Sumptuary Law* (Basingstoke, 1996).

Isherwood, Robert, 'Entertainment in the Parisian Fairs in the Eighteenth Century', *Journal of Modern History*, 53/1 (1981), 24–48.

Jensen, Claudia, *Musical Cultures in Seventeenth-Century Russia* (Bloomington, IN, 2009).

Jewell, Helen, *Education in Early Modern England* (Basingstoke, 1998).

Johnson, Emily D., *How St. Petersburg Learned to Study Itself: the Russian Idea of Kraevedenie* (University Park, PA, 2006).

Johnston, Trevor, 'The Reformation and Popular Culture', in Andrew Pettigrew (ed.), *The Reformation World* (London, 2000), 545–59.

Jones, Colin, *Paris: the Biography of a City* (London, 2006).

Jones, Jennifer, *Sexing La Mode: Gender, Fashion and Commercial Culture in Old Regime France* (London, 2004).

Jones, Robert, 'Getting the Goods to St Petersburg: Water Transport from the Interior, 1703–1811', *SR*, 43 (1984), 413–433.

Jong, Erik, *Nature and Art: Dutch Garden and Landscape Architecture, 1650–1740* (Philadelphia, PA, 2000).

Kaganov, Grigorii, '"As in the Ship of Peter"', *SR*, 50/4 (1991), 755–67.

Kaganov, Grigorii, *Sankt-Peterburg: Obrazy prostranstva* (Moscow, 1995).

Kahan, Arcadius, 'The Costs of "Westernisation" in Russia: the Gentry and the Economy in the Eighteenth Century', *SR*, 25 (1966), 40–66.

Kahan, Arcadius, *The Plow, the Hammer, and the Knout: An Economic History of Eighteenth-Century Russia* (Chicago, IL, 1985).

Kamenskii, Aleksandr B., *The Russian Empire in the Eighteenth Century: Searching for a Place in the World*, ed. and transl. David M. Griffiths (Armonk, NY, 1997).

Kaufmann, Thomas DaCosta, *Court, Cloister, and City: the Art and Culture of Central Europe, 1450–1800* (Chicago, IL, 1995).

Kavanagh, Thomas, *Dice, Cards, Wheels: a Different History of French Culture* (Philadelphia, PN, 2005).

Keenan, Paul, 'The Function of Fashion: Women and Clothing at the Russian Court, 1700–1762', in Wendy Rosslyn and Alessandra Tosi (eds), *Women in Eighteenth-Century Russian Culture and Society* (Basingstoke, 2007), 125–43.

Keenan, Paul, 'The Summer Gardens in the Social Life of St Petersburg, 1725–61', *SEER*, 88/1–2 (2010), 134–55.

Keenan, Paul, 'Card-playing and Gambling in Eighteenth-Century Russia', *European History Quarterly*, 42/3 (2012), 385–402.

Keller, Elena E.. *Prazdnichnaia kul'tura Petersburga: ocherki istorii* (St Petersburg, 2001).

Kelly, Catriona, *Petrushka: the Russian Carnival Puppet Theatre* (Cambridge, 1990).

Kelly, Catriona, *Refining Russia: Advice Literature, Polite Culture, and Gender from Catherine to Yeltsin* (Oxford, 2001).

Kepsu, Saul, *Peterburg do Peterburga: istoriia ust'ia Nevy do osnovaniia goroda Petra* (St Petersburg, 2000).

Khazin, Oleg A., *Pazhi, kadety, iunkera: istoricheskii ocherk* (Moscow, 2002).

Khmyrov, Mikhail D., *Grafinia Ekaterina Ivanovna Golovkina i eia vremia, 1701–91 goda* (St Petersburg, 1867).

Kholodov, Efim G., *Teatr i zriteli: stranitsy istorii russkoi teatral'noi publiki* (Moscow, 2000).

Khoteev, Pavel I., 'Frantsuzskaia kniga v biblioteke Peterburgskoi Akademii nauk (1714–1742 gg.)', in Sergei P. Luppov (ed.), *Frantsuzskaia kniga v Rossii v XVIII v. Ocherki istorii* (Leningrad, 1986), 5–58.

Kirsanova, Raisa M., *Russkii kostium i byt XVIII – XIX vekov* (Moscow, 2002).

Kizevetter, Aleksandr A., *Posadskaia obshchina v Rossii XVIII stoletiia* (Moscow, 1903).

Klingensmith, Samuel, *The Utility of Splendor: Ceremony, Social Life, and Architecture at the Court of Bavaria, 1600–1800* (Chicago, IL, 1993).

Kliuchevskii, Vasilii O., *Peter the Great*, transl. Liliana Archibald (London, 1968).

Klochkov, Mikhail V., *Naselenie Rossii pri Petre Velikom po perepisiam togo vremeni* (St Petersburg, 1911).

Kollmann, Nancy, 'The Seclusion of Elite Muscovite Women,' *Russian History/Histoire Russe*, 10 (1983), 170–87.

Komelova, Galina N., *Vidy Peterburga i ego okrestnostei serediny XVIII veka. Graviury po risunkam M. Makhaeva* (Leningrad, 1968).

Konechnyi, Albin M., 'Peterburgskie narodnye gulian'ia na maslenoi i paskhal'noi nedeliakh', in Natal'ia V. Iukhneva (ed.), *Peterburg i guberniia: istoriko-etnograficheskie issledovaniia* (Leningrad, 1989), 5–20.

Kopanev, Nikolai A., 'Frantsuzskie knigi v Letnem dome imperatritsy Elizavety Petrovny', in A. A. Zaitseva and Sergei P. Luppov (eds), *Kniga i biblioteki v Rossii v XIV – pervoi polovine XIX veka* (Leningrad, 1982), 26–41.

Kopanev, Nikolai A., 'Repertuar priozvedenii F. M. Vol'tera v Peterburgskoi akademicheskoi knizhnoi lavke v seredine XVIII v. (1731–61 gg.)', in G. V. Bakhareva and Sergei P. Luppov (eds), *Kniga i knigotorgovlia v Rossii v XVI–XVIII vv.* (Leningrad, 1984), 80–93.

Korsakov, D., 'Kniaginia Natal'ia Dolgorukaia', *Istoricheskii vestnik*, 23/2 (1886), 263–82.

Kosheleva, Ol'ga E., *Liudi Sankt-Peterburgskogo ostrova petrovskogo vremeni* (Moscow, 2004).

Kotilaine, Jarmo and Marshall Poe (eds), *Modernizing Muscovy: Reform and Social Change in Seventeenth-Century Russia* (London, 2005).

Kurukin, Igor' V., *Epokha 'Dvorskikh Bur': ocherki politicheskoi istorii poslepetrovskoi Rossii, 1725–1762 gg.* (Riazan', 2003).

Kuznetsov, Mikhail, *Prostitutsiia i sifilis v Rossii: istoriko–statisticheskiia izsledovaniia* (St Petersburg, 1871).

Ladurie, Emmanuel LeRoy, *Saint-Simon and the Court of Louis XIV* (Chicago, IL, 2001).

Leach, Robert and Victor Borovsky (eds), *A History of Russian Theatre* (Cambridge, 1999).

Lebedeva, I. N., 'Leib-medik Petra I i Robert Areskin i ego biblioteka', in Sergei P. Luppov and Boris B. Piotrovskii (eds), *Russkie biblioteki i ikh chitatel'* (Leningrad, 1983), 98–105.

Lebedianskii, Mikhail S., *Graver Petrovskoi epokhi Aleksei Zubov* (Moscow, 1973).

LeDonne, John, 'Ruling Families in the Russian Political Order, 1689–1825', *Cahiers du Monde russe et sovietique* (1987), 233–322.

LeDonne, John, *Absolutism and Ruling Class: the Formation of the Russian Political Order, 1700–1825* (Oxford, 1991).

Letopis' Rossiiskoi Akademii Nauk. Tom I: 1724–1802, ed. N. I. Nevskaia (St Petersburg, 2000).

Levin, Eve, *Sex and Society in the World of the Orthodox Slavs, 900–1700* (Ithaca, NY, 1989).

Lincoln, W. Bruce, *Sunlight At Midnight: St Petersburg and the Rise of Modern Russia* (Oxford, 2001).

Linder, Isaak M., *Shakhmaty na Rusi*, 2nd ed. (Moscow, 1975).

Lipski, Alexander, 'A Re-Examination of the "Dark Era" of Anna Ioannovna', *American Slavic and East European Review*, 15 (1956), 477–88.

Lisaevich, Irina I., *Pervyi arkhitektor Peterburga* (Leningrad, 1971).

Little, Meredith, and Natalie Jenne, *Dance and the Music of J. S. Bach* (Bloomington, IN, 1991).

Logunova, Marina, *Pechal'nye ritualy imperatorskoi Rossii* (Moscow, 2011).

Lotman, Iurii M., *Besedy o russkoi kul'ture: Byt i traditsii russkogo dvorianstva (XVIII – nachalo XIX veka)* (St Petersburg, 2002).

Luppov, Sergei P., *Istoriia stroitel'stva Peterburga* (Moscow, 1957).

Luppov, Sergei P., *Kniga v Rossii v pervoi chetverti XVIII veka* (Leningrad, 1973).

Luppov, Sergei P., *Kniga v Rossii v poslepetrovskoe vremia: 1725–1740* (Leningrad, 1976).

Luppov, Sergei P. and M. S. Fillipov (eds), *Istoriia Biblioteki Akademii nauk SSSR, 1714–1964* (Leningrad, 1964).

McClellan, James, *Science Reorganized: Scientific Societies in the Eighteenth Century* (New York, 1985).

McNeill, William, *Keeping Together in Time: Dance and Drill in Human History* (Cambridge, MA, 1995).

Malcolmson, Robert, *Popular Recreations in English Society, 1700–1850* (Cambridge, 1973).

Malinovskii, Konstantin V., *Sankt-Peterburg XVIII veka* (St Petersburg, 2008).

Mansel, Philip, *Dressed to Rule: Royal and Court Costume from Louis XIV to Elizabeth II* (New Haven, CT, 2005).

Marker, Gary, *Publishing, Printing, and the Origins of Intellectual Life in Russia, 1700–1800* (Princeton, NJ, 1985).

Marker, Gary, 'Russian Journals and their Readers in the Late Eighteenth Century', *Oxford Slavonic Papers*, 19 (1986), 88–101.

Marker, Gary, *Imperial Saint: the Cult of St Catherine and the Dawn of Female Rule in Russia* (DeKalb, IL, 2007).

Martin, Russell, *A Bride for the Tsar: Bride-Shows and Marriage Policies in Early Modern Russia* (DeKalb, IL, 2012).

Massie, Robert, *Peter the Great: His Life and World* (New York, 1981).

Matthee, Rudi, 'Anti-Ottoman Politics and Transit Rights: the Seventeenth-Century Trade in Silk between Safavid Iran and Muscovy', *Cahiers du Monde russe*, 35/4 (1994), 739–61.

Mazaev, Anatolii I., *Prazdnik kak sotsial'no-khudozhestvennoe iavlenie: opyt istoriko-teoreticheskogo issledovaniia* (Moscow, 1978).

Meehan-Waters, Brenda, *Autocracy and Aristocracy: the Russian Service Elite of 1730* (New Brunswick, NJ, 1982).

Melton, James van Horn, *Absolutism and the Eighteenth-Century Origins of Compulsory Schooling in Prussia and Austria* (Cambridge, 1988).

Melton, James van Horn, *The Rise of the Public in Enlightenment Europe* (Cambridge, 2001).

Miers, David, *Regulating Commercial Gambling: Past, Present, and Future* (Oxford, 2004).

Mikhailov, Grigorii V., 'Graviura A. Zubova "Svad-ba Petra I": realnost' i vymysel', *Panorama iskusstv*, 11 (1988), 25–38.

Mikhnevich, Vladimir O., 'Istoriia kartochnoi igry na Rusi', *Istoricheskii vestnik*, 83/1 (1901), 141–61; 83/2 (1901), 559–87.

Miloradovich, Grigorii A., *Materialy dlia istorii pazheskago Ego Imperatorskago Velichestva korpusa, 1711–1875* (Kiev, 1876).

Molchanov, Nikolai N., *Diplomatiia Petra Velikogo* (Moscow, 1990).

Monas, Sidney, 'Anton Divier and the Police of St Petersburg', in Morris Halle (ed.), *For Roman Jakobson: Essays on the Occasion of his Sixtieth Birthday* (The Hague, 1956), 361–66.

Mordvinova, Zinaida E., 'Smol'nyi institut v epokhu imperatritsy Ekateriny II (1764–96)', *Istoricheskii vestnik*, 136/6 (1914), 987–1001.

Motley, Mark, *Becoming a French Aristocrat: the Education of the Court Nobility, 1580–1715* (Princeton, NJ, 1990).

Muir, Edward, *Ritual in Early Modern Europe*, 2nd edition (Cambridge, 2005).

Mukerji, Chandra, *Territorial Ambitions and the Gardens of Versailles* (Cambridge, 1997).

Mulryne, James, Helen Watanabe-O'Kelly and Margaret Shewring (eds), *Europa triumphans: Court and Civic Festival in Early Modern Europe* (Aldershot, 2004), 2 vols.

Mumford, Lewis, *The Culture of Cities* (London, 1938).

Munck, Thomas, *Seventeenth-Century Europe: State, Conflict and the Social Order in Europe, 1598–1700* (Basingstoke, 1990).

Munck, Thomas, *The Enlightenment: a Comparative Social History, 1721–1794* (London, 2000).

Munro, George, *The Most Intentional City: St. Petersburg in the Reign of Catherine the Great* (Madison Cranbury, NJ, 2008).

Munting, Roger, *An Economic and Social History of Gambling in Britain and the USA* (Manchester, 1996).

Muravyeva, Marianna, 'Forms and Methods of Violence against Women in Eighteenth-Century Russia: Law against Morality', *SGECRN*, 26 (2008), 15–19.

Muzykal'nyi Peterburg. Entsiklopedicheskii slovar': XVIII vek (St Petersburg, 1999–2000), 3 vols.

Nekrylova, Anna F., *Russkie narodnye gorodskie prazdniki, uveseleniia i zrelishcha: konets XVIII – nachalo XX veka* (St Petersburg, 2004).

Neverov, Oleg, '"His Majesty's Cabinet" and Peter I's Kunstkammer', in Oliver Impey and Arthur McGregor (eds), *The Origins of Museums: the Cabinet of Curiosities in Sixteenth- and Seventeenth-Century Europe* (Oxford, 1985), 54–61.

Nevile, Jennifer (ed.), *Dance, Spectacle, and the Body Politick, 1250–1750* (Bloomington, IN, 2008).

Nicolosi, Riccardo, *Peterburgskii panegirik XVIII veka: mif – ideologiia – ritorika*, transl. M. N. Zharova (Moscow, 2009).

Ogarkova, Natal'ia A., *Tseremonii, prazdnestva, muzyka russkogo dvora* (St Petersburg, 2004).

Okenfuss, Max, 'Technical Training in Russia under Peter the Great', *History of Education Quarterly*, 13 (1973), 325–45.

Okenfuss, Max, *The Discovery of Childhood in Russia: the Evidence of the Slavic Primer* (Newtonville, MA, 1980).

Orden, Kate van, *Music, Discipline, and Arms in Early Modern France* (Chicago, IL, 2005).

Owens, Samantha, Barbara Reul, and Janice Stockigt (eds), *Music at German Courts, 1715–1760: Changing Artistic Priorities* (Woodbridge, 2011).

Parchevskii, Georgii F., *Karty i kartezhniki* (St Petersburg, 1998).

Parker, W. H., 'Europe: How Far?', *The Geographical Journal*, 126/3 (1960), 278–97.

Parkhomenko, V. P. (comp.), *Siiatel'nye zheny: biografii i rodoslovnaia stats-dam i freilin russkogo dvora, po spiskam P. F. Karabanova* (St Petersburg, 1992).

Parlett, David, *A History of Card Games* (Oxford, 1991).

Pavlenko, Nikolai I., *Ekaterina I* (Moscow, 2004).

Pekarskii, Petr P., *Nauka i literatura v Rossii pri Petre Velikom* (St Petersburg, 1862), 2 vols.

Pekarskii, Petr P., *Istoriia Imperatorskoi Akademii Nauk v Peterburge* (St Petersburg, 1870–3), 2 vols.

Peterson, Claes, *Peter the Great's Administrative and Judicial Reforms: Swedish Antecedents and the Process of Reception* (Stockholm, 1979).

Petrov, Petr N., *Istoriia Sankt-Peterburga s osnovaniia goroda do vvedeniia v deistvie vybornogo gorodskogo upravleniia po uchrezhdeniiam o guberniiakh: 1703–1782* (St Petersburg, 1884).

Petrukhintsev, Nikolai N., 'Stanovlenie Kadetskogo korpusa pri Anne Ioannovne, 1731–1741 gg.', *Trudy Gosudarstvennogo Ermitazha. Tom XXXVII. Pervyi Kadetskii Korpus vo dvortse Menshikova: K 275-letiiu osnovanie* (St Petersburg, 2007), 132–44.

Picard, Lisa, *Dr. Johnson's London: Life in London, 1740–1770* (London, 2000).

Pinkard, Susan, *A Revolution in Taste: the Rise of French Cuisine, 1650–1800* (Cambridge, 2010).

Pisarenko, Konstantin A., *Povsednevnaia zhizn' russkogo dvora v tsarstvovanie Elizavety Petrovny* (Moscow, 2003).

Plumley, Nicholas, 'The Royal Mathematical School, Christ's Hospital', *History Today*, 23/8 (1973), 581–7.

Pocock, J. G. A., 'Some Europes in their History', in Anthony Pagden (ed.), *The Idea of Europe: From Antiquity to the European Union* (Cambridge, 2002), 55–71.

Poe, Marshall, *A People Born to Slavery: Russia in Early Modern European Ethnography, 1476–1748* (Ithaca, NY, 2000).

Poe, Marshall, 'The Sexual Life of Muscovites: Evidence from the Foreign Accounts', *Russian History/Histoire Russe*, 35 (2008), 408–27.

Pogosian, Elena, *Petr I – arkhitektor rossiiskoi istorii* (St Petersburg, 2001).

Pogosian, Elena, '"I nevozmozhnoe vozmozhno": svad'ba shutov v ledianom dome kak fakt ofitsial'noi kul'tury', *Trudy po russkoi i slavianskoi filologii. Literaturovedenie*, 4 (2001), 80–109.

Pogosian, Elena, 'Masks and Masquerades at the Court of Elizaveta Petrovna (1741–42)', in Steven Usitalo and William Benton Whisenhurst (eds), *Russian and Soviet History: From the Time of Troubles to the Collapse of the Soviet Union* (Lanham, MD, 2008), 34–50.

Pollak, Martha, *Cities at War in Early Modern Europe* (Cambridge, 2010).

Porter, Roy, *English Society in the Eighteenth Century* (London, 1991).

Postnikov, Aleksandr V., *Russia in Maps: a History of the Geographical Study and Cartography of the Country* (Moscow, 1996).

Pumpianskii, Lev V., 'Mednyi vsadnik i poeticheskaia traditsiia XVIII veka', *Pushkin: Vremennik Pushkinskoi komissii*, 4–5 (1939), 91–124.

Puppe, Roland, 'Saxon Baroque Gardens (1694–1733): Nature's Entertainment Palaces', in Michel Conan (ed.), *Baroque Garden Cultures: Emulation, Sublimation, Subversion* (Washington DC, 2005), 213–44.

Pyliaev, Mikhail I., *Staryi Peterburg: razskazy iz byloi zhizni stolitsy* (St Petersburg, 1889).

Pyliaev, Mikhail I., *Staroe zhit'e: ocherki i razskazy* (Moscow, 1990).

Raeff, Marc, *Origins of the Russian Intelligentsia: the Eighteenth-Century Nobility* (New York, 1966).

Raeff, Marc, 'The Well-Ordered Police State and the Development of Modernity in Seventeenth- and Eighteenth-Century Europe: An Attempt at a Comparative Approach', *American Historical Review*, 80 (1975), 1221–43.

Raeff, Marc, *The Well-Ordered Police State: Social and Institutional Change through Law in the Germanies and Russia, 1600–1800* (New Haven, CT, 1983).

Raffensberger, Christian, *Reimagining Europe: Kievan Rus' in the Medieval World* (Cambridge, MA, 2012).

Ravel, Jeffrey, *The Contested Parterre: Public Theater and French Political Culture, 1680–1791* (Ithaca, NY, 1999).

Riasanovsky, Nicholas, *The Image of Peter the Great in Russian History and Thought* (Oxford, 1985).

Riasanovsky, Nicholas, *Russian Identities: a Historical Survey* (Oxford, 2005), 151–60.

Ribeiro, Aileen, *Dress in Eighteenth-Century Europe, 1715–1789*, 2nd edition (New Haven, CT, 2002).

Ribeiro, Aileen, *Dress and Morality*, 2nd edition (Oxford, 2003).

Rickman, Johanna, *Love, Lust, and License in Early Modern England: Illicit Sex and the Nobility* (Aldershot, 2008).

Ridder-Symoens, Hilde de (ed.), *A History of the University in Europe* (Cambridge, 1996), Volume 2.

Roche, Daniel, *The Culture of Clothing: Dress and Fashion in the Ancien Régime*, transl. Jean Birrell (Cambridge, 1994).

Roslavleva, Natal'ia P., *Era of the Russian Ballet* (London, 1966).

Rougle, William, 'António Manuel de Vieira and the Russian Court, 1697–1745', in Roger Bartlett, Anthony Cross and Karen Rasmussen (eds), *Russia and the World of the Eighteenth Century* (Bloomington, IN, 1988), 577–90.

Rudé, George, *Hanoverian London* (London, 1971).

Sander, Elizabeth Clara, *Social Dancing in Peter the Great's Russia* (Hildesheim, 2007).

Schaich, Michael (ed.), *Monarchy and Religion: the Transformation of Royal Culture on Eighteenth-Century Europe* (Oxford, 2007).

Schieder, Theodor, *Frederick the Great*, ed. and transl. Sabina Berkeley and Hamish Scott (London, 2000).

Schulze, Ludmilla, 'The Russification of the St Petersburg Academy of Sciences and Arts in the Eighteenth Century', *British Journal for the History of Science*, 18 (1985), 305–35.

Schuyler, Eugene, *Peter the Great, Emperor of Russia: a Study of Historical Biography* (New York, 1967), 2 vols.

Semenova, Lidiia N., *Ocherki istorii byta i kul'turnoi zhizni Rossii pervaia polovina XVIII v.* (Leningrad, 1982).

Semenova, Lidiia N., *Byt i naselenie Sankt-Peterburga (XVIII vek)* (St Petersburg, 1998).

Sementsov, Sergei V. et al., *Sankt-Peterburg na kartakh i planakh pervoi poloviny XVIII veka* (St Petersburg, 2004).

Semevskii, Mikhail I., *Tsaritsa Katerina Alekseevna, Anna i Villem Mons, 1692–1724* (Leningrad, 1990).

Semevskii, Mikhail I., *Tsaritsa Praskov'ia, 1664–1723* (Leningrad, 1991).

Semmens, Richard, *The Bals Publics at the Paris Opéra in the Eighteenth Century* (Hillsdale, NY, 2004).

Shamin, Stepan M., *Kuranty XVII stoletiia: evropeiskaia pressa v Rossii i vozniknovenie russkoi periodicheskoi pechati* (Moscow, 2011).

Sharymov, Aleksandr M., *Predystoriia Sankt-Peterburga. 1703 god. Kniga issledovanii* (St Petersburg, 2004).

Shepelev, Leonid E., *Chinovnyi mir Rossii: XVIII – nachalo XX v.* (St Petersburg, 1999).

Shliapkin, Il'ia S., *Tsarevna Natal'ia Alekseevna i teatr ee vremeni* (St Petersburg, 1898).

Shubinskii, Sergei N., *Istoricheskie ocherki i rasskazy* (Moscow, 1995).

Shvidkovsky, Dmitrii, *Russian Architecture and the West* (New Haven, CT, 2007).

Sindalovskii, Naum A., *Legendy i mify Sankt-Peterburga* (St Petersburg, 1994).

Slovar' russkogo iazyka XVIII veka (St Petersburg, 1984–), 19 vols to date.

Smith, Douglas, *Working the Rough Stone: Freemasonry and Society in Eighteenth-Century Russia* (DeKalb, IL, 1999).

Smith, Hannah, *Georgian Monarchy: Politics and Culture, 1714–1760* (Cambridge, 2006).

Smith, Robert and David Christian, *Bread and Salt: a Social and Economic History of Food and Drink in Russia* (Cambridge, 1984).

Smuts, R. Malcolm, 'Public Ceremony and Royal Charisma: the English Royal Entry in London, 1485–1621', in A. Lee Beier, David Cannadine and James Rosenheim (eds), *The First Modern Society: Essays in English History in Honour of Lawrence Stone* (Cambridge, 1989), 65–93.

Spielman, John, *The City and Crown: Vienna and the Imperial Court, 1600–1740* (West Lafayette, IN, 1992).

Spielman, John, 'Status as Commodity: the Habsburg Economy of Privilege', in Charles Ingrao (ed.), *State and Society in Early Modern Austria* (West Lafayette, IN, 1994), 110–18.

Steele, Valerie, *The Corset: a Cultural History* (New Haven, CN, 2001).

Stites, Richard, *Serfdom, Society, and the Arts in Imperial Russia* (New Haven, CT, 2005).

Stolpianskii, Petr N., *Muzyka i muzitsirovanie v starom Peterburge* (Leningrad, 1989).

Stolpianskii, Petr N., *Peterburg: kak voznik, osnovalsia i ros Sankt-Piterburkh* (St Petersburg, 1995).

Storrs, Christopher (ed.), *The Fiscal-Military State in Eighteenth-Century Europe: Essays in Honour of P. G. M. Dickson* (Farnham, 2009).

Strong, Roy, *Art and Power: Renaissance Festivals, 1450–1650* (Woodbridge, 1984).

Svodnyi katalog katalog russkoi knigi grazhdanskoi pechati XVIII veka, 1725–1800 (Moscow, 1962–7), 5 vols.

Thompson, Ian, *The Sun King's Garden: Louis XIV, André Le Nôtre and the Creation of the Gardens of Versailles* (London, 2006).

Thyret, Isolde, *Between God and Tsar: Religious Symbolism and the Royal Women of Muscovite Russia* (DeKalb, IL, 2001).

Tiukhmeneva, Ekaterina A., *Iskusstvo triumfal'nykh vrat v Rossii pervoi poloviny XVIII veka* (Moscow, 2005).

Tiulichev, Dmitrii V., 'Sotsial'nyi sostav podpischikov "Sanktpeterburgskikh vedomostei" (seredina XVIII v.)', in A. A. Zaitseva (ed.), *Kniga v Rossii. XVI – seredina XIX veka: knigarasprostranenie, biblioteka, chitatel'* (Leningrad, 1987), 62–70.

Tlusty, B. Ann, *Bacchus and Civic Order: the Culture of Drink in Early Modern Germany* (London, 2001).

Tribe, Keith, 'Cameralism and the Science of Government', *Journal of Modern History*, 56 (1984), 263–84.

Tri veka Sankt-Peterburga. Entsiklopediia. Tom I: Os'mnadtsatoe stoletie (St Petersburg, 2003).

Troitskii, Sergei M., *Finansovaia politika russkogo absoliutizma v XVIII veke* (Moscow, 1966).

Troitskii, Sergei M., *Russkii absoliutizm i dvorianstvo v XVIII v.: formirovanie biurokratii* (Moscow, 1974).

Unger, Richard, *Beer in the Middle Ages and the Renaissance* (Philadelphia, PA, 2007).

Vasmer, Max, *Etimologicheskii slovar' russkogo iazyka*, ed. Boris A. Larin, transl. Oleg N. Trubachev (Moscow, 1986), 4 vols.

Veselago, Feodosii F., *Ocherk istorii morskago kadetskago korpusa* (St Petersburg, 1852).

Vincent, Susan, *Dressing the Elite: Clothes in Early Modern England* (Oxford, 2003).

Vnutrennii byt russkago gosudarstva s 17-go oktiabria 1740 goda po 25-e noiabria 1741 goda (Moscow, 1880), 2 vols.

Volkov, Nikolai E., *Dvor russkikh imperatorov v ego proshlom i nastoiashchem, v 4-kh chastiakh* (St Petersburg, 1900).

Voronikhina, Anna N., 'Triumfal'nye vorota 1742 g. v Sankt-Peterburge', in Tat'iana V. Alekseeva (ed.), *Russkoe iskusstvo barokko: materialy i issledovaniia* (Moscow, 1977), 159–72.

Vsevolodskii-Gerngross, Vsevolod N., *Teatral'nye zdaniia v Sankt-Peterburge v XVIII stoletii* (St Petersburg, 1910).

Vsevolodskii-Gerngross, Vsevolod N., *Istoriia teatral'nago obrazovaniia v Rossii. Tom I (XVII i XVIII vv.)* (St Petersburg, 1913).

Vsevolodskii-Gerngross, Vsevolod N., *Teatr v Rossii pri imperatritse Anne Ioannovne i imperatore Ioanne Antonoviche* (St Petersburg, 1914).

Vsevolodskii-Gerngross, Vsevolod N., *Istoriia russkogo teatra v dvukh tomakh* (Moscow-Leningrad, 1929), 2 vols.

Vsevolodskii-Gerngross, Vsevolod N., *Teatr v Rossii po imperatritse Elisavete Petrovne* (St Petersburg, 2003).

Vucinich, Alexander, *Science in Russian Culture* (London, 1965), 2 vols.

Vysotskii, Ivan P., *Sankt-Peterburgskaia stolichnaia politsiia i gradonachalstvo, 1703–1903* (St Petersburg, 1903).

Wakefield, Andre, *The Disordered Police State: German Cameralism as Science and Practice* (Chicago, IL, 2009).

Watanabe-O'Kelly, Helen, *Court Culture in Dresden: From Renaissance to Baroque* (Basingstoke, 2002).

Werrett, Simon, *Fireworks: Pyrotechnic Arts and Sciences in European History* (Chicago, IL, 2010).

Whaley, Joachim, *Germany and the Holy Roman Empire* (Oxford, 2012), 2 vols.

White, Jerry, *London in the Eighteenth Century: a Great and Monstrous Thing* (London, 2012).

Whittaker, Cynthia (ed.), *Russia Engages the World, 1453–1825* (Cambridge, MA, 2003).

Wiesner, Merry E., *Women and Gender in Early Modern Europe*, 2nd edition (Cambridge, 2000).

Williams, Alan, *The Police of Paris, 1718–1789* (Baton Rouge, LA, 1979).

Wilson, Peter, *Absolutism in Central Europe* (London, 2000).

Wirtschafter, Elise Kimerling, *Social Identity in Imperial Russia* (DeKalb, IL, 1997).

Wirtschafter, Elise Kimerling, *The Play of Ideas in Russian Enlightenment Theatre* (DeKalb, IL, 2003).

Wolff, Christoph, *Bach: Essays on His Life and Music* (Cambridge, MA, 1991).

Wolff, Larry, *Inventing Eastern Europe: the Map of Civilisation in the Mind of the Enlightenment* (Stanford, CA, 1994).

Wortman, Richard, *Scenarios of Power: Myth and Ceremony in Russian Monarchy* (Princeton, NJ, 1995), 2 vols.

Wortman, Richard, 'The Russian Coronation: Rite and Representation', *The Court Historian*, 9/1 (2004), 15–32.

Wroth, Warwick, *The London Pleasure Gardens of the Eighteenth Century* (London, 1896).

Zabelin, Ivan E., *Domashnii byt russkago tsarei v XVI I XVII stoletiiakh*, 3rd edition (Moscow, 1895), part 1.

Zakharine, Dmitri, 'Tanz– und Körperverhalten im kommunikativen Alltagsverkehr des 17.–19. Jh. Russland und Westeuropa im Vergleich', *Wiener Slawistischer Almanach*, 47 (2001), 139–205.

Zakharova, Ol'ga Iu., *Svetskie tseremonialy v Rossii XVIII-nachala XX v.* (Moscow, 2001).

Zanger, Abby, *Scenes From the Marriage of Louis XIV: Nuptial Fictions and the Making of Absolutist Power* (Stanford, CA, 1997).

Zelov, Dmitrii D., *Ofitsial'nye svetskie prazdniki kak iavlenie russkoi kul'tury kontsa XVII – pervoi poloviny XVIII veka* (Moscow, 2002).

Zguta, Russell, *Russian Minstrels: a History of the Skomorokhi* (Philadelphia, PA, 1978).

Zhivov, Viktor M., 'Kul'turnye reformy v sisteme preobrazovanii Petra I', in A. D. Koshelev (ed.) *Iz istorii russkoi kul'tury* (Moscow, 1996), vol. 3, 528–83.

Zitser, Ernest, *The Transfigured Kingdom: Sacred Parody and Charismatic Authority at the Court of Peter the Great* (Ithaca, NY, 2004).

Zitser, Ernest, 'New Histories of the Late Muscovite and Early Imperial Russian Court', *Kritika: Explorations in Russian and Eurasian History*, 6/2 (2005), 375–92.

Zodchie Sankt-Peterburga. XVIII vek (St Petersburg, 1997).

Key to Maps

1. Sts Peter and Paul Fortress and Cathedral.
2. Admiralty yard and fortress.
3. Cathedral of the Holy Trinity and Trinity Square.
4. Petrine Winter Palace.
5. St Aleksandr Nevskii monastery and seminary.
6. Tsaritsyn Meadow.
7. 'Old' Summer Palace.
8. 'First' Summer Gardens and its grotto.
9. 'Second' Summer Gardens.
10. 'Third' Summer Gardens and its orangery.
11. Church of St Isaac of Dalmatia.
12. 'Italian' Palace and Gardens.
13. Palace of Aleksandr D. Menshikov (1710–27); Cadet Corps building (1731–).
14. Palace of Aleksandr V. Kikin (1711–18); Naval Academy (1718–32).
15. Palace of Tsarevna Natal'ia Alekseevna, with her theatre nearby.
16. Nevskii Prospekt.
17. 'Green' (*Zelenyi*) Bridge
18. Academy of Sciences, library and Kunstkamera.
19. Twelve Colleges building (including the Senate).
20. 'New' Winter Palace.
21. 'Wooden' Winter Palace, including 'new' Opera House.
22. 'New' Summer Palace.
23. Gostinyi dvor.
24. 'Old' Royal Theatre (destroyed 1749).
25. Pontoon bridge.
26. Naval Cadet Corps building.
27. Fireworks theatre.
28. Exchange building.
29. Opera House.
30. Church of the Virgin of Kazan'.
31. Palace of Sergei G. Stroganov.
32. Anichkov Bridge.
33. Anichkov Palace.
34. Artillery Laboratory and its school.
35. Smol'nyi Cathedral and Palace.

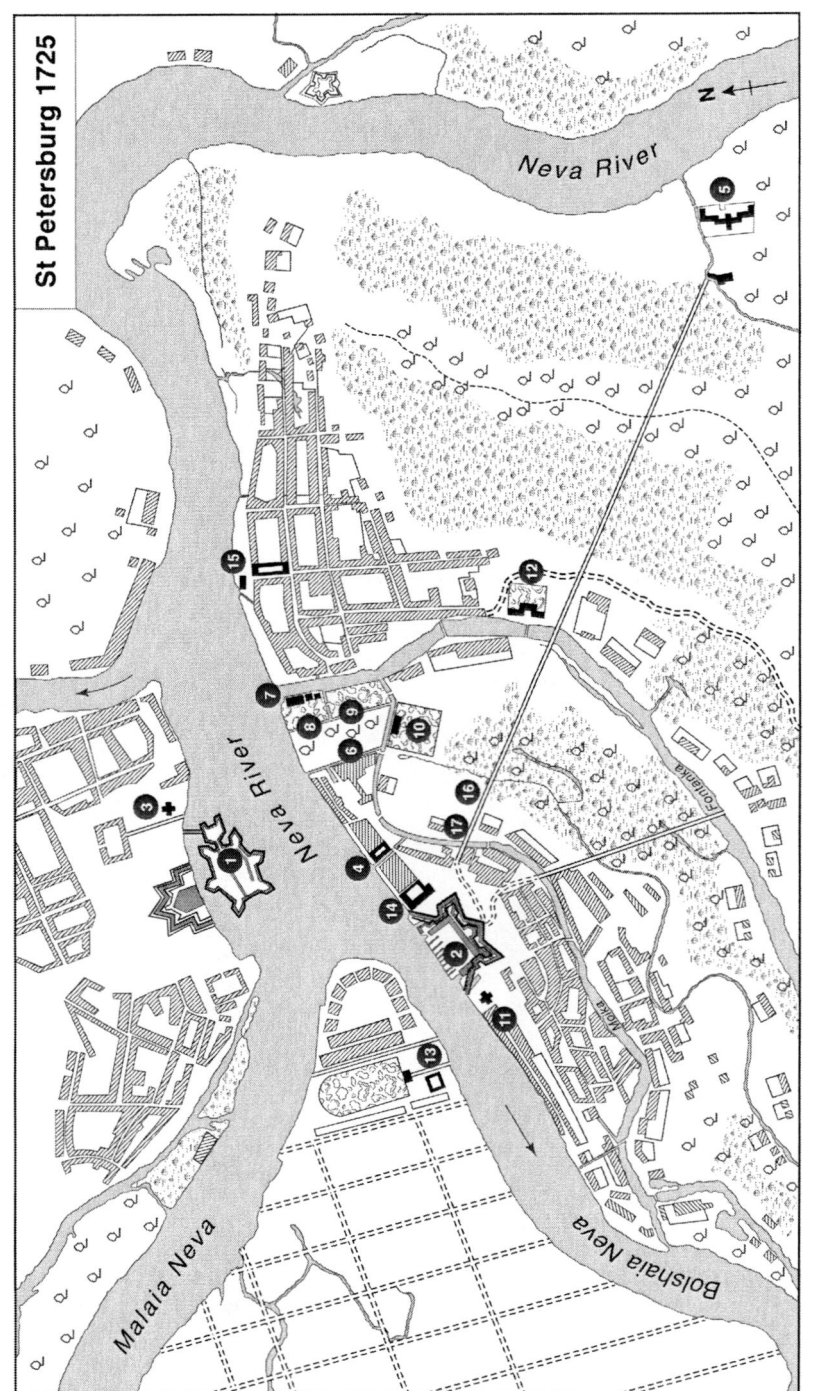

Map 1 St Petersburg, 1725
Source: Mina Moshkeri. Original map by Johann Baptist Homann.

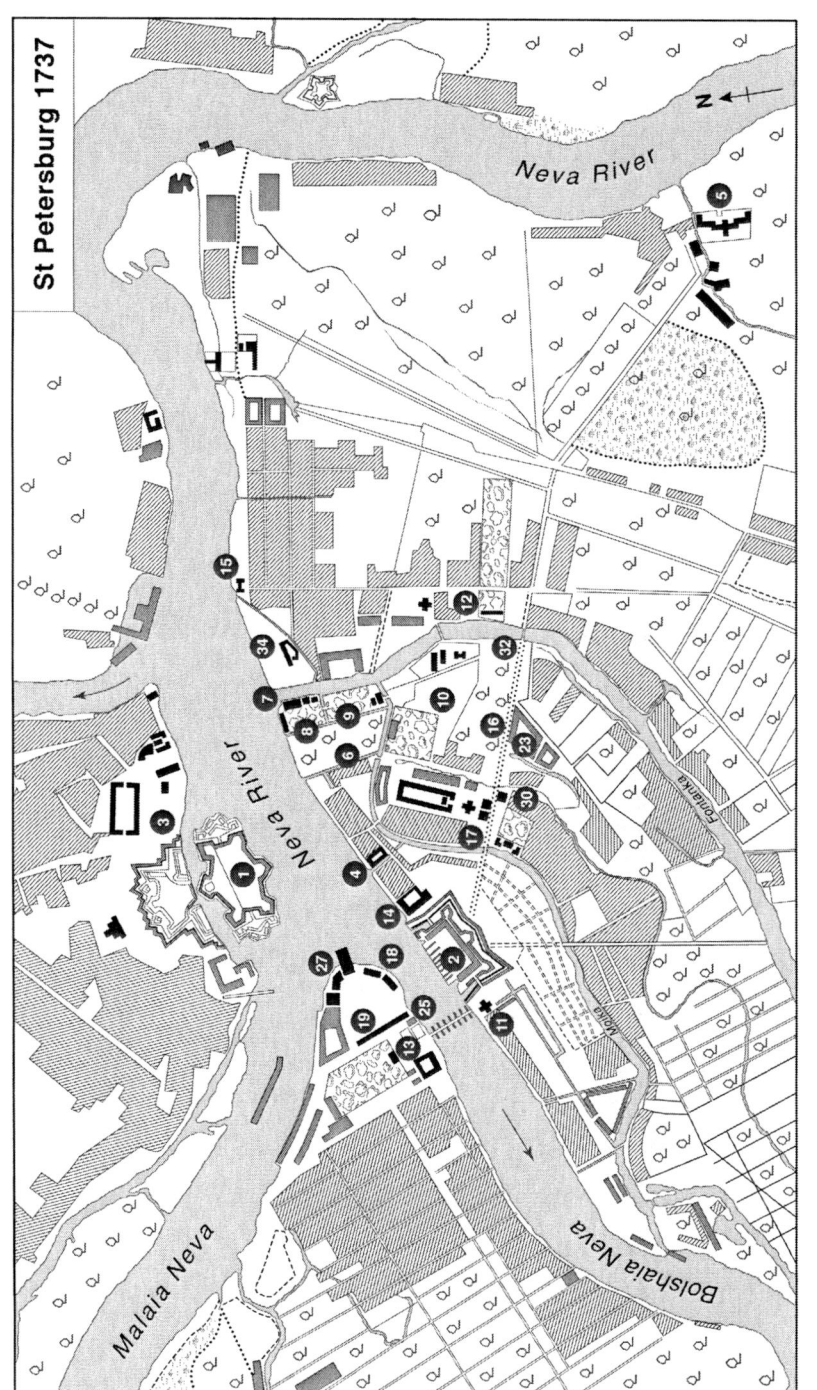

Map 2 St Petersburg, 1737
Source: Mina Moshkeri. Original map by Joseph Nicholas de L'Isle.

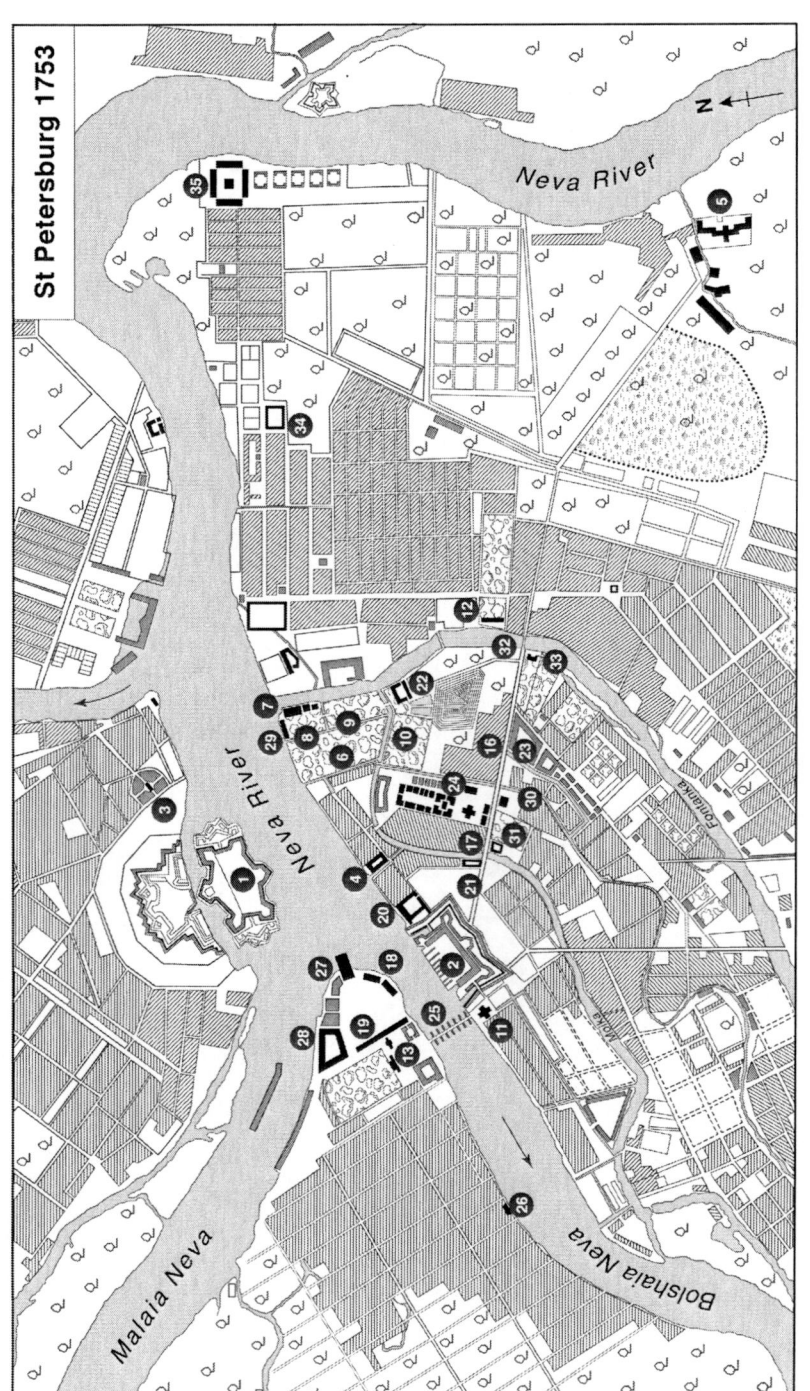

Map 3 St Petersburg, 1753

Source: Mina Moshkeri. Original map by John (Ivan) F. Truscott.

Index

Printed and bound in Great Britain by
CPI Antony Rowe, Chippenham and Eastbourne